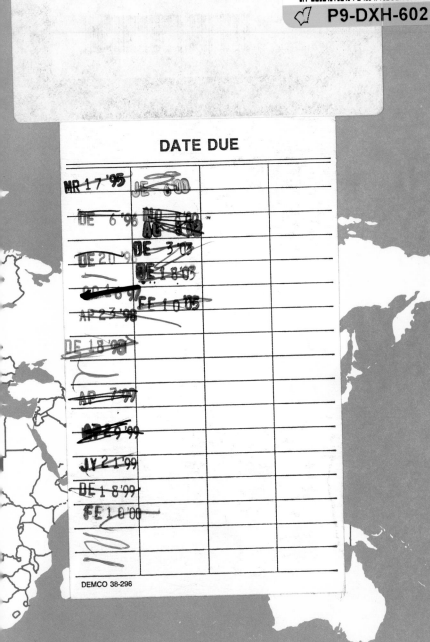

DATE DUE

MR 17 '95	DE 6 00		
DE 6 '96	NO 3 02 AG 8 02		
DE 20 '96	DE 3 03 DE 18 03		
AP 23 '98	FE 10 05		
DE 18 '98			
AP 7 '99			
MY 29 '99			
JY 21 '99			
DE 18 '99			
FE 10 '00			

DEMCO 38-296

Peru
a country study

Federal Research Division
Library of Congress
Edited by
Rex A. Hudson
Research Completed
September 1992

On the cover: Thumb-size figurine with movable nose piece and war club, headdress, and minuscule owl's-head necklace adorns gold and turquoise ear ornament found in a Moche tomb's sealed chamber.

Fourth Edition, 1993, First Printing, 1993.

Library of Congress Cataloging-in-Publication Data

Peru: a country study / Federal Research Division, Library of Congress ; edited by Rex A. Hudson. — 4th ed.
    p.   cm. — (Area handbook series, ISSN 1057-5294)
(DA Pam ; 550-42)
    "Supersedes the 1981 edition of Peru: a country study, edited by Richard F. Nyrop"—T.p. verso.
    "Research completed October 1992."
    Includes bibliographical references (pp. 339-377) and index.
    ISBN 0-8444-0774-7
——Copy 3 Z663.275 .P4   1993
    1. Peru.   I. Hudson, Rex A., 1947-   . II. Library of Congress. Federal Research Division. III. Area handbook for Peru. IV. Series. V. Series: DA Pam ; 550-42.
F3408.P4646   1993   93-19676
985—dc20   CIP

Headquarters, Department of the Army
DA Pam 550-42

Reprinted without alteration
on acid-free paper

♾ ™

Bernan Press
Lanham, Maryland
October 1993

Acknowledgments

The authors would like to acknowledge any contributions made by the writers of the 1981 edition of *Peru: A Country Study*. The authors and book editor of the present volume would also like to thank one of those writers in particular, James D. Rudolph, for kindly supplying the official 1989 Peru regionalization map, on which the corresponding map in this volume is based.

The authors are grateful to individuals in various agencies of the United States government, private institutions, and Peruvian diplomatic offices who gave their time, research materials, and special knowledge to provide information and perspective. Thanks also go to Ralph K. Benesch, who oversees the Country Studies—Area Handbook Program for the Department of the Army. None of these individuals, however, is in any way responsible for the work of the authors.

The book editor would like to thank members of the Federal Research Division who contributed directly to the preparation of the manuscript. These include Sandra W. Meditz, who reviewed all textual and graphic materials, served as liaison with the sponsoring agency, and provided numerous substantive and technical contributions; Marilyn L. Majeska, who reviewed editing and managed production; Andrea T. Merrill, who edited the tables; and Barbara Edgerton and Izella Watson, who did the word processing. Thanks also go to Cissie Coy, who edited the chapters; Beverly J. Wolpert, who performed the final prepublication editorial review; and Joan C. Cook, who compiled the index. Malinda B. Neale and Linda Peterson of the Library of Congress Printing and Processing Section performed the phototypesetting, under the supervision of Peggy Pixley.

David P. Cabitto provided invaluable graphics support, including preparation of several maps. He was assisted by Wayne Horne, who prepared the cover artwork; Harriett R. Blood, who prepared the topography and drainage map; and the firm of Greenhorne and O'Mara. Deborah Anne Clement designed the illustrations on the title page of each chapter.

Finally, the authors acknowledge the generosity of the individuals and the public and private agencies who allowed their photographs to be used in this study.

Contents

Chapter 2. The Society and Its Environment 59
Paul L. Doughty

Chapter 3. The Economy 137
John Sheahan

List of Figures

Preface

Like its predecessor, this study is an attempt to examine objectively and concisely the dominant historical, social, economic, political, and military aspects of contemporary Peru. Sources of information included scholarly books, journals, monographs, official reports of governments and international organizations, and numerous periodicals. Chapter bibliographies appear at the end of the book; brief comments on sources recommended for further reading appear at the end of each chapter. To the extent possible, place-names follow the system adopted by the United States Board on Geographic Names. Measurements are given in the metric system; a conversion table is provided to assist readers unfamiliar with metric measurements (see table 1, Appendix). A glossary is also included.

Spanish surnames generally are composed of both the father's and mother's family names, in that order, although there are numerous variations. In the instance of Alan García Pérez, for example, García is his patronymic and Pérez is his mother's maiden name. In informal use, the matronymic is often dropped, a practice that usually has been followed in this book, except in cases where the individual could easily be confused with a relative or someone with the same patronymic.

The body of the text reflects information available as of November 1992. Certain other portions of the text, however, have been updated. The Introduction discusses significant events that have occurred since the completion of research, the Country Profile includes updated information as available, and the Bibliography lists recently published sources thought to be particularly helpful to the reader.

Country Profile

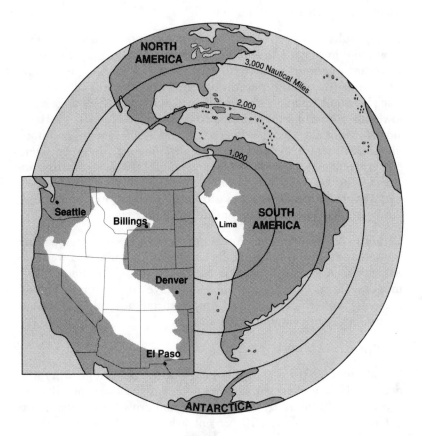

Country

Official Name: Republic of Peru (República del Perú).

Short Name: Peru.

Term for Citizens: Peruvian(s).

Capital: Lima.

Date of Independence: Declared July 28, 1821, from Spain; achieved, 1824.

NOTE—The Country Profile contains updated information as available.

Geography

Size: 1,285,216 square kilometers.

Topography: Western coast (Costa) mountainous and arid. Andes mountains in center (Andean highlands or Sierra) high and rugged. Less than one-fourth of Sierra, which includes cold, high-altitude grasslands (the puna), natural pasture. Puna widens into extensive plateau, Altiplano, adjoining Bolivia in southern Sierra. Eastern lowlands consist of semi-tropical and rugged cloud forests of eastern slopes (Montaña), lying between 800 and 3,800 meters; and jungle (Selva), which includes high jungle (*selva alta*), lying between 400 and 800 meters, and tropical low jungle (*selva baja*) of Amazon Basin, lying between 80 and 400 meters. Land use: 3 percent arable, 21 percent meadows and pastures, 55 percent forest and woodland, and 21 percent other, including 1 percent irrigated.

Climate: Varies from dry in western coastal desert to temperate in highland valleys; harsh, chilly conditions on puna and western Andean slopes; semi-tropical in Montaña; tropical in Selva. Uninhabited areas over 5,500 meters high have arctic climate. Rainy season ("winter") runs from October through April; dry season ("summer") in remaining months.

Society

Population: 22,767,543 in July 1992 with 2.0 percent growth rate; density, 17.8 persons per square kilometer. Projected population growth to 28 million by 2000 with annual growth rate of at least 2.1 percent. Population 70 percent urban in 1991.

Education and Literacy: Three-level, eleven-year educational system based on reforms made after the 1968 revolution. First preprimary level for children up to six years of age. Free, six-year primary education at second level (compulsory) for children between six and fifteen years of age. Five-year secondary education begins at age twelve. In 1990 gross primary school enrollment ratio was 126 percent, but only 58.6 percent of school-age children attended school. Over 27,600 primary schools in 1988; over 5,400 secondary schools in 1990. In 1990 Peru had twenty-seven national and nineteen private universities, all government-regulated and recipients of public funding. Estimated 85 percent literacy rate in 1990 (male 92 percent, female 79 percent) age fifteen and over.

Health: Peru's health indicators poor, with annual public health expenditure per capita of US$18 in 1985–90. In 1992 birth rate

27 births per 1,000 population; infant mortality rate 69 per 1,000 live births; life expectancy 63 years male, 67 years female. Over 25 percent of urban residences and about 80 percent of rural residences lacked potable water and sewerage, resulting in high death rates from infectious diseases. The cholera epidemic that began in 1990 ranked behind other more common diseases as cause of death (3,482 cholera deaths as of January 1993). In 1990–92 some 12 million Peruvians suffered extreme poverty. Malnutrition and starvation leading causes of illnesses. In 1991 about 1,200 children died weekly from malnutrition, while 38 percent of the survivors suffered chronic malnutrition. Total of 21,800 physicians in 1989 (1 per 1,000 persons). In early 1992, abortion considered one of the prime health threats for Peruvian women. According to the Ministry of Public Health, 43 percent of all maternal hospitalizations in Peru resulted from botched abortions. Abortion illegal in Peru except in cases where the mother's life is in danger. Reported total of 188 deaths from acquired immune deficiency syndrome (AIDS) and 493 cumulative AIDS cases as of September 30, 1991. Unlike elsewhere in the Andean area, there was a major change from 1989 to 1990 in the male/female AIDS ratio. While the number of cases reported in men remained stable over the 1989–90 period, the annual incidence among women more than tripled (from 13 to 50 from 1989 to 1990).

Religion: Predominantly (92.5 percent) Roman Catholic. Protestantism and Mormonism growing rapidly among urban poor and some indigenous tribes, although accounting for only about 4.5 percent of Peruvians in 1990. Other denominations in 1990 included the Anglican Communion; the Methodist Church, with about 4,200 adherents; and the Bahai Faith.

Official languages: Spanish and Quechua.

Ethnic Groups: Unofficial estimates: Native American, 45 percent; mestizo (mixed native American and European ancestry), 37 percent; white, 15 percent; black, Asian, and other, 3 percent. Other estimates put native Americans as high as 52.5 percent (Quechua, 47.1 percent; Aymara, 5.4 percent).

Economy

Gross Domestic Product (GDP): US$20.6 billion in 1991, or US$920 per capita. Real GDP per capita in 1990 US$2,622. GDP in 1991 in new soles (see Exchange Rate, this section) lower than recorded in 1980. Economic growth has declined markedly since

1950–65 period; estimated at 2.4 percent in 1991, minus 2.7 percent in 1992. Forecast for 1993: 2.5 percent real GDP growth. In 1990–91 symptoms of 1980s crisis continued, with sharply declining per capita output, worsening poverty, accelerating political violence, high levels of unemployment (15 percent) and underemployment (65 percent) and mounting external debt (US$19.4 billion in 1991). In 1990 women made up 33 percent of labor force. Foreign debt rose to US$21.6 billion in 1992. Labor force increased to 7.6 million by 1990. After Alberto K. Fujimori took office as president (1990–), inflation declined significantly to only 139 percent per year by the end of 1991, as compared with 7,650 percent in 1990, and 56.6 percent in 1992. Inflation forecast for 1993: 47 percent.

Agriculture: Production lagging behind population growth. Output per capita and share of output going to exports declined during 1980s. Accounted for only 10 percent of GDP in 1991. Agriculture employed 38 percent of labor force in 1991. New agrarian law passed in April 1991 amended 1969 Agrarian Reform Law by allowing private ownership of agricultural land by companies and individuals. Fish catch in 1989 totaled 10 million tons, but output fell 13 percent in 1991. Worsened by El Niño warm current, output fell 31 percent in first two months of 1992, but increased by 52 percent in the first quarter of 1993. Food imports estimated to cost Peru almost US$700 million in 1992, 64 percent more than in 1991.

Industry: After only 1.6 percent annual growth during 1980s, production, particularly basic medals, plummeted 23 percent in 1989. Mining, including petroleum, accounted for only 9 percent of GDP in 1988 but for nearly half of Peru's export earnings, with copper accounting for over one-fifth. Copper, silver, and iron outlook remained poor in 1991, when 13,500 miners lost their jobs as production slumped because of low world prices, low productivity, under-investment, strikes, and terrorism. Manufacturing accounted for 24 percent of GDP in 1991. Industry-commerce share of total employment 17 percent in 1991. Informal sector accounted for considerable production and personal services. Coca/cocaine industry added estimated 4 percent to value of GDP in 1989.

Energy: After increasing in the 1970s, oil production fell sharply in 1980–88 because of mismanagement, political violence, and price controls. Oil and gas industry remained moribund in early 1990s. Oil output totaled 41.8 million barrels in 1991, 11 percent lower than in 1990. Fujimori government sought new investment by foreign oil companies and ended monopoly by state oil firm. Resolution of disputes with two United States oil firms in 1991–92 improved Peru's relations with international community. In 1991 total electricity capacity 4,896,000 kilowatts; 15,851 million kilowatt hours produced, with 709 kilowatt hours per capita.

Services: Government made up about 8 percent of GDP in 1991. Construction, accounting for 6 percent of GDP in 1991, soared 18 percent in first two months of 1992. In April 1991, government liberalized banking system by suspending Central Bank's powers to set interest rates and allowing foreign banks to operate in Peru under same conditions as Peruvian banks. Services sector accounted for 45 percent of employment in 1991. Country's massive informal sector included more than half of total urban labor force.

Exchange Rate: The new sol, equivalent to 1 million intis, officially established as Peru's new currency on January 4, 1991. Replacement of inti became effective on July 1, 1991, at S/0.79 to US$1. In 1990 inti's exchange rate had reached 187,886 to US$1. New sol consists of 100 céntimos. After remaining heavily overvalued and unchanged against the dollar for six months, sol depreciated following the April 1992 coup from S/0.94 to US$1 to S/1.03 to US$1. As of December 31, 1992, the official rate was US$1 = 1.605 new soles.

Imports: Totaled US$3.5 billion in 1991, US$4.0 billion in 1992. In 1990 imported products included intermediate goods (45 percent), capital goods (32 percent), and consumer goods (11 percent). Terms of trade (see Glossary) index in 1990 was a low 78. In 1991 imports came from the United States (32 percent), Latin America (22 percent), European Community (17 percent), Switzerland (6 percent), Japan (3 percent). Under policy changes implemented by Fujimori government in September 1990 and March 1991, all direct quantitative restrictions on imports eliminated; rate of protection for industry cut from 83 percent to 24 percent; and tariff rates consolidated at three much lower levels: 15 percent for inputs into production, 20 percent for capital goods, and 25 percent for consumer goods.

Exports: Totaled US$3.3 billion in 1991, US$3.4 billion in 1992. Metals and petroleum most important products. In 1990 leading metal, copper, accounted for 22 percent of exports; zinc, 12 percent; lead, 6 percent; oil and oil products, only 8 percent; and nontraditional products, 30 percent. Fish meal exports in 1989 accounted for 12 percent of exports. Estimated illegal exports of coca/cocaine US$5.6 billion in 1989. Tariff structure and sol's overvaluation relative to dollar exacerbated long-running crisis for legal exporters. In 1991 legal exports destined to United States (22 percent), Latin America (12 percent), Japan (13 percent), European Community (28 percent), former Soviet Union (2 percent).

Balance of Payments: Total long-term debt of public and private sectors estimated US$13.9 billion at end of 1988, with 50 percent of long-term debt accounted for by public sector. After limiting debt-service payments to 10 percent of export earnings in 1985, Peru at odds with international creditors until 1991, when Fujimori government sought to smooth relations. On September 13, 1991, International Monetary Fund (IMF—see Glossary) approved Peru's economic stabilization program, securing Peru US$1.16 billion to clear its arrears from support group of countries to support balance of payments in 1991–92 and allowing rescheduling of US$6.6 billion of the US$7 billion external debt. International reserves exceeded US$1.4 billion by early 1992. Large amounts in loan funding from multilateral institutions delayed as a result of April 1992 coup. Trade deficit widened after import restrictions removed in a context of overvalued currency. In March 1993, Peru cleared its US$1.7 billion in arrears to the IMF and World Bank (see Glossary), clearing the way to an expected agreement with the Paris Club of official creditors.

Fiscal Year: Calendar year.

Fiscal Policy: Fujimori program implemented in August 1990 included limiting public-sector wages in terms of Peruvian currency; removal of subsidies; sharp increases in gas, utility, and food prices; strict government spending policies; and more efficient tax collection. Reversing his electoral position, Fuijmori adopted privatization program. Government's austerity measures won approval of international financial community, but financial stability threatened. Economy remained bogged in recession in first half of 1992. Government cut interest rates across the board in mid-March 1992, and borrowers in local currency paid about 8 percent per month. Bulk of privatization program began being implemented in early 1992, with 150 companies being considered for sale, including the state airline, or dismantlement (a total of 12 enterprises were privatized in 1992). In early 1992, government's 20 percent tax on interest from dollar savings deposits, designed to push down the value of sol, instead pushed up exchange rate and further squeezed liquidity.

Transportation and Communications

Ports: Lima's port of Callao services most shipping. Of country's seventeen deep-water ports, most in northern Peru. Five main river ports.

Railroads: System totaled 1,884 kilometers in 1990 (1,584 kilometers of standard gauge and 300 kilometers of narrow-gauge track).

Roads: System totaled 69,942 kilometers in 1991, including 7,459 kilometers of paved roads, 13,538 kilometers of gravel, and 48,945 kilometers of unimproved earth. Road maintenance haphazard and substandard, except for Pan American Highway and Trans-Andean Highway.

Airports: In 1991 Peru had 201 usable airports, 36 with permanent-surface runways. Jorge Chávez International Airport near Lima principal international airport.

Waterways: Totaled 8,600 kilometers of navigable tributaries of the Río Amazonas (Amazon River) and 208 kilometers of Lake Titicaca.

Telecommunications: Telephone system one of Latin America's least developed (544,000 telephones). Peru eliminated its telecommunications monopoly in November 1991 after concluding state companies had impeded modernization and hurt consumers, especially in rural areas. Broadcast stations included 273 AM, no FM, 140 TV, 144 shortwave.

Government and Politics

Government: On April 5, 1992, democratically elected President Fujimori staged military-backed self-coup, closing legislative and judicial branches and suspending 1979 constitution. Under 1979 constitution, executive power vested in president of the republic, elected for a five-year term. If no one presidential candidate received an absolute majority, the first- and second-place candidates ran in a runoff election. President could not serve two consecutive terms. Governed with a Council of Ministers that included a prime minister. Bicameral Congress had a 60-member Senate, elected on a district basis; and a 180-member Chamber of Deputies directly elected by proportional representation. Both houses elected for terms of five years coinciding with those of president and vice president. Only 6 percent of congressional seats occupied by women in 1991. Needed two-thirds vote to override presidential veto. Supreme Court of Justice highest judicial authority; twelve members nominated by president for life terms. At regional level, 1979 constitution mandated establishment of regional governments. Regionalization initiated in 1988 but stalled in 1992. Direct elections for municipalities held every three years and for regions, every five years. Under international pressure, Fujimori began transition to his reformed version of democracy with the establishment of the Democratic Constituent Congress (Congreso Constituyente Democrático—CCD) to serve as autonomous, single-chamber legislative body. Its eighty members were elected on November 22, 1992, in free and fair elections. Nationwide municipal elections held on January 29, 1993.

Politics: Peru's multiparty system traditionally has had numerous political parties. Virtually unknown, Fujimori ran for president in 1990 as outsider candidate of Peru's newest party, Cambio '90 (Change '90). With help from business and informal sectors and Evangelical grassroots organizers, Fujimori elected overwhelmingly by electorate that had lost faith in established political system. Succeeded populist Alan García Pérez, controversial head of left-of-center American Popular Revolutionary Party (Alianza Popular Revolucionaria Americana—APRA), Peru's oldest party. Impatient with legislative and judicial hindrance of free-market reforms, Fujimori staged self-coup on April 5, 1992, with full backing of armed forces, dissolving Congress, suspending 1979 constitution, and moving against political opposition led by García, who, accused of stockpiling weapons, fled into exile.

International Relations: In 1970s Peru's leftist military regime adopted independent, nonaligned course, expanding ties with communist world, particularly Soviet Union, becoming its largest military client in Latin America. Civilian government in 1980–85 deemphasized Peru's nonaligned stance and sought closer relationships with United States and Latin America. Under García, Peru reverted to anti-imperialist, openly confrontational strategy, straining relations with international financial community. Isolated stance on nonpayment of foreign debt, country's economic and insurgency crises, and cholera epidemic strained relations with neighbors. Fujimori sought to repair Peru's standing in international financial community and relations improved. Despite signing of drug accord in May 1991, relations with United States remained strained over Fujimori's reluctance to increase United States and Peruvian military efforts in eradicating coca fields and improving government's human rights record.

United States economic assistance to Peru has aimed at combatting narcotics. United States provided US$173 million in aid in fiscal year (FY) 1991 and US$129 million in FY 1992. About

US$85 million in additional Economic Support Fund (ESF) assistance appropriated in FY 1991 and FY 1992 was suspended in September 1991 because of human rights conditions imposed on the FY 1991 aid and because of the April 5, 1992, self-coup. United States FY 1993 foreign aid appropriation legislation prohibited FY 1993 military aid for Peru and reduced ESF assistance to US$40 million. Available FY 1993 United States support totaled US$245 million, including US$130 million in accumulated ESF assistance funds, US$25 million in development assistance, US$72 million in food aid, US$17.5 million in counternarcotics assistance, and US$0.7 million in International Military Education and Training (IMET) assistance. International community was also unwilling to provide credit or aid until restoration of democratic government. This attitude changed in March 1993 when Peru cleared its arrears with IMF. United States administration of President Bill Clinton subsequently released, in stages, suspended ESF assistance, specifically US$85 million in balance-of-payments support.

International Agreements and Membership: Member, Amazon Group; Andean Group; Customs Cooperation Council; Economic Commission for Latin America and the Caribbean; Food and Agriculture Organization; Group of Eleven; Group of Nineteen; Group of Twenty-Four; Group of Seventy-Seven; General Agreement on Tariffs and Trade; Inter-American Development Bank; International Atomic Energy Agency; International Bank for Reconstruction and Development; International Civil Aviation Organization; International Confederation of Free Trade Unions; International Development Association; International Fund for Agricultural Development; International Finance Corporation; International Labor Organization; IMF; International Maritime Satellite Organization; International Telecommunications Satellite Organization; International Criminal Police Organization; International Olympic Committee; International Organization for Migration; International Organization for Standardization; International Telecommunications Union; Latin American Economic System; Latin American Integration Association; League of Red Cross and Red Crescent Societies; Nonaligned Movement; Organization of American States; Agency for the Prohibition of Nuclear Weapons in Latin America and the Caribbean; Permanent Court of Arbitration; Rio Group; United Nations; United Nations Conference on Trade and Development; United Nations Educational, Scientific, and Cultural Organization; United Nations Industrial Development Organization; United Nations Iran-Iraq Military Observer Group; Universal Postal Union; World Confederation of Labor; World Federation of Trade Unions; World Health Organization; World Intellectual Property Organization; World Meteorological Organization; and World Tourism Organization.

National Security

Armed Forces: In 1992 included army (75,000), navy (22,000), and air force (15,000), with total strength of 112,000. Conscripts (69,000) made up 62 percent of armed forces (army, 69 percent; navy, 45 percent; air force, 47 percent). Creation of Ministry of Defense in 1986 unified armed forces under one ministry, eliminating separate service ministries. Military expenditure as a percentage of GDP in 1990 was 2.1 percent. Defense expenditures in 1991 totaled US$750 million. Defense budget in 1992 totaled US$656.8 million. A total of 18.5 percent of 1992 national budget earmarked for national security. Services traditionally provided excellent officer education and training, but Peru's deep financial crisis of the 1980s and 1990s affected program adversely.

Military Units: Army organized into twelve divisions (each consisting of four infantry battalions and artillery group), including one jungle operations, one cavalry, one special forces, one airborne, six motorized infantry, and two armored divisions. Army infantry, armored, and engineers forces organized into thirty-six battalions and nineteen groups. Army deployed into five military regions. Navy organized into Pacific Naval Force and Amazon River Force. Air force organized into some nine groups and twenty-two squadrons across country's three air defense zones.

Equipment: Soviet equipment predominated in army in 1990–92. Ground forces had significant armored capability, with 320 Soviet T-54, T-55, and T-62 tanks, as well as 110 French AMX–13 light tanks. Latin America's third-largest navy by late 1980s; navy's Pacific force had two cruisers, six destroyers, four missile frigates, nine submarines (plus one training submarine), and six missile attack craft. Latin America's third-largest air force by late 1980s; air force had advanced (mostly Soviet) equipment. Inventory included Sukhoi Su-22 and Canberra bombers, Mirage fighters, and Mi-24 attack helicopters.

Police: National Police, with 84,000 personnel in 1992, consisted of military-like General Police (at least 42,500); Technical Police, a plainclothes investigative and forensic group (at least 13,000); and Security Police, border guard and penitentiary force (at least 21,500)—all under Ministry of Interior. General Police organized into fifty-nine commands across five police regions—same regions as army's.

Antinarcotics Forces: National Police had primary responsibility for antinarcotics efforts, but army has been called on to drive insurgents out of coca-growing Upper Huallaga Valley. Police emphasized interdiction of cocaine and cocaine paste rather than eradication of coca plants. At end of July 1991, Peru signed two antidrug accords with United States linking drug fight with counterinsurgency. National Police in early 1990s had serious problems with corruption, repression, and hostile relations with army.

Paramilitary Forces: In response to insurgency challenge, central government encouraged creation of local community self-defense forces in rural areas, beginning in mid-1980s. Known as Peasant Patrols (*rondas campesinas*), these forces began receiving light arms from the army in 1991. Right-wing paramilitary squads included the Rodrigo Franco Command, formed in 1988 and linked to the Aprista minister of interior and APRA during the García government.

Insurgents: Two significant guerrilla organizations contested government authority in various parts of country. Shining Path (Sendero Luminoso), radical Maoist group that began operations in 1980, had an estimated 3,000 to 4,000 armed cadre in mid-1992. The Túpac Amaru Revolutionary Movement (Movimiento Revolucionario Túpac Amaru), which began activity in 1985, had between 750 and 1,000 under arms in 1992. Both groups suffered serious reverses in last quarter of 1992.

Introduction

ONCE THE CENTER of the powerful and fabulously wealthy Inca Empire, Peru in the early 1990s was an impoverished, crisis-prone country trying to cope with major societal, economic, and political changes. The strong undercurrents propelling these changes flowed from what historian Peter F. Klarén describes as Peru's historical "dualism": a wide racial, socioeconomic, and political division between the small white Criollo elite in Lima and the vast majority of the population, consisting of native Americans in the Andean interior and mestizos (those of mixed race; see Glossary), located mostly in the coastal cities. Until the 1980s, this dualism put Lima in sharp contrast to the native American interior. According to Klarén, however, this traditional dualism has been eroding both ethnically as a result of the increasing Andeanization of Lima and politically as a result of "the dispersion of power away from the traditional triumvirate of oligarchy, church, and armed forces."

Anthropologist José Matos Mar has noted that by the early 1990s the process of integration of Peru's native American population from the Andean highlands (Sierra) and jungle (Selva) regions had given Peru a new identity, one distinctly different from the traditionally dominant coast (Costa) culture of the Lima elites. Beginning in the mid-1970s, increasingly large numbers of highlanders began moving to Lima in search of work. This process was accelerated in the 1980s as mainly Quechua-speaking highlanders fled the growing violence of the Maoist-oriented Communist Party of Peru-Shining Path (Partido Comunista del Perú-Sendero Luminoso—PCP–SL, hereafter SL) and the army's harsh counterinsurgency measures. For anthropologist Paul L. Doughty, the Andeanization of Lima exemplifies a "reconquest" of Peru by the long-exploited native highlanders. This reconquest, however, has been confined to demographics and sociopolitical identity; the traditional socioeconomic chasm has remained and even widened.

In the early 1990s, the dualism model of analysis remained vaild in the case of Peru. Most of the former highlanders who had left the Andean countryside looking for a better life in Lima remained harshly marginalized (see Glossary). They survived in the capital's informal sector (see Glossary), living precariously in squalid conditions in makeshift shacks in the sprawling urban *barriadas* (see Glossary), known as *pueblos jóvenes,* or "young towns," on the hills that surround Lima. In mid-1992 at least 7 million people, or about one-third of the country's 22.7 million inhabitants, lived in Lima, which is now largely mestizo and native American, reflecting the new national identity of *mestizaje* (miscegenation). Despite Lima's Andeanization, the vast majority of the population still earns only a small percentage of the national income.

Peru's continuing dualism is symbolized by two prominent statues: the statue of Francisco Pizarro, the conqueror of the Incas and founder of Lima, in Lima's Government Center and the thirty-five-meter-high statue of Pachakuteq (Pachacuti Inca Yupanqui) erected near Cusco (Quechua: "Qosqo") in 1992. The economic elites in Lima have identified more closely with the heritage of their Spanish ancestry, including the tradition of treating the proud but humble descendants of the remarkable native American civilizations of ancient Peru with the same racial stereotypes and arrogant contempt. Essentially, the great majority of Peruvians remained marginalized in a resource-rich but economically impoverished and racially divided nation. As described by Italian naturalist Antonio Raimondi in 1874, Peru was still basically "a beggar sitting on a gold bench."

By 1990 Peru had changed far more significantly than many politicians in Lima realized as a result of the historic shift in its demographics and Lima's racial composition; the almost total disaffection of Peruvians with their political institutions, indeed, with democracy itself because of endemic governmental corruption and incompetence, particularly during the administration of Alan García Pérez (president, 1985–90); and the gradual disintegration of the state. For the first time since the demographic collapse of the native American population in the sixteenth and seventeenth centuries and the colonial subjugation of the country, Peru's national identity was more autochthonous than extraneous. These trends, combined with the increasing class divisions and antipathy within Peru's multiethnic society, created a ground swell in Peruvian politics and society that, ironically, propelled a politically unknown, second-generation Japanese-Peruvian (a nisei), Alberto Keinya Fujimori, to the presidency in July 1990.

Fujimori's parents arrived in Peru from Japan in the early 1930s, just before the Peruvian government ended Japanese immigration out of concern that Japanese immigrants were too competitive. His father prospered as a shopkeeper until anti-Japanese riots erupted in Lima in 1940 and the government closed the family business. Although his parents remained Buddhists, they allowed their son to grow up as a Roman Catholic and to attend Roman Catholic schools. Fujimori graduated first in his class from the National Agrarian University (Universidad Nacional Agraria—UNA) in

Lima in 1960. During his career as an agronomist and mathematics professor, Fujimori earned an M.A. in mathematics from the University of Wisconsin at Madison in the early 1970s and served as UNA's rector, as well as president of the national association of rectors, from 1984 to 1989. His hosting of a Lima television talk-show program on Peru's socioeconomic problems apparently inspired him to make a mid-life career change. Fujimori entered the presidential and senatorial races simultaneously in 1990 as the independent candidate of the new Change '90 (Cambio '90) party, an eclectic alliance of Protestant evangelicals, small-business owners, peasants, and shantytown dwellers. Doing better than expected as a candidate for president, he soon found himself battling another political neophyte—renowned novelist Mario Vargas Llosa.

After becoming involved politically in August 1987, when he protested the announced plan by populist García to nationalize all financial institutions and insurance companies, Vargas Llosa found himself heading the new Liberty Movement (Movimiento de Libertad). Alarmed over the antidemocratic and socialist direction his country was taking at the end of its first decade of democracy, Vargas Llosa gave up his cherished literary solitude for the tumultuousness of a presidential campaign, even though he was still ambivalent about getting further involved politically. Instead of becoming an independent candidate like Fujimori, however, Vargas Llosa, whose Peruvian campaign consultants were all upper class, made the strategic blunder of joining the center-right alliance called the Democratic Front (Frente Democrático—Fredemo). Fredemo had been formed in 1987 by two of the traditional opposition parties—Popular Action (Acción Popular—AP), headed by former president Fernando Belaúnde Terry (1965–68, 1980–85); and the Popular Christian Party (Partido Popular Cristiano—PPC), headed by Luis Bedoya Reyes. Because both the AP and PPC were discredited as oligarchical in the eyes of most Peruvians, Vargas Llosa compromised his image as an outsider and an advocate of change by joining Fredemo.

The candidacies of Fujimori and Vargas Llosa increasingly reflected Peru's widening socioeconomic and cultural divisions. The first electoral round, held in April 1990, showed that the electorate was polarizing between the large and rapidly growing poor majority, consisting of Spanish-speaking mestizos (constituting 37 percent of the population) and largely Quechua-speaking native Americans (45 percent) on one hand, and the small minority of Caucasians (15 percent), the well-off Criollo Peruvians, on the other. The white Criollo elite, which traditionally had held power, favored the patrician Vargas Llosa, culturally more European than Peruvian.

Vargas Llosa's popularity with the general public waned, however, as he began to be viewed as a protector of the traditional ruling class. In the first electoral round in April 1990, Fujimori came in second, only four points behind Vargas Llosa, who was still considered García's most likely successor.

Vargas Llosa's popularity soared when, exasperated by the bickering between his two party allies, he withdrew from Fredemo and went to Italy to accept a literary award. But the euphoria was short-lived. Peruvians felt betrayed when he rejoined Fredemo after the AP and PPC hastily reached an accord. His base of support in Lima, the center of political power, withered further as a result of his expensive and slick media blitz, which was culturally insensitive to Peru's predominantly nonwhite population. In addition, his exhausting, United States-style campaign tour of Peru's twenty-four departments aroused more curiosity than enthusiasm. Observers noted that Vargas Llosa talked above the heads of the voters and came across as too aloof, urbane, and privileged for the average Peruvian to be able to identify with him.

The two campaigns were worthy of an ironic political novel by Vargas Llosa himself. The agnostic, intellectual novelist found himself strongly supported by the Roman Catholic Church and, at least initially, the military. Tainted by his Fredemo alliance, however, he was widely seen by ordinary Peruvians as representative of the Criollo upper classes of Lima. His fanciful comment during a debate with Fujimori about how he would like to make Peru "like Switzerland" only heightened a public perception that he was out of touch with Peruvian reality. At the same time, he may have been too realistic for many poor Peruvians alarmed by his economic "shock" program.

By contrast, Fujimori, a devout Roman Catholic, gained the fervent support of the small evangelical Protestant community and the mass of poor Peruvians (his own 100,000-member Japanese community was ambivalent, fearful of an ethnic backlash should his presidency be a failure). He forged a tacit alliance with the military but called the Roman Catholic Church "medieval and recalcitrant" for its opposition to birth control. As an independent antipolitician, a Japanese-Peruvian, and a native of Lima's Barrios Altos, he was perceived as personifying not only change, but also the country's polyglot reality. His Japanese ancestry proved to be an asset, not only because Peruvians claimed to admire Japan more than any other nation, but also because Fujimori held out the prospect of an efficient, Japanese-assisted solution to Peru's problems. His advocacy of "work, honesty, and technology," foreign investment to increase productivity, economic development, and an end to food subsidies to make farming more profitable had popular appeal. The masses began to see Fujimori as someone who favored more democracy, greater openness, and less *politiquería* (petty politics) and authoritarianism than Vargas Llosa offered as head of the old-style Fredemo.

Fujimori stunned Vargas Llosa, as well as Peru and the world, by decisively winning the June 1990 runoff election. He received 56.5 percent of the popular vote and carried twenty-three of Peru's twenty-four departments. Vargas Llosa's Fredemo collected only 33.9 percent of the vote.

Fujimori won the 1990 elections in large measure because his army of unpaid volunteers ran a grassroots campaign that garnered 70 percent of the vote in the working-class districts of Lima. Political economist Carol Graham notes that "The 1990 electoral results reflected a total dissatisfaction and lack of faith on the part of the populace in traditional politicians and parties." Indeed, polls had revealed a general view that a decade of democracy had given Peruvians only corruption, ineptness, chaos, poverty, triple-digit inflation, disorder, hunger, and malnutrition. For example, a poll in June 1989 found that 96 percent of Peruvians had little or no confidence in the judicial process, and 75 percent thought that the National Congress was obstructing economic progress.

With Fujimori's assumption of office on July 28, 1990 (Peru's independence anniversary as well as Fujimori's birthday), Peru was no longer governed with the backing of a major political party, a factor that gave Fujimori unprecedented independence. Adopting a pragmatic approach to governing, Fujimori refused to make the traditional deals with any political parties. Ignoring the advisers who helped to get him elected, he recruited others to help him govern. He consulted specialists with international prestige, such as Harvard-trained economist Juan Carlos Hurtado Miller, who was named minister of economy and finance, and economist Hernando de Soto, author of *The Other Path,* an acclaimed book on Peru's informal economy, as well as relatively unknown figures of Asian origin.

Like a true politician, Fujimori then reversed a major campaign pledge by quickly adopting and implementing Vargas Llosa's draconian, neoliberal, economic austerity program in an attempt to bring the country's hyperinflation under control and reach an understanding with the international financial community. It was bitter medicine, but Peruvians accepted it stoically. Meanwhile, Fujimori's approval rating plummeted to 31 percent in July 1991, according to a poll conducted by Apoyo, a Lima-based private market research company. "Fujishock" proved to be effective, however. From 7,650 percent in 1990, inflation plunged to under 200 percent in 1991. But before that happened, Fujimori replaced Hurtado Miller as minister of economy and finance with Carlos Boloña Behr, a young economist with a doctorate from Oxford University. The troubled Andean nation hence entered the 1990s with Fujimori serving as one of its most efficient, if authoritarian, democratically elected civilian presidents. Aided by the success of his anti-inflationary measures, Fujimori soon improved his standing in the eyes of most Peruvians.

Despite his success in liberalizing the economy in his first year, Fujimori was unable to implement other economic priorities for lack of a legislative majority. The negative effects of his harsh economic policies were increased unemployment and poverty. Real incomes were cut in half in Fujimori's first year. By 1991, according to the United Nations Economic Commission for Latin America and the Caribbean (ECLAC—see Glossary), real wages in Peru had plummeted by two-thirds since 1987. In 1990-91 an additional 5 million Peruvians were pushed into extreme poverty, raising the overall figure to at least 13 million (60 percent of the population). Only the informal economy enabled these impoverished millions to survive. Nevertheless, each year about 60,000 children were reported to die from malnutrition and disease before their first birthday, and 75,000 before age five.

Peru's quality of life had declined drastically since the mid-1970s. In 1992 the Population Crisis Committee of the United States rated Lima, which has been growing by an estimated 400,000 new people annually, among the world's ten worst cities in quality-of-life factors. In the United Nations Development Programme's 1991 ranking of Peru's Human Development Index (HDI), a measure that combines per capita product with factors such as longevity and access to education, Peru ranked in seventy-eighth place worldwide, but fell to ninety-fifth place in the 1992 ranking of the HDI. Peru's socioeconomic statistics were generally grim. Only 13 percent of national income in the early 1990s went to the poorest 40 percent of the population. The poor were earning an average of US$200 a year in 1992. By 1990 the state spent US$12.50 per person on health and education, as compared with US$49 in 1981. Improving Peru's public education remained an uphill struggle for the Fujimori government. In 1990 less than 59 percent of school-age children attended school. During that year, almost 27,500 teachers, whose salary was less than US$60 a month, changed their professions. Most schools lacked even water, light, and sanitary facilities. In 1991, 16 percent of school children dropped out, according to the Ministry of Education.

Although the economy remained a major concern of Peruvians, about 68 percent of the citizens polled in a 1990 survey identified the SL as the nation's most serious problem. Political violence continued unabated during 1991–92. In 1991 Peru recorded 3,400 deaths from political violence, a 10 percent increase over 1990. Peru remained in a state of national insecurity for much of 1992 as a result of an economic depression and thirteen years of steadily increasing terrorism perpetrated by the SL. In 1992 political violence claimed 3,101 lives, with the SL and forces of public order responsible for 44 percent and 42 percent, respectively, of the dead. By the end of 1992, a total of 28,809 people had fallen victim to political violence since the SL began its terrorist war in 1980, according to the National Human Rights Coordinating Group. An estimated US$22 billion in property damage was a by-product of this violence.

Since beginning its terrorism during Peru's democratic elections in May 1980, the SL has been an implacable threat to the country's battered democracy. The widely reported urban terror perpetrated mainly by the SL, but also by the much smaller, pro-Cuban Túpac Amaru Revolutionary Movement (Movimiento Revolucionario Túpac Amaru—MRTA), combined with economic chaos, gave Peru the notoriety of being South America's most unstable nation. In September 1991, *Fortune* magazine rated Peru as the riskiest country in the world for investment, and the British newsletter *Latin American Special Reports* ranked it as the Latin American country with the highest political risk and the region's highest percentage of poor (60 percent).

By the early 1990s, more than half the population was living in "emergency military zones," where the security forces operated without accountability to the central government. Thus, the rural residents were caught between two brutal armies of occupation that terrorized them on a daily basis for any perceived sympathy to, or collaboration with, the other side. The army, the security forces, and the SL have all systematically perpetrated barbarous crimes against the rural population, with the female gender suffering no less than the male. The SL is one of the world's most brutal terrorist organizations, whose rural terror has been a major causative factor in the mass flight of Peruvians from the highlands to the cities, especially Lima, Arequipa, Cusco, and Ilo. Most Peruvians under twenty-four years of age were abandoning rural areas for Lima and other coastal cities, where they were emigrating in large numbers, mostly to the United States.

Viewing the SL insurgency through theoretical lenses, some political scientists, such as Cynthia McClintock and Gordon H.

McCormick, have depicted the SL as a peasant-based movement, a characterization that seemed to exaggerate the SL's limited support among the peasantry. Evidence to support the applicability of paradigms of peasant rebellion to the case of the SL was lacking. In the early 1990s, the SL was reliably reported to be a largely nonpeasant organization. It clearly lacked the degree of peasant support needed for mobilizing an indigenous uprising comparable to those of the eighteenth century, let alone a large enough fraction of the support needed in the *pueblos jóvenes* and other sectors to cause an urban uprising, as occurred in Nicaragua in 1979. SL militants consisted primarily of highly indoctrinated, poor, provincial, mestizo teenagers in shantytown strongholds. SL leaders were largely white, middle-class, university-educated ideologists from various professions. The fanatical, ultraviolent SL was as alien to the vast majority of nonviolent, nonpolitical Peruvian peasants and the urban poor as Cambodia's Khmer Rouge. Although it masqueraded as a political party and a peasant movement, the SL, like Pol Pot's Khmer Rouge, had succeeded only in depopulating the countryside through terror rather than in fomenting a popular peasant revolution.

The basic SL strategy supposedly was to "win" the countryside, then to "encircle" and "strangle" Lima. However, the SL's actual power, because of the nature of terrorism as the instrument of the weak, was derived more from pervasive fear perpetrated by small terrorist elements than by military strength. It was becoming increasingly evident that the SL had lost most of the coerced support that it once had among the peasantry and had failed to consolidate whatever supposed political control it had in the highlands, despite, or more likely because of, its savage terror tactics. It appeared that what McCormick described as the SL's "control" and "commanding position" in the Sierra essentially resulted from its filling of a power vacuum rather than from any defeat of the army by the guerrilla forces. These SL forces avoided any confrontation with the approximately 3,400 personnel that, according to McCormick, the army had in the field at any one time.

McCormick's conventional assessment in congressional testimony in March 1992 that the military "must serve as the principal weapon in the government's arsenal against the SL" neglected to take into account the increasingly stubborn peasant resistance to the SL. This was manifested in the proliferation of *rondas campesinas* (Peasant Patrols), which have served as legally recognized self-defense units for villages. For years the lightly armed *rondas* had been ineffective. However, during 1992 Fujimori began arming them on a larger scale, and they soon became more effective than the government's counterinsurgency forces in thwarting the SL's plans for Maoist-style domination of the countryside. The 1,500 *rondas* operating in the Mantaro Valley in 1992 dealt major setbacks to the SL in this strategic region, which is Lima's breadbasket. Some analysts, including McClintock and McCormick, have downplayed the significance of the *rondas;* others have viewed them in a more positive light, especially after the *rondas* underwent a transformation from passivity to a lethal manifestation of popular resistance to the SL. Anthropologist Carlos Iván Degregori has described the *rondas* as the Fujimori government's biggest success in the counterinsurgency war. By March 1992, more than 11,000 rifles and shotguns had been distributed among the 200,000 members of 526 officially registered *rondas* (which may actually number about 2,000), and the Fujimori government began handing out arms to newly created, *ronda*-like, urban self-defense groups as well. That September the government, also using the *rondas* as a model, provided about 1,400 shotguns to the Asháninka, the biggest ethnic minority in Peru's Amazonian region and the main target of SL terrorism against ethnic groups in Amazonia.

Raúl González, a sociologist and Senderologist, has noted that the SL began making Lima the focus of its terrorism in 1991 only after having lost in the countryside. As it intensified its violence in Lima, the SL appeared to be making strong psychological headway in its plan for seizing control of the national capital through the use of bullets and bombs instead of ballots. A poll taken in Lima in June 1991 by Apoyo found that 41 percent of respondents, totaling 15 percent of Lima's metropolitan population, were able to justify subversion as a result of poverty. The poll's most important finding had to do with the public's impression of the SL as a political group. The results suggested that an estimated 12 percent of respondents in the poorer areas of Lima were concealing their sympathies for the SL because they feared the security forces. SL leader Abimael Guzmán Reynoso ("Presidente Gonzalo") had a favorable rating of 17 percent in the poorest stratum, and an estimated 38 percent believed that the SL would be victorious. By September 1991, only 25 percent of Lima residents believed that the SL could be defeated, according to a survey published in *Quehacer*. The Lima poll results seemed to underscore Doughty's point that "the interrelated ills of poverty, inequity, and ethnoracial discrimination" are the basis for the SL's appeal. The resentment of Peru's native American and mestizo majority against the European elite that traditionally has ruled in Lima has been a driving force behind the SL insurgency.

Since it began in early 1991, the SL's campaign to infiltrate and radicalize Lima's shantytowns has had a clear impact on these huge population centers. A poll taken by Apoyo in mid-1991 found that 64 percent of Lima residents felt that subversive violence was the greatest violence-related problem in Peru, followed by drug trafficking (16 percent) and abuse of authority and repression (12 percent). The relatively low concern about repression seemed surprising considering that the United Nations Human Rights Commission ranked Peru as number one or two among the world's nations at causing its own people to "disappear" each year during the 1988–91 period. In 1990 the number of reported disappearances was 251, as compared with 440 in 1989. Other groups, such as Amnesty International, put disappearances two or three times higher. The United Nations Working Party on Disappeared Persons attributed 112 disappearances to Peru in 1992 (still the world's highest incidence).

In a 1991 editorial, Graham noted that the SL, "by targeting corrupt officials and allowing nongovernmental and health-care organizations to continue operating in Lima's shantytowns, was capitalizing on the erosion of state credibility caused by widespread corruption and violence." The SL's shantytown tactics turned violent, however, and by late 1991 or early 1992 the SL no longer fit this Robin Hood-like description. According to political scientist and Senderologist David Scott Palmer, the SL in early 1992 was fighting the local grassroots organizations—such as neighborhood committees, mothers' clubs, soup kitchens, and church-sponsored discussion groups—"hammer and tong" and imposing its own local organizations. The SL also began assassinating popular community leaders, such as María Elena Moyano, the courageous deputy mayor of Villa El Salvador—Lima's best-organized and largest shantytown (with 350,000 residents)—who had defiantly resisted the SL. As a result of thirty-two attacks in 1992, including ten assassinations of civic leaders, the SL attained control of Villa El Salvador's industrial park, many of its soup kitchens, and a local council. However, despite its efforts (which included assassinating Moyano's successor in January 1993), the SL failed to defeat the shantytown's popular organizations.

The increasing intensity of SL terrorism and frustration with congressional impediments to combatting it and supposedly drug trafficking were reported to be major motivations for Fujimori's military-backed self-coup (*autogolpe*) on April 5, 1992. Fujimori cast aside Peru's twelve-year-old formal democracy by suspending the constitution of 1979, dissolving Congress, and dismissing the National Council of Magistrates, the Tribunal of Constitutional

Guarantees, and the offices of the attorney general. He announced the installation of a Government of National Emergency and Reconstruction, headed by Oscar de la Puente Raygada Albela, president of the Council of Ministers and head of the Ministry of Foreign Relations.

Fujimori's abrogation of Peru's democratic system in a bloodless *autogolpe* apparently was more widely denounced outside of Peru than inside the country. Major United States newspapers called Fujimori a dictator. James A. Baker, then the United States secretary of state, called the self-coup "unjustified" and "an assault of democracy," and the United States suspended US$167 million in new aid assistance to Peru. The United States also scuttled a series of loans to Peru from industrialized countries and multilateral lending organizations.

A threat interrelated with the insurgency and corruption in the military and security forces and one that has concerned the United States government far more than the governments of Fujimori and his predecessors has been drug trafficking. This topic has been the dominant issue in United States-Peruvian bilateral relations because of Peru's status as the world's largest coca-leaf producer (accounting for about 65 percent of total production). In its first military training funding for Peru since 1965, the United States approved US$35 million in military equipment and training for the army and police forces in July 1991. The accord also provided for US$60 million in economic aid to assist coca growers to switch to other crops. Peruvians were generally unenthusiastic about the interception strategy, however. In 1990 only 11 percent of Peruvians surveyed considered drug trafficking as the nation's most serious problem. Echoing this sentiment, Fujimori favored the substitution of crops over forced eradication, in open disagreement with the United States.

In reaction to the *autogolpe,* the United States suspended all military and economic aid and reduced its counternarcotics presence in Peru by removing two large radar systems in Iquitos and Andoas and withdrawing twenty Special Forces troops, who had been training Peruvian police to combat drug traffickers. The Fujimori government expressed greater interest in United States assistance to the counterinsurgency effort than to the antidrug "war." Following his *autogolpe,* Fujimori pleaded in Washington for a US$300 million military aid package. But the administration of President George H.W. Bush was uninterested in Peru's plight. Although the army routed the MRTA from its bases of operation in the Middle Huallaga Valley in late 1992, the SL remained entrenched in Upper Huallaga and Central Huallaga.

For many Peruvians, the self-coup was a step forward, even though Peru's international shunning no doubt had a grave impact on the millions of Peruvians living in extreme poverty. Fujimori's *autogolpe* actually raised the hopes of many Peruvians, who approved of his dissolving Congress and the courts, which were widely seen as corrupt and detached from the people. According to a poll by the Lima-based Datum, only 16 percent opposed Fujimori's decision to modify the constitution, only 12 percent objected to his closing Congress, and only 2 percent faulted his intention to reorganize the judiciary, popularly known as the "Palace of Injustice." In the view of 85 percent, Fujimori would "structure a more efficient legislature," and 84 percent believed he would make the judiciary more honest. In the opinion of 75 percent, he would solve the economic crisis, and more than 50 percent believed he would defeat terrorism. An Apoyo poll taken at the end of April 1992 gave Fujimori a record 82 percent level of support. The sectors of society that were most vocal in supporting the *autogolpe* were the military, local businesspeople and exporters, and the urban middle and lower classes. Those sectors most opposed were the former parliamentarians, the political class, intellectuals, and sections of the media.

In McClintock's view, an important indicator of Peruvians' support for the former democracy was the high electoral turnout: approximately 80 percent of registered voters and 70 percent of all potential voters in 1985 and 1990. Voting was, to be sure, compulsory. According to surveys by Datum, more than half of those who voted in 1990 would not have bothered had voting not been mandatory. The fine of 20 new soles (about US$12; for value of the new sol, see Glossary) was a substantial penalty for most Peruvians, but the loss of a day's work to the bureaucracy to pay it was even worse.

Furthermore, the calls for a "return to democracy" tended to overlook the unrepresentative reality of Peruvian democracy as it had been practiced under the pseudo-democratic oligarchies of Belaúnde and García. As Graham points out, by 1990 Peru's democratic institutions—the Congress, the judiciary, and political parties—had become generally discredited and the viability of Peruvian democracy was threatened by "a crisis of representation." The members of the dissolved Congress were seen by most Peruvians as largely representing the white, wealthier residents of Lima. According to an Apoyo poll, Peru's citizens defined democracy as an elected president and a free press, with no mention of representative institutions. Additionally, Palmer notes that the number of provinces and department's under military control "substantially eroded the formal democratic reality."

Popular surveys amply demonstrated the public's distrust of Peru's democratic institutions. In a Lima poll conducted by Apoyo in 1991, only three of thirteen institutions listed—the Roman Catholic Church, the media, and the armed forces—generated more trust than distrust. Congress, which engendered the most distrust, was distrusted by 72 percent and trusted by only 19 percent. Following close behind was the judiciary, which was distrusted by 68 percent and trusted by only 22 percent. The presidency was distrusted by 61 percent and trusted by only 26 percent. The Council of Ministers was distrusted by 60 percent and trusted by only 24 percent. The National Police (Policía Nacional—PN) was distrusted by 61 percent and trusted by only 33 percent. Political parties inspired the trust of only 13 percent of polled citizens, whereas 76 percent distrusted them.

Low wages made both police personnel and judges, like many other public officials, susceptible to bribery and contributed to the inefficiency of the PN and the judiciary. A reported 1,300 policemen were dismissed in 1991, with many being sent to prison for involvement in offenses ranging from highway robbery to extortion and maltreatment of detainees.

Fujimori actively sought a reformed version of Peru's short-lived democracy, even "a profound transformation," not a return to it. In a remark quoted by the *New York Times,* political scientist Robert Pastor alluded to the inherent contradiction in the "return to democracy" argument. "Simply restoring the democratic status quo ante," Pastor said, "will not work because it was not working before." Bernard W. Aronson, the United States Department of State's assistant secretary for inter-American affairs, noted to Congress on May 7, 1992, that "ironically, nobody in Peru, whether the opposition or the Fujimori government, is arguing they should go back to the status quo ante of April 5; nobody is quarreling with the need for fundamental reforms." That, indeed, was Fujimori's announced plan. The question remained whether he was sincere in wanting to implement it in a timely manner, or would remain "emperor" for ten years. (Fujimori had quipped to a meeting of businesspeople in April 1992 that Peru needed an emperor.)

During the remainder of 1992, Fujimori seemed serious in his stated mission to "moralize" and reform what had been a corrupt and unrepresentative pseudo-democracy. In his speech to the Organization of American States (OAS—see Glossary) meeting in Nassau, the Bahamas, on May 18, and in his message to the nation on July 28, Fujimori committed himself to reestablishing full institutional democracy. He also underscored the main deficiency of the defunct democracy—the fact that representatives did not represent and were not accountable to their districts. He maintained that the country's political party system was basically undemocratic because the parties were dominated by professional cliques (*cúpulas*), who restricted membership and imposed their handpicked candidates for elective posts from closed lists (*listas cerradas*). He added that party influence had spread to virtually all social institutions, which were thus forced to be linked to the "partyocracy." Fujimori's conciliatory speech, combined with factors such as his domestic popularity, international pressure, and Boloña's efforts to win "reinsertion" in the international financial community helped to explain why the OAS's response to the self-coup was generally mild. The government of Japan, by conditioning Japanese aid on a swift return to democracy, reportedly was crucial in persuading Fujimori not to delay in carrying out his promise to create a new democratic system.

During 1992 Fujimori enacted reforms aimed at modernizing the whole political system, and he also sought to include the economic and social structures, including the educational system, in this modernization program. In the political arena, he proposed creating a system that would give power to the people rather than the leading cliques in the political parties. The centerpiece of the new system was the Democratic Constituent Congress (Congreso Constituyente Democrático—CCD), an autonomous, supposedly "sovereign," single-chamber body designed to temporarily replace the dissolved Congress, revise Peru's constitution of 1979, serve as a legislature until the end of Fujimori's legal term in July 1995, and reorganize the judiciary.

Fujimori quickly forged a consensus on the need for a reform of the judiciary and for establishing a mechanism to reform the constitution of 1979. A month after his self-coup, Fujimori put the prisons under the control of the National Police, restored order in them, and improved conditions for inmates. However, little headway was made to reduce the huge backlog of cases awaiting trial. In August 1992, he completed the tightening of the judicial system to deal more effectively with subversive groups by adopting the Colombian practice of trial by "faceless" judges. Fujimori's earlier martial law decree ensured that anyone charged with homicide would be tried by military tribunals. All other terrorist-related offenses would be tried summarily by the anonymous judges, who would sign their verdicts with code names. Terrorist offenses would be categorized as treason, punishable by a sentence of life imprisonment instead of the previous maximum of twenty-five years. Judicial reforms enacted by the CCD in March 1993 included a new system for the appointment of judges, a task previously performed in a politicized fashion by the National Council of Magistrates. The reform supposedly eliminated political interference by the executive and legislative branches in the designation of judges by giving the Council and the District Councils exclusive responsibility for the selection, appointment, and promotion of judges. Another reform was the creation of the School for Magistrates (Academia de la Magistratura).

Fujimori also sought to expedite the decentralization and deconcentration of power through the transfer of power and resources to local government. The establishment of regional governments in Peru had been proceeding slowly since 1980. Two weeks after his *autogolpe*, Fujimori dissolved the existing regional assemblies and regional councils of all regional governments, which he had lambasted as corrupt and inefficient forums that were obstructing his economic reforms. Most of the existing regional structures were controlled by left-of-center opposition parties, including García's American Popular Revolutionary Alliance (Alianza Popular Revolucionaria Americana—APRA).

The CCD was tasked with reassessing the interrupted regionalization process and deciding whether to retain the model prescribed by the 1988 Law on Regionalization Bases or set new guidelines that would correct the previous system's errors. The Fujimori government regarded the regionalization program as a bureaucratic nightmare and advocated a process of decentralization. It favored setting up four or five macroregions that would be able to coordinate large projects involving vast contiguous geographic areas. These macroregions would be intermediate units facilitating development, territorial organization, and administration between the central and municipal governments. The state would thus be organized into two levels: the central government, with regulatory and supervisory functions, and the municipal governments, for which the regional entity would serve an administrative function (although Lima and the constitutional province of Callao would have the same mayor, Callao would retain control of its own revenues and benefits). To this end, a decree established a Provisional Administrative Council (Consejo Administrativo Provisional) in each region.

Fujimori stated on several occasions during 1992 that no political or economic reforms would succeed unless the SL insurgency was defeated first. The SL and MRTA initially had welcomed the *autogolpe*, expecting that repression would further polarize the country. Instead, repression did not materialize and the SL suffered its first major reversal when the National Counterterrorism Division (Dirección Nacional Contra el Terrorismo—Dincote) finally caught up with Guzmán and other top SL leaders on September 16, 1992. Once again, the army was upstaged in the counterinsurgency war. Whereas Fujimori's support had slipped to a still impressive 65 percent in an Apoyo poll taken on July 12, 1992, when the SL offensive in Lima was intensifying, and to 60 percent in early August, an Apoyo poll published on September 20 gave him a healthy 74 percent level of support. In terms of political power in Peru, Guzmán was ranked number three in mid-1992 by *Debate* magazine's annual survey of power in Peru, as based on an opinion poll. Taking advantage of Guzmán's capture, Fujimori also launched a diplomatic campaign against the SL's networks in Europe and the United States. He described the networks as consisting of thirty-six organizations and about 100 members, mostly Peruvians, who acted as SL "ambassadors" responsible for distributing propaganda and raising funds.

In the wake of Guzmán's capture, the SL's prospects for seizing power seemed greatly diminished. Journalist Gustavo Gorriti Ellenbogen noted in Lima's centrist *Caretas* news magazine that while Guzmán was operating underground, his cult of personality was the SL's principal weapon. Gorriti added that with Guzmán's capture this cult became the SL's greatest point of vulnerability and probably will have "a corrosive and destructive effect on Shining Path." Dincote not only captured the SL's guiding light, thereby destroying his mythical status, but also effectively decapitated the SL's organizational leadership and dismantled its Lima apparatus, both of which were led to a large extent by women.

Peruvian women traditionally have been excluded from maledominated institutions at all levels of government and subjected to a multitude of other social injustices. Some of the more activist women have had a fatal attraction to the SL, which has vowed to sweep away these discredited governing structures and replace them with female-dominated "people's committees." The SL's female members proved to be as ruthless as its male members, and apparently more dominant. Before the arrests in September and October 1992, women had constituted a reported 56 percent of the SL's top leadership. In 1992 at least eight members of the SL's nineteen-member Central Committee were women. Also captured with Guzmán was Elena Albertina Iparraguirre Revoredo ("Miriam"), who occupied the number-two position in the SL's top decision-making body, the Politburo (which had various names). Captured documents enabled Dincote to neutralize the SL's Lima-based organization with the arrests of other key female leaders, such as Laura Zambrano Padilla ("Comrade Meche"), a former teacher who had headed the SL's Lima Metropolitan Committee, which planned and implemented terrorist actions in the capital. The right-of-center *Expreso* reported that the SL had lost about 70 percent of its ruling cadres because of the arrests. In October security forces captured four of the five top leaders of Popular Aid (Socorro Popular), another SL group responsible for SL military operations in Lima. Among those captured was Martha Huatay Ruiz ("Tota"), a lawyer and reportedly the SL's highest-ranking leader still at large. At the end of 1992, Fujimori claimed that 95 percent of the SL leadership had been captured and imprisoned for life.

In late June 1993, Dincote reported the new SL leadership in Lima to be María Jenny Rodríguez ("Rita"), first-in-command; Ostap Morote, second-in-command; and Edmundo Cox Beuzevilla, third-in-command. SL leaders in northern, southern, and central Peru were, respectively, Teresa Durand Araujo ("Juana," "Doris"), Margie Clavo ("Nancy"), and Oscar Ramírez Durand ("Feliciano"), the latter the son of an army general.

Despite the SL's leadership losses, its terrorist capability and clandestine military structure remained largely intact and continued to pose a serious threat. Funded with millions of dollars in drug "taxes," the SL entered a new phase of its multistaged war in the second half of 1992. It passed from what it grandly termed "strategic balance" (with the army) to "strategic offensive," which included striking at prominent targets in Lima. SL attacks actually intensified after Guzmán's arrest, although the statistics vary widely. De Soto's Legal Defense Institute (Instituto de Defensa Legal—IDL), itself the target of SL bomb attacks on two occasions, reported that the SL perpetrated 474 attacks nationwide in the three months after Guzmán's capture, killing 365 people, or about 25 percent more than in the three months preceding Guzmán's arrest. The Lima-based Institute for National Defense Research (Instituto para Investigaciones de la Defensa Nacional—Iniden) reported that 653 people were killed as a result of 502 terrorist attacks perpetrated during the three months that followed Guzmán's arrest. Peru's most violent month of 1992 was November, when 279 people were killed in 226 terrorist attacks, according to Iniden. The fatal casualties that month included seventy-five SL militants, ninety-two MRTA members, nine soldiers, thirteen members of the PN, and ninety civilians. The stepped-up violence reflected growing desperation on the part of both terrorist groups.

Fujimori continued to rely mainly on further militarization of the government's counterinsurgency efforts against the SL. However, many members of the military and PN—demoralized by low salaries, corruption, and obsolete equipment—lacked the sense of mission that their counterparts in Chile, Argentina, and Uruguay had when threatened by urban terrorism. Thus, in addition to the SL and MRTA, Fujimori had to cope with the everpresent threat of a military coup. Discontent within the ranks reportedly had been mounting during 1992 as a result of what military commanders viewed as the army's loss of institutional status, reduced prestige in society, low pay, and the military's politicization by the government. Former president Belaúnde called for a military coup against Fujimori to return the nation to democracy, implying that the military would graciously return to the barracks after overseeing a quick transition to democratic rule. (Having himself been overthrown by the military in 1968, Belaúnde sounded more like an oligarch than a democrat.)

Military resentment focused in particular on Vladimiro Montesinos Torres, a shadowy adviser of the presidency in internal security affairs accountable only to Fujimori. Montesinos has served as Fujimori's reputed intermediary with the faction of the military that has been Fujimori's main base of support. Montesinos reportedly was seen by the military as having obtained too much influence over promotions in the armed forces and too much power over the National Intelligence Service (Servicio de Inteligencia Nacional—SIN), which he designed. According to the London-based *Latin America Monitor,* Captain Montesinos was expelled from the army in 1976, allegedly for selling military secrets to foreigners (the charges were later dropped), and spent a year in prison for disobedience. He then earned a degree in criminal law and "amassed a fortune by defending and representing drug traffickers."

The degree of influence that Montesinos had in Fujimori's inner circle was reflected in *Debate's* 1991 annual survey, which put Montesinos in twelfth place. But in the Lima magazine's 1992 poll, Montesinos rose to fourth place. The negative press reports and the military resentment failed to sway Fujimori's unflinching confidence in Montesinos. Describing Montesinos as a "good friend," Fujimori somewhat implausibly denied that Montesinos supported any promotions or even that he served as an adviser. Given the military's fickle support of Fujimori, the Montesinos factor appeared to be a potentially risky test of Fujimori's authority over armed forces traditionalists and some congressmen. Palmer has posed pointed questions as to why the military has allowed itself to be subjected to Montesinos's machinations, and whether this is a sign of military weakness. Possible explanations appeared to be in Montesinos's ability to purge the military of any independent-minded officers and in Degregori's observation that the military's power had diminished. Moreover, as political scientist Enrique Obando has noted, a legislative decree of November 1991 gave Fujimori himself the power to choose the command of the armed forces, thereby making political loyalty a more important qualification than professional capability.

Thanks in no small part to Montesinos, Fujimori did not appear to be in the process of becoming a figurehead president like Uruguay's Juan María Bordaberry Arocena (1972–76), who gave free rein to the military to eliminate the urban Tupamaro guerrillas only to be later replaced by a military man. Although Fujimori was hardly immune from a similar fate, Graham's assertion that "the situation under Fujimori was one of de facto military control" seemed to be contradicted somewhat by Montesinos's influence, the military's continuing salary grievances, and Fujimori's success thus far in removing military commanders whenever they appeared to pose a potential threat to his authority. Nevertheless, as Graham points out, Fujimori's minister of interior and his minister of defense were both army generals. And the military clearly had become more politicized during the Fujimori administration. This fact was demonstrated by Fujimori's personal involvement in military promotions and by a political speech given in front of him by Major General Nicolás Hermoza Ríos, on taking over the Armed Forces Joint Command on January 2, 1992. Whether Fujimori would succeed in keeping the military at bay remained to be seen, but politicizing the institution risked dividing it. Fujimori publicly reiterated that "political power rules over the military, and the president is the supreme commander of the armed forces." Nevertheless, the depth of Fujimori's power over the military was still unclear in early 1993.

A lack of total control by Fujimori over the military was suggested by credible allegations that extremist elements of the army were operating with impunity by carrying out extralegal actions against suspected terrorists, without Fujimori's knowledge. During the García government, a paramilitary death squad called the Rodrigo Franco Command operated as an extralegal enforcement arm of the APRA under the direct control of the minister of interior. To the extent that Fujimori proves unable to rein in the military extremists, they could pose a potential threat to his authority and further jeopardize the human rights standing of his government. According to the United Nations, the number of "extra-judicial executions" was rising during Fujimori's government from 82 in 1990 to 99 in 1991 and 114 in 1992.

Discontent was rife in the Peruvian military in 1992. A pressing military issue in Peru seemed to be morale problems fueled by low military salaries. By 1992 monthly pay for a captain had declined to about US$120; a major, US$230; a colonel, between US$250 and US$300; and a general, between US$300 and US$500. Low pay presumably was a major reason for the high desertion rates, estimated during 1992 at 40 percent of conscripts and thirty-five trained officers a month. By the time of Fujimori's *autogolpe,* military unrest over low salaries reportedly had become intense, with a widening split between low-ranking and high-ranking officers. Indeed, in early 1992 a secretive cabal of middle-ranking officers, called Comaca (Commanders, Majors, and Captains), formed to plan rebellions against corrupt military leaders. Fujimori's failure to deliver on his pre-*autogolpe* promise to improve military pay was particularly upsetting to many soldiers and middle-ranking army officers, many of whom had expected significant salary increases in exchange for supporting the self-coup.

Fujimori took a risk by giving up his constitutional legitimacy and putting himself at the disposal of the military while co-opting the top military leadership. This fact became evident on November 13, 1992, when three recently retired generals, including the commander of the army, led a coup attempt that was crushed by the loyal military. The abortive action reportedly was motivated by a variety of factors, including grievances over low salaries and promotions and Fujimori's announced stand to punish navy officers involved in an embezzlement scandal. Another reported reason was his November 13 decree granting him direct authority to dismiss and assign all military officers above the rank of lieutenant (previously, officers could be removed only on retirement or for misconduct). Several of the coup plotters had been summarily retired from active service by Fujimori and Montesinos.

Fujimori claimed that opposition politicians were behind the coup attempt and that it was also a plot to prevent the CCD elections and to assassinate him. Whatever its motivations, he appeared to have calculated correctly that his popular support and the predominantly loyal military would obviate a military coup and that the armed forces did not want to take control and hence to assume responsibility for the nation's economic, social, and political crises (for which they already bore much blame from the disastrous period of military rule in 1968–80). Nevertheless, Fujimori's heavy-handed treatment of the coup members reportedly caused widespread resentment within the armed forces. Breaking with military tradition, the government incarcerated the conspirators in the civilian Canto Grande Prison instead of in a military prison. Brigade General Alberto Arciniega Huby, a member of the Military Tribunal that had summarily condemned Guzmán to life imprisonment and fined him about US$25 billion, fled into exile after being retired for criticizing the imprisonments of the coupists. (Two generals who led the coup attempt later received seven- to eight-year prison terms, and twenty-six other military officers were given prison sentences ranging from six months to seven years. However, eleven of the officers received presidential pardons in May 1993, and most others were expected to be pardoned as well.) In the analysis of Enrique Obando, the coup attempt constituted the beginning of a struggle in the army between "institutionalist" officers, represented by the coup members, and the "co-opted high command," a struggle likely to be a continuing source of instability for the government.

The election of the CCD's eighty members in a single nationwide district went ahead as scheduled on November 22, 1992. Fujimori's New Majority Movement (Movimiento Nueva Mayoría)-Change '90 coalition won control of the CCD by garnering 43 percent of the vote and 44 seats (almost the same number of seats that Change '90 had in the former 240-member Congress). Nevertheless, Fujimori had expected to win 50 seats. The eighteen other political groups that participated in the CCD elections did not include García's APRA and a number of other leftist parties, nor Belaúnde's AP or Vargas Llosa's Liberty Movement, all of which boycotted them. The conservative PPC contested the elections and won 7.7 percent of the vote, or nine seats. About 22 percent of the voters cast blank or deliberately spoiled ballots. In an internal CCD election held on December 29, New Majority's leader, Jaime Yoshiyama Tanaka, a Harvard-trained economist who had been serving as Fujimori's minister of energy and mines, was elected CCD president with 60 votes in favor (15 ballots were blank).

Some Peru analysts found fault with the CCD elections. McClintock accused Fujimori of "manipulating" them. In her view, the elections were "very problematical" because "there were many delays in the recognition of lists and the campaign time was very short." Critics also contended that the electoral rules were skewed in Fujimori's favor and that the CCD was designed to be subservient to executive authority. Nevertheless, 200 OAS observers determined that the elections were open and fair.

Despite the CCD elections, United States-Peruvian relations remained cool in late 1992. The United States lacked any apparent role or influence in Lima and did not even have an ambassador in Lima, in part because its ambassador's residence suffered extensive damage from a massive SL car bomb in February 1992 (a new ambassador was scheduled to assume the post in 1993). Following the CCD elections, Japan, attracted by Fujimori's ancestry and the absence of the United States, remained the major foreign player in Peru, providing US$400 million in aid in 1991 and substantial amounts in 1992 as well. The United States began to show some interest, however, by agreeing to jointly lead, with Japan, the Support Group (Grupo de Apoyo) for Peru for 1993. The administration of President Bill Clinton concluded in March 1993 that Peru's human rights record had improved sufficiently to justify United States assistance to Peru in the payment of its arrears with the International Monetary Fund (IMF—see Glossary) and the World Bank (see Glossary).

As in Bolivia, the United States strategy to interdict drugs and reduce coca-growing had made very little progress and lacked public support. By late 1992, less than one-half of 1 percent of raw cocaine reportedly was being intercepted, and coca-growing was expanding at a rapid rate. In contrast, legal agriculture remained stagnant. The United States Drug Enforcement Administration's largest and most important base in Latin America continued to operate at Santa Lucía in the Upper Huallaga Valley. According to Lima's *La República,* drug-trafficking activities had increased in the Huallaga region by late November 1992, aided by the protection of some army and PN forces in the area. Some independent journalists reportedly had been threatened and occasionally assassinated by narco-hit men for reporting on military corruption. In March 1993, Defense Minister Víctor Malca Villanueva informed the congressional drugs commission that seventy-four members of the armed forces were being tried for drug trafficking, but he denied that armed forces officers were paying bribes in order to serve in cocaine zones.

On the economic front, trends reportedly were beginning to tilt slightly in Fujimori's favor by the end of 1992, according to economist John Sheahan. Inflation was down from 60 percent a month at the end of García's presidency to 3.8 percent, mainly as a result of the tough economic-adjustment program introduced prior to the *autogolpe.* The accumulated inflation rate for 1992 amounted to 56.7 percent, the lowest rate in fifteen years. In addition, the US$22-billion debt was being serviced, the budget was being balanced, the nation's reserves had been restored to almost US$2 billion, privatization was proceeding, and Fujimori's incentives for foreign investment were technically among the most competitive in Latin America. The privatization process, which began in May 1992 with the government's announcement of its plans to sell off all 200 of its money-losing state companies, encountered a series of snags during the year. Nevertheless, Peru's first major sale of a state-owned industrial enterprise, the Hierroperú, S.A., mining company, went to a Chinese state-owned corporation,

l

making China the second-largest foreign investor in Peru, after the Southern Peru Copper Corporation.

The improving direction of some economic indicators, however, still did little to alleviate the plight of most Peruvians, who were consumed with the daily struggle for survival. The gross domestic product (GDP—see Glossary) fell in 1992 by about 3 percent, in a continuing recession. The lower class was living on survival wages and meager earnings, and the middle class was becoming increasingly impoverished. Per capita income had regressed to 1960s levels. In 1992 only 15 percent of Lima's work force was employed adequately, as compared with 60 percent in 1987. State employees reportedly were earning only 15 percent of what they did in 1988. By early 1993, the public sector had shed 500,000 employees since Fujimori's election, or about half of the country's total public-sector workforce. As a result of the government's attempts to modernize the agricultural sector by opening the market and eliminating credits and subsidies, many farmers were finding coca to be the only profitable crop. The expansion of coca-growing was accelerating ecological devastation in Amazonia. In short, the country's economic plight was profoundly altering Peru's society and environment.

Nevertheless, in late 1992 Sheahan saw some basis for optimism if more directive economic strategies were adopted to reduce poverty, to make the export sector more competitive (Peru's new sol had become overvalued as a result of excessive inflow of dollars, making exports less competitive), and to establish a stronger tax base. The latter, the Achilles' heel of the economy, was dependent on the willingness of middle- and upper-income groups to accept higher taxation, a necessity to avoid inflation, according to economist Jeffrey D. Sachs. Fujimori's sharp increase in property tax rates in 1991 created a public outcry, but inflation was brought under control. In Sheahan's analysis, Peru had nearly all the economic conditions needed for economic reactivation without inflation: underutilized capacity of the industrial sector, an abundance of skilled and unskilled labor, and growing capital imports needed for rising production.

How committed Fujimori was to fully reinstituting a democratic system remained to be seen. His government decreed somewhat prematurely on December 29, 1992, that it had ended the transitional stage to democracy with the installation of the CCD. The Fujimori government clearly improved its semi-legitimacy by holding the second national electoral process since the *autogolpe*—the municipal elections of January 29, 1993, which were also monitored by OAS observers. In contrast to the November 1989 municipal elections, which the SL disrupted by selective assassinations of mayors and mayoral candidates, some 12,000 candidates, spurning SL threats, registered without incident for the local 1993 elections in 187 provincial mayoralties and 1,599 district mayoralties, even in the SL's traditional stronghold of Ayacucho. The elections swept nonideological independents into office across the country, at the expense of candidates from the traditional political parties and Fujimori's New Majority Movement-Change '90 coalition of allied independents. This political trend was most evident in Lima, whose independent mayor, Ricardo Belmont Cassinelli, was reelected with nearly 48 percent of the votes. APRA, which had long dominated politics, did poorly in the municipal elections, winning only two mayoralties in its traditional stronghold in the north; its mayoral candidate in Lima received only 3 percent of the vote.

Contrary to the judgments of his foreign critics, Fujimori did not fit the mold of a traditional Latin American dictator. In a 1993 article, McClintock labeled Fujimori a "caudillo," a term usually denoting a military dictator (but occasionally a civilian one) interested in maintaining power at any cost, maximizing personal gain, and exercising extremely repressive rule. This generally accepted definition, although applicable to caudillos such as Nicaragua's General Anastasio Somoza Debayle and Chile's General Augusto Pinochet Ugarte, did not seem to fit Fujimori. His uncaudillo-like style of governing has been described as efficient, unconventional, anti-establishment, combative, brusque, astutely cautious, pragmatic, enigmatic, and low-profile. Fujimori has also been described by foreign journalists as an autocrat, a term denoting that he rules with unlimited power and influence. Yet, it seemed clear that his power over and influence with the military has been tenuous, and that he was not immune from being overthrown by the armed forces. His overthrow, moreover, would, as Degregori has warned, create a "political vacuum." That scenario could allow a real caudillo to take power.

Although he sought to emulate Pinochet's authoritarian implementation of a free-market economy, Fujimori's rule appeared to be no more than moderately repressive and far more responsive to international pressures to restore a democratic system. Few dictators or autocrats have been known to visit urban shantytowns and rural squatter settlements every week and to enjoy such high popularity ratings, as Fujimori has, to the consternation of the elites and his foreign critics. Polls throughout 1992 indicated that he continued to be viewed as one of Latin America's most popular presidents. According to a poll conducted in Lima by the Imasen Company in December 1992, Fujimori was maintaining his popularity at 63.3 percent. Even his countersubversive policy received a 74-percent approval rating in a poll conducted in Lima in January 1993.

An antipolitician and an authoritarian with a sense of mission, the professorial Fujimori seemed more like a president intent on "moralizing" and reforming Peru. He was clearly determined to make those in positions of responsibility accountable for violations of the public trust. "If we want moralization, we must be drastic," he told Peruvian journalists in an interview on January 2, 1993; "there are no partial solutions." He was particularly determined to make García an example by seeking to extradite him from Colombia to face trial for embezzlement of US$400,000 of state money and theft of US$50 million from the Central Bank during his term. Fujimori applied his reformist zeal as equally to the Ministry of Foreign Relations and the School of Diplomacy as to the legislative and judicial branches. Explaining that Peruvians had a right to expect results from the US$50 million per year spent by the ministry, Fujimori purged 117 diplomats (a fifth of the diplomatic corps), who failed to meet his standards; replaced the traditional system of political appointment of ambassadors with a merit-based system; and opened up the elitist School of Diplomacy to nondiplomats.

In early 1993, the Fujimori government appeared to be making some progress in pulling the economy out of its deep recession, despite another change in the post of minister of economy and finance. Carlos Boloña, who oversaw the deregulation of almost every aspect of economic activity, resigned over his opposition to Fujimori's plan to relax the rigid economic program. He was replaced on January 8 by Jorge Camet Dickman, Fujimori's former minister of industry, domestic trade, tourism, and integration and former head of Peru's most important business association. Camet vowed to continue Boloña's economic program, but with greater support to social sectors. Camet was known as a successful engineer and entrepreneur, but, unlike Boloña, he reportedly lacked any experience in negotiating international financial agreements. In the wake of Boloña's departure, annual inflation raised its head again, totaling 17.5 percent in the first quarter. However, Peru's first-quarter gross national product (GNP—see Glossary) grew 2.3 percent from the same period in 1992.

Fujimori seemed to be moving in the direction of building a reformed and more democratic governing system, and he fully expected to complete his term of office, barring an ill-conceived military coup by army officers on the payroll of drug traffickers or assassination by the extreme right or left. As of mid-June 1993, however, Graham's assertion that Fujimori's self-coup "played into

into the SL's strategy of provoking a coup in order to polarize society into military and nonmilitary camps'' fortunately had not yet been validated. The elections for a broadly based CCD and municipal governments were steps in the right direction, but the formal transition to a reformed democracy awaited the adoption of a new, improved constitution pending the holding of a national referendum. The draft of the new constitution, published in May 1993, contains 148 new articles, 93 modified articles, and 59 unchanged articles of the constitution of 1979.

Even with a new constitution, questions as to the CCD's autonomy would likely continue, and some freedoms normally expected of democracy probably would remain restricted. For example, although both Fujimori and General Juan Enrique Briones Dávila, the minister of interior, claimed in January 1993 that total freedom of the press existed throughout the nation, new legislation providing life sentences to journalists convicted of being ''apologists of terrorism'' was intimidating to reporters. Some limited press restrictions had been imposed, primarily against newspapers affiliated with the SL and the MRTA. Americas Watch, a New York-based human rights group, reported in early 1993 that ''Freedom of the press in Peru is steadily eroding in what appears to be a broad campaign by the Fujimori government to intimidate or silence critics and political opponents.'' In early 1993, Enrique Zileri Gibson, editor of the weekly news magazine *Caretas,* was barred from leaving the country, and his assets were frozen under the terms of his sentence for defaming Montesinos by characterizing him as a ''Rasputin.'' (If there is an indirect analogy between the illiterate mystic Rasputin and the well-informed Montesinos, it may be found in Rasputin's influence over Tsarina Alexandra on appointments and dismissals of high-ranking government officials and in Tsar Nicholas II's decision to ignore continued allegations of wrongdoing by Rasputin after expelling him once, only to have the tsarina return him to the palace.) Despite the Fujimori government's action against Zileri, *Caretas* continued to publish articles critical of the government and Fujimori in particular. Fujimori, for his part, continued to make himself accessible to the press by giving lengthy weekly interviews in which he has shown himself adept at putting a favorable ''spin'' on the news.

His critics notwithstanding, Fujimori was convinced that his authoritarian measures were rapidly pacifying Peru and setting the stage for a free-market economic boom in the mid-1990s. He was expected to continue pushing ahead with liberal policies, speeding up the privatization process, controlling inflation, and promoting the international reinsertion of Peru. Indeed, in sharp contrast to

Peru's standing in 1991, investor confidence in Peru was soaring by early 1993, buoyed by government progress against terrorism, the IMF's endorsement of the country's economic program, and Fujimori's liberal foreign investment regulations. Lima's stock index had risen in real terms by 138 percent, one of the highest rankings in terms of growth among world markets. France's Crédit Lyonnais (a state-owned bank slated to be privatized) became the first foreign bank in many years to assume majority control of a Peruvian bank, the Banco de Lima. Nevertheless, businesses still faced terrorist sabotage, deteriorating infrastructure, and miserable social conditions. It seemed doubtful that Peru would be able to imitate the example of its far more developed and democratic southern neighbor, Chile, whose economy was booming as a result of economic and political reforms. Peru's intractable problems, particularly the poverty of the great mass of Peruvians and the rapidly growing population rate, weighed heavily against the nation's emulation of Chile's rising level of development. But Fujimori, in contrast to his status quo predecessors, namely García and Belaúnde, appeared to be making progress in moving the country in the direction of significant political and economic reforms and eventual defeat of the SL and the MRTA (the latter was nearly neutralized in April 1993 with the recapture of a top leader, María Lucero Cumpa Miranda).

Peruvians, for their part, expected Fujimori to keep to his timetable of eliminating the SL threat by the end of his term on July 28, 1995. In 1992 Senderologists had differing views on the SL's chances of seizing power before the end of the twentieth century, as it had vowed to do. McCormick was among those who considered an SL victory by 2000 to be likely. Others, including Palmer, asserted that the Fujimori government was stronger than assumed, that the SL was weaker than assumed, and, thus, an SL takeover was unlikely. In the more blunt assessment of Raúl González, the SL's chances of seizing power were "nil." In April 1993, with most SL leaders in prison, the latter two views appeared to be closer to the mark. Nevertheless, the SL reportedly had decided on a strategy of total militarization and appeared to be still capable of continuing its terrorist activities indefinitely.

Peruvians also expected Fujimori to comply with the results of the 1995 presidential elections, even though his authoritarian tendencies seemed to run counter to his oft-stated intention to step down at the end of his term in 1995. In early January 1993, he signed some fifty decrees designed to consolidate presidential power before the CCD became operational that month. These decrees included a provision—approved by the CCD and included in the draft of the new constitution—for successive presidential reelection and the less justifiable power to dissolve Congress. With a 66 percent approval rating in June 1993, according to Apoyo, it seemed conceivable that Fujimori could complete his semi-legitimate term with a substantial measure of his extraordinary popularity intact. Although the Apoyo poll found that only 41 percent of the population would reelect him in the 1995 election, a Datum survey, also conducted in June 1993, showed that 58 percent supported his reelection in 1995. Should Fujimori decide in April 1995 to be a candidate, he could remain an "emperor," with a renewed mandate of legitimacy, for much of the decade by winning reelection. However, if he failed to restore full democratic freedoms and guarantees of respect for human rights, he risked renewed international isolation of Peru, which would likely have grave consequences for the economy, political stability, and the counterterrorism war.

June 30, 1993   Rex A. Hudson

Chapter 1. Historical Setting

Machupicchu ruins

As THE CRADLE of South America's most advanced native American civilizations, Peru has a rich and unique heritage among the nations of the southern continent. It encompasses a past that reaches back over 10,000 years in one of the most harsh and inhospitable, if spectacular, environments in the world—the high Andes of South America. The culmination of Andean civilization was the construction by the Incas, in little more than one hundred years, of an empire that spanned a third of the South American continent and achieved a level of general material well-being and cultural sophistication that rivaled and surpassed many of the great empires in world history.

Paradoxically, Peruvian history is also unique in another, less glorious, way. The Andean peoples engaged the invading Spaniards in 1532 in one of the first clashes between Western and non-Western civilizations in history. The ensuing Spanish conquest and colonialism rent the rich fabric of Andean society and created the enormous gulf between victors and vanquished that has characterized Peru down through the centuries. Indeed, Peru's postconquest, colonial past established a historic division—a unique Andean "dualism"—that formed the hallmark of its subsequent underdevelopment. Peru, like its geography, became divided economically, socially, and politically between a semifeudal, largely native American highland interior and a more modernized, capitalistic, urbanized, and mestizo (see Glossary) coast. At the apex of its social structure, a small, wealthy, educated elite came to dominate the vast majority of Peruvians, who, by contrast, subsisted in poverty, isolation, ignorance, and disease. The persistence of this dualism and the inability of the Peruvian state in more recent times to overcome it have prevented not only the development but also the effective integration and consolidation of the Peruvian nation to this day.

Another unique feature of Peru is the role that outsiders have played in its history. Peru's formal independence from Spain in 1824 (proclaimed on July 28, 1821) was largely the work of "outsiders," such as the Venezuelan Simón Bolívar Palacios and the Argentine José de San Martín. In 1879 Chile invaded Peru, precipitating the War of the Pacific (1879-83), and destroyed or carried off much of its wealth, as well as annexing a portion of its territory. Foreigners have also exploited Peru's natural resources, from silver in the colonial period to guano and nitrates in the

3

nineteenth century and copper, oil, and various industrial metals in the twentieth century. This exploitation, among other things, led advocates of the dependency theory to argue that Peru's export-dependent economy was created and manipulated by foreign interests in a nefarious alliance with a domestic oligarchy.

Although foreigners have played controversial roles throughout Peruvian history, internal demographic changes since the middle of the twentieth century have shaped contemporary Peru in other fundamental ways. For example, the total population grew almost threefold from over 7 million in 1950 to nearly 20 million in 1985, despite slowing down in the 1970s. This growth reflected a sharp jump after World War II in fertility rates that led to an average annual increase in the population of 2.5 percent. At the same time, a great wave of out-migration swept the Sierra. Over the next quarter century, Peru moved from a rural to an essentially urban society. In 1980 over 60 percent of its work force was located in towns and cities. The capital, Lima, had one-third of the total population, and the coast had three-fifths. This monumental population shift resulted in a dramatic increase in the informal economy (see Glossary) because Peru's formal economy was unable to expand fast enough to accommodate the newcomers. In 1985 half of Lima's nearly 7 million inhabitants lived in informal housing, and at least half of the country's population was employed or underemployed in the informal sector.

The demographic changes during the previous quarter century led anthropologist José Matos Mar to describe the 1980s as a great *desborde popular* (overflowing of the masses). Once the proud bastion of the dominant Creole (white American-born) classes, Lima became increasingly Andeanized in ways that have made it virtually unrecognizable to a previous generation of inhabitants. In some ways, this trend of Andeanization suggests that the old dualism may now be beginning to erode, at least in an ethnic sense. Urbanization and *desborde popular* also tended to overwhelm the capacity of the state, already weak by historical standards, to deliver even the basic minimum of governmental services to the vast majority of the population.

As these demographic changes unfolded, Peru experienced an increasing "hegemonic" crisis—the dispersion of power away from the traditional triumvirate of oligarchy, church, and armed forces. This dispersion occurred when the longstanding power of the oligarchy came to an abrupt end in the 1968 military "revolution." The ensuing agrarian reform of 1969 destroyed the economic base of both the export elite and the *gamonales* (sing. *gamonal;* rural bosses—see Glossary) in the Sierra. Then, after more than a decade, the

4

military, in growing public disfavor, returned to the barracks, opening the way, once again, to the democratic process.

With the resumption of elections in 1980, a process that was reaffirmed in 1985 (and again in 1990), "redemocratization" confronted a number of problems. The end of military rule left in its wake an enormous political vacuum that the political parties—absent for twelve years and historically weak—and a proliferating number of new groups were hard-pressed to fill. Even under the best of circumstances, given Peru's highly fragmented and heterogeneous society, as well as its long history of authoritarian and oligarchical rule, effective democratic government would have been difficult to accomplish. Even more serious, redemocratization faced an increasingly grave threat from a deepening economic crisis that began in the mid-1960s. Various economic factors caused the country's main engine for sustained economic growth to stall. As a result of the ensuing economic stagnation and decline, real wages by 1985 approached mid-1960 levels.

Finally, redemocratization was also threatened from another quarter—the emergence, also in 1980, of the Shining Path (Sendero Luminoso—SL) guerrilla movement, Latin America's most violent and radical ongoing insurgency. By 1985 its "people's war" had claimed about 6,000 victims, most of them innocent civilians killed by the guerrillas or the army. Resorting to extraordinarily violent means, the SL succeeded in challenging the authority of the state, particularly in the more remote areas of the interior, where the presence of the state had always been tenuous—the more so now because of the absence of the *gamonal* class. Violence, however, was a thread that ran throughout Andean history, from Inca expansion, the Spanish conquest and colonialism, and countless native American insurrections and their suppression to the struggle for independence in the 1820s, the War of the Pacific, and the long-term nature of underdevelopment itself.

Andean Societies Before the Conquest
Pre-Inca Cultures

The first great conquest of Andean space began some 20,000 years ago when the descendants of the original migrants who crossed the land bridge over what is now the Bering Straits between the Asian and American continents reached northern South America. Over the next several millennia, hunter-gatherers fanned out from their bridgehead at Panama to populate the whole of South America. By about 2500 B.C., small villages inhabited by farmers and fishermen began to spring up in the fertile river valleys of the north coast of Peru.

These ancient Peruvians lived in simple adobe houses, cultivated potatoes and beans, fished in the nearby sea, and grew and wove cotton for their clothing. The catalyst for the development of the more advanced civilizations that followed was the introduction of a staple annual crop—maize (corn)—and the development of irrigation, both dating from around the thirteenth century B.C. The stabilization of the food supply and ensuing surplus formed the foundation for the development of the great civilizations that rose and fell across the Andes for more than a thousand years prior to the arrival of the Europeans.

The Incas, of course, were only the most recent of these highly developed native American cultures to evolve in the Andes. The earliest central state to emerge in the northern highlands (that is, a state able to control both highland and coastal areas) was the Kingdom of Chavín, which emerged in the northern highlands and prospered for some 500 years between 950 B.C. and 450 B.C. Although it was originally thought by Julio C. Tello, the father of Peruvian archaeology, to have been "the womb of Andean civilization," it now appears to have had Amazonian roots that may have led back to Mesoamerica.

Chavín was probably more of a religious than political pan-Andean phenomenon. It seems to have been a center for the missionary diffusion of priests who transmitted a particular set of ideas, rituals, and art style throughout what is now north-central Peru. The apparent headquarters for this religious cult in all likelihood was Chavín de Huántar in the Ancash highlands, whose elaborately carved stone masonry buildings are among the oldest and most beautiful in South America. The great, massive temple there, oriented to the cardinal points of the compass, was perceived by the people of Chavín to be the center of the world, the most holy and revered place of the Chavín culture. This concept of God and his elite tied to a geographical location at the center of the cosmos—the idea of spatial mysticism—was fundamental to Inca and pre-Inca beliefs.

After the decline of the Chavín culture around the beginning of the Christian millennium, a series of localized and specialized cultures rose and fell, both on the coast and in the highlands, during the next thousand years. On the coast, these included the Gallinazo, Mochica, Paracas, Nazca, and Chimú civilizations. Although each had their salient features, the Mochica and Chimú warrant special comment for their notable achievements.

The Mochica civilization occupied a 136-kilometer-long expanse of the coast from the Río Moche Valley and reached its apogee toward the end of the first millennium A.D. The Mochica built

6

A Moche ceramic sculpture
Courtesy Embassy of Peru,
Washington

an impressive irrigation system that transformed kilometers of barren desert into fertile and abundant fields capable of sustaining a population of over 50,000. Without benefit of the wheel, the plough, or a developed writing system, the Mochica nevertheless achieved a remarkable level of civilization, as witnessed by their highly sophisticated ceramic pottery, lofty pyramids, and clever metalwork. In 1987 near Sipán, archaeologists unearthed an extraordinary cache of Mochica artifacts from the tomb of a great Mochica lord, including finely crafted gold and silver ornaments, large, gilded copper figurines, and wonderfully decorated ceramic pottery. Indeed, the Mochica artisans portrayed such a realistic and accurately detailed depiction of themselves and their environment that we have a remarkably authentic picture of their everyday life and work.

Whereas the Mochica were renowned for their realistic ceramic pottery, the Chimú were the great city-builders of pre-Inca civilization. Living in a loose confederation of cities scattered along the coast of northern Peru and southern Ecuador, the Chimú flourished from about 1150 to 1450. Their capital was at Chan Chan outside of modern-day Trujillo. The largest pre-Hispanic city in South America at the time, Chan Chan had 100,000 inhabitants. Its twenty square kilometers of precisely symmetrical design was surrounded by a lush garden oasis intricately irrigated from the Río Moche several kilometers away. The Chimú civilization lasted a comparatively short period of time, however. Like other coastal

7

states, its irrigation system, watered from sources in the high Andes, was apparently vulnerable to cutoff or diversion by expanding highland polities.

In the highlands, both the Tiwanaku (Tiahuanaco) culture, near Lake Titicaca in Bolivia, and the Wari (Huari) culture, near the present-day city of Ayacucho, developed large urban settlements and wide-ranging state systems between A.D. 500 and A.D. 1000. Each exhibited many of the aspects of the engineering ingenuity that later appeared with the Incas, such as extensive road systems, store houses, and architectural styles. Between A.D. 1000 and 1450, however, a period of fragmentation shattered the previous unity achieved by the Tiwanaku-Wari stage. During this period, scores of different ethnic-based groups of varying sizes dotted the Andean landscape. In the central and southern Andes, for example, the Chupachos of Huánuco numbered some 10,000, and the Lupacas on the west bank of Lake Titicaca comprised over 100,000.

The Incas

The Incas of Cusco (Cuzco) originally represented one of these small and relatively minor ethnic groups, the Quechuas. Gradually, as early as the thirteenth century, they began to expand and incorporate their neighbors. Inca expansion was slow until about the middle of the fifteenth century, when the pace of conquest began to accelerate, particularly under the rule of the great emperor Pachacuti Inca Yupanqui (1438–71). Historian John Hemming describes Pachacuti as "one of those protean figures, like Alexander or Napoleon, who combine a mania for conquest with the ability to impose his will on every facet of government." Under his rule and that of his son, Topa Inca Yupanqui (1471–93), the Incas came to control upwards of a third of South America, with a population of 9 to 16 million inhabitants under their rule. Pachacuti also promulgated a comprehensive code of laws to govern his far-flung empire, called Tawantinsuyu, while consolidating his absolute temporal and spiritual authority as the God of the Sun who ruled from a magnificently rebuilt Cusco.

Although displaying distinctly hierarchical and despotic features, Incan rule also exhibited an unusual measure of flexibility and paternalism. The basic local unit of society was the *ayllu* (see Glossary), which formed an endogamous nucleus of kinship groups who possessed collectively a specific, although often disconnected, territory. In the *ayllu,* grazing land was held in common (private property did not exist), whereas arable land was parceled out to families in proportion to their size. Because self-sufficiency was the ideal of Andean society, family units claimed parcels of land in different ecological niches in the rugged Andean terrain. In this way, they achieved what anthropologists have called "vertical complementarity," that is, the ability to produce a wide variety of crops— such as maize, potatoes, and quinoa (a protein-rich grain)—at different altitudes for household consumption.

The principle of complementarity also applied to Andean social relations, as each family head had the right to ask relations, allies, or neighbors for help in cultivating his plot. In return, he was obligated to offer them food and *chicha* (a fermented corn alcoholic beverage), and to help them on their own plots when asked. Mutual aid formed the ideological and material bedrock of all Andean social and productive relations. This system of reciprocal exchange existed at every level of Andean social organization: members of the *ayllus*, *curacas* (local lords) with their subordinate *ayllus*, and the Inca himself with all his subjects.

Ayllus often formed parts of larger dual organizations with upper and lower divisions called moieties, and then still larger units, until they comprised the entire ethnic group. As it expanded, the Inca state became, historian Nathan Wachtel writes, "the pinnacle of this immense structure of interlocking units. It imposed a political and military apparatus on all of these ethnic groups, while continuing to rely on the hierarchy of *curacas*, who declared their loyalty to the Inca and ruled in his name." In this sense, the Incas established a system of indirect rule that enabled the incorporated ethnic groups to maintain their distinctiveness and self-awareness within a larger imperial system.

All Inca people collectively worked the lands of the Inca, who served as representative of the God of the Sun—the central god and religion of the empire. In return, they received food, as well as *chicha* and coca leaves (which were chewed and used for religious rites and for medicinal purposes); or they made cloth and clothing for tribute, using the Inca flocks; or they regularly performed *mita* (see Glossary), or service for public works, such as roads and buildings, or for military purposes that enabled the development of the state. The Inca people also maintained the royal family and bureaucracy, centered in Cusco. In return for these services, the Inca allocated land and redistributed part of the tribute received—such as food, cloth, and clothes—to the communities, often in the form of welfare. Tribute was stored in centrally located warehouses to be dispensed during periods of shortages caused by famine, war, or natural disaster. In the absence of a market economy, Inca redistribution of tribute served as the primary means of exchange. The principles of reciprocity and redistribution, then, formed the organizing ideas that governed all relations in the Inca empire from community to state.

One of the more remarkable elements of the Inca empire was the *mitmaq* system. Before the Incas conquered the area, colonies of settlers were sent out from the *ayllus* to climatically different Andean terrains to cultivate crops that would vary and enrich the community diet. Anthropologist John V. Murra dubbed these unique Andean island colonies "vertical archipelagos," which the Incas adapted and applied on a large scale to carve out vast new areas of cultivation. The Incas also expanded the original Andean concept of *mitmaq* as a vehicle for developing complementary sources of food to craft specialization and military expansion. In the latter instance, Inca *mitmaq* were used to establish permanent garrisons to maintain control and order on the expanding Inca frontier. What "began as a means of complementing productive access to a variety of ecological tiers had become," in the words of Murra, "an onerous means of political control" under the Incas.

By the late fifteenth century and early sixteenth century, the Inca Empire had reached its maximum size. Such powerful states as the coastal Chimú Kingdom were defeated and incorporated into the empire, although the Chimús spoke a language, Yunga, that was entirely distinct from the Incas' Quechua. But as the limits of the central Andean culture area were reached in present-day Chile and Argentina, as well as in the Amazon forests, the Incas encountered serious resistance, and those territories were never thoroughly subjugated.

At the outset, the Incas shared with most of their ethnic neighbors the same basic technology: weaving, pottery, metallurgy, architecture, construction engineering, and irrigation agriculture. During their period of dominance, little was added to this inventory of skills, other than the size of the population they ruled and the degree and efficiency of control they attained. The latter, however, constituted a rather remarkable accomplishment, particularly because it was achieved without benefit of either the wheel or a formal system of writing. Instead of writing, the Incas used the intricate and highly accurate quipu (knot-tying) system of record-keeping. Imperial achievements were the more extraordinary considering the relative brevity of the period during which the empire was built (perhaps four generations) and the formidable geographic obstacles of the Andean landscape.

Viewed from the present-day perspective of Peruvian underdevelopment, one cannot help but admire a system that managed to bring under cultivation four times the amount of arable land

*Machupicchu—Incas' "lost city" discovered by American
historian Hiram Bingham, 1911
Courtesy Inter-American Development Bank*

11

cultivated today. Achievements such as these caused some twentieth-century Peruvian scholars of the indigenous peoples, known as *indigenistas* (indigenists), such as Hildebrando Castro Pozo and Luis Eduardo Valcárcel, to idealize the Inca past and to overlook the hierarchical nature and totalitarian mechanisms of social and political control erected during their Incan heyday. To other intellectuals, however, from José Carlos Mariátegui to Luis Guillermo Lumbreras, the path to development has continued to call for some sort of return to the country's pre-Columbian past of communal values, autochthonous technology, and genius for production and organization.

By the time that the Spaniards arrived in 1532, the empire extended some 1,860 kilometers along the Andean spine—north to southern Colombia and south to northern Chile, between the Pacific Ocean in the west and the Amazonian rain forest in the east. Some five years before the Spanish invasion, this vast empire was rocked by a civil war that, combined with diseases imported by the Spaniards, would ultimately weaken its ability to confront the European invaders. The premature death by measles of the reigning Sapa Inca, Huayna Cápac (1493–1524), opened the way for a dynastic struggle between the emperor's two sons, Huáscar (from Cusco) and the illegitimate Atahualpa (from Quito), who each had inherited half the empire. After a five-year civil war (1528–32), Atahualpa (1532–33) emerged victorious and is said to have tortured and put to death more than 300 members of Huáscar's family. This divisive and debilitating internecine conflict left the Incas particularly vulnerable just as Francisco Pizarro and his small force of adventurers came marching up into the Sierra.

The Spanish Conquest, 1532–72

Pizarro and the Conquistadors

While the Inca empire flourished, Spain was beginning to rise to prominence in the Western world. The political union of the several independent realms in the Iberian Peninsula and the final expulsion of the Moors after 700 years of intermittent warfare had instilled in Spaniards a sense of destiny and a militant religious zeal. The encounter with the New World by Cristóbal Colón (Christopher Columbus) in 1492 offered an outlet for the material, military, and religious ambitions of the newly united nation.

Francisco Pizarro, a hollow-cheeked, thinly bearded Extremaduran of modest hidalgo (lesser nobility) birth, was not only typical of the arriviste Spanish conquistadors who came to America, but also one of the most spectacularly successful. Having participated in the indigenous wars and slave raids on Hispaniola, Spain's first outpost in the New World, the tough, shrewd, and audacious Spaniard was with Vasco Núñez de Balboa when he first glimpsed the Pacific Ocean in 1513 and was a leader in the conquest of Nicaragua (1522). He later found his way to Panama, where he became a wealthy *encomendero* (see Glossary) and leading citizen. Beginning in 1524, Pizarro proceeded to mount several expeditions, financed mainly from his own capital, from Panama south along the west coast of South America.

After several failures, Pizarro arrived in northern Peru late in 1532 with a small force of about 180 men and 30 horses. The conquistadors were excited by tales of the Incas' great wealth and bent on repeating the pattern of conquest and plunder that was becoming practically routine elsewhere in the New World. The Incas never seemed to appreciate the threat they faced. To them, of course, the Spaniards seemed the exotics. "To our Indian eyes," wrote Felipe Guamán Poma de Ayala, the author of *Nueva crónica y buen gobierno* (New Chronicle and Good Government), "the Spaniards looked as if they were shrouded like corpses. Their faces were covered with wool, leaving only the eyes visible, and the caps which they wore resembled little red pots on top of their heads."

On November 15, 1532, Pizarro arrived in Cajamarca, the Inca's summer residence located in the Andean highlands of northern Peru, and insisted on an audience with Atahualpa. Guamán Poma says the Spaniards demanded that the Inca renounce his gods and accept a treaty with Spain. He refused. "The Spaniards began to fire their muskets and charged upon the Indians, killing them like ants. At the sound of the explosions and the jingle of bells on the horses' harnesses, the shock of arms and the whole amazing novelty of their attackers' appearance, the Indians were terror-stricken. They were desperate to escape from being trampled by the horses, and in their headlong flight a lot of them were crushed to death." Guamán Poma adds that countless "Indians" but only five Spaniards were killed, "and these few casualties were not caused by the Indians, who had at no time dared to attack the formidable strangers." According to other accounts, the only Spanish casualty was Pizarro, who received a hand wound while trying to protect Atahualpa.

Pizarro's overwhelming victory at Cajamarca in which he not only captured Atahualpa, but devastated the Inca's army, estimated at between 5,000 and 6,000 warriors, dealt a paralyzing and demoralizing blow to the empire, already weakened by civil war. The superior military technology of the Spaniards—cavalry, cannon, and above all Toledo steel—had proved unbeatable against a force, however large, armed only with stone-age battle axes, slings, and cotton-padded armor. Atahualpa's capture not only deprived the empire of leadership at a crucial moment, but the hopes of his recently defeated opponents, the supporters of Huáscar, were revived by the prospect of an alliance with a powerful new Andean power contender, the Spaniards.

Atahualpa now sought to gain his freedom by offering the Spaniards a treasure in gold and silver. Over the next few months, a fabulous cache of Incan treasure—some eleven tons of gold objects alone—was delivered to Cajamarca from all corners of the empire. Pizarro distributed the loot to his "men of Cajamarca," creating instant "millionaires," but also slighting Diego de Almagro, his partner who arrived later with reinforcements. This action sowed the seeds for a bitter factional dispute that soon would throw Peru into a bloody civil war and cost both men their lives. Once enriched by the Incas' gold, Pizarro, seeing no further use for Atahualpa, reneged on his agreement and executed the Inca—by garroting rather than hanging—after Atahualpa agreed to be baptized as a Christian.

Consolidation of Control

With Atahualpa dead, the Spaniards proceeded to march on Cusco. On the way, they dealt another decisive blow, aided by native American allies from the pro-Huáscar faction, to the still formidable remnants of Atahualpa's army. Then on November 15, 1533, exactly a year after arriving at Cajamarca, Pizarro, reinforced with an army of 5,000 native American auxiliaries, captured the imperial city and placed Manco Cápac II, kin of Huáscar and his faction, on the Inca throne as a Spanish puppet.

Further consolidation of Spanish power in Peru, however, was slowed during the next few years by both indigenous resistance and internal divisions among the victorious Spaniards. The native population, even those who had allied initially with the invaders against the Incas, had second thoughts about the arrival of the newcomers. They originally believed that the Spaniards simply represented one more in a long line of Andean power-contenders with whom to ally or accommodate. The continuing violent and rapacious behavior of many Spaniards, however, as well as the harsh overall effects of the new colonial order, caused many to alter this assessment. This change led Manco Cápac II to balk at his subservient role as a Spanish puppet and to rise in rebellion in 1536. Ultimately unable to defeat the Spaniards, Manco retreated to Vilcabamba in the remote Andean interior where he established an independent

Quechuan boy at Incan wall in Cusco
Courtesy Inter-American Development Bank

Inca kingdom, replete with a miniature royal court, that held out until 1572.

Native American resistance took another form during the 1560s with the millenarian religious revival in Huamanga known as Taki Onqoy (literally "dancing sickness"), which preached the total rejection of Spanish religion and customs. Converts to the sect expressed their conversion and spiritual rebirth by a sudden seizure in which they would shake and dance uncontrollably, often falling and writhing on the ground. The leaders of Taki Onqoy claimed that they were messengers from the native gods and preached that a pan-Andean alliance of native gods would destroy the Christians by unleashing disease and other calamities against them. An adherent to the sect declared at an official inquiry in 1564 that "the world has turned about, and this time God and the Spaniards [will be] defeated and all the Spaniards killed and their cities drowned; and the sea will rise and overwhelm them, so that there will remain no memory of them."

To further complicate matters for the conquerors, a fierce dispute broke out among the followers of Pizarro and those of Diego de Almagro. Having fallen out over the original division of spoils at Cajamarca, Almagro and his followers challenged Pizarro's control of Cusco after returning from an abortive conquest expedition to Chile in 1537. Captured by Pizarro's forces at the Battle of Salinas in 1538, Almagro was executed, but his supporters, who continued to plot under his son, Diego, gained a measure of revenge by assassinating Pizarro in 1541.

As the civil turmoil continued, the Spanish crown intervened to try to bring the dispute to an end, but in the process touched off a dangerous revolt among the colonists by decreeing the end of the *encomienda* system (see Glossary) in 1542. The *encomienda* had originally been granted as a reward to the conquistadors and their families during the conquest and ensuing colonization, and was regarded as sacrosanct by the grantees, or *encomenderos,* who numbered about 500 out of a total Spanish population of 2,000 in 1536. However, to the crown it raised the specter of a potentially privileged, neofeudal elite emerging in the Andes to challenge crown authority.

The crown's efforts to enforce the New Laws (Nuevos Leyes) of 1542 alienated the colonists, who rallied around the figure of Gonzalo Pizarro, the late Francisco's brother. Gonzalo managed to kill the intemperate Viceroy Don Blasco Núñez de la Vela, who, on his arrival, had foolishly tried to enforce the New Laws. In 1544 Pizarro assumed de facto authority over Peru. His arbitrary and brutal rule, however, caused opposition among the colonists, so that when another royal representative, Pedro de la Gasca, arrived in Peru to restore crown authority, he succeeded in organizing a pro-royalist force that defeated and executed Pizarro in 1548. With Gonzalo's death, the crown finally succeeded, despite subsequent intermittent revolts, in ending the civil war and exerting crown control over Spanish Peru.

It would take another two decades, however, to finally quell native American resistance. Sensing the danger of the Taki Onqoy heresy, the Spanish authorities moved quickly and energetically, through a church-sponsored anti-idolatry campaign, to suppress it before it had a chance to spread. Its leaders were seized, beaten, fined, or expelled from their communities. At the same time, a new campaign was mounted against the last Inca holdout at Vilcabamba, which was finally captured in 1572. With it, the last reigning Inca, Túpac Amaru, was tried and beheaded by the Spaniards in a public ceremony in Cusco, thereby putting an end to the events of the conquest that had begun so dramatically four decades earlier at Cajamarca.

The Colonial Period, 1550–1824

Demographic Collapse

Throughout the Americas, the impact of the Spanish conquest and subsequent colonization was to bring about a cataclysmic demographic collapse of the indigenous population. The Andes would be no exception. Even before the appearance of Francisco Pizarro on the Peruvian coast, the lethal diseases that had been introduced into the Americas with the arrival of the Spaniards—smallpox, malaria, measles, typhus, influenza, and even the common cold—had spread to South America and begun to wreak havoc throughout Tawantinsuyu. Indeed, the death of Huayna Cápac and his legitimate son and heir, Ninan Cuyoche, which touched off the disastrous dynastic struggles between Huáscar and Atahualpa, is believed to have been the result of a smallpox or measles epidemic that struck in 1530–31.

With an estimated population of 9 to 16 million people prior to the arrival of the Europeans, Peru's population forty years later was reduced on average by about 80 percent, generally higher on the coast than in the highlands (see table 2, Appendix). The chronicler Pedro de Cieza de León, who traveled over much of Peru during this period, was particularly struck by the extent of the depopulation along the coast. "The inhabitants of this valley [Chincha, south of Lima]," he wrote, "were so numerous that many Spaniards say that when it was conquered by the Marquis [Pizarro] and themselves, there were . . . more than 25,000 men, and I doubt that there are now 5,000, so many have been the inroads and hardships they have suffered." Demographic anthropologists Henry F. Dobyns and Paul L. Doughty have estimated that the native American population fell to about 8.3 million by 1548 and to around 2.7 million in 1570. Unlike Mexico, where the population stabilized at the end of the seventeenth century, the population in Peru did not reach its lowest point until the latter part of the eighteenth century, after the great epidemic of 1719.

War, exploitation, socioeconomic change, and the generalized psychological trauma of conquest all combined to reinforce the main contributor to the demise of the native peoples—epidemic disease. Isolated from the Old World for millennia and therefore lacking immunities, the Andean peoples were defenseless against the deadly diseases introduced by the Europeans. Numerous killer pandemics swept down from the north, laying waste to entire communities. Occurring one after the other in roughly ten-year intervals during the sixteenth century (1525, 1546, 1558–59, 1585), these epidemics did not allow the population time to recover and impaired its ability to reproduce itself.

The Colonial Economy

With the discovery of the great silver lodes at Potosí in Perú Alto (Upper Peru—present-day Bolivia) in 1545 and mercury at

Huancavelica in 1563, Peru became what historian Fredrick B. Pike describes as "Spain's great treasure house in South America." As a result, the axis of the colonial economy began to move away from the direct expropriation of Incan wealth and production and an attempt to sustain the initial Spanish population through the *encomienda* system to the extraction of mineral wealth. The population at Potosí in the high Andes reached about 160,000, its peak, in 1650, making it one of the largest cities in the Western world at the time. In its first ten years, according to Alexander von Humboldt, Potosí produced some 127 million pesos, which fueled for a time the Habsburg war machine and Spanish hegemonic political pretensions in Europe. Silver from Potosí also dynamized and helped to develop an internal economy of production and exchange that encompassed not only the northern highlands, but also the Argentine pampa, the Central Valley of Chile, and coastal Peru and Ecuador. The main "growth pole" of this vast "economic space," as historian Carlos Assadourian Sempat calls it, was the Lima-Potosí axis, which served as centers of urban concentration, market demand, strategic commodity flows (silver exports and European imports), and inflated prices.

If Potosí silver production was the mainspring of this economic system, Lima was its hub. "The city of the kings" (Los Reyes) had been founded by Pizarro as the capital of the new viceroyalty in 1535 in order to reorient trade, commerce, and power away from the Andes toward imperial Spain and Europe. As the outlet for silver bullion on the Pacific, Lima and its nearby port, Callao, also received and redistributed the manufactured goods from the metropolis for the growing settlements along the growth pole. The two-way flow of imports and exports through Lima concentrated both wealth and administration, public and private, in the city. As a result, Lima became the headquarters for estate owners and operators, merchants connecting their Andean trading operations with sources of supply in Spain, and all types of service providers, from artisans to lawyers, who needed access to the system in a central place. Not far behind came the governmental and church organizations established to administer the vast viceroyalty. Finally, once population, commerce, and administration interacted, major cultural institutions such as a university, a printing press, and theater followed suit.

The great architect of this colonial system was Francisco Toledo y Figueroa, who arrived in Lima in 1569, when its population was 2,500, and served as viceroy until 1581 (see table 3, Appendix). Toledo, one of Madrid's ablest administrators and diplomats, worked to expand the state, increase silver production, and generally

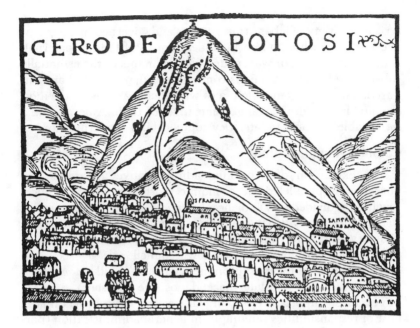

Woodcut of Potosí's Cerro Rico by Agustín de Zárate, 1555

reorganize the economy by instituting a series of major reforms during his tenure.

Native communities (*ayllus*) were concentrated into poorly located colonial settlements called *reducciones* (see Glossary) to facilitate administration and the conversion of the native Americans to Christianity. The Incan *mita* system was shifted from performing public works or military service to supplying compulsory labor for the mines and other key sectors of the economy and state. Finally, various fiscal schemes, such as the tribute tax to be paid in coin and the forced purchase of Spanish merchandise, were levied on the indigenous population in order to force or otherwise induce it into the new monetary economy as "free wage" workers. In these, as in many other instances, the Spaniards used whatever elements of the Andean political, social, and economic superstructure that served their purposes and unhesitatingly modified or discarded those that did not.

As a result of these and other changes, the Spaniards and their Creole successors came to monopolize control over the land, seizing many of the best lands abandoned by the massive native depopulation. Gradually, the land tenure system became polarized. One sector consisted of the large haciendas, worked by native peasant

19

serfs in a variety of labor arrangements and governed by their new overlords according to hybrid Andean forms of Iberian paternalism. The other sector was made up of remnants of the essentially subsistence-based indigenous communities that persisted and endured. This arrangement left Peru with a legacy of one of the most unequal landholding arrangements in all of Latin America and a formidable obstacle to later development and modernization.

Colonial Administration

The expansion of a colonial administrative apparatus and bureaucracy paralleled the economic reorganization. The viceroyalty was divided into audiences (*audiencias*—see Glossary), which were further subdivided into provinces or districts (*corregimientos*—see Glossary) and finally municipalities. The latter included a city or town, which was governed by a town council (*cabildo*—see Glossary) composed of the most prominent citizens, mostly *encomenderos* in the early years and later hacendados (see Glossary).

The most important royal official was the viceroy, who had a host of responsibilities ranging from general administration (particularly tax collection and construction of public works) and internal and external defense to support of the church and protection of the native population. He was surrounded by a number of other judicial, ecclesiastical, and treasury officials, who also reported to the Council of the Indies, the main governing body located in Spain. This configuration of royal officials, along with an official review of his tenure called the *residencia* (see Glossary), served as a check on viceregal power.

In the early years of the conquest, the crown was particularly concerned with preventing the conquistadors and other *encomenderos* from establishing themselves as a feudal aristocracy capable of thwarting royal interests. Therefore, it moved quickly to quell the civil disturbances that had racked Peru immediately after the conquest and to decree the New Laws of 1542, which deprived the *encomenderos* and their heirs of their rights to native American goods and services.

The early administrative functions of the *encomenderos* over the indigenous population (protection and Christianization) were taken over by new state-appointed officials called *corregidores de indios* (governors of Indians—see Glossary). They were charged at the provincial level with the administration of justice, control of commercial relations between native Americans and Spaniards, and the collection of the tribute tax. The *corregidores* (Spanish magistrates) were assisted by *curacas,* members of the native elite, who had been used by the conquerors from the very beginning as mediators between the native population and the Europeans. Over time the *corregidores* used their office to accumulate wealth and power. They also dominated rural society by establishing mutual alliances with local and regional elites such as the *curacas,* native American functionaries, municipal officials, rural priests (*doctrineros*), landowners, merchants, miners, and others, as well as native and mestizo subordinates.

As the crown's political authority was consolidated in the second half of the sixteenth century, so too was its ability to regulate and control the colonial economy. Operating according to the mercantilistic strictures of the times, the crown sought to maximize investment in valuable export production, such as silver and later other mineral and agricultural commodities, while supplying the new colonial market with manufactured imports, so as to create a favorable balance of trade for the metropolis. However, the tightly regulated trading monopoly, headquartered in Seville, was not always able to provision the colonies effectively. Assadourian shows that most urban and mining demand, particularly among the laboring population, was met by internal Andean production (rough-hewn clothing, foodstuffs, yerba mate tea, *chicha* beer, and the like) from haciendas, indigenous communities, and textile factories (*obrajes*—see Glossary). According to him, the value of these Andean products amounted to fully 60 to 70 percent of the value of silver exports and elite imports linking Peru and Europe. In any case, the crown was successful in managing the colonial export economy through the development of a bureaucratic and interventionist state, characterized by a plethora of mercantilistic rules that regulated the conduct of business and commerce. In doing so, Spain left both a mercantilist and export-oriented pattern and legacy of "development" in the Andes that has survived up to the present day, and which remains a problem of contemporary underdevelopment.

The Colonial Church

The crown, as elsewhere in the Americas, worked to solidify the Andean colonial order in tandem with the church to which it was tied by royal patronage dating from the late fifteenth century. Having accompanied Francisco Pizarro and his force during the conquest, the Roman Catholic friars proceeded zealously to carry out their mission to convert the indigenous peoples to Christianity. In this endeavor, the church came to play an important role in the acculturation of the natives, drawing them into the cultural orbit of the Spanish settlers. It also waged a constant war to extirpate native religious beliefs. Such efforts met with only partial success, as the syncretic nature of Andean Roman Catholicism today attests. With time, however, the evangelical mission of the church gave way to its regular role of ministering to the growing Spanish and Creole population.

By the end of the century, the church was beginning to acquire important financial assets, particularly bequests of land and other wealth, that would consolidate its position as the most important economic power during the colonial period. At the same time, it assumed the primary role of educator, welfare provider, and, through the institution of the Inquisition, guardian of orthodoxy throughout the viceroyalty. Together, the church-state partnership served to consolidate and solidify the crown authority in Peru that, despite awesome problems of distance, rough terrain, and slow communications, endured almost three centuries of continuous and relatively stable rule.

Silver production, meanwhile, began to enter into a prolonged period of decline in the seventeenth century. This decline also slowed the important transatlantic trade and diminished the importance of Lima as the economic hub of the viceregal economy. Annual silver output at Potosí, for example, fell in value from a little over 7 million pesos in 1600 to almost 4.5 million pesos in 1650 and finally to just under 2 million pesos in 1700. Falling silver production, the declining transatlantic trade, and the overall decline of Spain itself during the seventeenth century have long been interpreted by historians as causing a prolonged depression both in the viceroyalties of Peru and New Spain (see fig. 2). However, economic historian Kenneth J. Andrien has challenged this view, maintaining that the Peruvian economy, rather than declining, underwent a major transition and restructuring. After the decline in silver production and the transatlantic trade eroded the export economy, they were replaced by more diversified, regionalized, and autonomous development of the agricultural and manufacturing sectors. Merchants, miners, and producers simply shifted their investments and entrepreneurial activities away from mining and the transatlantic trade into internal production and import-substituting opportunities, a trend already visible on a small scale by the end of the previous century. The result was a surprising degree of regional diversification that stabilized the viceregal economy during the seventeenth century.

This economic diversification was marked by the rise and expansion of the great estates, or haciendas, that were carved out of abandoned native land as a result of the demographic collapse. The precipitous decline of the native population was particularly severe along the coast and had the effect of opening up the fertile

Church of San Antonio Abad in Cusco
Courtesy Inter-American Development Bank

bottom lands of the river valleys to Spanish immigrants eager for land and farming opportunities. A variety of crops were raised: sugar and cotton along the northern coast; wheat and grains in the central valleys; and grapes, olives, and sugar along the entire coast. The highlands, depending on geographic and climatic conditions, underwent a similar hacienda expansion and diversification of production. There, coca, potatoes, livestock, and other indigenous products were raised in addition to some coastal crops, such as sugar and cereals.

This transition toward internal diversification in the colony also included early manufacturing, although not to the extent of agrarian production. Textile manufacturing flourished in Cusco, Cajamarca, and Quito to meet popular demand for rough-hewn cotton and woolen garments. A growing intercolonial trade along the Pacific Coast involved the exchange of Peruvian and Mexican silver for oriental silks and porcelain. In addition, Arequipa and then Nazca and Ica became known for the production of fine wines and brandies. And throughout the viceroyalty, small-scale artisan industries supplied a range of lower-cost goods only sporadically available from Spain and Europe, which were now mired in the seventeenth-century depression.

If economic regionalization and diversification worked to stabilize the colonial economy during the seventeenth century, the benefits of such a trend did not, as it turned out, accrue to Madrid.

The crown had derived enormous revenues from silver production and the transatlantic trade, which it was able to tax and collect relatively easily. The decline in silver production caused a precipitous fall in crown revenue, particularly in the second half of the seventeenth century. For example, revenue remittances to Spain dropped from an annual average of almost 1.5 million pesos in the 1630s to less than 128,000 pesos by the 1680s. The crown tried to restructure the tax system to conform to the new economic realities of seventeenth-century colonial production but was rebuffed by the recalcitrance of emerging local elites. They tenaciously resisted any new local levies on their production, while building alliances of mutual convenience and gain with local crown officials to defend their vested interests.

The situation further deteriorated, from the perspective of Spain, when Madrid began in 1633 to sell royal offices to the highest bidder, enabling self-interested Creoles to penetrate and weaken the royal bureaucracy. The upshot was not only a sharp decline in vital crown revenues from Peru during the century, which further contributed to the decline of Spain itself, but an increasing loss of royal control over local Creole oligarchies throughout the viceroyalty. Lamentably, the sale of public offices also had longer-term implications. The practice weakened any notion of disinterested public service and infused into the political culture the corrosive idea that office-holding was an opportunity for selfish, private gain rather than for the general public good.

If the economy of the viceroyalty reached a certain steady state during the seventeenth century, its population continued to decline. Estimated at around 3 million in 1650, the population of the viceroyalty finally reached its nadir at a little over 1 million inhabitants in 1798. It rose sharply to almost 2.5 million inhabitants by 1825. The 1792 census indicated an ethnic composition of 13 percent European, 56 percent native American, and 27 percent *castas* (mestizos), the latter category the fastest-growing group because of both acculturation and miscegenation between Europeans and natives.

Demographic expansion and the revival of silver production, which had fallen sharply at the end of the seventeenth century, promoted a period of gradual economic growth from 1730 to 1770. The pace of growth then picked up in the last quarter of the eighteenth century, partly as a result of the so-called Bourbon reforms of 1764, named after a branch of the ruling French Bourbon family that ascended to the Spanish throne after the death of the last Habsburg in 1700.

In the second half of the eighteenth century, particularly during the reign of Charles III (1759–1788), Spain turned its reform efforts to Spanish America in a concerted effort to increase the revenue flow from its American empire. The aims of the program were to centralize and improve the structure of government, to create more efficient economic and financial machinery, and to defend the empire from foreign powers. For Peru, perhaps the most far-reaching change was the creation in 1776 of a new viceroyalty in the Río de la Plata (River Plate) region that radically altered the geopolitical and economic balance in South America. Upper Peru was detached administratively from the old Viceroyalty of Peru, so that profits from Potosí no longer flowed to Lima and Lower Peru, but to Buenos Aires. With the rupture of the old Lima-Potosí circuit, Lima suffered an inevitable decline in prosperity and prestige, as did the southern highlands (Cusco, Arequipa, and Puno). The viceregal capital's status declined further from the general measures to introduce free trade within the empire. These measures stimulated the economic development of peripheral areas in northern South America (Venezuela) and southern South America (Argentina), ending Lima's former monopoly of South American trade.

As a result of these and other changes, the economic axis of Peru shifted northward to the central and northern Sierra and central coast. These areas benefited from the development of silver mining, particularly at Cerro de Pasco, which was spurred by a series of measures taken by the Bourbons to modernize and revitalize the industry. However, declining trade and production in the south, together with a rising tax burden levied by the Bourbon state, which fell heavily on the native peasantry, set the stage for the massive native American revolt that erupted with the Túpac Amaru rebellion in 1780–82.

Indigenous Rebellions

An upsurge in native discontent and rebellion had actually begun to occur in the eighteenth century. To survive their brutal subjugation, the indigenous peoples had early on adopted a variety of strategies. Until recently, the scholarly literature inaccurately portrayed them as passive. To endure, the native Americans did indeed have to adapt to Spanish domination. As often as not, however, they found ways of asserting their own interests.

After the conquest, the crown had assumed from the Incas patrimony over all native land, which it granted in usufruct to indigenous community families, in exchange for tribute payments

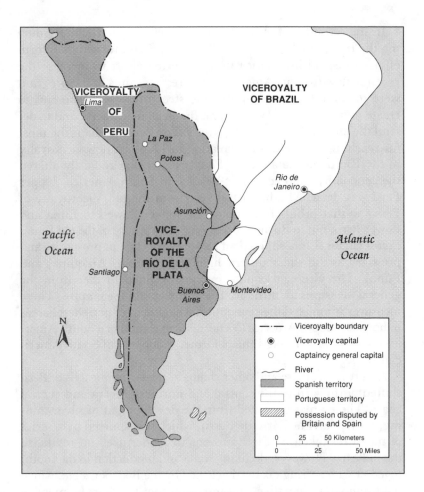

Source: Based on information from A. Curtis Wilgus, *Historical Atlas of Latin America,* New York, 1967, 112; and Aníbal Cueva García, ed., *Gran atlas geográfico del Perú y el mundo,* Lima, 1991, 69.

Figure 2. Three South American Viceroyalties, ca. 1800

and *mita* labor services. This system became the basis for a long-lasting alliance between the colonial state and the native communities, bolstered over the years by the elaboration of a large body of protective legislation. Crown officials, such as the *corregidores de indios,* were charged with the responsibility of protecting natives from abuse at the hands of the colonists, particularly the alienation of their land to private landholders. Nevertheless, the colonists and their native allies, the *curacas,* often in collusion with the *corregidores* and local priests, found ways of circumventing crown laws

and gaining control of native American lands and labor. To
ter such exploitation and to conserve their historical rights
land, many native American leaders shrewdly resorted to the legal
system. Litigation did not always suffice, of course, and Andean
history is full of desperate native peasant rebellions.

The pace of these uprisings increased dramatically in the eighteenth century, with five in the 1740s, eleven in the 1750s, twenty
in the 1760s, and twenty in the 1770s. Their underlying causes
were largely economic. Land was becoming increasingly scarce in
the communities because of illegal purchases by unscrupulous
colonists at a time when the indigenous population was once again
growing after the long, postconquest demographic decline. At the
same time, the native peasantry felt the brunt of higher taxes levied
by the crown, part of the general reform program initiated by
Madrid in the second half of the eighteenth century. These increased
tax burdens came at a time when the highland elite—*corregidores,*
priests, *curacas,* and Hispanicized native landholders—was itself increasing the level of surplus extracted from the native American
peasant economy. According to historian Nils P. Jacobsen, this
apparent tightening of the colonial "screw" during the eighteenth
century led to the "over-exploitation" of the native peasantry and
the ensuing decades of indigenous rebellions.

The culmination of this protest came in 1780 when José Gabriel
Condorcanqui, a wealthy *curaca* and mestizo descendant of Inca
ancestors who sympathized with the oppressed native peasantry,
seized and executed a notoriously abusive *corregidor* near Cusco.
Condorcanqui raised a ragtag army of tens of thousands of natives,
castas, and even a few dissident Creoles, assuming the name Túpac
Amaru II after the last Inca, to whom he was related. Drawing
on a rising tide of Andean millenarianism and nativism, Túpac
Amaru II raised the specter of some kind of return to a mythic
Incan past among the indigenous masses at a time of increased economic hardship.

Captured by royalist forces in 1781, Condorcanqui was brought
to trial and, like his namesake, cruelly executed, along with several relatives, in the main plaza in Cusco, as a warning to others.
The rebellion continued, however, and even expanded into the
Altiplano around Lake Titicaca under the leadership of his brother,
Diego Cristóbal Túpac Amaru. It was finally suppressed in 1782,
and in the following years the authorities undertook to carry out
some of the reforms that the two native leaders had advocated.

Independence Imposed from Without, 1808–24

Despite the Túpac Amaru revolts, independence was slow to
develop in the Viceroyalty of Peru. For one thing Peru was a

conservative, royalist stronghold where the potentially restless Creole elites maintained a relatively privileged, if dependent, position in the old colonial system.]At the same time, the "anti-white" manifestations of the Túpac Amaru revolt demonstrated that the indigenous masses could not easily be mobilized without posing a threat to the Creole caste itself.[Thus, when independence finally did come in 1824, it was largely a foreign imposition rather than a truly popular, indigenous, and nationalist movement.]As historian David P. Werlich has aptly put it, "Peru's role in the drama of Latin American independence was largely that of an interested spectator until the final act."

What the spectator witnessed prior to 1820 was a civil war in the Americas that pitted dissident Creole elites in favor of independence against royalists loyal to the crown and the old colonial order. The movement had erupted in reaction to Napoleon Bonaparte's invasion of Spain in 1808, which deposed Ferdinand VII and placed a usurper, Joseph Bonaparte, on the Spanish throne. In America the civil war raised the question of the very political legitimacy of the colonial government. When juntas arose in favor of the captive Ferdinand in various South American capitals (except in Peru) the following year, even though of relatively short duration, they touched off a process toward eventual separation that ebbed and flowed throughout the continent over the next fifteen years. This process developed its greatest momentum at the periphery of Spanish power in South America—in what became Venezuela and Colombia in the north and the Río de la Plata region, particularly Argentina, in the south.

Not until both movements converged in Peru during the latter phases of the revolt was Spanish control of Peru seriously threatened. General José de San Martín, the son of a Spanish army officer stationed in Argentina, had originally served in the Spanish army but returned to his native Argentina to join the rebellion. Once Argentine independence was achieved in 1814, San Martín conceived of the idea of liberating Peru by way of Chile. As commander of the 5,500-man Army of the Andes, half of which was composed of former black slaves, San Martín, in a spectacular military operation, crossed the Andes and liberated Chile in 1817. Three years later, his somewhat smaller army left Valparaíso for Peru in a fleet commanded by a former British admiral, Thomas Alexander Cochrane (Lord Dundonald).

Although some isolated stirrings for independence had manifested themselves earlier in Peru, the landing in Pisco of San Martín's 4,500-man expeditionary force in September 1820 persuaded the conservative Creole intendant of Trujillo, José Bernardo de Tagle y Portocarrero, that Peru's liberation was at hand and that he should proclaim independence. [It was symptomatic of the conservative nature of the viceroyalty that the internal forces now declaring for independence were led by a leading Creole aristocrat, the fourth marquis of Torre Tagle, whose monarchist sympathies for any future political order coincided with those of the Argentine liberator.]

[The defeat of the last bastion of royal power on the continent,] however, proved a slow and arduous task.] Although a number of other coastal cities quickly embraced the liberating army, San Martín was able to take Lima in July 1821 only when the viceroy decided to withdraw his considerable force to the Sierra, where he believed he could better make a stand. [Shortly thereafter, on July 28, 1821, San Martín proclaimed Peru independent and then was named protector by an assembly of notables.] However, a number of problems, not the least of which was a growing Peruvian resentment over the heavy-handed rule of the foreigner they dubbed "King José," stalled the campaign to defeat the royalists. As a result, [San Martín decided to seek aid from Simón Bolívar Palacios, who had liberated much of northern South America from Spanish power.]

The two liberators met in a historic meeting in Guayaquil in mid-1822 to arrange the terms of a joint effort to complete the liberation of Peru [Bolívar refused to agree to a shared partnership in the Peruvian campaign, however, so a frustrated San Martín chose to resign his command and leave Peru for Chile and eventual exile in France.] With significant help from San Martín's forces, Bolívar then proceeded to invade Peru, where he won the Battle of Junín in August 1824.] But it remained for his trusted lieutenant, thirty-one-year-old General Antonio José de Sucre Alcalá, to complete the task of Peruvian independence by defeating royalist forces at the hacienda of Ayacucho near Huamanga (a city later renamed Ayacucho) on December 9, 1824.] This battle in the remote southern highlands effectively ended the long era of Spanish colonial rule in South America (see also Colonial Period, ch. 5).

Postindependence Decline and Instability, 1824–45

Peru's transition from more than three centuries of colonial rule to nominal independence in 1824 under President Bolívar (1824–26) proved tortuous and politically destablizing. [Independence did little to alter the fundamental structures of inequality and underdevelopment based on colonialism and Andean neofeudalism.] Essentially, independence represented the transfer of power from Spanish-born whites (*peninsulares*) to sectors of the elite Creole class, whose aim was to preserve and enhance their privileged socioeconomic status.

29

However, the new Creole elite was unable to create a stable, new constitutional order to replace the crown monolith of church and state. Nor was it willing to restructure the social order in a way conducive to building a viable democratic, republican government. Ultimately, the problem was one of replacing the legitimacy of the old order with an entirely new one, something that many post-colonial regimes have had difficulty accomplishing.

Into the political vacuum left by the collapse of Spanish rule surged a particularly virulent form of Andean caudillismo. Caudillo strongmen, often officers from the liberation armies, managed to seize power through force of arms and the elaboration of extensive and intricate clientelistic alliances. Personalistic, arbitrary rule replaced the rule of law, and a prolonged and often byzantine struggle for power was waged at all levels of society. The upshot was internal political fragmentation and chronic political instability during the first two decades of the postindependence era. By one count, the country experienced at least twenty-four regime changes, averaging one per year between 1821 and 1845, and the constitution was rewritten six times.

This is not to say that larger political issues did not inform these conflicts. A revisionist study by historian Paul E. Gootenberg shows in great detail how the politics of trade (free or protectionist) and regionalism were central to the internecine caudillo struggles of the period. In this interpretation, nationalist elites—backing one caudillo or another—managed to outmaneuver and defeat liberal groups to maintain a largely protectionist, neomercantilistic, post-colonial regime until the advent of the guano boom at mid-century. This view stands in opposition to the dominant interpretation of the period, according to which unrestricted liberalism and free trade led to Peru's "dependency" on the international economy and the West.

However bewildering the chaotic era of the caudillo can be divided into several distinct periods. In the first, Bolívar tried, unsuccessfully, to impose a centralist and utopian liberal government from Lima. When events in Colombia caused him to relinquish power and return to Bogotá in 1826, his departure left an immediate vacuum that numerous Peruvian strongmen would try to fill. One of the most successful in terms of tenure was the conservative General Agustín Gamarra (1829–34) from Cusco, who managed to crush numerous rebellions and maintain power for five years. Then full-scale civil wars carried first General Luis de Orbegoso (1834–35) and then General Felipe Salaverry (1835–36) into the presidential palace for short terms. The power struggles reached such a chaotic state by the mid-1830s that General Andrés de Santa Cruz y Calahumana marched into Peru from Bolivia to impose the Peru-Bolivia Confederation of 1836-39. This alliance upset the regional balance of power and caused Chile to raise an army to defeat Santa Cruz and restore the status quo ante, which, in effect, meant a resumption of factional conflict lasting well into the 1840s.

[The descent into chronic political instability, coming immediately after the destructive wars for independence (1820-24), accelerated Peru's general postindependence economic decline.] During the 1820s, silver mining, the country's traditional engine of growth, collapsed, and massive capital flight resulted in large external deficits. By the early 1830s, the silver-mining industry began to recover, briefly climbing back to colonial levels of output in the early 1840s. Economic recovery was further enhanced in the 1840s as southern Peru began to export large quantities of wool, nitrates, and, increasingly, guano.

[On the other hand, the large-scale importation of British textiles after independence virtually destroyed the production of native artisans and *obrajes,* which were unable to compete with their more technologically advanced and cost-efficient overseas competitors. For the most part, however, the economy continued in the immediate decades after independence to be characterized by a low level of marketable surplus from largely self-sufficient haciendas and native communities.]

The expansion of exports during the 1840s did help, finally, to stabilize the Peruvian state, particularly under the statesmanlike, if autocratic, leadership of General Marshal Ramón Castilla (1845-51, 1855-62). Castilla's rise to power, coming as it did at the onset of the guano boom, marked the beginning of an age of unparalleled economic growth and increasing political stability that effectively ended the country's postindependence decline. Indeed, to many observers, Peru during the so-called guano age (1845-70) seemed uniquely positioned to emerge as the preeminent country in all of South America.

The Guano Era, 1845-70

Consolidation of the State

The guano boom, made possible by the droppings from millions of birds on the Chincha Islands, proved to be a veritable bonanza for Peru, beginning in the 1840s. By the time that this natural resource had been depleted three decades later, Peru had exported some 12 million tons of the fertilizer to Europe and North America, where it stimulated the commercial agricultural revolution. On the basis of a truly enormous flow of revenue to the state (nearly

US$500 million), Peru was presented in the middle decades of the nineteenth century with a historic opportunity for development. Why this did not materialize, but rather became a classic case of boom-bust export dependence, has continued to be the subject of intense discussion and debate. Most analysts, however, concur with historian Magnus Mörner that "guano wealth was, on the whole, a developmental opportunity missed."

On the positive side, guano-led economic growth—on average 9 percent a year beginning in the 1840s—and burgeoning government coffers provided the basis for the consolidation of the state. With adequate revenues, Castilla was able to retire the internal and external debt and place the government on a sound financial footing for the first time since independence. That, in turn, shored up the country's credit rating abroad (which, however, in time proved to be a double-edged sword in the absence of fiscal restraint). It also enabled Castilla to abolish vestiges of the colonial past— slavery in 1854 and the onerous native tribute—modernize the army, and centralize state power at the expense of local caudillos.

Failed Development

The guano bonanza also set in motion more negative trends. Castilla "nationalized" guano in order to maximize benefits to the state but in so doing reinforced aspects of the old colonial pattern of a mercantilist political economy. The state then consigned the commercialization of guano to certain favored private sectors based in Lima that had foreign connections. This action created a nefarious and often collusive relationship between the state and a new "liberal" group of guano consignees.

Soon, this increasingly powerful liberal plutocracy succeeded in reorienting the country's trade policy away from the previous nationalist and protectionist era toward export-led growth and low tariffs (see Historical Background, ch. 3). Capital investment derived from the guano boom and abroad flowed into the export sector, particularly sugar, cotton, and nitrate production. The coast now became the most economically dynamic region of the country, modernizing at a pace that outstripped the Sierra. Coastal export-led growth not only intensified the uneven and dualist nature of Peruvian development, but subjected the economy to the vicissitudes of world trade. Between 1840 and 1875, the value of exports surged from 6 million pesos to almost 32 million, and imports went from 4 to 24 million pesos. On the face of it, the liberal export model, based on guano, pulled Peru out of its postindependence economic stagnation and seemed dramatically successful. However, while great fortunes were accruing to the new coastal plutocracy, little thought was given to closing the historical inequalities of wealth and income or to fostering a national market for incipient home manufacturing that might have created the foundation for a more diversified and truly long-term economic development.

What proved a greater problem in the short term was the state's increasing reliance and ultimate dependence on foreign loans, secured by the guano deposits, which, however, were a finite and increasingly depleted natural resource. These loans helped finance an overly ambitious railroad and road-building scheme in the 1860s designed to open up Peru's natural, resource-rich interior to exploitation. Under the direction of American railroad engineer Henry Meiggs (known as the ''Yankee Pizarro''), Chinese workers constructed a spectacular Andean railroad system over some of the most difficult topography in the world. But the cost of constructing some 1,240 kilometers of railroad, together with a litany of other state expenditures, caused Peru to jump from last to first place as the world's largest borrower on London money markets.

Peru also fought two brief but expensive wars. The first, in which Peru prevailed, was with Ecuador (1859–60) over disputed territory bordering the Amazon. However, Castilla failed to extract a definitive agreement from Ecuador that might have settled conclusively the border issue, so it continued to fester throughout the next century. More successful was the Peruvian victory in 1866 over Spain's attempts to seize control of the guano-rich Chincha Islands in a tragicomic venture to recapture some of its lost empire in South America.

By the 1870s, Peru's financial house of cards, constructed on guano, finally came tumbling down. As described by Gootenberg, ''Under the combined weight of manic activity, unrestrained borrowing, dismal choice of developmental projects, the evaporation of guano, and gross fiscal mismanagement, Peru's state finally collapsed. . . .'' Ironically, the financial crisis occurred during the presidency of Manuel Pardo (1872–76), the country's first elected civilian president since independence and leader of the fledgling antimilitary Civilista Party (Partido Civilista—PC).

By the 1870s, economic growth and greater political stability had created the conditions for the organization of the country's first political party. It was composed primarily of the plutocrats of the guano era, the newly rich merchants, planters, and businesspeople, who believed that the country could no longer afford to be governed by the habitual military ''man on horseback.'' Rather, the new age of international trade, business, and finance needed the managerial skills that only civilian leadership could provide. Their candidate was the dynamic and cosmopolitan Pardo, who, at age thirty-seven, had already made a fortune in business and served with distinction as treasury minister and mayor of Lima. Who better, they asked, at a time when the government of Colonel José Balta (1868–72) had sunk into a morass of corruption and incompetence, could clean up the government, deal with the mounting financial problems, and further develop the liberal export-model that so benefited their particular interests?

However, the election of the competent Pardo in 1872 and his ensuing austerity program were not enough to ward off the impending collapse. The worldwide depression of 1873 virtually sealed Peru's fate, and as Pardo's term drew to a close in 1876, the country was forced to default on its foreign debt. With social and political turmoil once again on the rise, the Civilistas found it expedient to turn to a military figure, Mariano Ignacio Prado (1865–67, 1876–79), who had rallied the country against the Spanish naval attack in 1865 and then served as president. He was reelected president in 1876 only to lead the country into a disastrous war with its southern neighbor Chile in 1879.

The War of the Pacific, 1879–83

The war with Chile developed over the disputed, nitrate-rich Atacama Desert. Neither Peru, nor its ally, Bolivia, in the regional balance of power against Chile, had been able to solidify its territorial claims in the desert, which left the rising power of Chile to assert its designs over the region. Chile chose to attack Bolivia after Bolivia broke the Treaty of 1866 between the two countries by raising taxes on the export of nitrates from the region, mainly controlled by Chilean companies. In response, Bolivia invoked its secret alliance with Peru, the Treaty of 1873, to go to war.

Peru was obligated, then, to enter a war for which it was woefully unprepared, particularly since the antimilitary Pardo government had sharply cut the defense budget. With the perspective of hindsight, the outcome with Peru's more powerful and better organized foe to the south was altogether predictable. This was especially true after Peru's initial defeat in the naval Battle of Iquique Bay, where it lost one of its two iron-clad warships. Five months later, it lost the other, allowing Chile to gain complete control of the sea lanes and thus to virtually dictate the pace of the war. Although the Peruvians fought the superior Chilean expeditionary forces doggedly thereafter, resorting to guerrilla action in the Sierra after the fall of Lima in 1881, they were finally forced to conclude a peace settlement in 1883. The Treaty of Ancón ceded to Chile in perpetuity the nitrate-rich province of Tarapacá and provided that the provinces of Tacna and Arica would remain in Chilean possession for ten years, when a plebiscite would be held to decide their final fate (see fig. 3). After repeated delays, both countries finally agreed in 1929, after outside mediation by the United States, to a compromise solution to the dispute by which Tacna would be returned to Peru and Chile would retain Arica. For Peru, defeat and dismemberment by Chile in war brought to a final disastrous conclusion an era that had begun so auspiciously in the early 1840s with the initial promise of guano-led development (see also Postindependence: Military Defeat and Nation-Building, ch. 5).

Recovery and Growth, 1883–1930
The New Militarism, 1886–95

After a period of intense civil strife similar to the political chaos during the immediate postindependence period half a century earlier, the armed forces, led by General Andrés Avelino Cáceres (1886–90, 1894–95), succeeded in establishing a measure of order in the country. Cáceres, a Creole and hero of the guerrilla resistance to the Chilean occupation during the War of the Pacific, managed to win the presidency in 1886. He succeeded in imposing a general peace, first by crushing a native rebellion in the Sierra led by a former ally, the respected native American *varayoc* (leader) Pedro Pablo Atusparía (see Landlords and Peasant Revolts in the Highlands, ch. 2). Cáceres then set about the task of reconstructing the country after its devastating defeat.

The centerpiece of his recovery program was the Grace Contract, a controversial proposal by a group of British bondholders to cancel Peru's foreign debt in return for the right to operate the country's railroad system for sixty-six years. The contract provoked great controversy between nationalists, who saw it as a sellout to foreign interests, and liberals, who argued that it would lay the basis for economic recovery by restoring Peru's investment and creditworthiness in the West. Finally approved by Congress in 1888, the Grace Contract, together with a robust recovery in silver production (US$35 million by 1895), laid the foundations for a revival of export-led growth.

Indeed, economic recovery would soon turn into a sustained, long-term period of growth. Nils Jacobsen has calculated that "Exports rose fourfold between the nadir of 1883 and 1910, from 1.4 to 6.2 million pounds sterling and may have doubled again until 1919; British and United States capital investments grew nearly tenfold between 1880 and 1919, from US$17 to US$161 million."

Source: Based on information from David P. Werlich, *Peru: A Short History,* Carbondale,
Illinois, 1978, 110–11.

*Figure 3. Territorial Adjustments among Bolivia, Chile, and Peru, 1874–
1929*

However, he also notes that it was not until 1920 that the nation fully recovered from the losses sustained between the depression of 1873 and the postwar beginnings of recovery at the end of the 1880s. Once underway, economic recovery inaugurated a long period of stable, civilian rule beginning in 1895.

The Aristocratic Republic, 1895–1914

The Aristocratic Republic began with the popular "Revolution of 1895," led by the charismatic and irrepressible José Nicolás de Piérola (1895–99). He overthrew the increasingly dictatorial Cáceres, who had gained the presidency again in 1894 after having placed his crony Colonel Remigio Morales Bermúdez (1890–94) in power in 1890. Piérola, an aristocratic and patriarchal figure, was fond of saying that "when the people are in danger, they come to me." Although he had gained the intense enmity of the Civilistas in 1869 when, as minister of finance in the Balta government, he had transferred the lucrative guano consignment contract to the foreign firm of Dreyfus and Company of Paris, he now succeeded in forging an alliance with his former opponents. This alliance began a period known as the Aristocratic Republic (1895–1914), during which Peru was characterized not only by relative political harmony and rapid economic growth and modernization, but also by social and political change.

From the ruins of the War of the Pacific, new elites had emerged along the coast and coalesced to form a powerful oligarchy, based on the reemergence of sugar, cotton, and mining exports, as well as the reintegration of Peru into the international economy. Its political expression was the reconstituted Civilista Party, which had revived its antimilitary and proexport program during the period of intense national disillusion and introspection that followed the country's defeat in the war. By the time the term of Piérola's successor, Eduardo López de Romaña (1899–1903), came to an end, the Civilistas had cleverly managed to gain control of the national electoral process and proceeded to elect their own candidate and party leader, the astute Manuel Candamo (1903–1904), to the presidency. Thereafter, they virtually controlled the presidency up until World War I, although Candamo died a few months after assuming office. Elections, however, were restricted, subject to strict property and literacy qualifications, and more often than not manipulated by the incumbent Civilista regime.

The Civilistas were the architects of unprecedented political stability and economic growth, but they also set in motion profound social changes that would, in time, alter the political panorama. With the gradual advance of export capitalism, peasants migrated and became proletarians, laboring in industrial enclaves that arose not only in Lima, but in areas of the countryside as well. The traditional haciendas and small-scale mining complexes that could be connected to the international market gave way increasingly to modern agroindustrial plantations and mining enclaves. With the advent of World War I, Peru's international markets were temporarily disrupted and social unrest intensified, particularly in urban centers where a modern labor movement began to take shape.

Impact of World War I

The Civilistas, however, were unable to manage the new social forces that their policies unleashed. This fact first became apparent in 1912 when the millionaire businessman Guillermo Billinghurst (1912–14)—the reform-minded, populist former mayor of Lima—was able to organize a general strike to block the election of the official Civilista presidential candidate and force his own election by Congress. During his presidency, Billinghurst became embroiled in an increasingly bitter series of conflicts with Congress, ranging from proposed advanced social legislation to settlement of the Tacna-Arica dispute. When Congress opened impeachment hearings in 1914, Billinghurst threatened to arm the workers and forcibly dissolve Congress. The threat provoked the armed forces under Colonel Oscar Raimundo Benavides (1914–15, 1933–36, and 1936–39) to seize power.

The coup marked the beginning of a long-term alignment of the military with the oligarchy, whose interests and privileges it would defend up until the 1968 revolution of General Juan Velasco Alvarado (1968–75). It was also significant because it not only ended almost two decades of uninterrupted civilian rule, but, unlike past military interventions, was more institutional than personalist in character. Benavides was a product of Piérola's attempt to professionalize the armed forces under the tutelage of a French military mission, beginning in 1896, and therefore was uncomfortable in his new political role. Within a year, he arranged new elections that brought José de Pardo y Barreda (1904–1908, 1915–19) to power.

A new round of economic problems, deepening social unrest, and powerful, new ideological currents toward the end of World War I, however, converged to bring a generation of Civilista rule to an end in 1919. The war had a roller coaster effect on the Peruvian economy. First, export markets were temporarily cut off, provoking recession. Then, when overseas trade was restored, stimulating demand among the combatants for Peru's primary products, an inflationary spiral saw the cost of living nearly double between 1913 and 1919.

This inflation had a particularly negative impact on the new working classes in Lima and elsewhere in the country. The number of workers had grown sharply since the turn of the century—by one count rising from 24,000, or 17 percent of the capital's population in 1908, to 44,000, or 20 percent of the population in 1920. Similar growth rates occurred outside of Lima in the export enclaves of sugar (30,000 workers), cotton (35,000), oil (22,500), and copper. The Cerro de Pasco copper mine alone had 25,500 workers. The growth and concentration of workers was accompanied by the spread of anarcho-syndicalist ideas before and during the war years, making the incipient labor movement increasingly militant. Violent strikes erupted on sugar plantations, beginning in 1910, and the first general strike in the country's history occurred a year later.

Radical new ideologies further fueled the growing social unrest in the country at the end of the war. The ideas of the Mexican and Russian revolutions, the former predating the latter, quickly spread radical new doctrines to the far corners of the world, including Peru. Closer to home, the *indigenista* (indigenous) movement increasingly captured the imagination of a new generation of Peruvians, particularly urban, middle-class mestizos who were reexamining their roots in a changing Peru. *Indigenismo* (indigenism) was promoted by a group of writers and artists who sought to rediscover and celebrate the virtues and values of Peru's glorious Incan past. Awareness of the indigenous masses was heightened at this time by another wave of native uprisings in the southern highlands. They were caused by the disruption and dislocation of traditional native American communities brought about by the opening of new international markets and reorganization of the wool trade in the region.

All of these social, economic, and intellectual trends came to a head at the end of the Pardo administration. In 1918–19 Pardo faced an unprecedented wave of strikes and labor mobilization that was joined by student unrest over university reform. The ensuing worker-student alliance catapulted a new generation of radical reformers, headed by Víctor Raúl Haya de la Torre—a young, charismatic student at San Marcos University—and José Carlos Mariátegui—a brilliant Lima journalist who defended the rights of the new, urban working class—to national prominence.

The Eleven-Year Rule, 1919–30

The immediate political beneficiary of this turmoil, however, was a dissident Civilista, former president Augusto B. Leguía y

Salcedo (1908–12, 1919–30), who had left the party after his first term. He ran as an independent in the 1919 elections on a reform platform that appealed to the emerging new middle and working classes. When he perceived a plot by the Civilistas to deny him the election, the diminutive but boundlessly energetic Leguía (he stood only 1.5 meters tall and weighed a little over 45 kilograms) staged a preemptive coup and assumed the presidency.

Leguía's eleven-year rule, known as the *oncenio* (1919–30), began auspiciously enough with a progressive, new constitution in 1920 that enhanced the power of the state to carry out a number of popular social and economic reforms. The regime weathered a brief postwar recession and then generated considerable economic growth by opening the country to a flood of foreign loans and investment. The economic growth allowed Leguía to replace the Civilista oligarchy with a new, if plutocratic, middle-class political base that prospered from state contracts and expansion of the government bureaucracy. However, it was not long into his regime that Leguía's authoritarian and dictatorial tendencies appeared. He cracked down on labor and student militancy, purged the Congress of opposition, and amended the constitution so that he could run, unopposed, for reelection in 1924 and again in 1929.

Leguía's popularity was further eroded as a result of a border dispute between Peru and Colombia involving territory in the rubber-tapping region between the Río Caquetá and the northern watershed of the Río Napo. Under the United States-mediated Salomón-Lozano Treaty of March 1922, which favored Colombia, the Río Putumayo was established as the boundary between Colombia and Peru (see fig. 4). Pressured by the United States to accept the unpopular treaty, Leguía finally submitted the document to the Peruvian Congress in December 1927, and it was ratified. The treaty was also unpopular with Ecuador, which found itself surrounded on the east by Peru.

The orgy of financial excesses, which included widespread corruption and the massive build-up of the foreign debt, was brought to a sudden end by the Wall Street stock market crash of 1929 and ensuing worldwide depression. Leguía's eleven-year rule, the longest in Peruvian history, collapsed a year later. Once again, the military intervened and overthrew Leguía, who died in prison in 1932.

Meanwhile, the onset of the Great Depression galvanized the forces of the left. Before he died prematurely at the age of thirty-five in 1930, Mariátegui founded the Peruvian Socialist Party (Partido Socialista Peruano—PSP), shortly to become the Peruvian Communist Party (Partido Comunista Peruano—PCP), which set about the task of political organizing after Leguía's fall from power.

Although a staunch Marxist who believed in the class struggle and the revolutionary role of the proletariat, Mariátegui's main contribution was to recognize the revolutionary potential of Peru's native peasantry. He argued that Marxism could be welded to an indigenous Andean revolutionary tradition that included *indigenismo,* the long history of Andean peasant rebellion, and the labor movement.

Haya de la Torre returned to Peru from a long exile to organize the American Popular Revolutionary Alliance (Alianza Popular Revolucionaria Americana—APRA), an anti-imperialist, continent-wide, revolutionary alliance, founded in Mexico in 1924. For Haya de la Torre, capitalism was still in its infancy in Peru and the proletariat too small and undeveloped to bring about a revolution against the Civilista oligarchy. For that to happen, he argued, the working classes must be joined to radicalized sectors of the new middle classes in a cross-class, revolutionary alliance akin to populism. Both parties—one from a Marxist and the other from a populist perspective—sought to organize and lead the new middle and working classes, now further dislocated and radicalized by the Great Depression. With his oratorical brilliance, personal magnetism, and national-populist message, Haya de la Torre was able to capture the bulk of these classes and to become a major figure in Peruvian politics until his death in 1980 at the age of eighty-six.

Mass Politics and Social Change, 1930–68
Impact of the Depression and World War II

After 1930 both the military, now firmly allied with the oligarchy, and the forces of the left, particularly APRA, became important new actors in Peruvian politics. This period (1930–68) has been characterized in political terms by sociologist Dennis Gilbert as operating under essentially a "tripartite" political system, with the military often ruling at the behest of the oligarchy to suppress the "unruly" masses represented by APRA and the PCP. Lieutenant Colonel Luis M. Sánchez Cerro and then General Benavides led another period of military rule during the turbulent 1930s.

In the presidential election of 1931, Sánchez Cerro (1931–33), capitalizing on his popularity from having deposed the dictator Leguía, barely defeated APRA's Haya de la Torre, who claimed to have been defrauded out of his first bid for office. In July 1932, APRA rose in a bloody popular rebellion in Trujillo, Haya de la Torre's hometown and an APRA stronghold, that resulted in the execution of some sixty army officers by the insurgents. Enraged, the army unleashed a brutal suppression that cost the lives of at

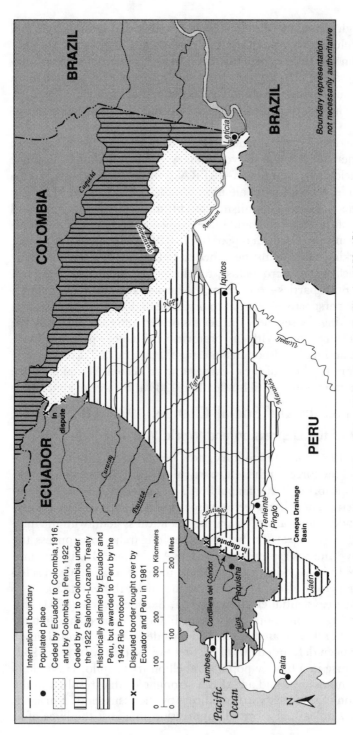

Source: Based on information from David P. Werlich, *Peru: A Short History*, Carbondale, Illinois, 1978, 171.

Figure 4. Peru's Northern Boundary Disputes in the Twentieth Century

least 1,000 Apristas (APRA members) and their sympathizers (partly from aerial bombing, used for the first time in South American history). Thus began what would become a virtual vendetta between the armed forces and APRA that would last for at least a generation and on several occasions prevented the party from coming to power.

Politically, the Trujillo uprising was followed shortly by another crisis, this time a border conflict with Colombia over disputed territory in the Leticia region of the Amazon. Before it could be settled, Sánchez Cerro was assassinated in April 1933 by a militant Aprista, and Congress quickly elected former president Benavides to complete Sánchez Cerro's five-year term. Benavides managed to settle the thorny Letícia dispute peacefully, with assistance from the League of Nations, when a Protocol of Peace, Friendship, and Cooperation was signed in May 1934 ratifying Colombia's original claim. After a disputed election in 1936, in which Haya de la Torre was prevented from running and which Benavides nullified with the reluctant consent of Congress, Benavides remained in power and extended his term until 1939.

During the 1930s, Peru's economy was one of the least affected by the Great Depression. Thanks to a relatively diversified range of exports, led by cotton and new industrial metals (particularly lead and zinc), the country began a rapid recovery of export earnings as early as 1933. As a result, unlike many other Latin American countries that adopted Keynesian and import-substitution industrialization (see Glossary) measures to counteract the decline, Peru's policymakers made relatively few alterations in their long-term model of export-oriented growth.

Under Sánchez Cerro, Peru did take measures to reorganize its debt-ridden finances by inviting Edwin Kemmerer, a well-known United States financial consultant, to recommend reforms. Following his advice, Peru returned to the gold standard, but could not avoid declaring a moratorium on its US$180-million debt on April 1, 1931. For the next thirty years, Peru was barred from the United States capital market.

Benavides's policies combined strict economic orthodoxy, measures of limited social reform designed to attract the middle classes away from APRA, and repression against the left, particularly APRA. For much of the rest of the decade, APRA continued to be persecuted and remained underground. Almost from the moment APRA appeared, the party and Haya de la Torre had been attacked by the oligarchy as antimilitary, anticlerical, and ''communistic.'' Indeed, the official reason often given for APRA's proscription was its ''internationalism'' because the party began as a continent-wide alliance "against Yankee imperialism"—suggesting that it was somehow subversively un-Peruvian.

Haya de la Torre had also flirted with the Communists during his exile in the 1920s, and his early writings were influenced by a number of radical thinkers, including Marx. Nevertheless, the 1931 APRA program was essentially reformist, nationalist, and populist. It called, among other things, for a redistributive and interventionist state that would move to selectively nationalize land and industry. Although certainly radical from the perspective of the oligarchy, the program was designed to correct the historical inequality of wealth and income in Peru, as well as to reduce and bring under greater governmental control the large-scale foreign investment in the country that was high in comparison with other Andean nations.

The intensity of the oligarchy's attacks was also a response to the extreme rhetoric of APRA polemicists and reflected the polarized state of Peruvian society and politics during the Depression. Both sides readily resorted to force and violence, as the bloody events of the 1930s readily attested—the 1932 Trujillo revolt, the spate of prominent political assassinations (including Sánchez Cerro and Antonio Miró Quesada, publisher of *El Comercio*), and widespread imprisonment and torture of Apristas and their sympathizers. It also revealed the oligarchy's apprehension, indeed paranoia, at APRA's sustained attempt to mobilize the masses for the first time into the political arena. At bottom, Peru's richest, most powerful forty families perceived a direct challenge to their traditional privileges and absolute right to rule, a position they were not to yield easily.

When Benavides's extended term expired in 1939, Manuel Prado y Ugarteche (1939–45), a Lima banker from a prominent family and son of a former president, won the presidency. He was soon confronted with a border conflict with Ecuador that led to a brief war in 1941. After independence, Ecuador had been left without access to either the Amazon or the region's other major waterway, the Río Marañón, and thus without direct access to the Atlantic Ocean. In an effort to assert its territorial claims in a region near the Río Marañón in the Amazon Basin, Ecuador occupied militarily the town of Zarumilla along its southwestern border with Peru. However, the Peruvian Army (Ejército Peruano—EP) responded with a lightning victory against the Ecuadorian Army. At subsequent peace negotiations in Rio de Janeiro in 1942, Peru's ownership of most of the contested region was affirmed.

On the domestic side, Prado gradually moved to soften official opposition to APRA, as Haya de la Torre moved to moderate the party's program in response to the changing national and international environment brought on by World War II. For example, he no longer proposed to radically redistribute income, but instead proposed to create new wealth, and he replaced his earlier strident "anti-imperialism" directed against the United States with more favorable calls for democracy, foreign investment, and hemispheric harmony. As a result, in May 1945 Prado legalized the party that now reemerged on the political scene after thirteen years underground.

The Allied victory in World War II reinforced the relative democratic tendency in Peru, as Prado's term came to an end in 1945. José Luis Bustamante y Rivero (1945–48), a liberal and prominent international jurist, was overwhelmingly elected president on the basis of an alliance with the now legal APRA. Responding to his more reform- and populist-oriented political base, Bustamante and his Aprista minister of economy moved Peru away from the strictly orthodox, free-market policies that had characterized his predecessors. Increasing the state's intervention in the economy in an effort to stimulate growth and redistribution, the new government embarked on a general fiscal expansion, increased wages, and established controls on prices and exchange rates. The policy, similar to APRA's later approach in the late 1980s, was neither well-conceived nor efficiently administered and came at a time when Peru's exports, after an initial upturn after the war, began to sag. This resulted in a surge of inflation and labor unrest that ultimately destabilized the government.

Bustamante also became embroiled in an escalating political conflict with the Aprista-controlled Congress, further weakening the administration. The political waters were also roiled in 1947 by the assassination by Aprista militants of Francisco Graña Garland, the socially prominent director of the conservative newspaper *La Prensa*. When a naval mutiny organized by elements of APRA broke out in 1948, the military, under pressure from the oligarchy, overthrew the government and installed General Manuel A. Odría (1948–50, 1950–56), hero of the 1941 war with Ecuador, as president.

Rural Stagnation and Social Mobilization, 1948–68

Odría imposed a personalistic dictatorship on the country and returned public policy to the familiar pattern of repression of the left and free-market orthodoxy. Indicative of the new regime's hostility toward APRA, Haya de la Torre, after seeking political asylum in the Embassy of Colombia in Lima in 1949, was prevented by the government from leaving the country. He remained a virtual prisoner in the embassy until his release into exile in 1954. However, along with such repression Odría cleverly sought to undermine APRA's popular support by establishing a dependent, paternalistic relationship with labor and the urban poor through a series of charity and social welfare measures.

At the same time, Odría's renewed emphasis on export-led growth coincided with a period of rising prices on the world market for the country's diverse commodities, engendered by the outbreak of the Korean War in 1950. Also, greater political stability brought increased national and foreign investment, particularly in the manufacturing sector. Indeed, this sector grew almost 8 percent annually between 1950 and 1967, increasing from 14 to 20 percent of gross domestic product (GDP—see Glossary). Overall, the economy experienced a prolonged period of strong, export-led growth, amounting on average to 5 percent a year during the same period (see Historical Background, ch. 3).

Not all Peruvians, however, benefited from this period of sustained capitalist development, which tended to be regional and confined mainly to the more modernized coast. This uneven pattern of growth served to intensify the dualistic structure of the country by widening the historical gap between the Sierra and the coast. In the Sierra, the living standard of the bottom one-quarter of the population stagnated or fell during the twenty years after 1950. In fact, the Sierra had been losing ground economically to the modernizing forces operative on the coast ever since the 1920s. With income distribution steadily worsening, the Sierra experienced a period of intense social mobilization during the 1950s and 1960s.

This fact was manifested first in the intensification of rural-urban migration and then in a series of confrontations between peasants and landowners. The fundamental causes of these confrontations were numerous. Population growth, which had almost doubled nationally between 1900 and 1940 (3.7 million to 7 million), increased rapidly to 13.6 million by 1970. Such growth turned the labor market from a state of chronic historical scarcity to one of abundant surplus. With arable land constant and locked into the system of latifundios (see Glossary), ownership-to-area ratios deteriorated sharply, increasing peasant pressures on the land.

Peru's land-tenure system remained one of the most unequal in Latin America. In 1958 the country had a high coefficient of 0.88 on the Gini index, which measures land concentration on a scale of 0 to 1. Figures for the same year show that 2 percent of the country's landowners controlled 69 percent of arable land. Conversely, 83 percent of landholders holding no more than 5 hectares controlled only 6 percent of arable land. Finally, the Sierra's terms of trade (see Glossary) in agricultural foodstuffs steadily declined because of the state's urban bias in food pricing policy, which kept farm prices artificially low (see Employment and Wages, Poverty, and Income Distribution, ch. 3).

Many peasants opted to migrate to the coast, where most of the economic and job growth was occurring. The population of metropolitan Lima, in particular, soared. Standing at slightly over 500,000 in 1940, it increased threefold to over 1.6 million in 1961 and nearly doubled again by 1981 to more than 4.1 million. The capital became increasingly ringed with squalid *barriadas* (shanty-towns—see Glossary) of urban migrants, putting pressure on the liberal state, long accustomed to ignoring the funding of government services to the poor.

Those peasants who chose to remain in the Sierra did not remain passive in the face of their declining circumstances but became increasingly organized and militant. A wave of strikes and land invasions swept over the Sierra during the 1950s and 1960s as campesinos demanded access to land. Tensions grew especially in the Convención and Lares region of the high jungle near Cusco, where Hugo Blanco, a Quechua-speaking Trotskyite and former student leader, mobilized peasants in a militant confrontation with local *gamonales*.

While economic stagnation prodded peasant mobilization in the Sierra, economic growth along the coast produced other important social changes. The postwar period of industrialization, urbanization, and general economic growth created a new middle and professional class that altered the prevailing political panorama. These new middle sectors formed the social base for two new political parties—Popular Action (Acción Popular—AP) and the Christian Democratic Party (Partido Demócrata Cristiano—PDC)—that emerged in the 1950s and 1960s to challenge the oligarchy with a moderate, democratic reform program. Emphasizing modernization and development within a somewhat more activist state framework, they posed a new challenge to the old left, particularly APRA.

For its part, APRA accelerated its rightward tendency. It entered into what many saw as an unholy alliance (dubbed the *convivencia,* or living together) with its old enemy, the oligarchy, by agreeing to support the candidacy of conservative Manuel Prado y Ugarteche in the 1956 elections, in return for legal recognition. As a result, many new voters became disillusioned with APRA and flocked to support the charismatic reformer Fernando Belaúnde Terry (1963–68, 1980–85), the founder of the AP. Although Prado won, six years later the army intervened when its old enemy, Haya de la Torre (back from six years of exile), still managed, if barely, to defeat the upstart Belaúnde by less than one percentage point in the 1962 elections. A surprisingly reform-minded junta of the armed forces headed by General Ricardo Pérez Godoy held power for a year (1962–63) and then convoked new elections. This time Belaúnde, in alliance with the Christian Democrats, defeated Haya de la Torre and became president.

Belaúnde's government, riding the crest of the social and political discontent of the period, ushered in a period of reform at a time when United States president John F. Kennedy's Alliance for Progress (see Glossary) was also awakening widespread expectations for reform throughout Latin America. Belaúnde tried to diffuse the growing unrest in the highlands through a three-pronged approach: modest agrarian reform, colonization projects in the high jungle or Montaña, and the construction of the north-south Jungle Border Highway (*la carretera marginal de la selva,* or *la marginal*), running the entire length of the country along the jungle fringe. The basic thrust of the Agrarian Reform Law of 1969, which was substantially watered down by a conservative coalition in Congress between the APRA and the National Odriist Union (Unión Nacional Odriísta—UNO), was to open access to new lands and production opportunities, rather than dismantle the traditional latifundio system. However, this plan failed to quiet peasant discontent, which by 1965 helped fuel a Castroite guerrilla movement, the Movement of the Revolutionary Left (Movimiento de la Izquierda Revolucionaria—MIR), led by rebellious Apristas on the left who were unhappy with the party's alliance with the country's most conservative forces.

In this context of increasing mobilization and radicalization, Belaúnde lost his reformist zeal and called on the army to put down the guerrilla movement with force. Opting for a more technocratic orientation palatable to his urban middle class base, Belaúnde, an architect and urban planner by training, embarked on a large number of construction projects, including irrigation, transportation, and housing, while also investing heavily in education. Such initiatives were made possible, in part, by the economic boost provided by the dramatic expansion of the fishmeal industry. Aided by new technologies and the abundant fishing grounds off the coast, fishmeal production soared. By 1962 Peru became the leading fishing nation in the world, and fishmeal accounted for fully one-third of the country's exports (see Structures of Production, ch. 3).

Belaúnde's educational expansion dramatically increased the number of universities and graduates. But, however laudable, this policy tended over time to swell recruits for the growing number

Municipal election headquarters in the Military
Geography Institute, Lima, 1966
Courtesy Paul L. Doughty

of left-wing parties, as economic opportunities diminished in the face of an end, in the late 1960s, of the long cycle of export-led economic expansion. Indeed, economic problems spelled trouble for Belaúnde as he approached the end of his term. Faced with a growing balance-of-payments problem, he was forced to devalue the sol (for value—see Glossary) in 1967. He also seemed to many nationalists to capitulate to foreign capital in a final settlement in 1968 of a controversial and long-festering dispute with the International Petroleum Company (IPC) over La Brea y Pariñas oil fields in northern Peru. With public discontent growing, the armed forces, led by General Velasco Alvarado, overthrew the Belaúnde government in 1968 and proceeded to undertake an unexpected and unprecedented series of reforms.

Failed Reform and Economic Decline, 1968–85
Military Reform from Above, 1968–80

The military intervention and its reformist orientation represented changes both in the armed forces and Peruvian society. Within the armed forces, the social origins of the officer corps no longer mirrored the background and outlook of the Creole upper

49

classes, which had historically inclined the officers to follow the mandate of the oligarchy. Reflective of the social changes and mobility that were occurring in society at large, officers now exhibited middle- and lower middle class, provincial, and mestizo or *cholo* (see Glossary) backgrounds. General Velasco, a *cholo* himself, had grown up in humble circumstances in the northern department of Piura and purportedly went to school barefoot.

Moreover, this generation of officers had fought and defeated the guerrilla movements in the backward Sierra. In the process, they had come to the realization that internal peace in Peru depended not so much on force of arms, but on implementing structural reforms that would relieve the burden of chronic poverty and underdevelopment in the region. In short, development, they concluded, was the best guarantee for national security. The Belaúnde government had originally held out the promise of reform and development, but had failed. The military attributed that failure, at least in part, to flaws in the democratic political system that had enabled the opposition to block and stalemate reform initiatives in Congress. As nationalists, they also abhorred the proposed pact with the IPC and looked askance at stories of widespread corruption in the Belaúnde government.

Velasco moved immediately to implement a radical reform program, which seemed, ironically, to embody much of the original 1931 program of the army's old nemesis, APRA. His first act was to expropriate the large agroindustrial plantations along the coast. The agrarian reform that followed, the most extensive in Latin America outside of Cuba, proceeded to destroy the economic base of power of the old ruling classes, the export oligarchy, and its *gamonal* allies in the Sierra. By 1975 half of all arable land had been transferred, in the form of various types of cooperatives, to over 350,000 families comprising about one-fourth of the rural population, mainly estate workers and renters (*colonos*). Agricultural output tended to maintain its rather low pre-reform levels, however, and the reform still left out an estimated 1 million seasonal workers and only marginally benefited campesinos in the native communities (about 40 percent of the rural population).

The Velasco regime also moved to dismantle the liberal, export model of development that had reached its limits after the long postwar expansion. The state now assumed, for the first time in history, a major role in the development process. Its immediate target was the foreign-dominated sector, which during the 1960s had attained a commanding position in the economy. At the end of the Belaúnde government in 1968, three-quarters of mining, one-half of manufacturing, two-thirds of the commercial banking system, and one-third of the fishing industry were under direct foreign control.

Velasco reversed this situation. By 1975 state enterprises accounted for more than half of mining output, two-thirds of the banking system, a fifth of industrial production, and half of total productive investment. Velasco's overall development strategy was to shift from a laissez-faire to a "mixed" economy, to replace export-led development with import-substitution industrialization. At the same time, the state implemented a series of social measures designed to protect workers and redistribute income in order to expand the domestic market.

In the realm of foreign policy, the Velasco regime undertook a number of important initiatives. Peru became a driving force not only behind the creation of an Andean Pact (see Glossary) in 1969 to establish a common market with coordinated trade and investment policies, but also in the movement of nonaligned countries of the Third World. Reflecting a desire to end its perceived dependency economically and politically on the United States, the Velasco government also moved to diversify its foreign relations by making trade and aid pacts with the Soviet Union and East European countries, as well as with Japan and West European nations. Finally, Peru succeeded during the 1970s in establishing its international claims to a 200-nautical-mile territorial limit in the Pacific Ocean.

By the time Velasco was replaced on August 29, 1975, by the more conservative General Francisco Morales Bermúdez Cerrutti (1975–80), his reform program was already weakening. Natural calamities, the world oil embargo of 1973, increasing international indebtedness (Velasco had borrowed heavily abroad to replace lost investment capital to finance his reforms), over-bureaucratization, and general mismanagement had undermined early economic growth and triggered a serious inflationary spiral. At the same time, Velasco, suffering from terminal cancer, had become increasingly personalistic and autocratic, undermining the institutional character of military rule. Unwilling to expand his initial popularity through party politics, he had created a series of mass organizations, tied to the state in typically corporatist (see Glossary) and patrimonialist fashion, in order to mobilize support and control the pace of reform. However, despite his rhetoric about creating truly popular, democratic organizations, he manipulated them from above in an increasingly arbitrary manner. What had begun as an unusual populist type of military experiment evolved into a form of what political scientist Guillermo O'Donnell calls "bureaucratic authoritarianism," with increasingly authoritarian and personalistic characteristics that were manifested in "Velasquismo."

Velasco's replacement, General Morales Bermúdez, spent most of his term implementing an economic austerity program to stem the surge of inflation. Public opinion increasingly turned against the rule of the armed forces, which it blamed for the country's economic troubles, widespread corruption, and mismanagement of the government, as well as the general excesses of the "revolution." Consequently, Morales Bermúdez prepared to return the country to the democratic process.

Elections were held in 1978 for a Constituent Assembly empowered to rewrite the constitution. Although Belaúnde's AP boycotted the election, an array of newly constituted leftist parties won an unprecedented 36 percent of the vote, with much of the remainder going to APRA. The Assembly, under the leadership of the aging and terminally ill Haya de la Torre (who would die in 1980), completed the new document in 1979. Meanwhile, the popularity of former president Belaúnde underwent a revival. Belaúnde was decisively reelected president in 1980, with 45 percent of the vote, for a term of five years.

Return to Democratic Rule, 1980-85

Belaúnde inherited a country that was vastly different from the one he had governed in the 1960s. Gone was the old export oligarchy and its *gamonal* allies in the Sierra, and the extent of foreign investment in the economy had been sharply reduced. In their place, Velasco had borrowed enormous sums from foreign banks and so expanded the state that by 1980 it accounted for 36 percent of national production, double its 1968 share. The informal sector of small- and medium-sized businesses outside the legal, formal economy had also proliferated.

By 1980 Belaúnde's earlier reforming zeal had substantially waned, replaced by a decidedly more conservative orientation to government. A team of advisers and technocrats, many with experience in international financial organizations, returned home to install a neoliberal economic program that emphasized privatization of state-run business and, once again, export-led growth. In an effort to increase agricultural production, which had declined as a result of the agrarian reform, Belaúnde sharply reduced food subsidies, allowing producer prices to rise.

However, just as Velasco's ambitious reforms of the early 1970s were eroded by the 1973 worldwide oil crisis, Belaúnde's export strategy was shattered by a series of natural calamities and a sharp plunge in international commodity prices to their lowest levels since the Great Depression. By 1983 production had fallen 12 percent and wages 20 percent in real terms while inflation once again surged.

Juan Velasco Alvarado
Courtesy, Embassy of Peru,
Washington

Francisco Morales
Bermúdez Cerrutti
Courtesy Embassy of Peru,
Washington

53

Unemployment and underemployment was rampant, affecting perhaps two-thirds of the work force and causing the minister of finance to declare the country in "the worst economic crisis of the century." Again, the government opted to borrow heavily in international money markets, after having severely criticized the previous regime for ballooning the foreign debt. Peru's total foreign debt swelled from US$9.6 billion in 1980 to US$13 billion by the end of Belaúnde's term.

The economic collapse of the early 1980s, continuing the long-term cyclical decline begun in the late l960s, brought into sharp focus the country's social deterioration, particularly in the more isolated and backward regions of the Sierra. Infant mortality rose to 120 per 1,000 births (230 in some remote areas), life expectancy for males dropped to 58 compared with 64 in neighboring Chile, average daily caloric intake fell below minimum United Nations standards, upwards of 60 percent of children under five years of age were malnourished, and underemployment and unemployment were rampant. Such conditions were a breeding ground for social and political discontent, which erupted with a vengeance in 1980 with the appearance of the Shining Path (Sendero Luminoso—SL).

Founded in the remote and impoverished department of Ayacucho by Abimael Guzmán Reynoso, a philosophy professor at the University of Huamanga, the SL blended the ideas of Marxism-Leninism, Maoism, and those of José Carlos Mariátegui, Peru's major Marxist theoretician. Taking advantage of the return to democratic rule, the deepening economic crisis, the failure of the Velasco-era reforms, and a generalized vacuum of authority in parts of the Sierra with the collapse of *gamonal* rule, the SL unleashed a virulent and highly effective campaign of terror and subversion that caught the Belaúnde government by surprise.

After first choosing to ignore the SL and then relying on an ineffective national police response, Belaúnde reluctantly turned to the army to try to suppress the rebels. However, that proved extremely difficult to do. The SL expanded its original base in Ayacucho north along the Andean spine and eventually into Lima and other cities, gaining young recruits frustrated by their dismal prospects for a better future. To further complicate pacification efforts, another rival guerrilla group, the Túpac Amaru Revolutionary Movement (Movimiento Revolucionario Túpac Amaru—MRTA), emerged in Lima.

Counterinsurgency techniques, often applied indiscriminately by the armed forces, resulted in severe human rights violations against the civilian population and only created more recruits for the SL. By the end of Belaúnde's term in 1985, over 6,000

Peruvians had died from the violence, and over US$1 billion in property damage had resulted (see Changing Threats to National Security, ch. 5). Strongly criticized by international human rights organizations, Belaúnde nevertheless continued to rely on military solutions, rather than other emergency social or developmental measures that might have served to get at some of the fundamental, underlying socioeconomic causes of the insurgency (see Shining Path and Its Impact, ch. 2).

The severe internal social and political strife, not to mention the deteriorating economic conditions, manifested in the Shining Path insurgency may have contributed in 1981 to a flare-up of the border dispute with Ecuador in the disputed Marañón region. Possibly looking to divert public attention away from internal problems, both countries began a brief, five-day border skirmish on January 28, 1981, the eve of the anniversary of the signing of the Protocol of Rio de Janeiro (see Glossary) on January 29, 1942. Peruvian forces prevailed, and although a ceasefire was quickly declared, it did nothing to resolve the two opposing positions on the issue of the disputed territory. Essentially, Peru continued to adhere to the Rio Protocol by which Ecuador had recognized Peruvian claims. On the other hand, Ecuador continued to argue that the Rio Protocol should be renegotiated, a position first taken by President José Velasco Ibarra in 1960 and adhered to by all subsequent Ecuadorian presidents.

Along with these internal and external conflicts, Belaúnde also confronted a rising tide of drug trafficking during his term. Coca had been cultivated in the Andes since pre-Columbian times. The Inca elite and clergy used it for certain ceremonies, believing that it possessed magical powers. After the conquest, coca chewing, which suppresses hunger and relieves pain and cold, became common among the oppressed indigenous peasantry, who used the drug to deal with the hardships imposed by the new colonial regime, particularly in the mines. The practice has continued, with an estimated 15 percent of the population chewing coca on a daily basis by 1990.

As a result of widespread cocaine consumption in the United States and Europe, demand for coca from the Andes soared during the late 1970s. Peru and Bolivia became the largest coca producers in the world, accounting for roughly four-fifths of the production in South America. Although originally produced mainly in five highland departments, Peruvian production has become increasingly concentrated in the Upper Huallaga Valley, located some 379 kilometers northeast of Lima. Peasant growers, some 70,000 in the valley alone, are estimated to receive upwards of US$240 million annually for their crop from traffickers—mainly Colombians who oversee the processing, transportation, and smuggling operations to foreign countries, principally the United States.

After the cultivation of coca for narcotics uses was made illegal in 1978, efforts to curtail production were intensified by the Belaúnde government, under pressure from the United States. Attempts were made to substitute other cash crops, and police units sought to eradicate the plant. This tactic only served to alienate the growers and to set the stage for the spread of the SL movement into the area in 1983–84 as erstwhile defenders of the growers. By 1985 the SL had become an armed presence in the region, defending the growers not only from the state, but also from the extortionist tactics of the traffickers. The SL, however, became one of the wealthiest guerrilla movements in modern history by collecting an estimated US$30 million in "taxes" from Colombian traffickers who controlled the drug trade.

As the guerrilla war raged on and with the economy in disarray, Belaúnde had little to show at the end of his term, except perhaps the reinstitution of the democratic process. During his term, political parties had reemerged across the entire political spectrum and vigorously competed to represent their various constituencies. With all his problems, Belaúnde had also managed to maintain press and other freedoms (marred, however, by increasing human rights violations) and to observe the parliamentary process. In 1985 he completed his elected term, only the second time that this had happened in forty years.

After presiding over a free election, Belaúnde turned the presidency over to populist Alan García Pérez of APRA who had swept to victory with 48 percent of the vote. Belaúnde's own party went down to a resounding defeat with only 6 percent of the vote, and the Marxist United Left (Izquierda Unida—IU) received 23 percent. The elections revealed a decided swing to the left by the Peruvian electorate. For APRA García's victory was the culmination of more than half a century of political travail and struggle.

Peru at the Crossroads

As García took office on July 28, 1985—at thirty-six the youngest chief executive to assume power in Peru's history—he seemed to awaken hope among Peruvians for the future. Although he had no previous experience in elected office, he possessed, as his decisive electoral victory illustrated, the necessary charisma to mobilize Peruvians to confront their problems. At the same time, the governing APRA party won a majority in the new Congress, assuring the new president support for his program to meet the crisis.

The crisis seemed daunting indeed. The foreign debt stood at over US$13 billion, real wages had eroded by 30 percent since 1980, prices for Peru's exports on the world market remained low, the economy was gripped in recession, and guerrilla violence was spreading. The future of Peru's fledgling redemocratization now hinged on García's ability to reverse these trends and, at bottom, to restore sustained economic growth and development (see The García Government, 1985–90, ch. 4).

* * *

There are a number of good, general histories of Peru. These include Magnus Mörner's *The Andean Past,* David P. Werlich's *Peru: A Short History,* and Michael Reid's *Peru: Paths to Poverty.* The reader should also consult the chapters on Peru in the authoritative, multi-volume, *Cambridge History of Latin America* (CHLA), edited by Leslie Bethell. A good general introduction to the colonial period is Mark A. Burkholder and Lyman L. Johnson's *Colonial Latin America.* The works of John V. Murra are seminal on the pre-Columbian period, a good introduction being his chapter ''Andean Societies Before 1532,'' in the CHLA. Most useful on the Incas and the Conquest are the brilliant works of Nathan Wachtel, *The Vision of the Vanquished,* and John Hemming's *The Conquest of the Incas.* A powerful account in defense of the native population after conquest is Felipe Guamán Poma de Ayala's *Letter to a King,* while the mestizo chronicler Garcilaso de la Vega's *Royal Commentaries of the Incas and General History of Peru* constitutes the first truly Peruvian vision of the Andes. Particularly incisive works on the colonial system are Karen Spalding's *Huarochirí: An Andean Society under Inca and Spanish Rule* and Steve J. Stern's *Peru's Indian Peoples and the Challenge of Spanish Conquest.*

The postindependence period has received innovative treatment in Paul E. Gootenberg's *Between Silver and Guano* and Nils P. Jacobsen's *Mirages of Transition.* Rosemary Thorp and Geoffrey Bertram's *Peru 1890–1977* is the standard source on twentieth-century economic development. Richard C. Webb and Graciela Fernández Baca de Valdéz's *Perú en números* provides important statistics on twentieth-century Peru. Four chapters in the CHLA cover the period since 1821: Heraclio Bonilla's ''Peru and Bolivia,'' Peter F. Klarén's ''Origins of Modern Peru, 1880–1930,'' Geoffrey Bertram's ''Peru: 1930–1962,'' and Julio Cotler's ''Peru since 1960.'' Incisive analyses on APRA can be found in Klarén's *Moderniza-tion, Dislocation, and Aprismo,* Steve Stein's *Populism in Peru,* and Fredrick B. Pike's *The Politics of the Miraculous in Peru.* Relations with the United States are surveyed adroitly by Pike in *The United States and the Andean Republics*. The military revolution of 1968 receives important attention from Cynthia McClintock and Abraham F. Lowenthal (eds.) in *The Peruvian Experiment Reconsidered* and in Alfred Stepan's *The State and Society*. The crisis of the early 1980s is analyzed by José Matos Mar's *Un desborde popular*. (For further information and complete citations, see Bibliography.)

Chapter 2. The Society and Its Environment

Mochican ceremonial gold mask

PERUVIANNESS (*PERUANIDAD*) has often been debated by Peruvian authors who evoke patriotism, faith, cultural mystique, and other allegedly intrinsic qualities of nationality. Peru, however, is not to be characterized as a homogeneous culture, nor its people as one people. Peruvians speak of their differences with certainty, referring to *lo criollo* ("of the Creole"), *lo serrano* ("of the highlander"), and other special traits by which social groups and regions are stereotyped. The national creole identity incorporates a combination of unique associations and ways of doing things *a la criolla.*

The dominant national culture emanating from Lima is urban, bureaucratic, street-oriented, and fast-paced. Yet the identity that goes with being a *limeño* (a Limean) is also profoundly provincial in its own way. In the first half of the twentieth century, the Lima cultural character transcended class values and ranks and to a significant degree was identified as the national Peruvian culture. The great migrations from 1950 to 1990 altered that personality substantially. By 1991 the national character, dominated by the urban style of Lima, was complicated by millions of highlanders *(serranos),* whose rural Spanish contrasts with the fast slurring and slang of the Lima dialect. Highland music is heard constantly on more than a dozen Lima radio stations that exalt the regional cultures, give announcements in Quechua, and relentlessly advertise the new businesses of the migrant entrepreneurs. The places mentioned and the activities announced are in greater Lima, but unknown to the *limeño.* The new *limeño,* while acquiring creole traits, nevertheless presents another face, one with which the Lima native does not closely relate and does not understand because few true *limeños* actually visit the provinces, much less stay there to live. Nor do they visit the sprawling "young towns" (*pueblos jóvenes*—see Glossary) of squatters that are disdained or even feared. Urban Hispanic Peruvians have always been caught in the bind of contradiction, at once claiming the glory of the Inca past while refusing to accept its descendants or their traditions as legitimately belonging in the modern state. In the early 1990s, however, this change was taking place, desired or not.

Events have been forcing the alteration of traditions in both the coast (Costa) and highlands (Sierra) in a process that would again transform the country, as did both conquest and independence. The peoples of the Altiplano and valleys of the Andean heartland—

long exploited and neglected and driven both by real needs and the quest for respect and equity—have surged over the country in a "reconquest" of Peru, stamping it with their image.

For respect and equity to develop, the white and mestizo (see Glossary) elites will have to yield the social and economic space for change and reconcile themselves to institutional changes that provide fairness in life opportunities. Up to 1991, the *serranos* had seized that space from a reluctant nation by aggressive migration, establishing vast squatter settlements and pushing hard against the walls of power. As with the Agrarian Reform Law of 1969, the elites and special interests that benefited from traditional socioeconomic arrangements had protected these old ways with few concessions to wider public and national needs. For the *cholo* (see Glossary), Peru's generic "everyman," to gain a place of respect, well-being, and a sense of progress will be a test of endurance, experiment, and sacrifice as painful and difficult as any in the hemisphere. With the agony of terroristic and revengeful revolution perpetrated by the Shining Path (Sendero Luminoso—SL) and the Túpac Amaru Revolutionary Movement (Movimiento Revolucionario Túpac Amaru—MRTA), on the one hand, and the chaotic collapse of the institutional formal economy, on the other, average Peruvians from all social groups were caught between the proverbial "sword and wall."

Just as the highland migration to the urban coast was the major avenue for social change through the 1980s, increasing numbers of Peruvians sought to continue this journey away from the dilemmas of their homeland by moving to other countries. About 700,000 had emigrated by 1991, with over 40 percent going to the United States. Catholic University of Peru professor Teófilo Altamirano has documented the new currents of mobility that went from Lima, Junín, and Ancash to every state in the United States, with heaviest concentrations in New Jersey, New York, California, and Florida. In 1990 about 300,000 of Altamirano's compatriots (*paisanos*) lived—either legally or not—in the United States.

In the early 1990s, Peru's identity as a nation and people was becoming more complex and cosmopolitan, while the distinctive traits of the culture were being broadened, disseminated, and shared by an increasingly wider group of citizens. The crosscurrents to these trends were configured around the struggle for retention and status of the native cultures: the Quechua, the Aymara, and the many tribal societies of Amazonia. Whereas tens of thousands deliberately embarked on life-plans of social mobility by altering their persona from *indio* (Indian) to *cholo* to mestizo in moving from the native American caste to upper-middle class, a new alternative for some was to use ethnic loyalty and identity as a device of empowerment and, thus, an avenue for socioeconomic change. How Peruvian institutions, state policy, and traditions adjusted to these trends would determine what Peruvians as a society would be like in the twenty-first century.

Environment and Population

Natural Systems and Human Life

Peru is a complex amalgam of ancient and modern cultures, populations, conflicts, questions, and dilemmas. The land itself offers great challenges. With 1,285,216 square kilometers, Peru is the nineteenth largest nation in area in the world and the fourth largest Latin American nation. It ranked fifth in population in the region, with 22,767,543 inhabitants in July 1992. Centered in the heart of the 8,900-kilometer-long Andean range, Peru's geography and climates, although similar to those of its Andean neighbors, form their own peculiar conditions, making the region one of the world's most heterogeneous and dynamic. Peru's principal natural features are its desert coast; the forty great snow-covered peaks over 6,000 meters in altitude, and the mountain ranges they anchor; Lake Titicaca, which is shared with Bolivia, and at 3,809 meters above sea level the world's highest navigable lake; and the vast web of tropical rivers like the Ucayali, Marañón, and Huallaga, which join to form the Río Amazonas (the Amazon) above Peru's "Atlantic" port of Iquitos (see fig. 5).

The Costa, Sierra, and Selva (*selva*—jungle), each comprising a different and sharply contrasting environment, form the major terrestrial regions of the country. Each area, however, contains special ecological niches and microclimates generated by ocean currents, the wide range of Andean altitudes, solar angles and slopes, and the configurations of the vast Amazonian area. As a consequence of these complexities, thirty-four ecological subregions have been identified.

Although there is great diversity in native fauna, relatively few animals lent themselves to the process of domestication in prehistoric times. Consequently, at the time of European arrival the only large domesticated animals were the llamas and alpacas. Unfortunately, llamas and alpacas are not powerful beasts, serving only as light pack animals and for meat and wool. The absence of great draft animals played a key role in the evolution of human societies in Peru because without animals such as horses, oxen, camels, and donkeys, which powered the wheels of development in the Old

World, human energy in Peru and elsewhere in the Americas could not be augmented significantly. As far as is known, the enormous potential in hydrologic resources in preconquest times was tapped only for agricultural irrigation and basic domestic usage. Through the elaborate use of massive irrigation works and terracing, which appeared in both highland and coastal valleys in pre-Chavín periods (1000 B.C.), the environment of the Andes was opened for intensive human settlement, population growth, and the emergence of regional states.

The development of Andean agriculture started about 9,000 years ago, when inhabitants began experimenting with the rich vegetation they utilized as food gatherers. Each ecological niche, or "floor," begins about 500 to 1,000 meters vertically above the last, forming a minutely graduated and specialized environment for life. The central Andean area is, thus, one of the world's most complex biospheres, which human efforts made into one of the important prehistoric centers of plant domestication. Native domesticated plants number in the hundreds and include many varieties of such important crops as potatoes, maize (corn), lima beans, peppers, yucca or manioc, cotton, squashes and gourds, pineapples, avocado, and coca, which were unknown in the Old World. Dozens of varieties of fruits and other products, despite their attractive qualities, are little known outside the Andean region.

Conquest of the Aztec alliance in Mexico and the Inca Empire (Tawantinsuyu) in the Andes gave impetus to one of the most important features of the colonial process, the transfer of wealth, products, and disease between the hemispheres. Andean plant resources, of course, contributed significantly to life in Europe, Africa, and Asia. Although attention has usually focused on the hoards of Inca gold and silver shipped to Spain and thus funneled to the rest of Europe, the value of Andean potatoes to the European economy and diet probably far exceeded that of precious metals. By the same token, the Spanish conquerors introduced into the New World wheat, barley, rice, and other grains; vegetables like carrots; sugarcane; tea and coffee; and many fruits, such as grapes, oranges, and olives. The addition of Old World cattle, hogs, sheep, goats, chickens, and draft animals—horses, donkeys, and oxen—vastly increased Andean resources and altered work methods, diets, and health. The trade-off in terms of disease was one-sided; measles, malaria, yellow fever, cholera, whooping cough, influenza, smallpox, and bubonic plague, carried by rats, arrived with each ship from Europe. The impact of these diseases was more devastating than any other aspect of the conquest, and they remain major scourges for the majority of Peruvians.

The Coastal Region

Peru's coast is a bleak, often rocky, and mountainous desert that runs from Chile to Ecuador, punctuated by fifty-two small rivers that descend through steep, arid mountains and empty into the Pacific. The Costa is a strange land of great dunes and rolling expanses of barren sand, at once a desert but with periods of humidity as high as 90 percent from June to September, when temperatures in Lima average about 16 degrees Celsius. Temperatures along the coast rise near the equator in the north, where the summer can be blazingly hot, and fall to cooler levels in the south. If climatic conditions are right, there can be a sudden burst of delicate plant life at certain places on the lunar-like landscape, made possible by the heavy mist. Normally, however, the mist is only sufficient to dampen the air, and the sand remains bleakly sterile. These conditions greatly favor the preservation of delicate archaeological remains. The environment also facilitates human habitation and housing because the climate is tolerable and the lack of rain eases the need for water-tight roofing.

Humans have lived for over 10,000 years in the larger coastal valleys, fishing, hunting, and gathering along the rich shoreline, as well as domesticating crops and inventing irrigation systems. The largest of these littoral oases became the sites of towns, cities, religious centers, and the seats of ancient nations. Although migration from the highlands and other provincial regions has long occurred, the movement of people to the Costa was greatly stimulated by the growth of the fishing industry, which transformed villages and towns into frontier-like cities, such as Chimbote. In the early 1990s, over 53 percent of the nation's people lived in these sharply delimited coastal valleys (see table 4, Appendix). As the population becomes ever more concentrated in the coastal urban centers, people increasingly overrun the rich and ancient irrigated agricultural lands, such as those in the Rímac Valley where greater Lima is situated, and the Chicama Valley at the site of the city of Trujillo. Although the region contains 160,500 square kilometers of land area, only 4 percent, or 6,900 square kilometers of it, is arable. By 1990 population growth had increased the density of habitation to 1,715 persons for each square kilometer of arable land (see table 5, Appendix). Throughout all the coastal valleys, human settlements remain totally dependent on the waters that flow from the Andes along canals and aqueducts first designed and built 3,000 years ago. Here, uncontrolled and unplanned urban growth competes directly with scarce and vitally needed agricultural land, steadily removing it from productive use.

The Andean Highlands

The Sierra is the commanding feature of Peru's territory, reaching heights up to 6,768 meters. Hundreds of permanently glaciated and snowcapped peaks tower over the valleys. The steep, desiccated Pacific flank of the Andes supports only a sparse population in villages located at infrequent springs and seepages. In contrast, tropical forests blanket the eastern side of the Andes as high as 2,100 meters. Between these extremes, in the shadows of the great snowpeaks, lie the most populous highland ecological zones: the intermontane valleys (*kichwa*) and the higher uplands and grassy puna or Altiplano plateaus. Approximately 36 percent of the population lives in thousands of small villages and hamlets that constitute the rural hinterland for the regional capitals and trading centers. More than 15 percent of Peruvians live at altitudes between 2,000 and 3,000 meters, 20 percent live between 3,000 and 4,000 meters, and 1 percent regularly reside at altitudes over 4,000 meters.

Although rich in mineral resources, such as copper, lead, silver, iron, and zinc, which are mined at altitudes as high as 5,152 meters, the Andes are endowed with limited usable land. The highlands encompass 34 percent of the national territory, or 437,000 square kilometers, but only 4.5 percent of the highlands, or 19,665 square kilometers, is arable and cultivated. Nevertheless, this area constitutes more than half the nation's productive land. About 93,120 square kilometers of the Sierra is natural pasture over 4,000 meters in altitude, too high for agriculture. The 4.5 percent of arable land, therefore, has fairly dense populations, particularly in Puno, Cajamarca, and in valleys such as the Mantaro in Junín Department and Callejón de Huaylas in Ancash Department. The highland provinces have a population density of 460 persons per square kilometer of habitable, arable land.

The best areas for cultivation are the valleys, which range from 2,000 to 3,500 meters in altitude. Although many valleys have limited water supplies, others, because of glacial runoffs, enjoy abundant water for irrigation. In the protected valleys, the dry climate is temperate, with no frost or great heat. In the high plateau or puna regions above 3,900 meters, the climate is cold and severe, often going below freezing at night and seldom rising above 16°C by day. A myriad of native tubers thrives at altitudes from 2,800 meters to almost 4,000 meters, including over 4,000 known varieties of the potato, oca, and *olluco,* as well as grains such as quinoa. The hardy native llamas and alpacas thrive on the tough *ichu* grass of the punas; European sheep and cattle, when adapted, do well at lesser altitudes.

A view of Huaraz and the Cordillera Blanca
Courtesy Inter-American Development Bank

For the Peruvians, there are two basic Andean seasons, the rainy season, locally referred to as winter *(invierno)*, from October through April and the dry season of summer *(verano)* in the remaining months. Crops are harvested according to type throughout the year, with potatoes and other native tubers brought in during the middle to late winter and grains during the dry season. The torrential rains of the winter months frequently cause severe landslides and avalanches, called *huaycos,* throughout the Andean region, damaging irrigation canals, roads, and even destroying villages and cities. In the valley of Callejón de Huaylas, the city of Huaraz (Huarás) was partially destroyed in 1941 by just such a catastrophe, an event repeated a few kilometers away in 1962, when the town of Ranrahirca was annihilated by a *huayco* that killed about 3,000 people.

The formidable terrain of the Andes, where the land may fall away from 5,000 meters to 500 meters and then rise to almost 7,000 meters in a space of 50 kilometers as the condor flies, poses a ubiquitous challenge to any modern means of transport. Thus, the Andean region was not penetrated by wheeled vehicles until railroads were built in the latter half of the nineteenth century. Moreover, most of the nation did not see wheels until the dirt road system was under construction in the 1920s. To build the system, President Augusto B. Leguía y Salcedo (1908–12, 1919–30) revived a national system of draft labor harkening back to the Inca's conscripted labor force, or *mita* (see Glossary), used for road and bridge building in ancient times.

High-Altitude Adaptations

As with the Himalayan mountains, the Andes impose severe conditions and many limitations on life. Consequently, Andean people are physically adapted to the heights in special ways. In contrast to persons born and raised at sea level, those living at Andean altitudes 2,500 meters or more above sea level have as much as 25 percent more blood that is more viscous and richer in red cells, a heart that is proportionately larger, and specially adapted, larger lungs, with an enhanced capacity to take in oxygen from the rare atmosphere. Biological adaptations have permitted the native highlanders to work efficiently and survive successfully in the Andean altitudes for 20,000 years.

The first important scientific research on high-altitude biology was undertaken by the Peruvian physician-scientist Carlos Monge Medrano in the 1920s. He showed that coca-leaf chewing played a role in aiding the metabolism in high-altitude populations. More recent studies have shown that coca chewing significantly aids in metabolizing high carbohydrate foods like potatoes, yucca, and corn, which are traditional staples in the Andean region, thus providing the chewer with more rapid energy input from his meals. Supposed narcotic effects of coca-leaf chewing are nil because enzymes in the mouth convert coca into atropine-like substances, unlike substances involved in cocaine. Anthropologists Catherine Allen and Roderick E. Burchard have also demonstrated the central role traditional coca use plays in Andean communities as a medicine, ritual substance, and an element in economic and social affairs.

The Amazonian Tropics

The Selva, which includes the humid tropics of the Amazon jungle and rivers, covers about 63 percent of Peru but contains only about 11 percent of the country's population. The region begins high in the eastern Andean cloud forests, called the *ceja de montaña* (eyebrow of the jungle), or Montaña or Selva Alta, and descends with the rush of silt-laden Andean rivers—such as the Marañón, Huallaga, Apurímac, and Urubamba—to the relatively flat, densely forested, Amazonian plain. These torrential rivers unite as they flow, forming the Amazon before reaching the burgeoning city of Iquitos. Regarded as an exotic land of mystery and promise throughout much of the twentieth century, the Selva has been seen in Peru as the great hope for future development, wealth, and the fulfillment of national destiny. As such, it became President Fernando Belaúnde Terry's "Holy Grail" as he devoted the energies of his two administrations (1963–68, 1980–85) to promoting colonization, development schemes, and highway construction across the Montaña and into the tropical domain.

Human settlements in the Amazonian region are invariably riverine, clustering at the edges of the hundreds of rivers and oxbow lakes that in natural conditions are virtual fish farms in terms of their productivity. The streams and rivers constitute a serpentine network of pathways plied by boats and canoes that provide the basic transport through the forest. Here, the Shipibo, Asháninka (Campa), Aguaruna, and other tribes lived in relative independence from the Peruvian state until the mid-twentieth century. Although the native people have cleverly exploited the extraordinary riverine environment for at least 5,000 years, both they and the natural system have been under relentless pressures of population, extractive industries, and the conversion of forest into farm and pasture. Amazonian forest resources are enormous but not inexhaustible. Amazonian timber is prized worldwide, but when the great cedar, rosewood, and mahogany reserves are cut, they are rarely replaced.

Peru's tropics are also a fabled source for traditional medicinal plants, such as the four types of domesticated coca, which are prized through the entire Andean and upper Amazonian sphere, having been widely traded and bartered for 4,500 years. Unfortunately, coca's traditional uses as a beneficial drug for dietary, medical, and ritual purposes, and, in the early twentieth century, as a primary flavoring for cola drinks have given way to illegal plantings on a large scale for cocaine production. All of the new, illegal plantations are located in Peru's upper Amazon drainage and have seriously deteriorated the forests, soils, and general environment where they exist. The use of chemical sprays and the widespread clearing of vegetation to eliminate illegal planting has also created unfortunate and extensive environmental side-effects.

In the early 1990s, the Selva was still considered an important potential source for new discoveries in the medicinal, fuel, and mineral fields. Petroleum and gas reserves have been known to exist in several areas, but remained difficult to exploit. And, in Peru's southern Amazonian department of Madre de Dios, a gold rush has been in progress since the 1970s, producing a frontier boom effect with various negative repercussions. The new population attracted to the region has placed numerous pressures on the native tribal communities and their lands.

All of these intrusions into the fragile Amazon tropics were fraught with environmental questions and human dilemmas of major scale. In this poorly understood environment, hopes and development programs have often gone awry at enormous cost. In their wake, serious problems of deforestation, population displacement, challenge to the tribal rights of the native "keepers of the forest," endless infrastructural costs, and the explosive expansion of cocaine capitalism have emerged. In the 1963–90 period, Peru looked to the tropics as the solution for socioeconomic problems that it did not want to confront in the highlands. In the early 1990s, it was faced with paradox and quandary in both areas.

The Maritime Region

A maritime region constitutes a fourth significant environment within the Peruvian domain. The waters off the Peruvian coast are swept by the Humboldt (or Peruvian) Current that rises in the frigid Antarctic and runs strongly northward, cooling the arid South American coastline before curving into the central Pacific near the Peru-Ecuador border. Vast shoals of anchovy, tuna, and several varieties of other valued fish are carried in this stream, making it one of the world's richest commercial fisheries (see Structures of Production, ch. 3). The importance of guano has diminished since the rise of the anchovy fishing industry. The billions of anchovy trapped by modern flotillas of purse seiners guided by spotter planes and electronic sounding devices are turned into fish meal for fertilizer and numerous other industrial uses. Exports of fish meal and fish products are of critical importance for Peru's economy. For this reason, changes in the environmental patterns on the coast or in the adjacent ocean have devastating consequences for employment and, therefore, national stability. The periodic advent of a warm current flowing south, known as El Niño (The Christ-child), and intensive fishing that has temporarily depleted the seemingly boundless stocks of anchovy have caused major difficulties for Peru.

Natural Disasters and Their Impact

Severely affecting conditions on both land and sea, El Niño is yet another peculiarity of the Peruvian environment. This stream of equatorial water periodically forces its way southward against the shoreline, pushing the cold Humboldt Current and its vast fishery deeper and westward into the ocean, while bringing in exotic equatorial species. El Niño is not benign, even though named after the Christ-child because it has often appeared in December. Instead, over cycles of fifteen to twenty-five years, El Niño disrupts the normally rainless coastal climate and produces heavy rainfalls, floods, and consequent damages. The reverse occurs in the highlands, where drought-like conditions occur, often over two-to-five-year periods, reducing agricultural production. The impact of this phenomenon came to be more fully understood only in the 1980s, and it has been shown to influence Atlantic hurricane patterns as well. Moreover, archaeological research by Michael Edward Moseley has demonstrated that El Niño turbulence probably led to the heretofore unexplained collapses of apparently prosperous ancient Andean societies. From 1981 to 1984, Peruvians experienced severe destruction from this perturbation; the destruction clearly contributed to the rapidly deteriorating socioeconomic conditions in the country.

Another major environmental variable is the activity of the Nazca plate, which abuts Peru along the Pacific shore and constantly forces the continental land mass upward. Although volcanism created numerous thermal springs throughout the coastal and highland region and created such striking volcanic cones as El Misti, which overlooks the city of Arequipa, it also poses the constant threat of severe earthquakes.

In the Sierra, much farmland rests at the foot of great, unstable mountains, such as those overlooking the spectacular valley of Callejón de Huaylas, which is replete with the evidence of past avalanches and seismic upheaval. It is also one of the most productive agricultural areas in the highlands. On May 31, 1970, an earthquake measuring 7.7 on the Richter scale staggered the department of Ancash and adjacent areas. A block of glacial ice split from the top of El Huascarán, Peru's tallest mountain (6,768 meters), and buried the provincial capital of Yungay under a blanket of mud and rock, killing about 5,000 people. In the affected region, 70,000 persons were killed, 140,000 injured, and over 500,000 left homeless. It was the most destructive disaster in the history of the Western Hemisphere and had major negative effects on the national economy and government reform programs at a critical moment during the administration of Juan Velasco Alvarado (1968–75).

In precolonial times, the Incas and their ancestors had long grappled with the seismic problem. Many archaeologists have attributed the special trapezoidal character of Inca architecture to precautions against earthquakes. The first name of the founder of the Inca empire, Pachacuti Inca Yupanqui, means "cataclysm." The Incas understood their terrain. Since 1568 there have been over 70 significant earthquakes in Peru, or one every six years, although each year the country registers as many as 200 lesser quakes. As an expression of their own powerlessness in the face of such events, many

Peruvians pray for protection to a series of earthquake saints. Among such saints are Cusco's Señor de los Temblores (Lord of the Tremors), revered since a disaster in 1650, and the Señor de los Milagros (Lord of Miracles), worshipped in Lima and nationwide since a quake in 1655.

People, Property, and Farming Systems

Human adaptation to the high altitudes, coastal desert, and tropical jungles requires specialized knowledge and skill in addition to the physiological adjustments noted to cope with altitudinal stress. Over the course of thousands of years, people invented elaborate irrigation systems to take advantage of the potential productivity in the coastal valleys. Visitors to even the smallest coastal valleys can still find elaborate evidence of these ancient public works. Many of these networks are still in use or form the basis of rebuilt systems that provide water to the lucrative commercial agriculture now practiced. Both in prehistoric times and now, the key to social and political affairs in these and all other coastal valleys is access to water, effective irrigation technology, and the ability to keep a large labor force at the task of construction and maintenance.

The coastal valleys from colonial times to the present have been dominated by extensive systems of plantation agriculture, with powerful elite families in control of the land and water rights. The principal crops harvested under these regimes are sugarcane and cotton, with a mixture of other crops, such as grapes and citrus, also being planted. Before the Agrarian Reform Law of 1969, about 80 percent of the arable coastal land was owned by 1.7 percent of the property owners. Despite the dominance of the great coastal estates, there were, and still are, thousands of smaller farms surrounding them, producing a wide variety of food crops for the urban markets and for subsistence. Since land reform, ownership of the great plantations has been transferred to the employees and workers, who operate them as a type of cooperative. The coastal farmland is extremely valuable because of the generous climate, flat lands, and usually reliable irrigation waters, without which nothing would succeed. These advantageous conditions are supplemented by the use of excellent guano and fish-meal fertilizers. As a result, the productive coastal land, amounting to only 3.8 percent of the national total, including pasture and forest, yields a reported 50 percent of the gross agricultural product.

In the intermontane Andean valleys, there is a wide variety of farming opportunities. The best lands are those that benefit year round from the constant flow of melting glacial waters. Most farming depends on the advent of the rains, and farmers must plan their

Destruction from the earthquake of May 31, 1970, in Ancash Department
Courtesy Inter-American Development Bank
Remnants of Yungay, Callejón de Huaylas Valley, buried by the 1970 ice
avalanche from El Huascarán
Courtesy Paul L. Doughty

75

affairs accordingly. In many areas, farmers have built reservoir and canal systems, but, for the most part, they must time their planting to coincide with the capricious onset of the rainy season. Where irrigation works are operative, as on the coast, farmers are joined in water-management districts and irrigation boards, which govern water flow, canal maintenance, and enforcement of complex water rights, rules, and customs.

Over 70 percent of the smallest farms are less than five hectares in size, with the great majority of them found in the Andean highlands. A typical peasant household with such a small property cannot harvest anything but the most minimum subsistence from it and inevitably must supplement household earnings from other sources, with most or all family members working. The adequacy of each small farm and its dispersed *chacras* (plots of land used for gardening) of course varies with water supply, altitude, soil fertility, and other local factors. The best irrigated farmland in the *kichwa* valleys tends to be highly subdivided in the competition for a rural subsistence base. The largest land holdings are the property of corporate communities, such as the numerous Peasant Communities (Comunidades Campesinas) and Peasant Groups (Grupos Campesinos). In 1990 these official forms of common entitlement, as opposed to individual private ownership, accounted for over 60 percent of pasture lands, much of which lies in the punas of the southern Andes.

The ecological mandates of the Andean environment thus structure the day-to-day farming activities of all highlanders and the character of their domestic economies. Research conducted by anthropologist Stephen B. Brush showed how peasant farmers traditionally have utilized the different ecological niches at their disposal. At the highest altitudes of production, animals are grazed and specialized tubers grown. At the intermediate altitudes are found grains like wheat, barley, rye, and corn, as well as pulses such as broad beans, peas, and lentils, along with a wide variety of vegetables, including onions, squashes, carrots, hot *rocoto* peppers, and tomatoes. At still lower levels, tropical fruits and crops prosper.

Some communities have direct access to all of these production environments, whereas others may be confined to one zone only. Traditionally, the strategy of families, the basic social units of production and consumption, is to arrange access to products from the different zones through the social mechanisms available to them. Particular *chacras* serve as virtual chess pieces as families buy and sell property, or enter into sharecropping arrangements in order to obtain access to specific cropping areas. Marital arrangements may also be made with specific properties in mind. Thus, the system

Ichu, an Aymara village above Lake Titicaca
Courtesy Paul L. Doughty

of small farms (*minifundios*—see Glossary) will invariably involve a confusing but systematic pattern of holdings.

In Huaylas, Ancash Department, for example, farmers owning small but highly productive irrigated *chacras* at about 2,700 meters cultivate corn, vegetables, and alfalfa. Slightly higher irrigated property is devoted to grains, and, higher still, *chacras* are devoted to potatoes, oca and other tubers, and quinoa. Above the cultivated land and on the nonirrigated hillsides, cattle and sheep are grazed on communally held open ranges and puna. In the deep protected gorges and canyons on the fringes of the district, small *chacras* at altitudes of 1,500 meters produce a variety of tropical crops. Consequently, within a relatively small area a single family may own or have usufruct rights to a checkerboard of small *chacras,* whose total area does not exceed four or five hectares, but whose range of production provides a diverse nutritional subsistence base.

For this reason, attempts to unify smallholdings to make them more efficient can likely yield the opposite effect in terms of the household economy. This is, in fact, what happened in many areas after the Agrarian Reform Law of 1969 was implemented, prohibiting sharecropping and restricting the geographical range of ownership in order to achieve hoped for economies of scale (see Glossary). After the initial attempts to enforce the new, well-meaning laws, the

77

minifundio system began to reemerge as peasants discovered ways to circumvent its restrictions, which inadvertently limited their ownership and use of *chacras* to a narrow range of ecological zones (see Structures of Production, ch. 3).

In other areas, such as those described by anthropologist Enrique Mayer in the Huánuco region, the relatively compressed ecology found in Huaylas gives way to one spread out over the eastern flanks of the Andes, stretching down eventually to the Selva. In contrast to the confining peasant farms of Huaylas, farmers in the Huánuco region develop barter and trade relations across the production zones, permitting them to exchange their farm produce, such as potatoes, for other crops grown at different levels.

Although most Andean farmers are independent producers, there are various types of large holdings, of which three are particularly important: the manorial estate, the *minifundio* and family farm, and the corporate community holding. Historically, the most significant holdings relative to socioeconomic power were the great manorial properties known as haciendas, which averaged over 1,200 hectares in size but often exceeded 20,000 hectares prior to being eliminated during the 1969–75 land reform. At the time the land reform began, 1.3 percent of the highland farm owners held over 75 percent of the farm and grazing lands, while 96 percent of the farmers held ownership of but 8.5 percent of the farm area. The corporate community holdings are in the form of land held in common title by a Peasant Community. After the land reform, groups of communities were organized as corporate bodies by the government to enable them, in theory, to combine lands and resources to gain the advantages of an economy of scale. These organizations and the Peasant Communities, reportedly numbering 5,500 in 1991, assumed titles to the haciendas expropriated during the reform period.

By contrast, the population living in the Selva is engaged in a totally different set of agroecological patterns of activity. The native peoples of the tropics, living in riverine settings for the greater part, depend on fishing, hunting, and selective gathering from the forest. They also engage in highly effective horticulture, usually in a system known as slash-and-burn (see Glossary). Long thought to be a destructive and inefficient method of farming, studies have revealed it to be quite the contrary. In this system, the tribal farmer usually exploits a particular plot for only a three-to-five-year period and then abandons it to open another fresh area. This practice allows the vegetation and thin soil to recuperate before the farmer returns to use it again in ten to twenty years. Another facet of the system is that all fields are used in a pattern of multicropping. In this approach, as many as fifteen different crops are intermingled in such a way that each plant complements the others in terms of nutrients used or returned to the soil. The arrangement also provides a disadvantageous environment for plant diseases and insect pests. Another common horticultural system employed along the river banks in the dry season takes advantage of extensive silt deposits left by the seasonal floods. On such open plots, farmers tend to monocrop or, at least, to reduce the number of varieties sown.

Human Settlement and Population Through Time

The special configuration and character of Peru's modern society owe their start to the Spanish conquest, when Europeans and Africans came into sexual contact with what had been a racially homogeneous population. In its own conquests, however, the Inca Empire had embraced a wide range of cultural groups that spoke over fifty languages and practiced diverse customs. As a multicultural state, the Incas had grappled with the problem of tribal diversity and competition, often resolving their disagreements with conquered peoples through violence and repression. Another Inca solution to such dilemmas was to forcibly relocate recalcitrant populations to more governable locations and replace them with trustworthy communities. Peoples resettled in this manner were called *mitimaes,* and the process contributed significantly to the complications of Andean ethnicity. In addition to these measures, the Incas often took the children of local leaders and other key personages as hostages to guarantee political tranquility. In some ways, then, the Inca experience harshly prefigured the Spanish conquest.

With the arrival of conquering migrants from the Old World, new mixed races were born. The initial importance of these offspring of whites and Africans with native American mothers was minimal, however, because of the ''great dying'' of the indigenous population instigated by European diseases and the subsequent collapse and demoralization of the native society and economy. The continuous impact of repressive colonial regimes did not permit any resurgence of native vitality or organization, although there were a number of rebellions and revolts. Under these conditions, Peru reached its nadir in 1796, near the end of the colonial period, when fewer than 1.1 million inhabitants were counted. This figure marked a fall from an estimated pre-Columbian total of at least 16 million, although some scholars think the figure may be twice that number, and others less. Peru recovered slowly, only slightly exceeding its minimally estimated preconquest population size in 1981 (see table 2, Appendix).

The critical factors in population growth since the mid-nineteenth century have been the rapid emergence of the mestizo population, which grew at a rate of over 3 percent per year throughout the colonial period until the 1980s, and the reduction but not the disappearance of sweeping epidemic diseases. Another factor that played a role in this increase was the influx of foreign migrants from Europe, and especially from China and, more recently, Japan. The rate of growth became very high during the twentieth century owing to a number of factors. The then dominant mestizo and other mixed populations were obviously more resistant to the diseases to which the native peoples, lacking natural immunities, succumbed. The mestizos also enjoyed important cultural advantages in a colonialist society, which actively discriminated against the native population on racial and ethnic grounds. From conquest to the present, it has been the fate of the native peoples not to prosper.

The Spanish colonial policy regarding population management in the viceroyalty, as throughout the hemisphere, was to create bureaucratic order through an official hierarchy of caste, with obligations and privileges attached thereto. The system attempted to keep people sorted out according to genealogical history and place of birth. Thus, Europeans ranked first, followed by all others: a male offspring of a European and a native American was called a mestizo, or *cholo;* of a European and African, a mulatto; of an African and a native American, a *zambo;* of a mestizo and *indio,* a *salta atrás* (jump backward). The order encompassed all of the combinations and recombinations of race, with over fifty commonly used terms, many of which—such as mestizo, mulatto, *zambo, cholo,* criollo, *indio, negro* (Negro or black), and *blanco* (white)—survive in common usage today. For both white Europeans and Africans, there were two categories—those born in the Old World were called *peninsulares* and *bosales,* respectively, whereas those of both races born in Peru were called criollos (Creoles). In the case of whites, the fact that Creoles were lower in rank than their peninsular counterparts was resented and contributed eventually to the overthrow of colonial rule.

There were six basic castes in Colonial Peru: Spaniards, native Americans, mestizos, Negroes, mulattos, and *zambos.* In theory, these categories defined a person's place of residence and occupation, taxes, obligations to the viceroyalty under the *mita,* which churches and masses could be attended, and which parts of the towns could be entered. Sumptuary laws determined the nature of one's clothing as well, and prohibited natives in particular from riding horses, using buttons, having weapons, and even owning mirrors and playing stringed instruments. Such a system was hard, if not impossible, to keep on track, and its rules and powers were irregularly applied. Nevertheless, vestiges of the colonial social caste system and its associated behavior and attitudes linger in present-day Peruvian society in many ways.

Although largely replaced along the coast by mestizos, Afro-Peruvians, and Chinese laborers, the native peoples survived biologically as well as culturally in the highlands. Their survival was attributed to many factors: the sheer numbers of their original population; their relative isolation, resulting in part from the collapse of the society and inefficiency of the colonial regimes; and the assumption of the kind of passive defensive posture of silence and apparent submissive behavior that has been characterized as a "weapon of the weak." In numerous cases, communities managed to place themselves under the wing of religious orders and, ironically, the hacienda system, with its conditions of serfdom. This situation developed with the demise of the system of serfdom called the *encomienda* (see Glossary) and the state monopoly of selling goods to the native peoples called the *repartimiento* (see Glossary). If nothing more, by becoming serfs on the haciendas, native Americans were defended by landlords, who were inclined to protect their peons from exploitation by others and especially from having to serve in the *mita de minas* (the mine labor draft—see Glossary). Consequently, the bastions of highland indigenous culture have been the small, isolated mountain villages and hamlets; dispersed farming and pastoral communities; and haciendas, where populations were encapsulated under protective exploitation and ignored by their absentee landlords.

Settlement Patterns

In pre-Columbian eras, the highland population was ensconced on ridges, hillsides, and other locations that did not interfere with farming priorities. Large ceremonial buildings, temples, or administrative centers, were, however, located in central locations, often apart from the residences of average persons. By the time of conquest, the Incas had rearranged settlements to suit their own vision of administrative needs in conquered areas. Thus, Inca planners and architects constructed special towns and cities, such as Huánuco Viejo, to accommodate their needs.

With Viceroy Francisco Toledo y Figueroa's colonial reforms in the late sixteenth century, however, the traditional Andean settlement patterns were drastically altered through the establishment of settlements called reductions (*reducciones*—see Glossary), which were located in the less advantageous areas, and the founding of new Spanish towns and cities. The reduction system forced native Americans to settle in nucleated villages and towns, which were easily controlled by their masters, the *encomenderos* (see Glossary), as well as by clergy and regional governors (*corregidores de indios*— see Glossary). The Spaniards also established their own towns, which were off-limits to most native peoples except for occasional religious celebrations or for work assignments. These towns eventually became home to the dominant mestizos. As the municipal and economic centers of each district and province, these mestizo towns (*poblachos mestizos*) remain the dominant settlements, constituting the district and provincial capitals throughout the country. Today, virtually all of the small towns and villages throughout the highlands are either the product of the reduction system of forced relocation or were established as Spanish colonial municipalities.

The striking similarities among settlements in terms of design and architecture are no accident. Almost all settlements thus exhibit the grid pattern or model of rectangular blocks arranged around a town square, universally known as the arms plaza (*plaza de armas*). This design reflects the military dimension of the conquest culture, the central place in an encampment being where armaments were kept when not deployed. By direct analogy, it also demonstrates and symbolizes central authority and power. Typically, then, the most important residents lived close to the *plaza de armas,* in the most prominent houses. Status, conferred by birth, race, and occupation, was confirmed by a central urban residence. In modern practice, status has continued to be reflected in a hierarchy of urban residence descending from Lima to the departmental, provincial, and district capitals. No one of importance or power is rural.

Urban, Rural, and Regional Populations

The change in distribution from rural to urban has been profound: the urban population rose from 47 percent in 1961 to an estimated 70 percent in 1990. By that time, Peru's population had reached a point where its configurations were thus substantially different than they were a generation earlier, largely because of the enormous growth of metropolitan Lima, which includes the seaport of Callao. Indeed, four of the largest political districts of greater Lima began as squatter settlements and now would rank among the nation's top ten cities if they had been counted separately. The leading cities in Peru represent a mix of old colonial places—Lima, Arequipa, Trujillo, Cusco (Cuzco), Piura, and Ica—and newly emergent ones, such as Huancayo, Chimbote, Iquitos, and Juliaca, whose new elites derive mostly from the highly

Plaza de Armas, Cusco, with La Merced church in background
Courtesy Inter-American Development Bank

mobile provincial middle and lower classes (see table 6, Appendix). In the Sierra, Juliaca, because of its role in marketing and transportation, surpassed the departmental capital of Puno in both size and importance to become the most important city south of Cusco.

Burgeoning cities, such as the industrial port of Chimbote, had a kind of raw quality to them in the early 1990s, with blocks and blocks of recently constructed one- and two-story buildings and a majority of streets neither paved nor cobbled. As the site of Peru's prestige industry—an electrically powered steel mill—and as a major port for the anchovy industry, Chimbote attracted bilingual mestizos and *cholos,* who continued to pour into the city from the highlands of Ancash, especially the provinces of Huaylas, Corongo, Pallasca, and Sihuas. The migrants' dynamism, powered by a will to progress and modernize, built the city from a quaint seaside town of 4,200 residents in 1940 to 296,000 in 1990, with neither the approval nor significant assistance of government planners or development programs. Although the energy and growth of Chimbote was impressive, the lack of urban infrastructure in the basic services, absence of attention to environmental impacts, and totally inadequate municipal budgets led directly to converting Chimbote Bay, the best natural port on Peru's coast, into a cesspool of industrial

83

and urban wastes (meters thick in places). Even smaller coastal boom towns, such as Supe, have suffered the same outcomes. It was not surprising that the 1991 cholera outbreak should have started in Chimbote.

Just as the cities have grown, the rural sector's share of the population has declined. Nevertheless, in the early 1990s there were still more persons living in the rural regions than ever before in the nation's history. In fact, the rural population in 1991 equaled the total population of the country in 1961.

At first, the country seemed to relish its growth even though the population explosion distressed the urbane sensibilities of the elite and the comfortable middle classes. Through its increase in size, Peru gained stature internationally and maintained a superiority of sorts vis-à-vis Ecuador, Bolivia, and Chile, its regional rivals. It could be maintained that Peru's policy was to let the population problem "solve itself" through spontaneous migration by which people found their own solutions for the maldistribution of wealth, services, resources, and power. The vast and growing squatter settlements in Lima, however, gave many serious pause, and alternatives were proposed (see Employment and Wages, Poverty, and Income Distribution, ch. 3).

Demography of Growth, Migration, and Work

Significant in different ways were the divisions according to the major ecological zones. In 1990 the coastal region held 53 percent of the nation's peoples; the highlands, 36 percent; and the Selva, the other 11 percent. This distribution pattern marked an abrupt change from almost thirty years earlier when the figures for coast and highlands were nearly the reverse. These shifts obviously had significant implications for the nation in terms of government, the economy, and social relations. For example, the agricultural sector had two parts: the mechanized high-export production of the coastal plantations and cooperatives, and the intensively farmed small-holdings of the Sierra, which have depended most heavily on hand labor and have been essentially unchanged in technology since the colonial period. Although the highland farm technology was effective, Andean production was undermined by urbanward migrations and the revolution and repression of the 1980s.

Within the contexts of these significant demographic changes, the general growth of the population has been constant since its low point at the end of the colonial period. Between 1972 and 1981, the country grew by 25 percent. The increase may have been greater between 1981 and 1991, reaching over 30 percent, if projections were correct (see fig. 6). The increase ran counter to the anticipated benefits stemming from the continued drop in fertility rates, which declined from 6.7 children born per woman in 1965 to 3.3 in 1991, and in birthrates, which dropped from a high of 45 births per 1,000 in 1965 to 27 per 1,000 in 1992. The crude death rates, however, despite the many problems in health care, fell over this same period from 16 to 7 per 1,000, basically matching the decline in the birthrate and retaining the actual rate of population growth near its same level as before. Life expectancy for males in Peru has increased from fifty-one years in 1980 to estimates of sixty-three years in 1991, second lowest in South America after Bolivia. Demographers projected that Peru's population would reach 28 million by the year 2000 and 37 million in 2025 if these rates continued. Contemporary dilemmas paled before the problems posed by such estimates. A significant lowering in infant deaths would markedly increase the overall growth rate and accompanying problems posed to institutions, services, and resources.

Population Policy and Family Planning

The issue of slowing population growth through the systematic implementation of modern birth-control methods had remained low-key since the late 1960s but erupted during the 1980s, as a result of pressure coming particularly from women. Research in the early 1980s showed that over 75 percent of women wished to use contraceptives, but over 50 percent did not do so out of fear and uncertainty about their effects or because of the disapproval of the spouse. In this context, the 1985 Law of the National Population Council came into being under the premise that although abortion and voluntary sterilization were excluded, all other "medical, educational, and information services about family planning guarantee that couples and all persons can freely choose the method for control of fecundity and for family planning." The proposed law was opposed in 1987 by the Assembly of Catholic Bishops, which retained its opposition to artificial methods and "irresponsible philosophies." Implementation of the law, however, began that year, setting targets for lowering fecundity rates to 2.5 children per family by the year 2000 and greatly amplifying the availability of clinical resources and contraceptives. In addition to government programs, there were sixteen private organizations promoting various aspects of the policy by 1988.

In 1986 a reported 46 percent of women of child-bearing age were using some form of contraception, but it was not known what percentage of men used contraceptives. The data on the incidence of abortions was not compiled until the 1980s, but according to hospital reports, in 1986 there were 31,860 abortions performed

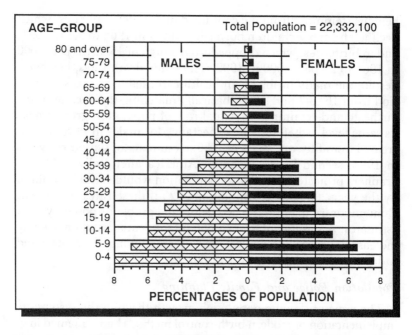

Source: Based on information from Richard Webb and Graciela Fernández Baca de Valdez (eds.), *Perú en números, 1990,* Lima, 1990, 105.

Figure 6. Estimated Population by Age and Sex, 1990

for life-threatening sociomedical reasons, which represented almost 43 percent of all hospital cases involving obstetrical procedures. The estimated rate of clandestine abortions, however, was reportedly at the high rate of 143 cases per 1,000 pregnancies, despite a law that in theory prohibited such interventions. A survey in 1986 of women's attitudes toward contraception and family planning showed that over 27 percent of women would halt their family size after one child, 69 percent would limit their family to two, and over 80 percent desired no more than three children. It was clear from this response that Peruvian women wanted to limit family size and that their demands for increased state and private services would continue to rise.

During the 1975–90 period, contraceptives became more widely available throughout Peru, being distributed or sold nationwide through Ministry of Health programs and private clinics, pharmacies, and even by street vendors in marketplaces. Pharmacies were the most common source of both information about and supply of contraceptives. Not surprisingly, use of birth-control techniques increased sharply with socioeconomic status, educational level, and urban coastal residence.

Lima and the Patterns of Migration

The first Belaúnde administration (1963–68) initiated concerted efforts to develop the Amazon Basin through its ambitious Jungle Border Highway (*la carretera marginal de la selva* or *la marginal*) program, the organization of colonization projects, and special opportunity zones to steer highland migrants in that direction and away from the coast. Belaúnde's Selva-oriented program thus tended to divert investments away from the Sierra, even though much was done there on a small local scale through the self-help Popular Cooperation (Cooperación Popular) projects. In hindsight, the resulting degradation of the tropical biosphere in the wake of these schemes created new sets of problems that were far from anyone's mind in 1964. Unfortunately, the net result of these expensive and sweeping efforts at tropical development has not been as planned. Significant changes in the direction of migration did not take place, and the jungle perimeter road system covering hundreds of kilometers was often used as landing strips by airborne drug traffickers and for military maneuvers.

Just as there are strong "pull" factors that attract persons to Lima and the other major cities, there are also many conditions that "push" people out of their communities: the loss or lack of adequate farmland, natural disasters such as earthquakes and landslides, lack of employment options, and a host of personal reasons. In addition, since the outbreak of terrorist activities by the Shining Path movement in 1980 and subsequent military reactions, over 30,000 persons have been dislocated from towns and villages in the Ayacucho and Huancavelica highlands, most of them gravitating to Ica or Lima.

The profound changes during the 1950–90 period, spurred by sheer increases in numbers, largely resulted from a desire for better life opportunities and progress. The significant demographic change that took place was the migration from rural areas to the cities, especially Lima. Five major features gave this great migration a particular Peruvian character: the concentration of people in Lima and other coastal cities, the regional heterogeneity of the migrants, the tendency of people to follow their family and *paisanos* to specific places, the development of migrant organizations, and the willingness of migrants to assist their homelands.

The migrants, searching for employment and better living conditions, went predominantly from the provinces to the national capital, creating a megalopolis out of Lima and Callao. In 1990 greater Lima had over 30 percent of all Peruvians as residents. On the north coast, cities such as Piura, Chiclayo, and Trujillo have attracted persons from their own regions in considerable numbers; significant growth has occurred in the southern highland cities of Arequipa, Juliaca, and Cusco, as well as in the remote jungle city of Iquitos. Despite rates of increase averaging more than 330 percent between 1961 and 1990, these cities drew few people compared to the numbers of persons drawn to greater Lima. In 1990 Lima was 14 percent larger than the next 24 cities combined, and 58 percent of all urban dwellers lived in greater Lima. As such, Lima had become one of the world's leading cities in terms of its level of primacy, that is, its overwhelming demographic dominance with respect to the next largest urban centers.

Lima's development as a "primate" city (megalopolis) began taking shape during the nineteenth century when the nation was recuperating from the disastrous War of the Pacific (1879–83) with Chile. This trend accelerated dramatically after about 1950, when the fishing industry began its expansion and Peru started to industrialize its urban economy in a determined manner. Thus, throughout most of this long period, no less than a third of the capital's residents were born elsewhere.

Lima's dominance has been more than demographic. In the late 1980s, the metropolis consumed over 70 percent of the nation's electrical energy; had 69 percent of its industry, 98 percent of private investment, and 83 percent of bank deposits; yielded 83 percent of the nation's taxes; had 42 percent of all university students, taught by 62 percent of all professors; and had 73 percent of the nation's physicians. Over 70 percent of the country's wages were paid out in Lima to 40 percent of all school teachers, 51 percent of public employees, and equivalent percentages of the skilled labor force and other urban workers. From television and radio stations to telephones, most consumer goods, recreational facilities, and other items of modern interest were also concentrated in Lima. In short, if Peru had it, it came first to Lima and more often than not was unavailable elsewhere.

Government, too, has been totally centralized in the capital since the establishment of the viceregal court in the sixteenth century. The centrality of Lima in colonial times was so significant that persons committing crimes were often punished by exiling them from the capital for various periods of time; the farther away, the worse the penalty. This notion still underlies much of the cultural concept of social value in Peru today. Everyone living outside of greater Lima is automatically a provincial (*provinciano*), a person defined as being disadvantaged and, perhaps, not quite as civilized as a *limeño*. Under such circumstances, it is hardly surprising that Lima has attracted the vast majority of Peruvians hoping to improve their lives, whether looking for employment, seeking an education, or attempting to influence bureaucratic decisions and win assistance for their communities. Lima has been both hated and loved by *provincianos,* who have been engaged in unequal struggle for access to the nation's wealth and power. The factor of primacy loomed as one of Peru's most significant problems, as the nation attempted to decentralize various aspects of the government under a reorganization law promulgated in March 1987 (see Regionalism and Political Divisions, this ch.).

Another aspect of the migration had to do with its heterogeneity of origin in terms of both place and sociocultural features. At the beginning of the twentieth century, most of the provincial migrants were fairly homogeneous representatives of local elites and relatively prosperous sectors of provincial urban capitals. The last decades of the century, however, have seen a marked growth in the social and cultural diversity of the migrants. Between 1950 and 1990, increasing numbers of persons came from villages and hamlets, not the small district capitals, and thus were more representative of the bilingual and bicultural population, referred to as *cholos.* Whereas in the earlier years of this period, it was unusual to hear migrants speaking the Quechua or Aymara languages on the street, by 1990 it was commonplace to hear these languages used for commerce and general discourse in Lima. This change occurred mostly after 1970, when the populist military regime of Juan Velasco Alvarado began a strong effort to legitimize the native tongues. And thus, it has also become more common to see persons retaining various aspects of their regional clothing styles, including hats and colorful skirts, and in, general, not discarding those cultural class markers that were so denigrated a short generation earlier.

A third migratory pattern was that people invariably followed in the footsteps of relatives and fellow *paisanos.* Once a village had a few *paisanos* established in the city, they were soon followed by others. During the course of Peruvian migration, relatively few persons simply struck out on the migratory adventure alone. Thus, the society of migrants was not a collection of alienated "lost souls," but rather consisted of groups of people with contacts, social roles, and strong cultural and family ties.

This fact produced the fourth dimension of the Peruvian migratory process: the propensity of migrants to organize themselves into effective voluntary associations. The scale and pattern of these associations distinguished the process in Peru from that in most other countries. The organizations have taken several forms, but the two most outstanding examples are found in the squatter settlements and regional clubs that have proliferated in all the largest cities, particularly Lima. The process of urban growth in Lima has produced an urban configuration that conforms to no central plan. Without access to adequate housing of any type, and without funds or available loans, migrants set about developing their own solutions by establishing organizations of their own, occasionally under the sponsorship of APRA. They planned a takeover of unoccupied land at the fringes of the city and, with the suddenness and effectiveness of a military attack, invaded the property, usually on a Saturday night.

Once on the land, the migrants laid out plots with precision and raised temporary housing in a matter of hours. Called by the somewhat deprecatory term *barriada* (see Glossary), the shantytowns quickly developed both an infrastructural and a sociopolitical permanence, despite initial official disapproval and police harassment. At first, the land invasions and *barriada* formation provoked enormous unease among traditional *limeños* and especially in the halls of government. The *barriadas* were wildly characterized as dangerous slums by the Lima middle- and upper classes, which felt threatened by the squatters. Research by anthropologists José Matos Mar and William Mangin demonstrated beyond doubt, however, that these "spontaneous settlements" were, in fact, solutions to grave urban problems. Subsequent research by anthropologist Susan Lobo established that such settlements were civilly organized and rapidly assumed positive urban attributes under the squatters' own initiatives.

In 1990 there were over 400 of these large settlements surrounding Lima and Callao, containing at least half of Lima's population. Over time, many of them—such as San Martín de Porres, Comas, and Pamplona Alta—had become new political districts within the province of Lima, with their own elected officials and political power. Political scientists Henry A. Deitz and David Collier have called attention to squatter organizations as mechanisms of empowerment for persons otherwise denied a base or place in the political system. An important step for the squatters was the acquisition of the skill and the ability to exercise influence in the corridors of bureaucratic power. As these settlements and their organizations gained public legitimacy in the 1960s, the Velasco government, on assuming power in 1968, soon renamed them *pueblos jovenes,* a name which was quickly adopted and has remained.

The regional club aspect of Peru's urban migration was not as obvious a phenomenon as the ubiquitous squatter settlements. The need for a social life, as well as the desire to maintain contact with the home community, friends, and relatives, had moved migrants

El Agustino, a northern Lima district and "young town"
Courtesy Inter-American Development Bank

from particular villages and towns to create representative organizations based on their common place of origin. As a result, according to Teófilo Altamirano, in 1990 there were over 6,000 such clubs in greater Lima, with hundreds more to be found in the other major cities. Not only have these clubs provided an important social venue for migrants, but they also have served as a vehicle by which members could give not insubstantial assistance to their homeland (*terruño*), when called for.

Regionalism and Political Divisions

The formidable mountain ranges, deep chasms, and deserts that partition the habitable regions of Peru contribute greatly to the formation and maintenance of political and social identities by facilitating or obstructing communication, as well as by creating economic diversity through zonal specializations. Archaeologists and ethnohistorians have identified some forty-four different highland cultures and thirty-eight more in coastal valleys that existed at the time of the rise of the Inca Empire in the fifteenth century. Tawantinsuyu (Land of the Four Quarters) retained these preexisting ethnogeographic zones in one form or another, according to anthropologist Michael Moseley, establishing at least eighty ethnically distinct political provinces throughout the empire's vast territory.

The policies of the Tawantinsuyu presaged subsequent geo-political territorial arrangements. The "quarters" were unequal in size and population, but roughly corresponded to the cardinal directions. Each region began with its cobbled roadway leaving the "navel" of the city of Cusco, whose perimeters shaped a symbolic Andean puma. To the north, Chinchaysuyu encompassed most of the coast and highlands of modern Peru, from Nazca, and eventually with conquest, to what is now northern Ecuador. In terms of the divisions of the Inca Empire, 68 percent of Peruvians in 1990 lived in Chinchaysuyu. To the south stretched the vast region of the puna and Lake Titicaca Basin called the Collasuyu. With the Inca conquests, the Collasuyu quarter extended to the Río Maule in what is now central Chile. To the east and west were two relatively small quarters, the Antisuyu and Cuntisuyu, respectively. The former occupied the forested semitropical highland region called Montaña, and the latter, the arid mountains and coast encompassing present-day Arequipa and adjacent departments. Seen in this perspective, 41 percent of the people lived in four departments occupying the central region of the country, with 27 percent in the northern area, 23 percent in the south, and 8 percent in the Amazonian departments of the east in 1990. These four modern quarters of Peru often have been utilized in the context of planning studies.

The Spaniards reorganized the Tawantinsuyu on discovering that the highland Inca capitals at Cusco and Cuenca (Ecuador) and their own first choice of Jauja near present-day Huancayo suited neither their physiological nor political needs. When they founded Lima, the Spaniards turned the Inca spatial concepts upside down: centrality and place were reoriented as Cusco became a province and no longer was the "navel of the universe" from which all roads departed. Despite this change, Spanish viceregal organization educed its structure from longstanding ethnolinguistic and ecological realities. The Spaniards formed provinces (*corregimientos*—see Glossary), which later became intendancies (*intendencias*), as well as Catholic dioceses or parishes.

With independence, the colonial territories were again redefined, but in most cases, the "new" politico-administrative boundaries still recalled ancient cultural and linguistic outlines. The republic carried forward many operational aspects of the colonial administrative units. Throughout their national history, Peruvians have demonstrated a propensity to revise their political affairs both with respect to leadership and the boundaries within the nation. In 1980 the department of Ucayali was created by splintering off two provinces from the Selva department of Loreto, a reflection of development and population increases in that immense tropical region.

*Uru children
(descendants of the Lupacas)
in a totora-reed hut on Lake
Titicaca's floating island
Courtesy Harvey W. Reed*

Moreover, after the census in 1981, six new provinces in Cajamarca, Ancash, and Ucayali departments and twenty new districts were created in various parts of the country through legislative acts. The new districts included six in the populous highland department of Cajamarca; three each in Ucayali, Puno, and Ancash; two in the province of Lima; and others in the departments of Huánuco and Cusco. Each time a census occurs, political and social identities are further refined, usually building on old traditions of similitude, as well as a desire for separate political representation and control.

The result was a nation divided into a political hierarchy of 24 departments, 159 provinces, and 1,717 districts, each with its urbanized capital symbolized by a plaza bordered by a "mother church" and municipal office. Peruvians invariably identify themselves as being from one of these divisions, as the place of birth, and thus everyone carries a locality identity as a *limeño* from Lima, a *chalaco* from Callao, a *cuzqueño* from Cusco, a *huaracino* from Huaraz, and so forth, down to the smallest hamlet. The political fissioning thus reflects a strong geocultural identity and bonding, manifested by the establishment and activities of thousands of regional and local clubs and associations by migrants from these places who live in cities throughout the country.

Provincial migrants, especially those in greater Lima, play important and often key roles in the creation of new political divisions back in their homelands, as was the case by 1990 in the highland district of Santo Toribio in the province of Huaylas. The new district was the result of political antagonisms originating in colonial times between the small mestizo district capital of Huaylas and its rural hinterland of Santo Toribio. After more than sixty years of plots and counterplots in Lima and in the *patria chica* (hometown or "little homeland"), the partisans of Santo Toribio, represented by migrants in Lima, finally won out over the Huaylas district lobby made up of migrants from the town that sought to maintain district unity.

In this maneuvering, the national political parties were used as the fulcrum on which the scales were tipped. The municipal government of Huaylas was held by members of the Popular Action (Acción Popular—AP) party, whereas the Santo Toribio interests were aligned with the American Popular Revolutionary Alliance (Alianza Popular Revolucionaria Americana—APRA) party, which took power nationally under Alan García Pérez (president, 1985–90). This scenario is replicated throughout the highlands and is at the core of virtually all such alterations in political boundaries. In most cases, the imbroglio develops as rural villagers, native Americans, and *cholos* vie for power with the mestizo townspeople who have dominated them for centuries.

The same struggle has accompanied the dramatic growth of greater Lima, to which migrants from the provinces have gone to seek access to power, as well as education and jobs. Understanding the political structure of Lima is in itself a study in the process of empowerment. The city of Lima is actually a collection of municipalities. Instead of the two municipal districts of colonial time—Lima and Rímac—by 1961 Lima contained fifteen district municipalities, and by 1990 it had grown to thirty-three, all the result of migration. Like all their provincial counterparts, each municipal district has its plaza, elected mayor and council, and municipal functions. The government of the province of Lima unites them and coordinates the metropolis as an urban entity. The rest of metropolitan Lima consists of the constitutional province of Callao, the old colonial port. Callao is fused with the capital by a continuous blanket of housing projects, squatter settlements, and industries through which one passes en route to Jorge Chávez International Airport from Lima. Even so, in early 1991 there were still small patches of irrigated farmland at the northern fringe of Callao Province, awaiting the next spurt of urban growth to engulf them.

The administrative system of departments, provinces, and districts is under the central authority of the national executive, that is, the president and prime minister. As such, the decisions and policy inevitably and ultimately descend from a government overwhelmed by the needs, demands, and power of Lima. The centralization of power is resented and regarded as anachronistic, a problem that has provoked debate since 1860 about the wisdom of decentralization and how it might be accomplished.

The reorganization decree promulgated by the García government in March 1987 put forth a plan to decentralize the nation and establish new administrative zones, regrouping the present twenty-four departments into twelve larger regions with legislative, administrative, and taxing powers (see Local and Regional Government, ch. 4). Interestingly, the names Inca, Wari (Huari), and Chavín have been applied to areas where those ancient cultures once thrived. If the system becomes fully installed, it will dramatically alter Peru as a nation and would be the most significant change in structure since independence. In the early 1990s, few Peruvians yet understood how the new system would work or what its impact would be. Because of many uncertainties created by the unstable political and economic conditions of the 1980s, both the Congress and the government of President Alberto K. Fujimori (1990–) postponed putting the full plan into effect, although some aspects of the program had begun (see Local and Regional Government, ch. 4).

Culture, Class, and Hierarchy in Society

A large part of Peru's complicated modern social system started with the hierarchical principles set down in colonial times. They remain as powerful guidelines for intergroup and interpersonal behavior. Peru's ethnic composition, however, is mixed. In the early 1990s, Europeans of various background made up 15 percent of the population, Asians from Japan and China and Africans formed 3 percent, the mestizo population constituted 37 percent, and the native Americans made up 45 percent, according to various United States and British reference sources. However, it is difficult to judge the composition of the native population because census data have generally undercounted or frequently failed to identify ethnic groups successfully. Even using language as the primary criterion does not take bilingualism adequately into account and omits other aspects of cultural behavior altogether. Thus, although Cajamarca Department is 98-percent Spanish-speaking, the bulk of the rural population lives in a manner identical to those classified as native people because they speak Quechua. The question as to who is a native has been an oft-debated issue. But how the individual chooses to classify his or her cultural identity is determined by the forces of society that give ethnic terms their social meaning. Because of

Peruvian society's longstanding negative attitudes and practices toward native peoples, persons who have become socially mobile seek to change their public identity and hence learning Spanish becomes critical. Denial of the ability to speak Quechua, Aymara, or other native languages often accompanies the switch.

Another separate dimension of the "Indian problem" so widely discussed by Peruvian essayists has to do with the natives living in the Selva and high Selva, or Montaña, regions of the country. The tribal peoples have a tenuous and generally unhappy relationship with Peruvians and the state, evolved from long experience along the tropical frontier. The Incas and their predecessors ventured only into the fringes of the region called Antisuyu, and the Spanish followed their pattern. The inhabitants were known collectively as savages (*chunchos*). In documents they are politely referred to as jungle people (*selvícolas* or *selváticos*). Thought to be savage, wild, and dangerous but usually described as "simple" and innocent, they are also widely considered to possess uncanny powers of witchcraft and healing. Here, the sixteenth-century concept of the "noble savage" vies with equally old notions that these are lazy, useless people who need to get out of the way of progress. Indeed, modern currents of developmental change, the expanding drug trade, oil exploration, the clearing of the forest, and the search for gold in Madre de Dios Department have placed native peoples under great pressures for which they are little prepared. The Selva tribes, like native highlanders, Afro-Peruvians, and other people "of color," are those who feel the discriminatory power of the colonial legacy as well as modern stresses, especially if they are poor. In demographic terms, the impact of poverty and oppression has been, and remains, considerable. Thus, the mortality rates of native peoples and especially their children are much higher than those of the general population. Tribal peoples are still widely susceptible to numerous uncontrolled infectious diseases and outside the religious missions have little or no access to scientific medical care.

The tribal peoples of the lower Selva along the major rivers have endured the stress and danger of contact with outside forces longer than those groups located at the upper reaches of the streams. It is in these "refuge areas" that most of the present tribal populations survive (see fig. 7). More than any other sector of the population, the rural peoples of the Selva, and especially the tribal groups, live at the fringe of the state both literally and figuratively, being uncounted, unserved, and vulnerable to those who would use the area as their own. According to anthropologist Stéfano Varese, there are about 50 tribes numbering an estimated 250,000

persons and maintaining active communities, scattered principally throughout the departments of Loreto, Amazonas, Ucayali, Huánuco, and Madre de Dios. The national census, however, has lowered its estimates from 100,830 in 1961 to 30,000 in 1981 for the tribal peoples, even though field studies have not supported such conclusions.

In the Selva, tribal lands in the early 1990s were in even more jeopardy than the Quechua and Aymara farmland in the Sierra. Although community rights were acknowledged, if not respected, in the Andes, outsiders have virtually never accepted this fact in the case of the Amazonian peoples. Nevertheless, apparently many tribal societies, such as the Shipibo, have held their traditional hunting, fishing, and swidden lands in continuous usufruct for as long as 2,000 years. As a result of the land reforms under the Velasco government, however, laws established the land rights of Amazonian native communities. Consequently, some groups, such as the Cocama-Cocamilla, have been able to secure their agroecological base.

The Afro-Peruvians who came as slaves with the first wave of conquest remained in that position until released from it by Marshal Ramón Castilla (1845–51, 1855–62) in 1854. During their long colonial experience, many Afro-Peruvians, especially the mulattos and others of mixed racial parentage, were freed to assume working-class roles in the coastal valleys. Even fewer blacks than Europeans settled in the highland towns and for virtually all the colonial epoch remained concentrated in the central coastal valleys. Lima's colonial population was 50 percent African during much of the era. Indeed, the term "criollo" was originally identified with native-born blacks and acquired much of its special meaning in association with urban, streetwise behavior. The social status of blacks in many ways paralleled that of the native Americans in rank and role in society.

Completing the human resource mix in Peru were the immigrants from Europe and Asia. The former arrived with the advantages of conquest; the latter arrived first as indentured laborers and later as Japanese and Taiwanese immigrants who pursued careers in truck farming, commerce, and business. The Chinese who were brought to Peru from Macao and other ports between 1849 and 1874 numbered about 90,000. The Chinese influx occurred in the same period as the United States' importation of Chinese workers, and many of the latter were eventually shipped from San Francisco to Lima. Most Chinese eventually survived their indentures and took up residence in the coastal towns where they established themselves as active storekeepers and businesspeople. The growth of the Japanese presence in Peru began early in the twentieth century and quietly increased over the 1970–90 period. In 1990 Japanese immigrants constituted the largest foreign group in Peru and were rapidly integrating into Peruvian culture, gaining positions from president (Fujimori) to popular folk singer (the "Little Princess from Yungay"). In the middle range of Peruvian class structure, the Chinese and especially the Japanese have achieved status and mobility in ways the native peoples have not.

The key to understanding Peruvian society is to view aspects of its dynamic ethnoracial character as a set of variables that constantly interplays with socioeconomic factors associated with social class configurations. Thus, a native American might acquire the Spanish language, a university education, a large amount of capital, and a cosmopolitan demeanor, but still continue to be considered an *indio* (Indian) in many circles and thus be an unacceptable associate or marital companion. Yet, there is opportunity for socioeconomic mobility that permits ambitious individuals and families to ascend the hierarchy ranks in limited ways and via certain pathways. Such mobility is easier if one starts on the ladder as a mestizo or a foreigner, but especially if one is white.

Indigenous Peoples

The word *indio*, as applied to native highland people of Quechua and Aymara origin, carries strong negative meanings and stereotypes among mestizo and white Peruvians. For that reason, the ardently populist Velasco regime attempted with some success to substitute the term peasant (campesino) to accompany the many far-reaching changes his government directed at improving the socioeconomic conditions in the highlands. Nevertheless, traditional usage has prevailed in many areas in reference to those who speak native languages, dress in native styles, and engage in activities defined as native. Peruvian society ascribes to them a caste status to which no one else aspires.

The ingrained attitudes and stereotypes held by the *mistikuna* (the Quechua term for mestizo people) toward the *runakuna* (native people—the Quechua term for themselves) in most highland towns have led to a variety of discriminatory behaviors, from mocking references to "brute" or "savage" to obliging native Americans to step aside, sit in the back of vehicles, and in general humble themselves in the presence of persons of higher status. The pattern of ethnoracist denigration has continued despite all of the protests and reports, official policies, and compelling accounts of discrimination described in Peruvian novels published since the beginning of the twentieth century.

*Aymara girls at a
community fiesta on
Lake Titicaca's Taquili Island
Courtesy Elayne Zorn,
Inter-American Foundation*

The regions and departments with the largest populations of native peoples are construed to be the most backward, being the poorest, least educated, and less developed. They are also the ones with the highest percentages of Quechua and Aymara speakers. The reasons for the perpetuation of colonial values with respect to autochthonous peoples are complex; they involve more than a simple perseverance of custom. The social condition of the population owes its form to the kinds of expectations embedded in the premises and workings of the nation's institutions. These are not easily altered. Spanish institutions of conquest were implanted into colonial life as part of the strategy for ruling conquered peoples: the indigenous people were defeated and captured and thus, as spoils of war, were as exploitable as mineral wealth or land. In the minds of many highland mestizos as well as better-off urbanites, they still are.

Although the Spanish crown attempted to take stern control over civic affairs, including the treatment, role, and conditions of native Americans who were officially protected, the well-intended regulations were neither effective nor accepted by creole and immigrant interests. Power and status derived from wealth and position, are considered not only to come from money and property, but also from the authority to exercise control over others. Functionaries of the colonial regime paid for their positions so that they could exact the price of rule from their constituent populations.

Encomenderos, corregidores, and the numerous bureaucrats all held dominion over segments of the native population and other castes, which were obliged to pay various forms of tribute. With the decline of the colonial administration and the failure of the many attempts at reform to control the abuses of the native peoples, Peru's political independence saw a transfer of power into the hands of white Creoles and mestizos, the latter of whom made up the majority of Peru's citizens in the early 1990s.

The growth of large estates with resident serf populations was an important feature of this transition period. The process benefited from the new constitutional policies decreeing the termination of the Indigenous Community (Comunidad Indígena)—the corporate units formerly protected by the crown. The subsequent breakup of hundreds of communities into individually owned properties led directly to these lands being purchased, stolen, or usurped by eager opportunists in the new society. The most critical native American franchise was thus lost as entire communities passed from a relatively free corporate status to one of high vulnerability, subject to the whims of absentee landlords. Although the development of haciendas occurred rapidly after the demise of the colonial regime, the system of debt serfdom had long been in place in the form of the *encomienda* system. Under the *encomienda* system, the crown in place assigned property and natives to reward particular individuals for their service to the crown. Institutions such as the church and public welfare societies that aided the poor by operating hospitals and orphanages also benefitted from the *encomienda* system. Debt peonage constituted the basic labor arrangement by which landlords of all types operated their properties nationwide. The system endured until it was abolished by the land reform of 1969.

Legacy of Peonage

Although a thing of the past, the numbing effects of four centuries of peonage on Peruvian society should not be underestimated. One archetypical Andean estate operated at Vicos, Ancash Department, from 1594 to 1952, before it became part of Peru's first land-reform experiment. The 17,000-hectare estate and the landlord's interests were managed by a local administrator, who employed a group of straw bosses, each commanding a sector of the property and directing the work and lives of the 1,700 peons (*colonos*) attached to the estate by debt. Dressed in unique homespun woolen clothing that identified them as *vicosinos* (residents of Vicos), each *colono* family lived in a house it built but did not own. Rather, it owed the estate three days of labor per week, and more if demanded, in exchange for a small subsistence plot and limited rights to graze animals on the puna. Grazing privileges were paid for by dividing the newborn animals each year equally between *colono* and landlord. For the work, a symbolic wage (*temple*) of twenty centavos (about two cents in United States currency of the time) and a portion of coca and alcohol were given to each peon. In addition, peons were obliged to provide other services on demand to the administrator and landlord, such as pasturing their animals, serving as maids and servants in their homes, running errands of all types, and providing all manner of labor from house construction to the repair of roads. The landlord might also rent his peons to others and pay no wage.

To enforce order on the estate, the administrator utilized "the fist and the whip." Vicos had its own jail to which *colonos* were sent without recourse to any legal process; fines, whippings, and other punishments could be meted out arbitrarily. As individuals, the *colonos* were subject to severe restrictions, not being allowed to venture outside of the district without permission, or to organize any independent activities except religious festivals, weddings, and funerals that took place in the hacienda's chapel and cemetery, only occasionally with clerical presence. The only community-initiated activities allowed were those under the supervision of the parish church.

Outside the protection of the estate, peons correctly felt themselves to be vulnerable to exploitation and feared direct contact with those *mistikuna* whom they regarded as dangerous, even to the extent of characterizing whites and powerful mestizos as *pishtakos,* mythical bogeymen who kill or rape natives. In protecting themselves from the threats of this environment, *vicosinos,* like tens of thousands of other *colonos* across the Andes, chose to employ the "weapons of the weak," by striking a low profile, playing dumb, obeying, taking few initiatives, and in general staying out of the way of mestizos and strangers they did not know, reserving their own pleasures and personalities for the company of family and friends.

Peonage under the hacienda functioned in a relatively standard fashion throughout Peru, with variations between the coastal plantations, on the one hand, and the highland estates and ranches, on the other. On some highland estates, conditions were worse than those described; in others they were not as restrictive or arbitrary. Although called haciendas, the coastal plantations were far more commercialized, being given to the production of goods for export or the large urban markets. Under these more fluid socioeconomic circumstances, the plantation workers, called *yanaconas* (after the

Incan class of serfs called *yanas*), who permanently resided on the estates, also had access to subsistence plots. Moreover, they usually had "company" housing, schools, and access to other facilities specified under a signed labor contract often negotiated through worker unions.

Nevertheless, there were lingering connections to the highland manorial system. Because plantation crops, such as sugarcane and cotton, require a large labor force for harvests and planting, workers are seasonally recruited from the highland peasantry for these tasks. In some instances, owners of coastal plantations also possessed highland estates from which they might "borrow" the needed seasonal workers from among the *colonos* they already controlled in peonage and pay them virtually nothing. In most cases, however, the coastal plantations simply hired gangs of peasant farmers for the short term, using professional labor contractors to do the job. For thousands of young men, this became an important first experience away from their family and village, serving as a rite of passage into adulthood. It also constituted an important step for many in developing the labor and life skills needed to migrate permanently to the coast. Employment on the coastal plantations offered the highland farmer the opportunity to use mechanized equipment and different tools, observe agricultural procedures guided by scientific principles and experts, and work for wages that greatly surpassed what he might earn in the villages. For most farm workers, it was the only chance to actually accumulate money.

Elites

Concentrated in the provincial, departmental, and national capitals, Peru's upper class was the other side of the coin of peonage. The Quechua or Aymara native population was powerless, submissive, and poor; the Hispanics were the regional and national elites, dominant, and wealthy. The inheritors of colonial power quickly reaffirmed their political, social, and economic hegemony over the nation even though the Peruvian state itself was a most unstable entity until the presidency of Ramón Castilla. They continued to strike the posture of conquerors toward the native peoples, justifying themselves as civilized, *culto* (cultured), and urbane, as well as *gente decente* (decent people), in the customary phrase of the provincial town. Such presumption of status is a powerful but unwritten code of entitlement. It permits one to expect to have obedient servants, to be deferred to by those of lesser station, and to be the first to enjoy opportunity, services of the state, and whatever resources might be available.

The modern national upper classes of Peru are today a more diverse population than was the case even at the end of the nineteenth century. They have remained essentially identified with the Costa, even though they have controlled extensive property in the highlands and Selva. Nevertheless, these elites are highly conscious of class integrity; social life unfolds in the context of private clubs and specialized economic circles. The predilection of the upper-class families to show the strength of their lineages is revealed not only in the use of full names, which always contain both one's father's and mother's last names in that order, but also the *apellidos* (last names) of important grandparental generations. Thus, magazine society pages report names like José Carlos Prado Fernandini Beltrán de Espantoso y Ugarteche, in which only Prado is the last name in the American sense. Use of the family pedigree to demonstrate rank is common among the elite when the names are clearly associated with wealth and power.

As Peruvians have become more cosmopolitan, foreign names from Britain, Italy, Austria, and Germany have appeared with increasing frequency among those claiming upper-class credentials, leading to the conclusion that it is easier to reach elite status from outside Peru than to ascend from within the society. There are, of course a number of families who can trace their lineages to the colonial period. However, families of nineteenth- and early twentieth-century immigrants constitute about 40 percent of Peru's most elite sector, indicating a surprising openness to cosmopolitan mobility. In a 1980s list of Peru's national elite containing over 250 family names, for example, only one of clearly Quechua origins could be identified.

The racial composition of the upper class is predominantly white, although a few mestizos are represented, especially at regional levels. The social structure of the country follows a Lima-based model. The national upper class is located almost exclusively in the province of Lima; the second stratum of elites is provincial, residing in the old principal regional cities, such as Arequipa, Trujillo, and Cusco, but not in Huancayo, Chimbote, or Juliaca, whose populations are predominantly of highland mestizo and *cholo* origins. Upper-class status in provincial life generally does not equate with the same levels in Lima, but rather to a middle level in the national social hierarchy.

Traditionally, the upper classes based their power and wealth on rural land ownership and secondarily on urban industrial forms of investment. This situation has changed in part through the rise of business, industry, banking, and political opportunities, and also because of the Agrarian Reform Law of 1969, which forced dramatic changes in land tenure patterns. It was, however, a change as difficult to make as any that could be imagined: the fabled landed oligarchy greatly feared any alterations in its property rights, which included the *colonos* and *yanaconas* attached to both highland and coastal estates. Their control over Peru's power, purse, and peasantry bordered on the absolute until the second half of the twentieth century, when the great highland migrations took hold of coastal cities and industrial growth exploded. Ensuing social and political demands could no longer be managed from behind the traditional scenes of power.

Vested interests of the landed upper class were ensconced in the National Agrarian Association (Sociedad Nacional Agraria—SNA). Until the first government of Fernando Belaúnde, it had been impossible to discover just what the property and investment interests of this group were because government files on these subjects were closed and, indeed, had never been publicly scrutinized. All of this changed abruptly after the peasant land invasions of estates in 1963, when the need for solutions overcame the secrecy. In 1966 economic historian Carlos Malpica Silva Santisteban identified the landed oligarchy as a relatively small group, with 190 families owning 54 percent of the irrigated coast and 36 families or persons holding 63 percent of titled land in the Selva, for a total of over 3 million hectares. In the highlands, the data were similar in content but hard to verify.

Although upper-class wealth was founded on rural properties, it is evident that elite urban, mining, and industrial interests were also extensive. An indefatigable compiler of data on Peru's elites, Malpica annotated an extensive catalog of modern business and banking concerns showing the concentration of economic control in the hands of a tiny group of elite families, many being familiar traditional members of the oligarchy, now deprived of their land base by the agrarian reform. Of the seventy-nine families holding significant blocks of shares in the twelve principal insurance and banking operations in 1989, almost 50 percent were descended from the aforementioned European immigrant groups. Despite this Eurocentric trend, descendants of Japanese and Chinese immigrants have also entered the economic elites, if not with the equivalent social status. At least one Chinese-Peruvian family, which holds substantial banking, commercial, and industrial investments, descends from immigrants who arrived as indentured laborers in the nineteenth century.

Military Classes

The militarily connected population has developed into a significant national sector. Playing an ever more important social role, the military (*los militares*) has, in effect, emerged as a subsociety. Its special attributes and arrangements set it apart from other social classes as a powerful special interest elite, with its own allegiances and identity, sense of mission, and objectives developed in coherent, relatively independent ways from other national policy and planning processes. No other groups within the population, with the possible exception of the cabals of the oligarchy, can be so characterized.

The people involved in ancillary activities probably approach 1 million, or 4 percent of the nation's population. Included in these activities were military industries, medical services, civilian business managers and employees, service and maintenance personnel, and members of family networks who benefitted from having one of their number in the armed forces. The military domain commands 20 percent of central-government expenditures, 5 percent more than education, the next largest share of the national budget, and much more than health services, which claimed 5.8 percent in 1988. Indeed, Peru's military expenditures of US$106 per capita exceeded three times the average expenditure per capita of all other South American nations in 1988. Over a twenty-year period, between 1972 and 1992, the military budget gained 38 percent in its share of the national budget, whereas education dropped by 35 percent and health gained by less than 5 percent.

Professionalization has involved areas that few have analyzed but that constitute the major reward system for professional career officers and noncommissioned personnel. These are the elaborate infrastructure and exclusive services for personnel and their families, including beach resorts and hotels, consumer discount cooperatives, casinos and clubs, schools of several types and levels, hospitals and general medical services, insurance coverages, recreational facilities, and a variety of other programs. In addition, there are extensive housing subdivisions in Lima for the officer corps and other military employees, named for the military branches that they serve. Members of the military also benefit from special retirement provisions and a plethora of other benefits that are unavailable to others in the society at large.

The sphere of military activities includes an extremely active internal social calendar of commemorative events that bond the members and their families more tightly to group interests. In sum, the Peruvian military constitutes a virtually encapsulated society within the larger one and competes with advantage for the public funds vis-à-vis other interests by operating its own industries, sponsoring its own research and advanced study, and engaging in civic-action programs that often replicate the assigned work of civilian

107

institutions, such as the Ministry of Agriculture. Consequently, the ubiquitous and well-established institutions of military society pervade Peruvian life at every turn and are regarded with skepticism by many who see them as depriving civilian needs of essential resources (see also The Armed Forces in Society and Politics, ch. 5).

Urban Classes

Between the extremes of wealth and power represented by the white upper class and the native caste is the predominantly mestizo and *cholo* population, which largely comprises the lower and middle sectors of rural and urban society. These are the most numerous and diverse sectors, constituting the core of Peruvian national society in culture, behavior, and identity. Together, these sectors include a wide range of salaried working-class families, persons in business and commercial occupations, bureaucrats, teachers, all military personnel (except those related to elite families), medical, legal, and academic professionals, and so forth. In terms of occupation, residence, education, wealth, racial, and ethnic considerations, the population is diverse, with few clear-cut markers differentiating one segment from another. Yet, there are obvious differences among the regions of the country that combine with those indicators to suggest a person's social position in relation to others. The importance of the regions derives from the fact that the urban and rural areas of the Sierra are, as a whole, measurably poorer than the Costa and Selva, and the various occupational groups less well-off in proportion. As in the case of the provincial upper class, being middle class in the regional context does not necessarily mean the same thing in the capital, although being marked as lower class would translate to the same category in Lima or Trujillo.

An important study by anthropologist Carlos E. Aramburu and his colleagues in 1989 provides a graphic outline of how levels of living vary throughout the nation. Analyzing the 1981 census, they ranked the 153 provinces on the basis of five variables: the proportion of households without any modern household appliance; the average per capita income; the percentage of illiterate women over fifteen years of age; the number of children between six and nine years of age who regularly worked; and the rate of infant mortality. These indicators were representative of involvement in the economy, participation in state-operated institutions, and access to health services, each of which is critical for marking advances in the level of living from the perspective of the modern state. Only nine of the 100 highland provinces were represented among those in the top two levels of wealth, and only Arequipa was in the top rank. In contrast to the Selva provinces, which lacked any rank, eighteen of the twenty-eight coastal provinces registered in the top third of provinces according to wealth. At the other end of the scale, all but three of the poorest fifty-three provinces with 20 percent of the population were in the highlands, and none were on the coast. These data, when juxtaposed with the distribution of monolingual Quechua and Aymara speakers, confirm the poverty status of Peru's native population at the bottom of the socioeconomic scale.

Thus, the provincial upper classes, with few exceptions, do not equate with the Lima-based national elite, whose socioeconomic position is vastly enhanced by their status as Lima residents and, subsequently, by their international connections. The same can be said for the other middle and lower sectors of the provincial population in comparison to Lima. In a very real sense then, Peru has two levels of class structure layered in between the national extremes of the oligarchic elites and the rural native peasantry: one in the context of Lima's primacy, the other with reference to the rest of the nation.

Although the role of racial phenotypes and associated ethnic behaviors is clearly seen at the extreme poles of Peruvian society, it is somewhat obscured in the middle sectors. In general, the more closely one approximates the ideal of Euro-American appearance, the greater the social prestige and status derived. On the other hand, Peru is a country whose majority population is darker skinned, with distinctive facial and bodily features. The varied shades of meaning attached to the designations mestizo and *cholo* are as much socioeconomic and cultural in import as they are racial. Thus, in the Peruvian vernacular phrase, "money whitens" one's self-concept and expectations.

With other non-native groups, such as the Japanese, Chinese, and Afro-Peruvians, status and class considerations are structured somewhat differently, yet exhibit the same tendencies toward ethnoracist marking. Just how strongly stereotypes have prevailed over facts was witnessed by the 1990 presidential election of the Japanese-Peruvian Alberto Fujimori, who was constantly referred to as *el chinito* (the little Chinaman). Racial terms are frequently employed in normal discourse in ways that many foreigners find uncomfortable. Afro-Peruvians are referred to as *zambos negritos,* or more politely as *morenos* (browns). In many instances, this terminology implies behavioral expectations and stereotypes, and yet in others the same term is simply used as an impartial means of description.

Aspects of Family Life

Much has been said about kinship and family in Latin America. The "Peruvian family" is of course not a homogeneous entity, but rather reflects both ethnic and socioeconomic factors. If there is a generalization to be made, however, it is that families in Peru, no matter what their status, show a high degree of unity, purpose, and integration through generations, as well as in the nuclear unit. The average size for families for the nation as a whole is 5.1 persons per household, with the urban areas registering slightly more than this and, contrary to what might be expected, rural families, especially in the highlands, being smaller, with a national average size of 4.9 persons. This apparent anomaly runs counter to the expected image of the rural family because the highland families that constitute the bulk of rural households have been deeply affected by the heavy migration of their members to the cities, coastal farms, and Selva colonizations.

The roles of the different family members and sexes tend to follow rather uniform patterns within social class and cultural configurations. In terms of family affairs, Hispanic Peruvian patterns are strongly centered on the father as family head, although women increasingly occupy this titular role in rural as well as urban areas. Women serve as family heads in 20 percent of all households. As is the pattern in other countries, women have increasingly sought wage and salaried work to meet family needs. This, coupled with the fact that social and economic stress has forced a departure from the traditional model of male-centered households, means that the patriarchal family is gradually losing its place as the model of family life. Contributing to these changes is the neolocality of nuclear families living in cities, that is, located apart from the families of either spouse, and the loss of male populations in rural areas through migration and various poverty-related conditions that lead men to abandon their families. Families are patricentric, and the male head of household is considered the authority. His wife respects his position, yet exercises considerable control over her own affairs with respect to property and marketing. This gender and lineage hierarchy is to be seen as families walk single-file to market, each carrying their bundles, the husband leading the way, followed by his wife and then the children.

In many Quechua communities, the ancient kinship system of patrilineages (called *kastas* in some areas) survives. It is thought to have been the basis for the Incaic clan village, the *ayllu* (see Glossary). In a patrilineal system, wives belong to their father's lineage and their children to their father's side of the family tree. This

Aymara woman, with daughter,
filling a cántara *in Platería,*
a village near Puno
Courtesy Inter-American
Development Bank

practice differs from the Hispanic system, which is bilateral, that is, includes one's mother's kin as part of the extended family, as in the British system. If native Americans follow a patrilineal system, families are at odds with the formal requirement of Peruvian law, which demands the use of both paternal and maternal names as part of one's official identity, thus forcing the bilateral pattern on them.

In many Hispanic mestizo homes, fathers exercise strong authoritarian roles, controlling the family budget, administering discipline, and representing the group interest to the external world. Mothers in these homes, on the other hand, often control and manage the internal affairs in the household, assigning tasks to children and to the female servant(s) present in virtually every urban middle- and upper-class home. For children school is de rigueur, and the more well-to-do, the more certain it is that they attend a private school, where the educational standards approach or equal good schools in other countries. The home is prized and well-cared for, with patios and yards protected by glass-studded walls and, in recent years, by electrical devices to keep out thieves.

The lower-class household in the urban areas—such as Lima, Trujillo, or Arequipa—presents the other side of this coin. In metropolitan Lima, 7 percent of the population lives in a *tugurio* (inner-city barrio) and 47 percent in a squatter settlement. In 1990 the older *pueblos jóvenes* erected in the 1950s had the look of concrete

111

middle-class permanency, with electricity, water, and sewerage. The newer invaded areas, however, had a raw and dusty look: housing appeared ramshackle, made of bamboo matting (*esteras*) and miscellaneous construction materials scrounged from any available source. Here, as in the *tugurios,* the domestic scene reveals a constant scramble for existence: the men generally leave early in the morning to travel via long bus routes to reach work sites, often in heavy construction, where without protective gear, such as hard hats or steel-toed shoes, they haul iron bars and buckets of cement up rickety planks and scaffolding. With an abundance of men desperate for work, modern buildings are raised more with intensive labor than machinery.

Women's roles in the squatter settlements cover a wide variety of tasks, including hauling water from corner spigots and beginning the daily preparation of food over kerosene stoves. In the 1975–91 period, the food supply for substantial numbers of the urban lower class in Lima and other coastal cities came from the United States Food for Peace (Public Law 480) programs administered by private voluntary organizations. Women also keep their wide-ranging family members connected, seeking the food supply with meager funds, and doing various short-term jobs for cash. According to social scientist Carol Graham, the poor urban areas have a high percentage of female-headed households, as well as a large number of abandoned mothers who are left with the full responsibility for supporting their households and raising the children.

Urban Informal Sector

In 1990 the vast "informal sector" (see Glossary) of Lima's economy was the most striking feature of its commercial life. There, 91,000 street vendors, 54 percent of them women, sold food in the streets or public squares of central Lima or the residential area of Miraflores, the upscale mecca of the city. Street vendors have been a part of Lima life and culture since early colonial times, and the city government has persistently attempted to remove them to fixed market places. Nevertheless, street commerce in Lima throughout the colonial period and until the twentieth century was generally regarded as a colorful, folkloric aspect of urban life and was often depicted in period paintings and descriptions. Since the great migrations began in the early 1950s, however, the city elites have come to disdain the street vendors who swarm over the Rímac Bridge every afternoon. As Hernando de Soto has abundantly documented in *El otro sendero (The Other Path),* this freewheeling entrepreneurial sector of the labor force was, in the 1980s, producing the equivalent of almost 40 percent of the national income. As "unregistered" business, this activity is outside the control of the national economic institutions, whose cumbersome and often corrupt bureaucratic regulations stifle initiatives, especially if one lacks resources to pay all the bribes and formal start-up costs. In the circumstances of 1991, the public need to participate in the economy had, in essence, neutralized and bypassed the official system (see Nonparty Organizations, ch. 4).

Domestic Servants

The urban middle-class family without servants is incomplete. Although household servants constitute a major element in the urban informal economic sector, they are rarely analyzed as part of it. The retaining, training, disciplining, or recruiting of domestic help is constantly in progress under the supervision of the wife of the household head. One of the most common sights in Lima is therefore the small printed sign in front of houses reading "Se necesita muchacha" ("girl needed").

There is a constant flow of young highland migrant women to urban areas, and a very large portion of them seek domestic positions on first arriving in Lima. Although census figures were dated, it appeared that about 18 percent of all women employed in metropolitan Lima in 1990 were domestic servants. Domestic service work of course pays poorly, and social and sexual abuse appear often to accompany such employment. Nevertheless, in the absence of other alternatives, migrant women find these jobs temporarily useful in providing "free" housing and a context for learning city life, while also having some opportunity to attend night school to learn a profession, such as tailoring or cosmetology, two of the more popular fields. As domestic work has been increasingly regulated, the term *empleada* (employee) has begun to replace the use of *muchacha* as the term of reference. Over the 1960–91 period, households have been obliged to permit servants to attend school and to cover other costs, such as social security.

Godparenthood

Family life at all levels of society is nourished by an ample number of ceremonial events marking all rites of passage, such as birthdays, anniversaries, graduations, or important religious events, such as baptisms, confirmations, and marriages. Family life is thus marked by small fiestas celebrating these events and passages. In this context, Peruvians have greatly elaborated the Roman Catholic tradition of godparenthood (*padrinazgo*) to encompass more occasions than simply celebration of the sacraments of the church, although following the same format. The parties involved include the child or person sponsored in the ceremony, the parents, and the godparents, who are the sponsors and protectors. The primary relationship in this triad is between the godchild (*ahijado*) and the godparents (*padrinos*). The secondary bond of *compadrazgo* (see Glossary) is between the parents and godparents, who after the ceremony will forever mutually call each other *compadre* or *comadre*. For the child, the relationship with the godparents is expected to be one of benefit, with the *padrinos* perhaps assisting with the godchild's education, finding employment, or, at the least, giving a small gift to the child from time to time. For the *compadres,* there is the expectation of a formalized friendship, one in which favors may be asked of either party.

Ritual sponsorship has two dimensions with respect to its importance to family and community. On the one hand, the mechanism can be utilized to solidify social and family relations within a small cluster of relatives and friends, which is generally the case for families concerned with enclosing their social universe for various reasons. Among the top upper class, it may provide a way of concentrating power relations, business interests, or wealth; among the native caste, the inward selection of *compadres* may follow the need to protect one's access to fields or to guarantee a debt. On the other hand, many families deliberately choose *compadres* from acquaintances or relatives who can assist in socioeconomic advancement. In this fashion, the original religious institution has lent itself to social needs in a dynamic and flexible manner. In the more closed type of community setting, there are only five or six occasions for which godparents are selected; among more socially mobile groups, there may be as many as fifteen or more ways in which a family may gain *compadres*. Thus, it would not be unusual for the parents of a family with four children to count as many as forty or more different *compadres*. In a more conservative setting, the number might be less than ten for a similar family.

Rural Family and Household

Andean peasants, often maligned by those who discriminate against them as being lazy and poor workers, are the reverse of the stereotype. The peasant family begins its day at dawn with the chores of animal husbandry, cutting the eucalyptus firewood, fetching water, and a plethora of other domestic tasks. Field work begins with a trek to the often distant *chacras,* which may be located at a different altitude from the home and require several hours to reach. In instances where *chacras* are very distant from the home, farmers maintain rough huts in which to store tools or stay for

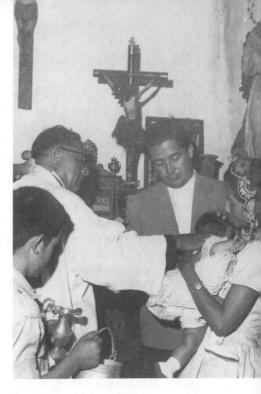

Baptism of a child
in a Lima church
Courtesy Paul L. Doughty

several days. Andean peasants of all ages and both sexes lead rigorous lives, hustling about steep pathways carrying loads of firewood, produce, and tools on their backs.

Although horses and mules are of greater market value than burros, they are more expensive to maintain, and thus burros are the most common beasts of burden in most of the highlands. Native Andean llamas and alpacas are commonly found in the central and southern Andes, where they are still widely used for transport, wool, and meat. Peasant women and girls, although carrying a burden, perpetually keep their hands at work spinning wool to be handwoven by local artisans into clothing, blankets, and ponchos. Although there are few who approach full self-sufficiency in the Andes (and none on the coast), the Andean peasants make, repair, invent, and adapt most of their tools; they also prepare food from grain they have harvested and animals they have raised and butchered.

Although modern amenities and appliances have found their way into most nonfarm households, the rural poor by necessity must conduct their affairs without these instruments of pleasure and work. Even though consumer items—such as electric irons, blenders (especially useful for making baby food), televisions, and radiocassette tape players—are keenly desired, surveys have shown that 25 percent of all Peruvian households possess none of these things. The great majority of households (more than 50 percent) lacking modern appliances were in the rural areas of the Andes. The contributions of many hands, therefore, are vital to the rural economy and household. The same survey by Carlos Aramburu and his associates also showed that the poorest and most rural areas were also the provinces that in demographic terms had the highest dependency ratios (the largest number of persons—the very young and the aged—who were only limited participants in the labor force). Consequently, the loss of youth to migration cuts deeply into the productive capacity of hundreds of families and their communities. In those districts in the central highlands especially, where the Shining Path has been active since the early 1980s, the absolute decline in work force numbers has left a third of the houses empty, fields in permanent fallow, and irrigation works in disrepair, losses which Peru could ill afford in view of its declining agricultural production and great dependency on imported foodstuffs, even in rural areas.

These demographic changes also threaten other community and family institutions like the use of festive and exchange-labor systems (*minka* and *ayni,* respectively) that have been such an integral part of the traditional peasant farm tradition. The *minka* involves a family working side by side with relatives and neighbors to plant or harvest, often with the accompaniment of musicians and always with ample basic food supplied by the hosts. On some occasions, invited workers may request token amounts of the harvest. Exchange labor, or *ayni,* is the fulfillment of an obligation to return the labor that someone else has produced. The communities of peasant farmers, whether native or *cholo,* utilize these mechanisms to augment family labor at critical times. *Minka* work crews, however, are often inefficient and overly festive, and their hosts are unable to keep activities task-oriented on a late afternoon. As a consequence, farmers who are mainly concerned with monetary profitability, tend to utilize paid temporary workers instead of the *minka,* whose ceremonial aspects are distracting. On the other hand, the purpose of the *minka* is obviously social and communal, as well as economic. Family economic activity in rural communities has invariably relied primarily on unpaid family labor, augmented by periodic cooperative assistance from relatives and neighbors to handle larger seasonal tasks.

Community Life and Institutions

The importance of developing and maintaining effective intracommunity relationships underlies many of the kinship traditions that are universal in Andean and Peruvian family life in small towns. Throughout the Andes, there has been a constant need for peasants to retain strong interpersonal and family bonds for

116

significant socioeconomic reasons. For centuries the peasantry suffered the constant loss of land until the Agrarian Reform Law of 1969 reversed the pattern. The stronger a community is tied together, the greater has been its ability to defend its interests against usurpers, a fact often shown in ethnographic studies throughout the region.

By practice and reputation, Andean villages and towns often enjoy reputations for cohesiveness, community action, and the good, simple life. The tight social relationships in Peru's towns and villages, peasant communities, and small cities, however, are not necessarily based on "rural" or agricultural needs and a positive community spirit. Even in small populations where everyone knows everyone else, or knows about them, there can be marked ethnic and social class differences and rivalries that afford many opportunities for disagreement and feuds. Although people share their culture, values, and participation in a community, family interests often clash over property ownership and *chacra* boundaries, local politics, and any of the myriad reasons why people might not like each other. Thus, small town life can be difficult when conflicts erupt: "pueblo chico, infierno grande" ("small town, big hell") is the expression used. There are, therefore, two contradicting images of small town life: one bucolic, tranquil, and good natured; the other, petty and conflictive. Both images are rooted in fact.

Catholicism and Community

Like many Latin American nations, Peru's predominant religion is Roman Catholicism, which after 460 years has remained a powerful influence in both state affairs and daily activities. Church activities and personnel are, of course, centered in Lima, and the cathedral is symbolically located on the east side of the Plaza de Armas to one side of the National Palace and the Municipality of Lima, which occupy the north and west quarters, respectively, of the central square from which all points in Peru are measured. The ceremonial functions of the state are integrated into the rites of the church, beginning with the inauguration of the president with high mass in the cathedral, Holy Week events, and the observances of major Peruvian saints' days and festivals, such as that of Santa Rosa de Lima (Saint Rose of Lima) and others. The institutional role of the church was established with conquest and the viceroyalty, but since independence it has slowly declined through losing its exclusive control over the domains of education, maintenance of vital statistics, marriages, and the organization of daily life around church rites. Nevertheless, the ceremonial aspects of the Catholic religion, moral dictates, and values are profoundly embedded in

Peruvian culture; parish priests and bishops play active roles in local affairs where they are present.

The policies of the church historically have been considered as very conservative, and the various parishes and bishoprics were great landlords, either managing their properties directly or renting them to other elites. Church districts with such properties were eagerly sought by ambitious clergy, many of whom even gained dubious reputations as hacendados (see Glossary). Throughout the highlands, the priesthood actively carried the colonial legacy in its dealings with the Quechua and Aymara peoples until the decade of the 1950s, when many foreign priests, notably the Maryknolls in Puno, began introducing substantial changes in these traditional patterns. Part of this development resulted in the emergence of a strongly populist and social activist theme among many clergy, such as Gustavo Gutiérrez, whose 1973 book, *A Theology of Liberation,* was perhaps to have greater political impact outside of Peru than in it. The changes, however, were considerable, and many priests and nuns worked to assist the poor in ways that marked a turnabout in both style and concept of duty from a short generation before. Although the Peruvian priesthood has been thus invigorated, the church remains unable to fill a large percentage of its parishes on a regular basis, in part because of the demand for clergy in Lima and the other coastal cities.

Roman Catholicism, as the official state religion, has played a major role in Peruvian culture and society since conquest, with every village, town, and city having its official church or cathedral, patron saint, and special religious days, which are celebrated annually. These kinds of activities are focal events for reaffirming social identity and play key roles in the life of all types and sizes of community. Participation in these events is spurred by both religious devotion and desire to serve in community functions for prestige and perhaps political purposes. The most notable of these activities are the patronal festivals that each settlement annually celebrates. Costs for these affairs vary greatly, depending on the size of the town or community. In the case of large cities like Ica or Cusco, expenses are impressive. To underwrite the costs, localities have each developed their own methods of "taxation," although none would call it that. The most common method is to obtain "volunteers," who agree to serve as festival sponsors, called *mayordomos* (see Glossary), who can enlist their family members to aid in the work of organizing and paying for community-wide celebrations. In small places, the *mayordomo* and his or her family may handle the costs within the group, even going into debt to do things properly. In large towns and cities, the festivals are often

A colonial church in Ayacucho
Courtesy Embassy of Peru

sponsored by the municipal government as well as the church, with *mayordomos* serving in only limited capacities. In many towns, there is a religious brotherhood (*hermandad*) or other organization that also takes part in this fashion. Peru's largest religious celebration, the Señor de los Milagros, which takes place in Lima during the month of October each year, is largely funded by the brotherhood of the Señor de los Milagros.

In communities that maintain strong native cultural traditions, Roman Catholicism is intricately mixed with facets of Incan beliefs and practices. The native populations hold firm animistic notions about the spirits and forces found in natural settings, such as the great snowpeaks where the *apus* (lords of sacred places) dwell. Many places are seen as inherently dangerous, emanating airs or essences that can cause illness, and are approached with care. The Incas and other Andean peoples revered the *inti* (sun) and *pacha mama* (earth mother), as well as other gods and the principal ancestral heads of lineages. The Spaniards, in converting the people to Catholicism, followed a deliberate strategy of syncretism that was used throughout the Americas. This process sought to substitute Christian saints for local deities, often using existing temple sites as the location of churches. Many of the biblical lessons and stories were conveyed through dramatic reenactments of those

119

events at fiestas that permitted people to memorize the tales and participate in the telling. Thousands of Andean fiestas are based on such foundations.

The annual celebrations of village patron saints' days often coincide with important harvest periods and are clearly reinterpretations of preconquest harvest observances disguised as Catholic feast days. In the south highlands, among such pastoral peoples as those of Q'eros, Cusco preserves many ancestral practices and lifeways. Elaborate rites to promote the fertility of their llama and alpaca herds are still undertaken. In other communities, religious rites that evoke natural and spiritual forces require sacrifices of animals, such as llamas or guinea pigs, the spillage of *chicha* or alcohol on sacred ground, or the burying of coca and other ritual items to please the *apus* or the *pacha mama*. In numerous highland areas, the Spanish introduced the Mediterranean custom of blood sports, such as bull-fighting, bullbaiting, and games of horsemanship in which riders riding at full gallop attempt to wring the necks of fowl or condors. José María Arguedas recounts these practices in his famous 1941 novel, *Yawar Fiesta*.

Andean religious practices conform to the sociocultural divisions of Peruvian society, with the Hispanicized coastal cities following general Roman Catholic practices, and the Andean towns and villages reflecting the syncretisms of conquest culture, which endure as strong elements in modern belief and worldview. The importance of these events is considerable because they evoke outpourings of devotion and emotional expressions of belief, while giving opportunity for spiritual renewal. They also function to tie the population together in their common belief and allegiance to the immortal figure of the saint, or *apu,* and thus constitute important bonding mechanisms for families and neighborhoods. From the major celebrations—such as those of two specifically Peruvian saints, Santa Rosa of Lima and San Martín of Porres (Saint Martin of Porres)—to the dozens of important regional figures, such as the Virgen de la Puerta (Virgin of the Door) in La Libertad Department and the revered saints and crosses in village chapels, these feast days have a singular role in social life. Indeed, not only do settlements have religious allegiances, but so, too, do public institutions. For example, the armed forces celebrate the day of their patroness, the Virgen de las Mercedes (Virgin of the Mercedes—Our Lady of Ransom), with pomp and high-level participation around the country.

Since about 1970, Protestantism has been winning converts in Peru at a relatively rapid rate among the urban poor and certain native populations (see The Church, ch. 4). Yet, Peruvians, like those in other Andean countries, have not been as receptive to Protestant entreaties to convert as have people in Central America. According to one study, only about 4.5 percent of Peruvians can be counted as Protestants, with the Church of Jesus Christ of Latterday Saints (Mormons) forming about a quarter of the number and the rest belonging to various other groups. To many, the appeal of Protestantism comes in reaction to the kinds of ceremonial obligations that have accompanied Roman Catholic practice and the failure of the traditional church to address adequately the pressing issues that were problems among the poor.

Most intensive Protestant missionary attention has been directed toward the tribal peoples of the Amazon Basin, where the Summer Institute of Linguistics (SIL), Wycliffe Bible Translators, and similar evangelical groups have long worked. In particular, the SIL has occupied a peculiar position in Peru through its long-running contracts with the Ministry of Education to educate the numerous tribes, such as the Shipibo, and assist the government in developing linguistically correct texts for several groups. Nevertheless, nationalistic public reaction to the SIL's activities has provoked many attempts to force the organization out of Peru. Because the force behind the evangelical movements emanates largely from the United States and because Roman Catholicism is the official state religion, there have been occasional hints of loyalist hostility with respect to zealous proselytizing.

Catholic cults have also bloomed throughout Lima's squatter settlements. The role of religion and the fact that the people themselves generate institutions of worship with relatively little external guidance is yet another expression of the migrants' striving for a sense of community in the difficult circumstances of Lima's squatter settlements.

Community Leadership

Throughout the highlands, there are vestiges of the colonial civic and religious organizations of "indirect rule" originally implanted by Spanish officials. Where they survive in Peru, principally in native communities, there are networks of villages tied together in an association broadly supervised by a parish priest or his surrogate. The village religious leaders, who are called by various names such as *alcaldes pedáneos* (lesser mayors) and *varayoq* or *envarados* (staff bearers), plan and carry out elaborate yearly festival cycles involving dozens of lesser special lay religious authorities. Often referred to as carrying a "burden" or responsibility (*cargo*), all of these village officials are selected annually by elaborate systems of prestige rankings based on prior experience and local values of devotion, honesty, reputation for work, and capacity to under-write the costs of office.

The principal officials in these hierarchies carry holy staffs of office, often made of *chonta* (tucuma) palm wood brought from the tropics and adorned with silver relics and symbols. The additional duties of the *varayoq* include the supervision of village morals, marriage, and the application of informal justice to offenders of village norms. Although specifically outlawed in several of Peru's older constitutions, the system has endured throughout the highlands. Changes have occurred, however, when communities, under pressures to modernize, abolished the *varayoq* institution. In other cases, the system has evolved into a more formal political apparatus, leaving the religious activities in the hands of the parish priest, lay brotherhoods, and other devotees. The multicommunity Peasant Patrols (*rondas campesinas*) in the highlands have acted as informal but powerful self-defense forces controlling rustling and, beginning in the 1980s, the intrusion of unwanted revolutionaries like the Shining Path. In aspects of their orientation and organization, they may aspire to resemble the *varayoq* as moral authorities.

The formal political and social organization of Peruvian towns and cities of course follows the outlines laid down in the constitution of 1979 and various laws enacted by the Congress. One of the somewhat confusing arrangements, however, pertains to the officially constituted corporate community enterprises, the Peasant Communities, and their offshoots—such as the Social Interest Agrarian Association (Sociedad Agrícola de Interés Social—SAIS) and the Social Property Enterprises (Empresas de Propiedad Social—EPS). There is disagreement over how these entities fit into the community and political picture because their constituencies overlap with the political divisions. The districts and provinces are political subdivisions with elected mayors and council members charged with administering their areas. Corporate communities are a form of agrarian cooperative business that own inalienable land, with memberships that are not necessarily restricted to a single residential unit like a town.

The Peasant Communities and other units conduct their affairs through a president, as well as administrative and vigilance committees elected by the general assembly of the membership. Community property and members (*comuneros*) are within the administrative domains of districts and provinces for all other civic purposes. In some areas, the boundaries of the Peasant Communities coincide with those of a district, as is frequently the case in the Mantaro Valley. In other areas, community lands occupy only a portion of the district; there may also be two separate Peasant

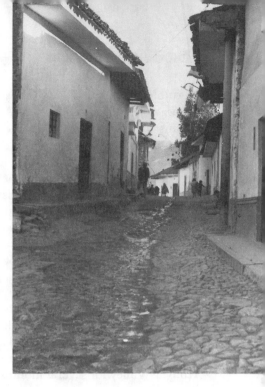

A street in the town of Huaraz,
Ancash Department
Courtesy Inter-American
Development Bank

Communities within a district, or districts with residents who do not belong to the corporate organization.

Members of Peasant Communities and other corporate groups constitute about 30 percent of all rural people and therefore have been a significant factor in economic and political affairs throughout the highlands and in some areas of the Costa, where the former plantations passed into workers' hands after 1969. On the coast, there have long been linkages between worker unions and the regional political powers, but in the Sierra these ties have not developed strongly. The exception is in the central highland department of Junín and in the southern department of Puno, where in the 1980s there were powerful, organized movements based on Peasant Communities and independent small farmers groups allied with political parties. The influence of these groups was, for the most part, localized.

Landlords and Peasant Revolts in the Highlands

In the great majority of highland provinces, political and economic leadership and power were based on traditional social elites, a landlord class that controlled the haciendas and, thus, very large proportions of the rural poor. In these contexts, powerful landlords (*terratenientes*) manipulated political affairs, either by themselves holding positions of authority, such as the prefectures, municipal offices, and key government posts, or influencing those who did. A tradition

123

of ruthlessness, greed, and abuse is associated with this system (*gamonalismo*) throughout Peru. A *gamonal* is a person to be feared because he has extraordinary and extralegal powers to protect his interests and act against others. Although the agrarian reform of 1969 did much to cut this power, local affairs in many districts and provinces have remained under such domination, to the deep resentment of the rural poor, who most directly feel its consequences.

Since the late nineteenth century, various regional movements have arisen to address abuse. Historian Wilfredo Kápsoli Escudero has documented thirty-two peasant revolts and movements from 1879 to 1965, a number that is not exhaustive but which contradicts the view that Peru's native peasantry was passive in accepting its serfdom. Characteristically, virtually all of these efforts were specifically directed against the abuses of *gamonales* and hacendados, at least in their initial phases. The forces in the 1885 Ancash uprising, led by Pedro Pablo Atusparía, an *alcalde pedáneo* from a village near Huaraz, eventually captured and held the Callejón de Huaylas Valley for several months before federal troops reclaimed it.

Most peasant revolts were not as dramatic, but all testified to the burgeoning feelings of frustration, anger, and alienation that had built up over the centuries. In part, this anger and frustration stemmed from the fact that native American communities had been deprived of their communal holdings after national independence, which meant that extensive holdings passed from community control to private elite interests. Demands for redress of this situation led to the reestablishment of the official Indigenous Community in 1920 during the second presidency of Augusto B. Leguía (1919–30). Subsequently, communities that could prove they at one time had held colonial title to land were permitted to repossess it, a long and arduous bureaucratic process in which the most successful communities were those with active migrants in Lima who could lobby the government.

Another response was President Manuel A. Odría's (1948–56) sanctioning of the Cornell-Peru project in which the Ministry of Labor and Indian Affairs, in collaboration with Cornell University in Ithaca, New York, would conduct a demonstration of community development and land reform at Hacienda Vicos in Ancash Department, starting in 1952. It was Peru's first such development program and received extensive publicity around the country. This situation provoked consternation among landlords and elite interests, which purposefully delayed the conclusion of the project. The *colonos* of Vicos became an independent community in 1962, when they were finally permitted to purchase the estate they and their ancestors had cultivated for others for 368 years.

With its widespread publicity, the Vicos project helped to whet appetites for change. At that time, several hundred hacienda communities like Vicos were requesting similar projects and the freedom to purchase their lands. When the reluctant government of oligarch Manuel Prado y Ugarteche (1939–45, 1956–62) and the slow and corrupt mechanisms of the bureaucracy could not meet these rising demands, an explosive situation developed. Peasant invasions of hacienda lands began a few days after Fernando Belaúnde assumed office as president in 1963. He had promised to organize a land reform, and the native communities, in their words, were "helping" him keep his word. Hundreds of estates were taken over by peasants, provoking a national crisis that eventually subsided when Belaúnde convinced communities that his administration would fulfill its promises. It did not happen.

However, on the "Day of the Indian," June 24, 1969, General Juan Velasco Alvarado (president, 1968–75), head of the populist "Revolutionary Government of the Armed Forces," decreed a sweeping and immediate land reform, ending serfdom and private latifundios (see Glossary) that included the sacrosanct coastal plantations. Hope and expectations on the part of the peasantry had never been higher, but the succeeding years brought back the frustration; serious problems resulted from natural disasters, the withdrawal of significant international credit and support from the United States for reform programs, bureaucratic failures, and a lack of well-trained personnel. After the Velasco government gave way to more conservative forces within the army in 1975, a retrenchment began. In this phase of the process, some haciendas, including several in Ayacucho Department, were returned to their former owners, provoking bitter disappointment and further alienation among the peasants.

Shining Path and Its Impact

The social history of the 1960s and 1970s is background for the emergence of the disturbing Shining Path (Sendero Luminoso—SL) movement. Its many violent actions have been directed against locally elected municipal officials and anyone designated as a *gamonal* in the departments of Ayacucho, Huancavelica, Apurímac, Junín, Huánuco, and portions of Ancash and Cusco departments, as well as some other areas designated as emergency zones where government control was deeply compromised. The Maoist-oriented SL opposed Lima as the metropolis that usurps resources from the rest of the nation. Like most past revolutionary movements (as opposed

125

to peasant revolts) acting on behalf of the poor, the SL leadership has consisted of disgruntled and angry intellectuals, mestizos, and whites, apparently from provincial backgrounds. Many adherents have been recruited from university and high-school ranks, where radical politicization has been a part of student culture since the late nineteenth century. Others have come from the cadres of embittered migrant youths living in urban lower-class surroundings, disaffected and frustrated school teachers, and the legions of alienated peasants in aggrieved highland provinces in Huancavelica, Ayacucho, and adjacent areas.

Peru's socioeconomic and political disarray has taken on its present pattern after four decades of extravagant demographic change, a truncated land reform that never received effective funding or ancillary support as needed in education, and incessant promises of development, jobs, and progress without fulfillment. The SL has sought to eliminate the perpetrators of past error to establish a new order of its own. The SL's vengeful approach appeared attractive to many, coming at a time when the migration pathway to social change appeared blocked, the ability to progress by this method stymied by the economic crisis, and rural development was at an all-time low ebb.

The immediate impact of the terror-inspiring violence of SL actions and the correspondingly symmetrical responses of the Peruvian Army (Ejército Peruano—EP) has had a devastating effect on rural and urban life, public institutions, and agricultural production, especially in the emergency zone department of Ayacucho. Since the SL's first brutal attack on the defenseless people of Chuschi, its actions and the violent reactions of the police and army have produced chaos throughout the central highlands and deep problems in Lima.

From 1980 to 1990, an estimated 200,000 persons were driven from their homes, with about 18,000 people killed, mostly in the department of Ayacucho and neighboring areas. In five provinces in Ayacucho, the resident population dropped by two-thirds, and many villages were virtual ghost towns. This migration went to Lima, Ica, and Huancayo, where disoriented peasants were offered little assistance and sometimes were attacked by the police as suspected Senderistas (SL members). Many communities have responded to SL attacks by organizing and fighting back. Towns or villages in La Libertad and Cajamarca departments, in particular, greatly amplified the system of *rondas campesinas*. Elsewhere, the army organized local militias and patrols to combat and ferret out SL cadres. Unfortunately, in addition to providing for defense all of these actions left room for abuses, and there were numerous

A school scene in Cusco
Courtesy Karen R. Sagstetter

cases of personal vendettas taking place that had little to do with the task.

There was no question that the SL's revolutionary terrorism was producing major disruptions and profound changes in Peruvian society. Surveys indicated that 71 percent of Peruvians agreed that poverty, social injustice, and the economic crisis were together the root cause of the SL's revolution, and that 68 percent identified the SL as the nation's most serious problem. Drug trafficking was ranked a distant second by only 11 percent of respondents. At least one conclusion, however, seemed abundantly clear: Peruvians had to address their longstanding and deeply interrelated ills of poverty, inequity, and ethnoracial discrimination if they hoped to take control of the situation.

Education, Language, and Literacy

The Education System

In Peru schooling is regarded as the sine qua non of progress and the key to personal advancement. In 1988 there were over 27,600 primary schools in Peru, one for virtually every hamlet with over 200 persons throughout the country (see table 7, Appendix). It is no exaggeration to say that the presence of a village school

127

and teacher is considered by the poor as the most important first step on the road to ''progress'' out of poverty and a state of disrespect, if not for themselves, for their children. Because of the historical ethnic and racial discrimination against native peoples, the village school became the instrument and method by which one could learn Spanish, the most important step toward reducing one's ''visibility'' as an identifiable object of denigration and being able to gain mobility out of the native American caste. The primary school also has provided the means to become a recognized citizen because the exercise of citizenship and access to state services require (in fact, if not officially) a basic ability to use written and spoken Spanish. Thus, the spread of primary schools owed much to the deep desire on the part of the native and rural poor to disassociate themselves from the symbols of denigration. The thrust of Peruvian education has been oriented toward this end, however subtly or even unconsciously. School policies encouraged the discarding of native American clothing and language, and the frequent school plays and skits burlesqued native peoples' practices, such as coca chewing or fiestas, or equated indigenous culture with drunkenness and, often, stupidity and poverty, while at the same time exhorting native children to ''lift themselves up.'' The opposite pole to being native American was to be Spanish-speaking, urban, white-collar, and educated.

The influence of these educational policies is reflected in the currents of social change sweeping Peru in the second half of the twentieth century. In the early 1960s, Peru was a nation where almost 39 percent of the population spoke native languages, half being bilingual in Spanish and half monolingual in a native tongue. By 1981 only 9 percent were monolingual, and 18 percent remained bilingual. In 1990 over 72 percent claimed to speak only Spanish, whereas in 1961, about 60 percent did. In 1990 Quechua was by far the dominant native language spoken in all departments, except Amazonas and Ucayali. Almost 80 percent of Aymara speakers lived in Puno, with many bilingual persons in Arequipa, greater Lima, Tacna, and Moquegua. About 85 percent of the population in 1991 was literate (see table 8, Appendix).

There are many technical and cultural difficulties associated with gathering and reporting information on native languages. Because of this, most experts have concluded that native languages are significantly underreported with respect to bilingualism. According to one study, native languages are the preferred means of communication even within those households whose adult members are bilingual. However, given the force of state policy in education and the many concomitant pressures on the individual, Quechua and Aymara will likely survive largely as second languages.

In the Sierra, where villages and communities are famous for their voluntary work, the majority of self-financed public community projects have been dedicated to the construction and maintenance of their *escuelitas* (little schools) with little assistance except from their migrant clubs and associations in Lima or other large cities. This overwhelming drive to change personal, family, and community conditions by means of education began at least 150 years ago, at a time when public education was extremely limited and private schooling was open to only the elite mestizo and white populations of the few major cities. In 1990, however, 28 percent of all Peruvians, over 5 million people, were matriculated in primary or secondary schools, which were now within reach of people even in the remotest of places.

In the mid-nineteenth century, aside from a few progressive districts that operated municipal schools, most educational institutions were privately operated. Individual teachers would simply open their own institutes and through modest advertising gain a clientele of paying students. There have been laws mandating public education since the beginning of the republic, but they were not widely implemented. In 1866 the minister of justice and education sought to establish vocational schools and uniform curricula for all public schools and to open schools to women. The Constitutional Congress in 1867 idealistically called for a secondary school for each sex in every provincial capital. With constitutional changes and renewed attempts to modernize, it became the obligation of every department and province to have full primary and secondary education available, at least in theory, to any resident. Primary education was later declared both free and compulsory for all citizens.

The Ministry of Education in Lima exercises authority over a sprawling network of schools for which it uniformly determines curricula, textbook content, and the general values that guide classroom activities nationwide. Because of the importance invested in education, the role of the teacher is respected, especially at the district level, where teachers readily occupy leadership positions. Because of this tendency, for many years teachers were prohibited from holding public office on the theory that they would, like priests, exercise an unusual level of influence in their districts. The power accruing to a teacher as the only person with postsecondary education in a small rural town can be considerable: the teacher is sought out to solve personal and village problems, settle disputes, and act as spokesperson for the community. Both men and women

129

have eagerly sought teaching positions because they have offered a unique opportunity for personal advancement. In a nation steeped in androcentric traditions, however, teaching has been especially important for women because it has been an avenue of achieving upward mobility, gaining respect, and playing sociopolitical roles in community affairs that have been otherwise closed to them.

Higher education is hence greatly respected. University professors symbolize a high order of achievement, and they are addressed as *profesor* or *profesora*. The same recognition of educational achievement is given to other fields as well. Anyone receiving an advanced degree in engineering is always addressed as engineer (*ingeniero*) or *doctor*. The titles are prestigious and valued and permanently identify one as an educated person to be rewarded with respect. The titles are therefore coveted, and on graduation the new status is often announced in *El Comercio,* Lima's oldest daily newspaper.

In 1990, in addition to its primary schools, Peru counted over 5,400 secondary schools (*colegios*) of all types. Although these too were widely distributed throughout the country, the best secondary schools were heavily concentrated in the major cities and especially in Lima. There, the elite private international institutions and Peruvian Catholic schools have offered excellent programs featuring multilingual instruction and preparation aimed at linking students with foreign universities. The private Catholic schools throughout the country, both primary and secondary, have been highly regarded for their efforts to instill discipline and character.

Because it is required by law that each provincial capital have a public secondary school, such schools historically have come to enjoy special status as surrogate intellectual centers in the absence of universities in their regions. The tradition of strong high school alumni allegiance is pronounced, with organizations and reunions commonplace and attachments to classmates (*condiscípulos*) enduring. The importance of a high school diploma is further emphasized by each graduating class, which bestows honor on some personage or event by naming its graduation after them. High school graduates take the selection of the class name as an opportunity to make a statement about things that concern them and choose one that embodies their thoughts. This custom is followed by university graduating classes as well.

Because people correlate social and economic well-being with educational achievement, schooling becomes essential not only for its functional usefulness but also for social reasons. The concept of education is infused with high intrinsic value, and educated people by definition are more cultivated (*culto*), worthy, and qualified to be admired as role models than others. Educated persons are thought to have the duty to speak out and address public issues on behalf of others less privileged; many students have accepted this responsibility as part of their student role.

The development of national identity is another area to which public education is firmly committed. In the wake of the devastating War of the Pacific—in which Peru lost territory, wealth, dignity, and pride—the emergent public school system became the major vehicle by which citizens established strong linkages to the state. Primary and secondary school curricula are thus heavily laden with patriotic, if not jingoistic, nationalism, elements of which are written into the nation's textbooks by the Ministry of Education. If nothing else, the primary school pupil learns that he or she is a Peruvian and that many of Peru's national heroes, such as Admiral Miguel Grau, Colonel Francisco Bolognesi, and Leonicio Prado, were martyrized on the nation's behalf by Chilean forces against whom one must be constantly on guard. Ecuador is viewed in this same tenor, but perceived as less menacing, constituting a vague threat to the nation's security or Amazonic oil rights.

The school calendar is thus filled with observances and ceremonies honoring national heroes and martyrs, including Túpac Amaru II (José Gabriel Condorcanqui). Parades, drum and bugle corps (*banda de guerra*—war band), and flag bearers spend dozens of hours in school yards preparing for the celebration of national holidays (*fiestas patrias*), national independence day affairs that are the feature of every district, province, and department capital each year on July 27 and 28. In Lima the tradition of *fiestas patrias* involves a major display of military forces and equipment accompanied by high school units parading the length of Avenida Brasil (Brazil Avenue) across Lima. Completing the essentially military focus on nationalism in the public schools is the pupil uniform, a military cadet-type outfit for boys that includes a cap introduced by the General Manuel Odría regime in the 1950s.

Universities

As the first university founded in the Americas in 1551, the National Autonomous University of San Marcos (Universidad Nacional Autónoma de San Marcos—UNAM) has had a long and varied history of elitism, reform, populism, controversy, respect, prestige, and, especially since the mid-1980s, conflict and confusion born of political divisions and broad social unrest. Although it remained the largest university in the nation, it had lost much of its former prestige by 1990. In the 1970–90 period, several smaller private institutions, such as the Pontifical Catholic University of Peru (Pontificia Universidad Católica del Perú), located in Lima,

131

have gained more stature. The major public universities are the specialized National Agrarian University (Universidad Nacional Agraria—UNA) in Lima's La Molina District and the National Engineering University (Universidad Nacional de Ingeniería), also in the Lima area. The most prestigious medical school is the private Cayetano Heredía in Lima.

Lima has captured most of the resources of higher education. Universities in Lima, which had 42 percent of all students, employed 62 percent of all faculty in the late 1980s. Nevertheless, there are universities in all but four of the departments. Although many of these are newly founded and poorly equipped, the demand for access to advanced study has provided them with a growing stream of students. The abandoned colonial University of Huamanga (Universidad de Huamanga) in Ayacucho is one of these, having been reopened in the late 1950s to fill an educational void for students drawn from impoverished and isolated Ayacucho Department. Although initiated on its modern course with high hopes, it has suffered from budgetary inadequacies, frustrated plans, and disgruntled students impatient for social change. During the late 1960s, it became the home to embittered revolutionaries, who emerged as the leaders of the SL movement.

The public schools have long been deeply influenced by political factionalism, which has divided the constitutionally established governing bodies of universities. Internal politics at San Marcos and other universities have involved complex alliance-making among administrators, staff, faculty, and the student body, as well as partisan political forces that crosscut these sectors with their own agendas. Thus, APRA, various communist factions, and other groups have played out their strategies, often with negative consequences or even little direct reference to the mission of education as such. APRA, however, did play a role in establishing the University of the Center (Universidad del Centro) in Huancayo and Federico Villareal in Lima, now the second-largest university. The present organization of the public universities was originally conceived as a result of the Latin American-wide university reform movement of the 1920s and 1930s which attempted to democratize the traditional, colonial-style elite traditions. What has evolved, however, has led to constant problems of paralytic conflict, student strikes, slogan mongering, and, often, closure of a university for one or more semesters at a time. As a result, the private universities, such as those tied to the Catholic Church and various segments of the upper-middle classes, have emerged as the most stable and best staffed institutions during the last twenty-five years.

Out of this milieu, one can begin to understand the political role of teachers and their organizations, such as the Trade Union of Education Workers of Peru (Sindicato Único de Trabajadores de la Enseñanza del Perú—SUTEP), the national teachers union. Most teachers attend teaching colleges before entering the classroom with their certificates, and many of these colleges, such as La Cantuta outside of Lima, have long been centers for radical politics. With teachers earning less than the average beginning police officer, discontent has run high among teachers for many years. Thus, given the importance and role of teachers in district schools nationwide, it is not surprising that SUTEP has been a strong voice in expressing its social and economic discontent or that the SL and MRTA had succeeded in recruiting followers from the ranks of SUTEP.

Health and Well-Being

In the early 1990s, Peru was hit by a cholera epidemic, which highlighted longstanding health care problems. Review of health statistics amply illustrates Peru's vulnerability to disease and the uneven distribution of resources to combat it. The most and the best of the health facilities were concentrated in metropolitan Lima, followed by the principal older coastal cities, including Arequipa, and the rest of the country. The differences among these regions were not trivial. Whereas Lima had a doctor for every 400 persons on average, and other coastal areas had a ratio of one doctor for every 2,000, the highland departments had one doctor for every 12,000 persons (see table 9, Appendix). The same levels of difference applied with respect to hospital beds, nurses, and all the medical specialties.

In the early 1990s, over 25 percent of urban residences and over 90 percent of rural residences lacked basic potable water and sewerage. Thus, the population has been inevitably exposed to a wide variety of waterborne diseases. The incidence of disease not surprisingly reflected the inequities evidenced in the health system: the leading causes of death by infectious diseases have varied from year to year, but invariably the principal ones have been respiratory infections, gastroenteritis, common colds, malaria, tuberculosis, influenza, measles, chicken pox, and whooping cough. The cholera epidemic, which began in 1990 and claimed international headlines, ranked well down the list of causes for death behind these others, which have been endemic and basically taken for granted. In a typical case, during one year in Huaylas District, which had a small clinic and often was fortunate enough to have a doctor in residence, 40 percent of all deaths registered were children below four years of age, who died because of a regional influenza epidemic.

Although Peru's infant mortality rate per 1,000 live births dropped from 130 to 80 over a 26-year period (1965–91), the rate in 1991 was still over twice the rate of Colombia and four times the rate of Chile. The mortality rate for children under 5 was also brought down greatly, from 233 per 1,000 in 1960 to 107 per 1,000 in 1991. Both measures for 1991 still exceeded all the other Latin American countries except Bolivia and Haiti. The only direct measure of social welfare that deteriorated was nutrition: calorie consumption per capita fell 5 percent from the average for 1964–66 to 1984–86. In 1988 calorie consumption was 2,269, as compared with 2,328 in 1987. Because calorie consumption levels generally parallel income levels, the decrease must have been concentrated at the level of the extremely poor (see table 10, Appendix).

Peru's lack of general well-being was further suggested by the nation's high and growing dependence on foreign food since 1975 through direct imports, which had increased 300 percent, and food assistance programs, which showed a tenfold increment. The United States has been by far the largest provider of food assistance to Peru through its multiple programs administered under the Food for Peace (Public Law 480) projects of the United States Agency for International Development (AID). During the 1980s, food aid amounted to over 50 percent of all United States economic assistance. The aid was delivered as maternal and child health assistance and food-for-work programs administered by CARE (Cooperative for American Relief), church-related private voluntary organizations, or by direct sale to the Peruvian government for urban market resale.

Peru's totally inadequate social security system, operated by the Peruvian Institute of Social Security (Instituto Peruano de Seguridad Social—IPSS), did not remain exempt from the Fujimori government's privatization policy. As a result of two legislative decrees passed in November 1991, Peru's system for providing social security retirement and health benefits underwent significant modification. The changes were similar to those made by the military government of Chile in the early 1980s, when employees were given a choice of either remaining with the existing system or joining private systems set up on an individual capitalization basis. The Fujimori government decided to adopt the Chilean social security model almost completely. The stated objectives were to permit open market competition, alleviate the government's financial burden by having it shared by the private sector, improve coverage and the quality of benefits, and provide wider access to other social sectors. Private Pension Funds Administrators (Administradoras de Fondos de Pensiones—AFPs) were expected to begin operating in

June 1993. A presidential decree in December 1992 ended the IPSS's monopoly on pensions. This action provided a boost to Peru's small and underdeveloped capital market by allowing the AFPs to invest in bonds issued by the government or Central Reserve Bank (Banco Central de Reservas—BCR, also known as Central Bank) as well as in companies.

The cholera and other health and social issues in Peru were interrelated closely with the country's steadily worsening environmental conditions. The high levels of pollution in large sectors of Lima, Chimbote, and other coastal centers had resulted from uncontrolled dumping of industrial, automotive, and domestic wastes that had created a gaseous atmosphere. The loss of irrigated coastal farmland to urban sprawl, erosion of highland farms, and the clearcutting of Amazonian forest all have conspired to impoverish the nation's most valuable natural resources and further exacerbate social dilemmas. Although Peru is endowed with perhaps the widest range of resources in South America, somehow they have never been coherently or effectively utilized to construct a balanced and progressive society. The irony of Peru's condition was captured long ago in the characterization of the nation as being a "pauper sitting on a throne of gold." How to put the gold in the pauper's pockets without destroying the chair on which to sit is a puzzle that Peruvians and their international supporters have yet to solve.

* * *

The literature on Peru is extensive. Particularly important have been the many monographs, books, and series issued under the aegis of research institutes, such as the Institute of Peruvian Studies (Instituto de Estudios Peruanos—IEP) and the Center for Development Studies and Promotion (Centro de Estudios y Promoción del Desarrollo—DESCO), and publishers such as Mosca Azul and the Pontificia Universidad Católica del Perú, to name but a few. Readers can find a lucid review of Incan and pre-Incan societies in Michael E. Moseley's *The Incas and Their Ancestors.* Henry F. Dobyns and Paul L. Doughty give an overview of national society in *Peru: A Cultural History.* Women's roles are thoroughly explored in B. Ximena Bunster and Elsa Chaney's study of market women, *Sellers and Servants,* and in Susan C. Bourque and Kay B. Warren's *Women of the Andes.* Stephen B. Brush's description of peasant life, *Mountain, Field, and Family,* gives a clear explanation of Andean farming. There are many excellent studies of the central highlands and Mantaro Valley, including Norman Long and Bryan R. Roberts's edited volume, *Miners, Peasants, and Entrepreneurs.* Susan Lobo discusses the social organization of Lima's squatter settlements in her monograph, *A House of My Own.* Peter Lloyd's comparative study of Lima's squatter settlements, *The "Young Towns" of Lima,* gives a strong overview of the results of migration. Teófilo Altamirano's studies of migration are especially good in showing the impacts of change, as is David Collier's *Squatters and Oligarchs* for dealing with the politics of settlement.

By far the most important analysis of demography and policy is Alberto Varillas Montenegro and Patricia Mostajo de Muente's *La situación poblacional peruana.* Successful early grassroots development work is described in Henry F. Dobyns, Paul L. Doughty, and Harold D. Lasswell's account of the Cornell Peru Project at Vicos in *Peasants, Power, and Applied Social Change.* The religious experiences of Peruvians are reviewed in Jeffrey L. Klaiber's *Religion and Revolution in Peru, 1824–1976;* and Manuel Marzal's *Los caminos religiosos de los inmigrantes en la gran Lima,* an excellent account of neighborhood-level Catholicism and Protestantism. The literature on Peasant Communities is large, but note should be made of Cynthia McClintock's *Peasant Cooperatives and Political Change in Peru,* which recounts the changes during the Velasco era. The special problems of coca and cocaine are well presented in Deborah Pacini and Christine Franquemont's *Coca and Cocaine* and in Edmundo Morales's *Cocaine: White Gold Rush in Peru.* (For further information and complete citations, see Bibliography.)

Chapter 3. The Economy

Figure on an Incan wool and cotton tapestry

THE PERUVIAN ECONOMY achieved a higher rate of economic growth than the average for Latin America from 1950 to 1965, but since then has turned from one of the more dynamic to one of the most deeply troubled economies in the region. Even in the period of rapid growth, Peru was characterized by exceptionally high degrees of poverty and inequality, and since the late 1980s poverty has become much worse. Major changes in economic strategy introduced in 1990 and 1991 offer new hope for future growth but have not been oriented toward reduction of poverty and inequality.

In the first post-World War II decades, Peru achieved an above-average rate of growth with low levels of inflation and with rising exports of its diversified primary products. Output per capita grew 2.9 percent a year in the decade of the 1950s and then 3.2 percent annually in the first half of the 1960s, compared with the regional growth rate of 2.0 percent for these fifteen years. As of 1960, income per capita was 17 percent above the median for Latin American countries. However, since the mid-1960s the economy has run into increasing difficulties. Output per capita failed to grow at all from 1965 to 1988, then fell below its 1965 level in 1989 and 1990. The previously moderate rate of inflation accelerated, balance-of-payments deficits became a chronic problem, and the country accumulated a deep external debt. As poverty worsened, political violence in the countryside and cities grew increasingly intense. The economy and the society as a whole seemed to lose coherence and any sense of direction.

The reasons for this deterioration from 1965 to 1991 are complex and very much open to debate. Many aspects of the debate center on two opposing conceptions of what national economic strategy and goals should be. One conviction is that the best course is to keep the economic system open to foreign trade and investment, to avoid extensive government intervention in the economy, and to rely mainly on private enterprise for basic decisions on production and investment. The contrary conception favors restricting foreign trade and investment while promoting an active government role in the economy to accelerate industrialization, to reduce inequality, and to control the actions of private investors. The conflict between these economic models is familiar in the experience of all Latin American countries. The failure to reconcile

139

them in Peru has been an important factor in the deteriorating economic performance since the mid-1960s.

At least five interacting problems have been important in the explanation of why the economy has deteriorated so badly since the mid-1960s. First, natural resource limits began to handicap further expansion of primary-product exports, requiring difficult changes in the structures of production and trade. Second, partly in response to these constraints, and partly as a matter of a growing conviction that the country needed to industrialize more rapidly, successive governments began to promote industrialization through protection against imports, reversing the country's traditional policy of relatively open trade. Third, dissatisfaction with widespread inequality and poverty encouraged attempts at radical social change, but the two governments that tried to lead the way—those of General Juan Velasco Alvarado (1968–75) and Alan García Pérez (1985–90)—failed to find any effective answers or to maintain viable macroeconomic policies. Fourth, the temporary move back toward a more open economy under the second government of Fernando Belaúnde Terry (1980–85) resulted in a surge of imports and an external crisis—mainly because of currency overvaluation and an excessively rapid rise in government spending—that again discredited this approach. And finally, rural violence took on a profoundly destructive character with the growth of the Shining Path (Sendero Luminoso—SL) and the cocaine industry. On top of those two sources of violence, weakening governmental capability to maintain order and worsening conditions of employment led to growing security problems in cities.

Deteriorating conditions since the mid-1960s need to be considered against the background of a deeply divided society and a considerable lag, compared with many other Latin American countries, in developing either a competitive industrial sector or a modern structure of public administration able to implement public policies effectively. These handicaps can be overstated. After all, the Peruvian economy functioned well up to the mid-1960s, and both private business and government officials have gained experience since then. As of the beginning of the 1990s, however, the country's prolonged decline had seriously undermined public confidence in the possibilities for recuperation and renewed growth.

The most evident symptoms of the crisis at the beginning of the 1990s were falling national output and income, high levels of unemployment and underemployment, worsening poverty and violence, accelerating inflation, and deep external debt. Under the Belaúnde administration, the external debt grew too high for Peru to meet scheduled service payments, although the government maintained the position that payments would be resumed when possible. Under the next government, García made a point of declaring that payments would be unilaterally limited to 10 percent of export earnings. His more aggressive position led to a near-total cutoff of external credit, which remained in effect throughout his term.

The government of Alberto K. Fujimori (1990–) adopted a drastic stabilization program to break out of this complex of problems by first attacking the forces driving inflation. The initial shock of the new measures, which more than doubled the consumer price level in a single day, nearly paralyzed markets and production. After a steep fall in output, the economy began to stabilize with a lower rate of inflation but without any strong signs of recovery. Although the Fujimori program included many lines of intended action beyond the initial shock, it remained incomplete in many respects. It raised a host of questions about what other policies would reactivate the economy while preventing any further burst of inflation, and how long it would take to restore something like Peru's earlier capacity for growth.

Growth and Structural Change
Historical Background

Through the nineteenth century and into the mid-twentieth century, the great majority of the Peruvian population depended on agriculture and lived in the countryside. By 1876 Lima was the only Peruvian city with over 100,000 people—only 4 percent of the population (see table 3, Appendix). Much of the impetus for economic growth came from primary exports (see Glossary). In common with the rest of Latin America up to the 1930s, Peru maintained an open economic system with little government intervention and few restrictions on either imports or foreign investment. Such investment became highly important in the twentieth century, especially in the extraction of raw materials for export.

For many Latin American countries, the impact of falling export prices and curtailed external credit in the Great Depression of the 1930s led to fundamental changes in economic policies. Many governments began to raise protection against imports in order to stimulate domestic industry and to take more active roles in shaping economic change. But Peru held back from this common move and kept on with a relatively open economy. That put it behind many other countries in post-World War II industrialization and led to increasing pressures for change. Significant protection started in the 1960s, accompanied by both new restrictions on foreign investment and a more active role of government in the economy.

One of the country's basic problems has been that the growth of population in the twentieth century outran the capability to use labor productively. The ratio of arable land to population—much lower than the average for Latin America—continued decreasing through the 1970s. Employment in the modern manufacturing sector did not grow fast enough to keep up with the growth of the labor force, let alone provide enough opportunities for people moving out of rural poverty to seek urban employment. The manufacturing sector's employment as a share of the labor force fell from 13 percent in 1950 to 10 percent in 1990.

Orientation Toward Primary-Product Exports

Peru's most famous exports have been gold, silver, and guano. Its gold was taken out on a large scale by the Spanish for many years following the conquest and is of little significance now, but silver remains an important export. Guano served as Europe's most important fertilizer in the mid-nineteenth century and made Peru for a time the largest Latin American exporter to Europe. The guano boom ran out about 1870, after generating a long period of exceptional economic growth (see The Guano Era, 1845–70, ch. 1). When the guano boom ended, the economy retreated temporarily but then recovered with two new directions for expansion. One was a new set of primary-product exports and the other a turn toward more industrial production for the domestic market.

The alternative primary exports that initially replaced guano included silver, cotton, rubber, sugar, and lead. As of 1890, silver provided 33 percent of all export earnings, sugar 28 percent, and cotton, rubber, and wool collectively 37 percent. Copper became important at the beginning of the twentieth century, followed on a smaller scale by petroleum after 1915. Then, in the post-World War II period, fish meal from anchovies caught off the Peruvian coast became yet another highly valuable primary-product export. Industrial products remained notably absent from Peru's list of exports until the 1970s. As late as 1960, manufactured goods were only 1 percent of total exports.

Manufacturing for the home market has had many ups and downs. The first major downturn came with the guano boom of the mid-nineteenth century. Foreign-exchange earnings from guano exports became so abundant and, therefore, imported goods so cheap that much of Peru's small-scale local industry went out of production. The end of the guano boom relieved this pressure, and in the 1890s a new factor, a prolonged depreciation of the currency, came into play to stimulate manufacturing. The currency was at that time based on silver, and falling world market prices for silver in this period acted to raise both import prices and export values (of products other than silver), relative to Peruvian costs of production. Without any overt change in national policies, Peru began a process of import-substitution industrialization (see Glossary) combined with stronger incentives for exports. Domestic entrepreneurs responded successfully, and the economy began to show promising signs of more diversified and autonomous growth.

This redirection of Peruvian development was in turn sidetracked in the 1900–1930 period, in part by a decision to abandon the silver-based currency and adopt the gold standard instead. The change was intended to make the currency more stable and, in particular, to remove the inflationary effect of depreciation. The change succeeded in making the currency more stable and to some degree in holding down inflation, but Peruvian costs and prices nevertheless rose gradually relative to external prices. That trend hurt exports and the trade balance, especially in the 1920s, but instead of devaluing the currency to correct the country's weakening competitive position, the government chose to borrow abroad to keep up its value.

As has been noted, many Latin American countries reacted to the Great Depression by imposing extensive import restrictions and by adopting more activist government policies to promote industrialization. But at that point, Peru departed from the common pattern by rejecting the trend toward protection and intervention. After a brief experience with populist-style controls from 1945 to 1948, Peru returned to the open-economy model and a basically conservative style of internal economic management, in sharp contrast to the growing emphasis on import substitution and government control in Argentina, Brazil, Chile, and Colombia.

Aided by the early recovery of some of its main exports in the 1930s, and then by development of new primary exports in the early post-World War II period, Peru had in many respects the most successful economy in Latin America up to the mid-1960s. But increasing pressure on the land from a rapidly growing population, accompanied by rising costs and limited supplies of some of the country's natural resources, began to intensify demands for change. One of the worst blows for continued reliance on growth of primary exports was a sudden drop in the fish catch that provided supplies for Peru's important fish meal exports; over-fishing plus adverse changes in the ocean currents off Peru cut supplies drastically in the early 1970s (see Structures of Production, this ch.). That reversal coincided with supply problems in copper mining. Costs had begun to rise steeply in the older mines, and development of new projects required such large-scale investment that the foreign companies dominant in copper hesitated to go ahead with them. Further, population pressure and increasing difficulties in raising output of food converted Peru into an importer for a rising share of its food supply and began to work against use of land for agricultural exports. Although new investment and better agricultural techniques could presumably have helped a great deal, it began to seem likely that the only way to maintain high rates of growth would be to shift the structure of the economy more toward the industrial sector.

Evolution of Foreign Investment

During its long period of attachment to an open economic system, Peru welcomed foreign investment and in some periods adopted tax laws specifically designed to encourage it. That is to say, until the 1960s the small fraction of Peruvians in a position to determine the country's economic policies welcomed foreign investment without paying much attention to growing signs of popular opposition. In the 1960s, many things changed. The major change for foreign investors was that growing criticism of their role in the economy led to nationalization of several of the largest firms and to much more restrictive legislation.

Foreign investment played a relatively minor role in the nineteenth century, although it included railroads, British interests in banking and oil, and United States participation in sugar production and exports. Its role grew rapidly in the twentieth century, concentrated especially in export fields. In 1901, just as Peruvian copper began to gain importance, United States firms entered and began buying up all but the smallest of the country's copper mines. The International Petroleum Company (IPC), a Canadian subsidiary of Standard Oil of New Jersey, established domination of oil production by 1914 through purchase of the restricted rights needed to work the main oil fields. The trend to foreign entry in manufacturing as well as finance and mining was stimulated by promotional legislation under the eleven-year government of Augusto B. Leguía y Salcedo (1908–12, 1919–30), an initially elected president turned dictator who regarded foreign investment as the key to modernization of Peru. That much-publicized partnership between a repressive government and foreign investors was to play an important role for the future of Peru, by feeding convictions that foreign investment was inescapably linked to control of the country by the few at the expense of the public.

By the end of the 1920s, foreign firms accounted for over 60 percent of Peru's exports. The Great Depression of the 1930s changed that by bringing new foreign investment to a halt and by driving down the prices of the products of foreign firms (chiefly copper) much further than those exported by Peruvian firms. That double effect brought the share of exports by foreign firms down to about 30 percent by the end of the 1940s. Foreign investment remained low in the first postwar years, both because investors in the industrialized countries were preoccupied at home and because it was not encouraged by the populist government in Peru from 1945 to 1948. After a military coup installed a conservative dictator in 1948, the government offered a renewed welcome to foreign investors, made particularly effective by the Mining Code of 1950. This law offered very favorable tax provisions and quickly led to an upsurge of new investment. History repeated itself: as in the 1920s, a repressive government turned to foreign investors for economic growth and for its own support, adding fuel to widespread public distrust of foreign firms.

Public opposition to foreign ownership focused particularly on the largest firms owning and exporting natural resources, above all in copper and petroleum. The IPC became the center of increasing conflict over the terms of its operating rights and its financial support of conservative governments. When Belaúnde (1963–68, 1980–85) took office as president in 1963, he promised to reopen negotiations over the contract with IPC, but he then delayed the question for years and finally backed away from this promise in 1968. His failure to act provoked the military coup led by General Velasco, this time from the left wing. The Velasco government promptly nationalized IPC and started a determined campaign to restrict foreign investment. Although the government subsequently moderated its hostility to foreign firms, continuing disputes and then the deterioration of the economy led some companies to withdraw and held foreign investment down to very low levels through the 1980s.

The redirection of economic strategy under the Fujimori government in 1990–91 included a return to welcoming conditions for foreign investment, providing a much more favorable legal context, and disavowing completely the control-oriented policies of the governments of Velasco and García. Several foreign oil companies responded immediately, although the disorganized state of the economy and the context of political violence discouraged any general inflow of new foreign investment.

Structures of Production

By official measures of their contributions to the gross domestic product (GDP—see Glossary) at current prices, agriculture and fishing accounted for 22 percent of total output in the 1950s but

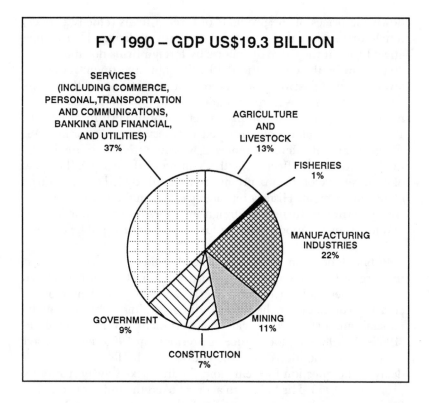

FY 1990 – GDP US$19.3 BILLION

SERVICES
(INCLUDING COMMERCE,
PERSONAL,TRANSPORTATION
AND COMMUNICATIONS,
BANKING AND FINANCIAL,
AND UTILITIES)
37%

AGRICULTURE
AND
LIVESTOCK
13%

FISHERIES
1%

MANUFACTURING
INDUSTRIES
22%

GOVERNMENT
9%

MINING
11%

CONSTRUCTION
7%

Source: Based on information from Banco Central de Reservas, *Memoria, 1990,* Lima, 1991.

Figure 8. Gross Domestic Product (GDP) by Sector, 1990

only 14 percent by 1990. Manufacturing fell slightly from 23 percent in the 1950s to 22 percent in 1990. The share of mining increased from 6 percent in the 1950s to 11 percent in 1990. Services, construction, and government combined rose from 52 percent in the 1950s to 53 percent by 1990 (see fig. 8).

All such measures are subject to uncertainty in all countries, but especially so in Peru. One reason is that Peru's national accounts have excluded illegal production of coca and its derivatives. Unofficial estimates suggest that their value in 1989 would have added 4 percent to GDP for the year and 11 percent to the official value of agricultural production. A second reason for doubt is that Peru has an exceptionally large informal sector (see Glossary) of unregulated activities, producing many services and some manufacturing outside of any official framework of reporting. Although the government includes estimates of such production in the national accounts and there is no systematic evidence that it has been either over- or underestimated, no one can be sure.

Agriculture

Perhaps the most important fact about the agricultural sector is that its production has not kept up with the growth of population. Total output of agriculture and fishing combined rose 63 percent between 1965 and 1988, but output per capita fell by 11 percent. Output per capita started falling in the early 1950s, climbed back up again to its 1950 level by 1970, then began a more pronounced and prolonged fall through the 1980s. Per capita output of food, as distinct from total agriculture, did better: it increased 1 percent during the period from the early 1980s to the late 1980s.

The downward trend in agricultural production per capita was accompanied by a fall in the share of output going to exports. From 1948 to 1952, Peru exported 23 percent of its agricultural output; by 1976 the export share was down to 8 percent. The trade balance for the agricultural sector remained consistently positive through the 1970s but then turned into an import surplus for the 1980s (see table 11, Appendix).

Although agricultural production in the aggregate failed to keep up with population growth, a few important products stood out as exceptions. With favorable support prices, output of rice increased at an annual rate of 7.9 percent in the 1980s. Changes in production techniques helped raise output of chickens and eggs at a rate of 6.5 percent in this period. The Ministry of Agriculture interpreted these positive results as evidence of what could be accomplished more generally with better incentives and improvement of agricultural techniques. For many crops, extremely wide variations in output per hectare, even in similar conditions of land and water supply, suggest that if effective extension services were implemented average productivity could be raised to levels closer to those achieved by leading producers (see People, Property, and Farming Systems, ch. 2). Contrary to the experience of many other countries in the region, productivity for most crops other than rice showed little or no improvement from 1979 to 1989.

Obstacles to increasing agricultural production include the poor quality of much of the country's land and the high degree of dependence on erratic supplies of water, plus the negative effects of public policies toward agriculture. Frequent recourse to price controls on food and in some periods to subsidized imports of food have hurt agricultural incentives as a byproduct of efforts to hold down prices for urban consumers. In general, government policies have persistently favored urban consumers at the expense of rural producers.

Another important set of questions bearing on agricultural productivity concerns the effects of the Agrarian Reform Law of 1969. The reform itself came long after the beginning of the decline in output per capita and was at first accompanied by a brief upturn. But the downtrend set in again from 1972 on and continued through the 1980s. The major question about the effects of the reform on productivity concerns the fact that most of the large estates taken away from prior owners were turned into cooperatives, made up of the former permanent workers on the estates. One problem was that the workers lacked management experience and a second was that incentives for individual participants were often unclear. Shares in earnings of the cooperative as a whole were not closely related to the individual member's time and effort, with the result that many of them concentrated on small parcels allocated to production for their own families rather than production for the cooperative. The performances of the cooperatives turned out to be highly varied. Some, particularly those with relatively good land and markets, were able to raise output and group earnings more successfully than the previous landowners. But many were not, and by the end of the 1970s many of the cooperatives were either bankrupt or close to becoming so. The tension between individual incentives and concern for the functions of the cooperative as a whole led to a general turn toward "decollectivization" at the end of the 1970s, breaking up the cooperatives into individual holdings. When the practice was made legal by the Belaúnde government in 1980, it spread rapidly.

The decollectivization has given Peruvian agriculture a much stronger component of individual family farming than it has ever had before. The large haciendas are gone, and the new farms are closer to a viable family-supporting size than has been true of the *minifundios* (see Glossary) of the Sierra. The consequences for agricultural productivity and growth were still unclear in 1991: incentives for individual effort were greater but the smaller production units may have lost some economies of scale (see Glossary). An econometric study of land productivity in north-coast agriculture, tracing output from prior cooperatives through individual results with the same land in the 1980s, brings out a wide variety of results rather than any great change in total. It shows that the individual holdings have on average done slightly better than the preceding cooperatives on the same land, chiefly by greater inputs of labor per hectare, but not enough better to make any convincing case of superiority. The authors of this study rightly emphasize that results in the 1980s cannot be explained adequately only in terms of farming practices because productivity was also adversely affected by the deterioration of the economic system as a whole.

In addition to the negative effects on agriculture of economy-wide disequilibrium in the 1980s, some areas were badly hurt in this period by increased violence and partial depopulation. The violence worsened from 1988 through 1990, driving people out of farms and whole villages and leaving productive land and equipment idle. In some of the worst-hit areas, production had fallen in half.

Fishing

Peru's rich fishery has been utilized since ancient times, but it was not until the post-World War II decades that an extensive export industry developed. Peru's fishing industry rapidly expanded in the 1950s to make the country the world's foremost producer and exporter of fish meal. Although a large variety of fish are caught offshore, the rapid growth was primarily in the catching of anchovies for processing into fish meal. The fish meal boom provided a major stimulus to the economy and accounted for more than a quarter of exports in the mid-1960s.

In the 1960s, however, there were indications that the nation's offshore fishing area was being overfished. Experts estimated that the fish catch should be about 8 to 9 million tons a year if overfishing was to be avoided. In 1965 the government attempted to limit the annual fish catch to 7 million tons but without success, partly because investments in ships and processing facilities greatly exceeded that level. By the late 1960s, a finite resource was being depleted. In 1970 the anchovy catch peaked at over 12 million tons.

Peru's rich fishing grounds are largely the result of the cold offshore Humboldt Current (Peruvian Current) that causes a welling up of marine and plant life on which the fish feed (see Natural Systems and Human Life, ch. 2). Periodically, El Niño (The Christchild), a warm-water current from the north, pushes farther south than normal and disrupts the flow of the Humboldt Current, destroying the feed for fish. In such years, the fish catch drops dramatically. The intrusion of El Niño occurred in 1965, 1972, and 1982–83, for example. The 1972 catch, a quarter its peak size, contributed to a crisis in the fish meal industry and the disappearance of fish meal as a leading Peruvian export during most of the 1970s.

In 1973 the government nationalized fish processing and marketing. However, the fish industry became a large drain on the government budget as the national fish company paid off former owners for their nationalized assets, reduced excess capacity, and processed a meager catch of less than 4 million tons. Partly to reduce the drain on revenue, in 1976 the government sold the fishing fleet back to private enterprise. Emphasis was also shifted away from fish meal, mainly from anchovies, to edible fish and exports of canned and frozen fish products.

The fishing industry recovered in the late 1970s, but the return of El Niño in 1982–83 devastated the industry until the mid-1980s. By 1986 the total fish catch exceeded 5.5 million tons and by 1988, 5.9 million tons, with exports of fish meal valued at US$379 million. The 1989 catch totaled 10 million tons, an increase of 34 percent over 1988, and fish meal exports were worth US$410 million. In late 1991, Congress passed a decree that eliminated all restrictions and monopolies on the production and marketing of fish products and encouraged investment in the industry.

Manufacturing

The industrial sector has had its problems too, especially in the 1980s. Manufacturing production grew more rapidly than the economy as a whole up to that decade. It increased at a compound annual rate of 3.8 percent between 1965 and 1980. But it grew only 1.6 percent a year from 1980 to 1988, and then plunged 23 percent in the ghastly economic conditions of 1989.

Of dominant importance in the 1980s were food processing, textiles, chemicals, and basic metals; food processing alone accounted for nearly one-third of total manufacturing output. For the period 1980–88, when total manufacturing production increased by only about 5 percent, food processing rose by nearly 23 percent. Production of basic metals went the other way, falling by almost 22 percent. Output of metal products and machinery, closely associated with capital goods and investment, fell by 7 percent from 1980 to 1988, and then fell by one-fourth between 1988 and December 1989 (see table 12, Appendix).

The weak picture for manufacturing in the 1980s did not result from any intrinsic obstacle on the side of productive capacity but from the overall weakness of the economy and of domestic markets. The sector's ability to increase production under better economic conditions was demonstrated by what happened between 1985 and 1987, in the successful first half of the García administration when aggregate demand was stimulated but inflation had not yet gotten out of control; manufacturing output shot up 34 percent between these two years.

The modern manufacturing sector has relied on relatively capital-intensive and import-intensive methods of production, failing to provide much help for employment. Manufacturing value increased from 20 to 22 percent of GDP between 1950 and 1990, but its share of total employment fell from 13 to 10 percent (see table 13, Appendix). Its dependence on imports of current inputs and capital equipment has probably resulted in large measure from the combination of an overvalued currency with high protection against competing imports. Overvaluation holds down the prices of imported equipment and supplies, making them artificially cheap relative to labor and other domestic inputs. Protection adds to the problem by allowing those firms that prefer the most modern possible equipment, even when it is more expensive than domestic alternatives, to pass on any extra costs to captive domestic consumers. In addition, protection saddled industrial firms themselves with high-cost inputs from other domestic firms, raising their costs to levels that have made it extremely difficult for even the most efficient to compete in export markets.

Growth of manufacturing, as of the whole economy, has been held back seriously by the failure so far to achieve any sustained growth of industrial exports. The sector acts as a drag on the possibilities of overall growth by using a great deal more of the country's scarce foreign exchange to import its supplies and equipment than it earns by its exports. This issue is key to future growth. Directing manufacturing production more toward exports would provide a new avenue for growth through sales to world markets and would also help relax the foreign-exchange constraints that so frequently hold back the whole economy.

Mining and Energy

The mining sector, including petroleum, accounted for only 9 percent of GDP in 1988 but nearly half of the country's export earnings. Its share of total exports increased from 45 percent in 1970 to 48 percent in 1988. Copper alone accounted for 24.4 percent of total export earnings in 1970 and 22.5 percent in 1988 (see fig. 9).

Mining developed as an export sector, first for precious metals and then chiefly for nonferrous metals needed by the industrialized countries rather than by non-industrialized Peru. Mining has always been an enclave, only weakly related to the domestic economy for its supplies or for its markets. But it has been a principal provider of the foreign exchange and tax revenue needed to keep the rest of the economy going. That key role made the dominance of foreign ownership, especially in copper and oil, a focus of bitter conflict for many years. The sector became the center of intense debate over dependency, exploitation, and national policy toward foreign investment.

Foreign investment was the main source of mining development up to the 1960s, starting from the turn of the century in copper and extending to a wide range of metals after the highly favorable Mining Code was enacted in 1950. The sector was divided between the largest mines, which produced roughly two-thirds of metal output and were owned by foreign firms, and the small- to medium-size mines, which supplied the other one-third of output and were under Peruvian ownership. Following the Mining Code of 1950, foreign investment flowed into iron ore, lead, zinc, and other minerals, and metals exports grew from 21 percent of total exports in 1951 to over 40 percent a decade later.

When the military overthrew the government of Belaúnde in 1968, the immediate issue was a conflict with IPC, the foreign firm dominating the oil industry. The Velasco regime quickly nationalized IPC and then in the 1970s also nationalized the largest copper mining corporation, Cerro de Pasco. It established the Peruvian State Mining Enterprise (Empresa Minera del Perú—Mineroperú) as the main state firm for development of copper and the Peruvian State Mineral Marketing Company (Mineroperú Comercial—Minpeco) as the new state mining marketing agency.

Output of metal products was erratic in the early 1970s but then took a big jump with completion of a major new copper-mining project, Cuajone, in 1976. By 1980 value added in the sector, at constant prices, was 1.5 times as high as in 1970. But then in the 1980s, value added began to fall, along with practically everything else. By 1988 it was 14 percent below the 1980 level. The decrease could be explained to some degree by the general disorganization of the economy, but more specific problems were caused by increased guerrilla violence interrupting supplies and deliveries, and by prolonged strikes.

Extraction, refining, and domestic marketing of oil were under control of the Petroleum Enterprise of Peru (Petroleos del Perú—Petroperú) from 1968 to 1991. Foreign firms have been allowed to participate in exploration for new fields, although negotiations over their rights often have proved to be difficult. One foreign firm, Belco Petroleum Corporation, maintained offshore production until 1985, when its operations were nationalized after a dispute over taxes with the García government.

Output of oil products increased greatly in the course of the 1970s: its value at constant prices was 2.7 times as high in 1980 as in 1970. But then oil production joined the collective downtrend: it fell sharply between 1980 and 1985 (see table 14, Appendix). Again, both the general disorganization of the economy and the increase in rural violence contributed to the decrease. Additionally controls

on prices of oil products held them far below costs of production in the second half of the 1980s. That fact put Petroperú deeply into deficit and constrained its ability to finance both production and exploration. In 1990 petroleum contributed US$263 million to the value of the country's exports. The major changes introduced by the Fujimori government in 1990–91 included invitations for new investment by foreign oil companies, ending the monopoly position of Petroperú. Several foreign oil companies immediately entered negotiations to begin exploration activities, either independently or in collaboration with Petroperú.

Services

The formally legalized side of the service sector includes both government and private services. Government services, measured by payments for inputs in the absence of any recognized standard of output, have grown remarkably fast. As evaluated in current prices, government services increased from 4 percent of GDP in the decade of the 1950s to 9 percent in 1990.

Among the private service-sector activities, retail and wholesale trade has been the most important, accounting for 13.7 percent of GDP in 1988. Financial and business services were next most important at 8.5 percent of GDP, followed by transport and communications at 7.4 percent. Electricity and water constituted a small share of output in 1988, at 1.3 percent of GDP, but they increased at a very high rate from 1970 to 1988: their output in 1988 was 3.4 times as high as in 1970. Although these formal service-sector activities have, for the most part, shown significant growth even during the difficult 1980s, national accounts indicated that the largest of them—retail and wholesale trade—did not grow at all between 1980 and 1988. But that official measure was not readily credible, given the country's population growth and especially the rapid growth of the urban population. The official measure apparently reflected the fact that a growing share of trade was being carried out by unregistered individuals and firms.

Official statistics on production and employment are always subject to many reservations in Peru, as in all developing countries, but especially so for the service sector. Much of what is going on among these activities is outside the formal framework of the economy and very difficult to measure. In 1990–91 many service activities were legally registered, reported sales and profits for tax purposes, and were in all respects within the formal accounting system of the economy. But many others were unregistered and might not even be known to exist as far as the government's statistics were concerned. That is true in any country for some activities, particularly those that operate against the law. It is also true on a massive scale in Peru for people who are just repairing shoes, making small items in their homes to sell in the streets, or in general trying to survive by activities that are perfectly normal and productive but not registered with the government. Peru has a massive informal sector, which includes more than half the total urban labor force. This sector accounts for a high proportion of personal services and retail sales activities, as well as considerable industrial production.

Exactly when and why these informal-sector activities moved from a marginal to a large share of the economy are open questions. One strongly argued view, associated particularly with the work of Hernando de Soto, author of *El otro sendero (The Other Path)*, is that regulatory activities of government proliferated from the 1960s onward, imposing intolerable costs on private business activities. A slightly different but consistent view is that the rapid growth of the informal sector coincided with increased business taxation, beginning at the end of the 1960s. The two interpretations fit each other, but the former lends itself more to a general argument against government regulation of business, without paying much attention to the fact that the growth of the informal sector means a shrinking tax base for the society.

Both of these analyses surely capture much of the causation behind the growth of the informal sector in Peru, but they may deflect attention from two other explanations that could be more important. One of them concerns the generalized deterioration of the economy and the consequent weak growth of job opportunities in formal-sector employment. With the rapid growth of the labor force, and a high rate of migration to the cities, the number of people looking for work far outpaced the number of formal job openings. The answer for those without regular employment in the formal sector has been to create self-employment activities of their own or to work for relatives in small-scale operations, often on a basis of family sharing rather than regular wage employment. These people do everything from selling coat hangers on sidewalks in the center of the city to putting together computers from discarded spare parts. In this view, the problem is not so much government regulation or excess taxation as it is one of macroeconomic failure of the economy as a whole. The informal sector may be in part a way to avoid regulation, but more fundamentally it is a necessary means of survival, a constructive answer on the individual level to lack of success at the level of the macroeconomy.

Still another interpretation that must be considered centers on the background of the migrants to the cities. They have been native

Americans and mestizos (see Glossary) from rural communities in which ways of earning a living are bound within traditional family and community relationships. Production is carried out on a self-employed or very small-scale basis with a minimum of the kinds of accounting, financial, and legal complications of modern society. The new migrants to the cities look for work and guidance from former migrants and especially relatives from the same communities who are carrying on much the same kinds of activities as they knew at home. They re-create in Lima the kinds of informal activities they have always known. In this view, the informal sector is largely a cultural phenomenon, by no means explicable in purely economic terms.

Succeeding governments have gone back and forth in their treatment of the informal sector, at times trying to crack down on unregistered vendors and their sources of supply, and at other times trying to provide them with information and technical help. The formal business sector might be expected to press for regulation of these activities because the legally registered firms must pay the higher costs of following regulations and paying taxes: competition is not even. But then the formal sector is itself divided. Because some of these firms cut their own costs by subcontracting activities to the informal sector, to some degree they share in the same profit from being outside the law. Everyone recognizes that the informal sector is the source of livelihood for a great many people without alternative opportunities and that helping to make them more productive could yield important gains for them and for Peru. The other side of the coin is that those in this sector pay no attention to the legal system, to health and safety regulations, or to the society's need for a tax base to support necessary public functions.

Banking

In 1987 the García government attempted to nationalize Peru's banks, financial institutions, and insurance companies. Under the legislation, which Congress approved despite a judicial ruling against the government's proposals, the government was to hold 70 percent of shares of nationalized banks, with the remaining 30 percent offered for sale to the public. The legislation excluded foreign banks operating in Peru from the nationalization program but prohibited them from opening any new branches in Peru. This set of proposals stimulated widespread public opposition and provoked a breakdown of cooperation between business leaders and the government. Private investment fell abruptly. García attempted to pursue the nationalization despite all the opposition, but adverse

*Morning rush hour on Avenida de los Héroes in Lima's low-income,
southern district of San Juan de Miraflores
Courtesy Inter-American Development Bank*

judicial rulings slowed implementation and finally killed the proposals.

In early 1991, Peru's financial system included four development banks, twenty-two commercial banks, eight credit firms (*financieras de crédito*), fifteen savings-and-loan mutuals (*mutuales*), twelve municipal savings-and-loans institutions, and the Savings Bank of Lima (Caja de Ahorros de Lima). In May 1991, the Fujimori government introduced a new package of economic measures designed to liberalize the banking system. The government suspended the powers of the Central Reserve Bank (Banco Central de Reservas, or BCR—hereafter Central Bank) to set interest rates and allowed them to float according to market forces. It also stipulated that in the future foreign banks would be able to operate in Peru under the same conditions as Peruvian banks. In addition, it amended the Agrarian Reform Law of 1969 by allowing farmers to put up their land as collateral for bank loans. When it went into effect in June 1991, the new banking law shook up the state banking sector, which employed 20,000 people and included six state-owned banks. The new law eliminated specialized banks, credit firms, and mortgage-lending mutuals, forcing them to reorganize as commercial banks.

Transportation and Communications

Peru's transportation sector has deteriorated seriously since the mid-1970s. In 1990 the national railroad network, managed by the National Railway Enterprise (Empresa Nacional de Ferrocarriles—Enafer), totaled 1,884 kilometers, including 1,584 kilometers of standard gauge and 300 kilometers of narrow gauge track. The national railway network consists of two major systems. The Central Railroad, with approximately 512 kilometers open, runs from Callao to Lima to La Oroya to Huancayo (see fig. 10). The highest railroad in the world, it crosses the central Andes and connects with the Cerro de Pasco Railroad and the narrower gauge Huancayo-Huancavelica Railroad, which runs to the mercury mines at Huancavelica. The second major railway, the Southern Railroad, with 1,073 kilometers open, runs from Mollendo to Arequipa to Juliaca and Puno—crossing the southern Andes and serving as a major link with Bolivia—and from Juliaca proceeds in a northwestern direction to Cusco (Cuzco). In addition, the Southern Peru Copper Corporation operates 219 kilometers of track, including five tunnels totaling 27 kilometers. The García government had planned to electrify the railroad system and extend the Central and Southern railroads, but lack of funds delayed implementation of these plans.

Passenger train service—often more comfortable and quicker than bus service—existed on the following lines: Lima-La Oroya-Huancayo, La Oroya-Cerro de Pasco, Huancayo-Huancavelica, Arequipa-Juliaca-Puno, Puno-Juliaca-Cusco, and Cusco-Machu picchu-Quillabamba. Lima's mass-transit electric train project has proceeded slowly.

A chronic lack of funds for road repair and construction has led to deterioration and, in places, disappearance of Peru's land transport infrastructure. Most of the high Sierra roads were narrow, unsurfaced, and subject to frequent landslides. In 1990 Peru's road system totaled almost 70,000 kilometers, including about 7,500 kilometers of paved roads, 13,500 kilometers of gravel, and 49,000 kilometers of unimproved earth. The most important highways are the paved Pan American Highway (2,495 kilometers), which runs southward from the Ecuadorian border along the coast to Lima and then south to Arequipa and Chile and is relatively well maintained; the Inca Highway (3,193 kilometers), which runs from Piura to Puno; the Jungle Border Highway (*la carretera marginal de la selva* or *la marginal*), which extends 1,688 kilometers from Cajamarca to Madre de Dios Department; and the mostly paved Trans-Andean or Central Highway (834 kilometers), which runs from Lima to Pucallpa on the Río Ucayali via La Oroya, Cerro de Pasco, Huánuco, and Tingo María.

By the mid-1980s, the Peruvian Army (Ejército Peruano—EP) had built 700 kilometers of a planned 2,000 kilometers of roads located mostly in frontier areas. Three of the sixteen road projects planned had been completed, and the thirteen other, longer roads were scheduled for completion in the 1990s. The Fujimori government expected to complete its ambitious US$300 million road-repair program by June 1994, more than a year earlier than it had expected. The program included repairs to 1,400 kilometers of the Pan American Highway and Central Highway and maintenance of 2,000 kilometers of the same roads.

Most shipping is through Lima's port of Callao. There are also seventeen deep-water ports, mainly in northern Peru—including Salaverry, Pacasmayo, and Paita—and in the south, including the iron ore port of San Juan. River ports are located at Borja, Iquitos, Pucallpa, Puerto Maldonado, and Yurimaguas. The government's National Ports Enterprise (Empresa Nacional de Puertos—Enapu) administers all coastal, river, and lake ports. In 1990 Peru's merchant marine totaled twenty-nine ships, including sixteen cargo ships; one refrigerated cargo ship; one roll-on/roll-off cargo ship; three petroleum, oils, and lubricants tankers; and eight bulk cargo ships. In addition, eight naval tankers and one naval cargo ship were sometimes used commercially. Inland waterways totaled 8,600 kilometers of navigable tributaries of the Amazon system and 208 kilometers of Lake Titicaca. Although the Fujimori government did not plan to privatize Enapu, it invited tenders from private operators to run port operations.

Peru had 27 large transport aircraft and 205 useable airports in 1990, 36 of which had permanent-surface runways. Of the 205 airports, there were 2 with runways over 3,659 meters, 24 with runways 2,440 to 3,659 meters, and 42 with runways 1,220 to 2,439 meters. The principal international airport is Jorge Chávez International Airport near Lima. Other international airports are Colonel Francisco Secada Vigneta Airport, near Iquitos; the new Velasco Astete Airport at Quispiquilla, near Cusco; and Rodríguez Ballón Airport, near Arequipa.

The Fujimori government planned to privatize the flag air carrier, the Air Transport Company of Peru (Empresa de Transporte Aéreo del Perú—Aeroperú). Forty percent of Aeroperú was offered in 1991 to a qualified foreign airline, 20 percent to Peruvian investors, and 10 percent to the airline's personnel, with the state holding on to the remaining 30 percent. Aeroperú, which was in a very poor state in 1991, has operated both internal services and international routes to other Latin American countries and the United States. Other domestic airlines with routes to Miami were Airlines of Peru (Aeronaves del Perú) and the Faucett Aviation Company (Compañía de Aviación Faucett). A new domestic airline, Aerochasqui, based in Arequipa, operated flights to and from Lima and elsewhere in Peru.

Peru's telecommunications were fairly adequate for most requirements, although its telephone system was one of the least developed in Latin America. The country had a nationwide radio relay system; 544,000 telephones; 273 AM radio stations; no FM stations; 140 television stations; and 144 shortwave stations. Since 1988 Peru has utilized the Pan American Satellite (PAS-1) and two Atlantic Ocean Intelsat (International Telecommunications Satellite Organization) earth stations, with twelve domestic antennas. In the late 1980s, the government granted the Peruvian Telephone Company (Compañía Peruana de Teléfonos—CPT), serving the Lima-Callao area, permission to offer facsimile, telex, data transmission, international long-distance telephone, and cellular telephone service. However, in November 1991 the Fujimori government eliminated the state's telecommunications monopoly, saying that the CPT and the National Telecommunications Enterprise of Peru (Empresa Nacional de Telecomunicaciones del Perú—Entelperú), responsible for telecommunications outside the Lima-Callao area, had impeded modernization and hurt consumers, especially in rural areas. The government also vowed to promote free competition in providing telecommunications services. It increased the capital of the CPT and Entelperú and offered a 40 percent stake in them to foreign bidders.

Tourism

Lima, with its Spanish colonial architecture, and Cusco, with its impressive stonework of pre-Inca and Inca civilizations, notably at Machupicchu, are the centers of Peru's ailing tourism industry. Lake Titicaca also constitutes a major tourist attraction. However, as a result of terrorism, insurgency, common crime, the 1990–91 cholera epidemic, and the April 1992 coup, tourism has declined drastically since 1988, when Peru received an estimated 320,000 foreign visitors and US$300 million in tourism earnings. One American tourist was murdered in Cusco in early 1990, and several others died in the late 1980s because of sabotage of a train line between Cusco and Machupicchu. Under sharply increased taxes on tourism imposed in 1989 in response to declining numbers of tourists, foreigners have had to pay far more than Peruvians for internal flights and visits to museums and archaeological sites. In 1989 six flights a day shuttled tourists between Cusco and Lima, but by late 1990 there were only two. Tourist arrivals in Peru continued to decline in 1990 and 1991.

According to the National Tourism Board (Cámara Nacional de Turismo—Canatur), tourism in the first half of 1992 was down 30 percent from the first semester of 1991, which, in turn, fell 70 percent from 1988, tourism's record year. A major blow to Lima's hotel business was the SL's car bomb attack in the exclusive Miraflores district on July 16, 1992, in which six major hotels suffered over US$1 million in damages. The number of tourists visiting Cusco and Machupicchu had dropped 76 percent since 1988.

Foreign Trade and the Balance of Payments

Foreign trade has always been a crucial factor in Peruvian economic growth, sometimes as a major stimulus and sometimes more as a source of disruptive shocks. Falling external demand can set the whole economy back quickly, and at all times import competition can constrain the development of domestic industries. Many Peruvians believe that the society would be healthier and the economy more dynamic if foreign trade were tightly restricted. Many others favor taking maximum advantage of the opportunities opened up by external trade, even if the structure of production were pulled toward export specialization at the cost of greater diversification and industrialization.

165

Export and Import Structures

Peru's exports and imports have been so volatile, owing both to external fluctuations and to internal problems, that it is hard to define what could be considered normal structures of trade. Measured in terms of dollars, exports rose greatly from 1970 to 1980, from US$1.0 billion to US$3.9 billion, but they then fell back to US$2.5 billion by 1986. Imports were less than exports in 1970, at US$700 million, but tripled in the next five years as a result of the heavy spending of the military government in that period. Imports were pulled back to US$1.7 billion by 1978, then jumped to US$3.8 billion in 1981 as the Belaúnde government both liberalized imports and increased its own spending. At the end of the decade, in 1989, the collapse of domestic economic activity pulled imports back down to US$2.0 billion, exactly where they had been a decade earlier. Because the same collapse of domestic sales encouraged increased attempts to export, Peru finished the decade with a record trade surplus of US$1.6 billion. The surplus was not so much an achievement as it was the result of failure to maintain economic growth (see table 15, Appendix).

In a comparison of exports of goods and services to GDP, the country's export ratio was 16 percent in 1965 but fell to 10 percent by 1988. Imports of goods and services were 19 percent of GDP in 1965 and 14 percent in 1988, giving the country a net resource inflow equal to 3 percent of GDP in the earlier year and 4 percent in 1988.

Taking 1988 as something close to a representative year (to avoid the particularly strained conditions of 1989 and 1990), exports of goods included US$1.4 billion worth of traditional products and US$0.8 billion of more diversified nontraditional products. Both of these values were, unhappily, below their levels as of 1980 (see table 16, Appendix). Metals and petroleum were by far the most important products. The principal metal products accounted for 50.6 percent of total commodity export earnings, with petroleum and its derivatives adding 8 percent. Copper stood out, as it has for many years, accounting for 22.3 percent of earnings in 1990, down slightly from more than 24 percent in 1970. Zinc exports climbed rapidly between these twenty years, reaching 12.6 percent of the total in 1990. A comparison of 1970 and 1990 somewhat misleadingly suggests strong growth for petroleum exports, from a negligible level in 1970 to 8 percent of total exports in 1990. This suggestion is misleading because oil exports actually reached their peak in 1980, at US$792 million and 20 percent of total exports. By 1990 their value had fallen, at much lower prices, to US$263 million.

Trucks passing a construction area on the northern coast-to-jungle Olmos-Corral Quemado road
Courtesy Inter-American Development Bank

Agricultural exports were much lower than those from the mining sector, but the four major products—coffee, cotton, fish meal, and sugar—added up to 19 percent of total exports in 1988. They did not show much growth between 1970 and 1988, rising only from US$462 to US$523 million over this eighteen-year period.

Peru's future growth prospects depend crucially on the ability to develop new exports, preferably manufacturing exports and more diversified, higher-value, primary products to supplement the traditional products. Manufacturing exports are free of the built-in limits of production imposed by dependence on exhaustible natural resources, and their markets are usually more stable than those for primary products. For Peruvian industrialists who have limited their focus mainly to protected domestic markets, manufactured goods offer both a competitive stimulus and important learning opportunities. If more Peruvian manufacturers enter export markets successfully, the prospects for growth of productivity and of entrepreneurial capacity could greatly improve.

Peruvian industrial firms seemed to be starting this important transition in the 1960–80 period, but then the new trend went into reverse. Exports of manufactured goods were US$743 million in 1980, but by 1987 they had fallen to US$540 million. In 1987 the manufacturing sector's imports of inputs for production and of capital equipment were nearly triple its exports.

The manufacturing sector's failure so far to raise exports even close to the level of its own imports is a crucial problem for Peru. The problem could in theory be resolved by changing two aspects of national economic policy that have worked powerfully to hold back industrial exports. One of the two key obstacles has been the high rate of effective protection for industrial products. High protection increases the profitability of selling to the home market rather than exporting and also makes it difficult to compete abroad because it raises the prices of inputs for Peruvian firms above the international prices available to competitors in other countries. Peruvian protection was greatly raised in the 1960s and then again, after temporary reductions, in the second half of the 1980s. As discussed below, the Fujimori government went back the other way: it simplified the tariff structure and made significant reductions for the products with the highest rates of protection. These changes should help to release constraints on manufacturing exports, but the likely results depend on the other key policy variable concerned, the exchange rate.

The second policy adverse to exports has been chronic overvaluation of the currency. With the Peruvian currency overvalued, the domestic currency equivalent of foreign-exchange earnings by exporters is held down; for most producers, exports become simply unprofitable. The currency has clearly been overvalued in the great majority of years since 1960, and especially so at the end of the 1980s. The degree of overvaluation was relatively low as of 1980, but the real exchange rate (see Glossary) fell nearly 50 percent from 1980 to 1989. Although there is room for a great deal of debate about how rapidly exports of manufactures could grow in response to a rising real exchange rate, there is no doubt that a falling rate can kill them off.

Imports are also responsive to changes in exchange rates, although they are more strongly affected by changes in the levels of domestic demand and economic activity, and in some periods by changes in degrees of import restriction. Domestic economic activity has a particularly direct effect because most imports consist of current inputs for production and capital equipment. The structure of imports in 1988 was fairly representative in this respect. Imports of consumer goods were only 10 percent of the total, reflecting the high import barriers in effect for them. Imports of current inputs for production of the private sector were 34 percent of the total, and similar imports by the public sector were equal to 23 percent of the total. Imports of machinery and equipment by the private sector were 23 percent and those by the public sector, 2 percent.

Imports of consumer goods became temporarily more important when the Belaúnde government relaxed restrictions on them in the early 1980s. Consumer goods imported by the private sector more than tripled between 1979 and 1982, increasing from 5 percent to 11 percent of a rapidly rising import total. But the trade deficit went up so swiftly in this period that restrictions were quickly restored. The experience led many Peruvians to conclude that the country could not afford to allow anything like free access to imports. An alternative view, apparently shared by the Fujimori government, is that the trade deficit resulted more from excess spending than from the reduction of restrictions, and that a more comprehensive and sustained opening of the economy could do a great deal to foster more competitive Peruvian industries.

Following this brief experiment with more open trade in the early 1980s, Peru returned to its preceding regime of high tariffs and multiple forms of direct import restriction. At the end of the García government, in June 1990, the average tariff rate was 66 percent. A more significant measure for the industrial sector is the rate of effective protection (see Glossary) for its products. As of July 1990, effective protection for the industrial sector averaged 82 percent. Individual industries had widely different levels of effective protection, ranging up to 130 percent for clothing. And in addition to such protection through tariffs, twenty different regulations authorized direct restrictions to prohibit or to apply quota limits to many products.

The Fujimori government introduced a revolution in trade policy in September 1990 and carried it still further with new changes in March 1991. All direct quantitative restrictions on imports were eliminated. The rate of effective protection for industry was cut from 83 percent to 44 percent in September and to 24 percent in March. The wildly dispersed tariff rates previously in effect were consolidated at three much lower levels: 15 percent for inputs into production, 20 percent for capital goods, and 25 percent for consumer goods.

Policies with respect to protection and exchange rates can make a great deal of difference to the evolution of exports and imports, and to the economy as a whole, but that is not to deny the independent importance of fluctuations in external demand and prices. A worldwide industrial boom invariably works to raise prices of metals and to create an export boom for Peru, just as a worldwide contraction acts to set it back. Peru's terms of trade (see Glossary) have always been highly volatile. Using 1978 as a base year equal to 100, the terms of trade index went as high as 150 and as low as 86 in the course of the 1970s (the higher the index, the better are the terms of trade for a given country). The index reached 153 in 1980 and then plunged to 66 in 1986, cutting more than half the purchasing power of a given volume of exports. The terms of trade then began a modest rise, to an index of 77 by 1989. These swings in relative prices apply above all to Peru's primary exports, especially metals. Their impacts on the Peruvian economy could be moderated considerably if the country manages to move toward an export structure based more on manufactured goods and less on primary exports.

Economic Implications of Coca

Production and exports of coca and its derivatives have many different effects on the Peruvian economy, all of them difficult to quantify because basic information cannot be checked in any dependable way. On the positive side, coca adds to the incomes of otherwise extremely poor peasant producers and also adds foreign exchange earnings that, at least in part, flow through to the legal economy and help finance imports. On the negative side, coca pulls human effort and land into production at the expense of possible alternative food production; holds down the price of foreign currency and therefore the incentives for legal exports; causes ecological damage from the chemical residues used to process cocaine; increases violence and the costs to the society of trying to restrain it; and aggravates corruption in the military, police, and civilian government. If coca production were to fall back to traditional levels of consumption by Andean peasants themselves, many Peruvians would lose income; if it continued at 1990–91 levels or grew, the society as a whole would be the poorer in terms of competitive strength in legal markets and in terms of civil order.

Neither Peru's national accounts nor its export data include any estimates for the value of coca leaf and its derivatives. A private statistical service, Cuánto S.A., estimates that income from coca added 7 percent to the officially calculated value of GDP in 1979 and 4 percent in 1989. Estimated drug exports averaged US$1.4 billion in the years 1979–82 and US$1.6 billion in 1986–89. Without counting coca, commodity exports in 1989 were US$3.7 billion. Counting coca, they were US$5.6 billion.

Considering the agricultural sector separately, these estimates suggest a strong impact, raising value added by about 11 percent as of 1989. That extra income goes in unknown proportions to dealers and processors (mostly Colombians); to third parties providing protection, including the Shining Path; and to peasant

Market day near Puno
Courtesy World Bank (Ramón Cerra)

producers. Even though the share going to peasant producers may
not be high, their incomes from coca can be more than seven times
as high per hectare of land than could be earned in the next most
profitable (legal) crop, coffee. Growers in the main producing
region, the Upper Huallaga Valley, are estimated to earn about
US$4,500 per year for each hectare in coca, compared with about
US$600 in coffee. Such differentials are mainly a matter of the high
market value of coca, but they also reflect the fact that this particular region of Peru is singularly well adapted to growth of coca
and poorly suited to most alternative crops. Coca would be an ideal
crop here, with low opportunity costs, if it were not for all its negative human and economic implications.

Government policies to restrain coca production and marketing
have been more in the realm of police and military action than that
of economics. One of the most appealing proposals within the range
of economic policies has been to promote alternative crops through
credit and technical assistance plus guaranteed purchasing at favorable prices. The two main drawbacks to developing such a program
have been the government's own lack of financial resources and
the enormous differentials between earnings from coca and those
possible from alternatives. The approach would have much more
of a chance for success if cocaine demand in the United States could

be reduced significantly, allowing the value of coca to fall. Absent such a change on the demand side, economic incentives in Peru work powerfully to keep up supply.

Balance of Payments and External Debt

Peru's balance of payments has been an almost constant problem since the early 1970s, or rather two kinds of problems alternating with each other. The most frequent difficulty is that the deficit on current account—the deficit for current trade and services—has increased too fast to be financed by feasible borrowing abroad. This situation is the common meaning of a "foreign-exchange crisis," and it has been a recurring problem in Peru. The opposite kind of difficulty is that it has been too easy to borrow abroad in some periods in which fiscal restraint plus currency devaluation might have served both to improve the current account and promote steadier growth. In certain periods, especially 1972–75 and 1980–83, the government has been able to borrow so much abroad that the plentiful supply of foreign exchange has reduced pressures to take such corrective action. External credit can be so tight that its scarcity cripples production or so abundant that it encourages waste and discourages desirable policy change.

Peru's current-account deficits and external borrowing to finance them were safely low fractions of GDP for the 1960s as a whole. For both 1971 and 1972, the deficits were barely 1 percent of GDP. But in the next several years, the rising fiscal deficits of the military government spilled over into generalized excess demand and the highest current-account deficits Peru had ever known. The deficit in 1975, at over US$1.5 billion, far exceeded the previous peak of US$282 million in 1967. It was equal to a record 10 percent of GDP. Peru's external debt correspondingly rose well beyond any level known before, pointing the way to the rocky road ahead.

The deep deficits on current account in 1974 and 1975 and their financing were examples of the second kind of problem mentioned earlier. Peru had fallen into rising fiscal deficits and currency overvaluation, but pressures to take corrective action were forestalled because the government could borrow readily abroad and avoid changing its policies. By 1975 the disequilibrium was so great that foreign creditors began to back off, creating a foreign-exchange crisis that forced the government to take corrective action. Fiscal and monetary restraints and devaluation were finally adopted. These measures plus good luck with export prices gradually cut down the external deficits and achieved a significant surplus on current account by 1979.

The new civilian government of President Belaúnde started in 1980 with a very small external deficit and promptly turned it into a very large one. Rapidly rising spending plus temporary import liberalization raised the current-account deficit from US$101 million in 1980 to over US$1.7 billion in 1981. Once again, the government's ability to borrow abroad, restored by the austerity of the late 1970s, proved to be costly to the country by permitting continued excess spending and currency overvaluation.

The Belaúnde administration was forced to adopt more restrained spending policies in its later years, slowing the economy but bringing the current-account deficit down again. It left the García government with a small surplus by 1985. Then the seemingly inexorable cycle went right back into action: the García government plunged into an expansion program that temporarily revived the economy but raised demand too fast for external balance. The surplus of 1985 was replaced by deficits in the range of US$1 billion to US$1.5 billion from 1986 through 1988. In 1989 the combination of internal disruption and a brief attempt to restrain demand brought down production and imports so sharply that the current account moved back into surplus. The surplus clearly reflected a severe setback to the economy, rather than an achievement based on macroeconomic balance and rising exports.

The external borrowing in these repeated periods of high current-account deficits naturally created a high level of external debt. External borrowing is normal for a developing country and can help increase the rate of economic growth by providing additional resources for investment. But the crucial questions concern degrees of borrowing and the country's ability to finance debt service out of its gains in productive capacity. In the periods described, Peru borrowed very heavily and was unable to make much headway in its capacity to finance imports plus debt service out of its export earnings. That combination led to major arrears in making scheduled debt-service payments.

Total long-term debt of the public and private sectors combined was estimated by the World Bank (see Glossary) at US$2.7 billion at the end of 1970 and US$13.9 billion at the end of 1988. At the latter level, it was equal to 56 percent of GDP. Peruvian estimates, including short-term debt as well, show totals of US$18.1 billion for 1988 and US$19.8 billion for 1989. The great increase in long-term debt between 1970 and 1988 resulted almost entirely from borrowing by the public sector. The public sector's long-term debt was equal to 12 percent of GDP in 1970 but 50 percent of GDP by 1988.

Actual payments of debt service have not been high proportions of exports or of GDP because both the Belaúnde government in its last years and the García government stopped trying to keep up with scheduled payments. Debt service had run at 2 percent of GDP and 12 percent of exports in 1970, when payments were being made on schedule, but they were only 1 percent of GDP and 8 percent of exports despite the much larger debt in 1988. Using the average rate of interest on Peruvian public debt in 1988 (7.6 percent), interest payments due would have been US$948 million; actual interest payments were US$164 million.

The Belaúnde government let scheduled debt payments slide by as quietly as possible. But President García converted the problem into a worldwide challenge to the creditor countries. In his inaugural address of July 1985, he declared that his obligations to the welfare of Peru came ahead of financial obligations to foreign creditors and announced that Peru would not allocate more than 10 percent of its export earnings to debt service. The International Monetary Fund (IMF—see Glossary) and the World Bank continued for some time to encourage multilateral negotiations instead of this unilateral limit, but when García persisted the IMF declared Peru to be ineligible for new credit.

The Fujimori government emphatically rejected García's position and requested renewed negotiations with external creditors. The government's willingness to negotiate and its accompanying programs of economic reform led the international financial agencies to resume discussions. Although the United States-led Support Group (Grupo de Apoyo) of nations failed to come up with the US$1.3 billion that Peru needed to clear its arrears with multilaterals, the IMF nevertheless decided in September 1991 to lend Peru the money to clear its arrears and then start new adjustment lending. This crucial step toward more normal relationships with the international financial and development agencies was once more put into question in April 1992, when the Fujimori government suspended democracy in Peru and the international agencies responded by suspending negotiations on external credit.

Employment and Wages, Poverty, and Income Distribution

In the first post-World War II decades, the economy was able to absorb the growing urban labor force fairly well, allowing real wages to rise and probably achieving some reduction in poverty. But from the early 1970s to the early 1990s, change has been downhill in such respects, with falling real wages, increasing poverty, and worsening indices of underemployment.

At a bus stop in downtown Lima
Courtesy Inter-American Development Bank

Employment

The Peruvian labor force increased from 3.1 million workers in 1960 to 5.6 million by 1980, and to 7.6 million by 1990. As it did so, the share of the labor force in agriculture steadily decreased, but the shares in manufacturing and mining failed to rise (see fig. 11). On balance, the decreases in the agricultural share had to be offset by increases in the share in service activities, some of them offering productive employment at above-poverty income levels but many of them not (see table 17, Appendix).

Peru's long process of transition away from a rural society was far from complete at the beginning of the post-World War II period. Fifty-nine percent of the labor force was still working in agriculture in 1950. That share fell to barely over half by 1960 and to 34 percent by 1990. The more surprising trend is that the share of the labor force in manufacturing also fell, from 13 percent in 1950 to 10 percent by 1990. Stable shares in both construction and mining meant that the shift out of agriculture went mainly toward services, pulling their share of employment up from 23 percent in 1950 to 50 percent by 1990.

The persistent decrease in the share of the labor force in agriculture could in theory have helped to alleviate rural poverty by leaving higher average land holdings to those remaining in agriculture.

175

But the absolute number of people trying to make a living from inadequate land holdings actually increased. The labor force in agriculture rose 52 percent between 1960 and 1990. In addition, emigration from agriculture exerted increasing pressure on labor markets in the cities, and the increase in rural workers kept earnings low in that sector.

A growing labor force need not drive wages down and in most instances does not, provided that investment and technical change keep opening up new opportunities for productive employment fast enough to absorb the larger number of workers. Peru managed to accomplish such growth in the first post-World War II decades, but from the early 1970s the trend went downward. As more and more workers tried to survive in the service sector by self-employment or work with families instead of formally registered firms, they created a rapidly growing informal sector. Workers in the informal sector are mostly employed, and they certainly add to national income, but their earnings are often below the poverty line.

Overt unemployment that can actually be counted has been only a small part of the problem. The overt unemployment level in Lima was an estimated 7 percent in 1980, rising to 8 percent by 1990. But estimates of underemployment in part-time or very low-income activities indicate that 26 percent of Lima's labor force was in this category in 1980, and fully 86 percent in 1990. Such measures are invariably somewhat arbitrary, depending on how underemployment is defined and measured. However, the fact that the share of Lima's labor force fitting the definition more than tripled between 1980 and 1990 is readily understandable in the light of the deterioration of the economy in the 1980s.

Wages

Real wages in Peru rose when the economy was advancing in the 1950s and 1960s but then began to go down persistently. From 1956 to 1972, average wages in manufacturing increased at an annual rate of 4.1 percent. But then from 1972 to 1980, they went back down at the rate of 3.6 percent a year, and from 1980 to 1989 they went further down at the rate of 5.2 percent a year. Although comparisons of real wage levels over long periods are inherently uncertain, given many changes in the structures of wages and prices, it seems evident that real wages in Peruvian manufacturing were much lower in 1989 than they had been a third of a century earlier.

Even in comparison with the sharp fall in manufacturing real wages during the 1980s, the concurrent plunge in real minimum wages for urban workers was appalling. While the average for manufacturing fell 58 percent from 1980 to 1989, the real minimum wage fell 77 percent; the purchasing power of the minimum wage in 1989 was less than one-fourth its level in 1980.

The minimum wage applies to legally employed workers in the formal sector. The much larger number of workers in the informal sector, not covered by the minimum wage, also lost purchasing power in the course of the 1980s but apparently not as drastically. An index of real earnings in the informal sector shows a decrease of 28 percent between December 1980 and December 1989. That index also shows extreme volatility. Real earnings rose steeply between December 1980 and December 1987, almost doubling in this period, and then plunged to a level far below the starting point.

Organized Labor

In labor markets as weak as those of Peru from the early 1970s onward, organized labor has not normally had any great bargaining power. It could affect the political balance, but it has not been able to do much to keep real earnings from falling when the economy declined. Peruvian labor has never been more than moderately organized in any case: unionization did not take off significantly until the political climate changed with the reformist military government of 1968. Labor has played a more active political role since that time, but has not so far been able to prevent deterioration of real wages (see Labor Unions, ch. 4).

Organized labor in Peru got off to a slow start in the interwar period (1919-40), compared with active unionism in Argentina, Chile, and Venezuela. Still, the textile workers, in the one sizable industry of the time, managed to defy the government and win a famous strike in 1919. They gave the credit to a student activist who stepped in to lead them and negotiated an impressive victory. The activist, Víctor Raúl Haya de la Torre, went on at the beginning of the 1930s to found the American Popular Revolutionary Alliance (Alianza Popular Revolucionaria Americana—APRA), the country's first mass-based political party. Haya de la Torre simultaneously promoted organization of labor through the Confederation of Peruvian Workers (Confederación de Trabajadores del Perú—CTP) and consolidated a close partnership between APRA and the CTP. The CTP was the dominant voice of labor until Haya de la Torre allied himself with the conservative side of the political spectrum during the 1960s. That move to the right then stimulated the growth of a rival Communist-led labor federation, the General Confederation of Peruvian Workers (Confederación General de Trabajadores del Perú—CGTP).

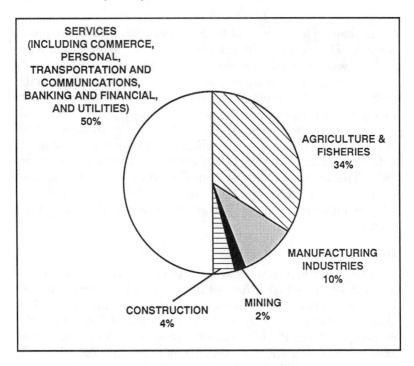

SERVICES
(INCLUDING COMMERCE,
PERSONAL,
TRANSPORTATION AND
COMMUNICATIONS,
BANKING AND FINANCIAL,
AND UTILITIES)
50%

AGRICULTURE &
FISHERIES
34%

MANUFACTURING
INDUSTRIES
10%

MINING
2%

CONSTRUCTION
4%

Source: Based on information from Richard Webb and Graciela Fernández Baca (eds.),
Perú en números, 1990, Lima, 1990, 303.

Figure 11. Employment by Sector, 1990

Neither APRA nor the labor movement made much headway under the conservative governments in office up to the 1960s. But after the reformist military government took power in 1968, unionization spread rapidly. More new unions were given legal recognition from 1968 to 1978 than in all prior Peruvian history: there were 2,152 recognized unions in 1968 and 4,500 by 1978. The new unions, less tied to APRA, began to strike out more on their own to undertake joint negotiations and demonstrations with community groups of all kinds. The military government began to regard unions less as allies and more as sources of opposition, and in fact labor became a center of resistance to military authority all through the 1970s.

Although the Velasco government was committed in many respects to support of popular organizations, its relationships with organized labor turned into conflicts in two fundamental ways. One was purely economic; the government was initially determined to prove its ability to avoid inflation, which it identified as evidence of the inherent weakness of civilian governments. Increase in wages was seen as a threat to control of inflation, and wages in general were considered a matter to be decided by government rather than unions.

The second and more general source of conflict was that the Velasco government had a strongly corporatist (see Glossary) conception of social order, in which labor unions had their place but had no business trying to change it. The government was deeply opposed to theories of class conflict. Labor and capital alike were expected to recognize that their interests had to be reconciled for the good of the society as a whole. The military welcomed and sponsored public organizations but distrusted any signs of excessive autonomy.

Once in open conflict with the two main labor confederations, the government tried to undercut them by creating a new one, the Federation of Workers of the Peruvian Revolution (Central de Trabajadores de la Revolución Peruana—CTRP; see Labor Unions, ch. 4). The new confederation received government help in getting favorable wage settlements and added to the scope of labor organization but had little effect in actually weakening the more independent unions.

In the economic contraction following 1975, labor played a more active role of social protest than ever before. The first general strike in the country's history, in July 1977, seemed to herald a new epoch in labor relations in Peru. Labor's support for left-oriented parties, no longer so predominantly for APRA, became evident in the elections of 1980. In terms of wage trends, the more active role of organized labor has not seemed to make much difference. Organized labor certainly did not stop the devastating fall of real wages in the 1980s. Still, average wages for workers under collective bargaining contracts have been much higher than those for workers without them. As of December 1986, the average wage for those with contracts was 2.2 times that of workers without them. That ratio fell to 1.7 by December 1989, as everyone's real wages plunged.

Poverty

Whether poverty is measured in terms of family income or in terms of social indicators, such as child mortality, it has been greater in Peru than would be expected on the basis of the country's average income per capita. Historically, this situation has been an expression of the country's exceptionally high degree of inequality. More recently, especially in the course of the 1980s, it increased even more than in the other major Latin American countries, chiefly because of the drastic deterioration of the economy's overall performance.

Measures of poverty based on family income are, of course, dependent on the particular income level chosen as a dividing line between the poor and the non-poor. Both the Economic Commission for Latin America and the Caribbean (ECLAC—see Glossary) and the World Bank draw two lines—one for a tightly restricted income level to define extreme poverty, or destitution, and a second cutoff for poverty in a less extreme sense. Destitution refers to income so low that it could not provide adequate nutrition even if it were spent entirely on food. Poverty in the less extreme sense takes as given the proportion of income spent on food in each society and compares that proportion to the level needed for adequate nutrition.

A comprehensive analysis of poverty in Latin America for 1970 concluded that fully 50 percent of Peruvian families were below the poverty line and 25 percent were below the destitution level. These proportions were both higher than Latin America's corresponding averages—40 percent in poverty and 19 percent in destitution. In Peru, as in the rest of Latin America, the incidence of poverty and destitution was much higher for rural than for urban families. Fully 68 percent of rural families were below the poverty line, compared with 28 percent of urban families.

A more recent ECLAC study provides new estimates of the incidence of poverty for 1980 and 1986. For Latin America, the share of families in poverty fell from 40 percent in 1970 to 35 percent in 1980 but then rose to 37 percent in the more difficult conditions of 1986. For Peru, the incidence of poverty also fell from 50 percent in 1970 to 46 percent in 1980, but then it increased to 52 percent by 1986, rising faster than the rest of the region.

As in 1970, the incidence of poverty and destitution in 1986 remained higher for rural than for urban families, but the differences had lessened. In 1970 the incidence of poverty for rural families was 2.4 times that for urban families; in 1986 the ratio was only 1.4 times. The proportion of rural families in poverty actually fell, from 68 percent to 64 percent, while that of urban families rose greatly, from 28 percent to 45 percent.

Cuánto S.A. has developed an ongoing monthly indicator of extreme poverty in Peru, combining measures of earnings by workers paid the minimum wage with earnings in the informal urban sector and in agriculture. Taking January 1985 as the starting point, this index shows a substantial fall in extreme poverty up to December 1987, in the first years of the García government's expansion. But then it shows a dramatic increase as the economy went rapidly downhill. At the end of the García administration, in June

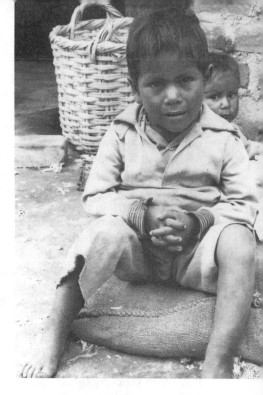

Children in La Molina,
a town south of Lima
Courtesy Inter-American
Development Bank

1990, the index was 91 percent higher than in December 1987 and
32 percent higher than its starting point in January 1985.

Income Distribution

The distribution of income in Peru has been exceptionally unequal for a long time, but by some measures the degree of inequality
apparently decreased between 1970 and 1985 (see table 18, Appendix). The main causes of inequality have changed as well, in
some ways for the better and in some for the worse.

In the pre-World War II years, the dominant causes of inequality were a very high concentration of ownership of land and access
to capital and to education, along with a sociopolitical structure
that condemned the indigenous rural population to bare subsistence with little chance of mobility. In the post-World War II period,
especially since the 1960s, access to education gradually has spread
to rural areas, and increased migration to the cities has opened
up new opportunities for people previously blocked in poverty-
stricken rural occupations. The Agrarian Reform Law of 1969
wiped out large private land holdings and led in the 1980s to a vastly
less unequal distribution of individual ownership (see the Velasco
Government, this ch.). The rise of production and export of coca
probably also played a role in raising rural incomes in the 1980s.

More positively, if only for a brief period from 1985 to 1987,
the agrarian policies of the García government helped stimulate

181

agricultural markets and production, and controls on prices in the industrial sector served to raise greatly the ratio of agricultural to industrial prices. As has been noted, the proportion of the rural population below the poverty line fell from 68 percent in 1970 to 64 percent by 1986, while that for urban families was rising from 28 percent to 45 percent. The positive change for rural families was small, and the negative change for urban families was large, but because urban poverty was initially less the degree of inequality between the rural and urban sectors decreased.

Other changes in the post-World War II years worked in the opposite direction, toward greater inequality. The turn to industrial protection raised profits of industrialists relative to other forms of income and also raised the prices of their products relative to those of the agricultural sector. Wages for organized workers in manufacturing rose relative to wages of lower-income rural and unorganized labor, as well. The pressure of a rapidly growing labor force against the society's limited openings for productive employment acted in general to keep downward pressure on labor income relative to property income. That imbalance worsened in the 1980s when the chaotic conditions of the economy as a whole made employment conditions more difficult.

During the period of exceptional economic growth from 1961 to 1972, the incomes of the poorest 60 percent of Peruvian families increased at a rate of 2.3 percent a year, just matching the rate of growth of national income. As growth weakened from the mid-1970s, both average real wages and minimum real wages began a prolonged decline, and total wages fell relative to incomes of property owners. But earnings of the lowest income groups in agriculture went up, slightly reducing the percentage of rural families falling below the poverty line. A World Bank study concludes that these changes reduced the degree of inequality between 1972 and 1985: the share of the poorest 60 percent increased from 18 to 27 percent of total income.

An alternative measure of inequality, the Gini index, shows a similar improvement. The higher the coefficient, the higher the degree of inequality. In the early 1960s and again in the early 1970s, Peru had either the highest or the second highest Gini coefficient for all the Latin American countries measured, at 0.61 for 1961 and 0.59 for 1972. By 1985 it had come down to 0.47, far below Brazil and only slightly higher than Colombia. These countries all have high inequality by world standards, but in 1985 Peru no longer stood out as the worst.

The latest estimate available, for 1988, suggests that inequality had increased slightly compared with 1985, with the Gini coefficient rising from 0.47 to 0.50. Although not a drastic change in itself, its connotations are worsened by the simultaneous rise in poverty. The latter may well be considered to be the more important matter: it would not mean much to reduce inequality if that just meant more equal sharing of greater poverty. The one clearly positive combination of indicators is that for the period 1980-85 the incidence of poverty fell, if only slightly, for the rural households who have always constituted the majority of Peru's poor.

Economic Policies and Their Consequences

Peru's long reliance on a relatively open economy allowed the country to reach a level of income per capita above the average for Latin America at the start of the 1960s but with exceptionally high degrees of poverty and inequality. Its open economy also left the country behind the leading countries of the region in terms of development of entrepreneurship and technology, as well as capacity of the public sector for effective policy implementation. Popular dissatisfaction and pressures for change had objective reasons behind them.

The military government of General Velasco changed the scene completely with its radical reforms of 1968-72. Peru has never been the same since. But the changes did not lead to any sustainable new economic strategy: the old balance was destroyed, but no viable new one was created to replace it. All the governments since Velasco have been trying to find new solutions by reversing their predecessors' policies, so far without notable success.

The Velasco Government

The economic strategy of the Velasco government was shaped by a concept frequently advocated in Latin America but rarely put into practice. The idea was to find a "third way" between capitalism and socialism, with a corporatist society much more inclusionary than that possible under capitalism but without rejecting private ownership or adopting any of the compulsory methods identified with communism. Under this strategy, land reform was designed to override existing property interests in order to establish cooperative ownership, rejecting both individual private farming and state farms. Promoting worker participation in ownership and management was intended to reshape labor relations. Foreign influences were reduced through tight restrictions on foreign investment and nationalization of some of the largest foreign firms. On a more fundamental plane, the Velasco government saw its mission as one of eliminating class conflict and reconciling differences among interest groups within its own vision of a cooperative society.

Land Reform

The most striking and thorough reform imposed by the Velasco government was to eliminate all large private landholdings, converting most of them into cooperatives owned by prior workers on the estates. The reform was intended to destroy the basis of power of Peru's traditional elite and to foster a more cooperative society as an alternative to capitalism. Such social-political purposes apparently dominated questions of agricultural production or any planned changes in patterns of land use. It was as if the questions of ownership were what mattered, not the consequences for output or rural incomes. In fact, the government soon created a system of price controls and monopoly food buying by state firms designed to hold down prices to urban consumers, no matter what the cost to rural producers.

As mentioned earlier, the cooperatives had very mixed success; and the majority were converted into individual private holdings during the 1980s. The conversions were authorized in 1980 by changes in the basic land-reform legislation and were put into effect after majority votes of the cooperative members in each case. The preferences of the people involved at that point clearly went contrary to the intent of the original reform. But the whole set of changes was not a reversion to the prereform agrarian structure. In fact, the conversions left Peru with a far less unequal pattern of landownership than it had prior to the reform and with a much greater role for family farming than ever before in its history.

Labor and Capital in the Industrial Sector

In line with its basic conception of social order, the military government also created a complex system of "industrial communities." Under this system, firms in the modern sector were required to distribute part of their profits to workers in the form of dividends constituting ownership shares. The intent was to convert workers into property owners and property ownership into a form of sharing for the sake of class reconciliation. But in practice, the system never functioned well. The firms did all they could to avoid reporting profits in order to postpone sharing ownership, sometimes by setting up companies outside the system to which they channeled profits, sometimes by adjusting the books, and in general by keeping one step ahead of intended regulations. A small fraction of the industrial workers gained shares in firms, but as a rule workers were not so much interested in long-term claims of ownership as they were in immediate working conditions and earnings. For organized labor, the whole approach seemed an

Harvesting hay near Huancayo, Junín Department
Courtesy International Labor Organization

attempt to subvert any role for union action and to make organization irrelevant. The system was not popular with either side. It was quickly abandoned when the more conservative wing of the military took power away from General Velasco in 1975.

Attempted reform of labor relations in the mid-1970s also included severe restrictions on rights to discharge workers once they passed a brief trial period of employment. A review process set up to examine disputes was implemented in a way that made discharges practically impossible. Businesspeople circumvented the restrictions to some degree by hiring workers on a temporary basis up to the point at which they would have to be kept and then letting them go before the restrictions applied. Businesspeople remained unremittingly hostile to this type of regulation, primarily on the grounds that it took away their main means of exercising discipline over their workers. This form of regulation was also eliminated shortly after Velasco lost power.

Protection and Promotion of Industry

Along with the intention of resolving internal class conflict, the Velasco government determined to lessen Peru's dependency on the outside world. The two most important components of the strategy were a drive to promote rapid industrialization and an attack on the role of foreign firms. In contrast to the industrialization strategies of most other Latin American countries, the intention of the Velasco regime was to industrialize without welcoming foreign investment.

The preceding Belaúnde administration had started Peru on the path of protection to promote industry, and in this respect the Velasco government reinforced rather than reversed the existing strategy. Beyond the usual recourse to high tariffs, Velasco's government adopted the Industrial Community Law of 1970 that gave any industrialist on the register of manufacturers the right to demand prohibition of any imports competing with his products. No questions of exceptionally high costs of production, poor product quality, or monopolistic positions fostered by excluding import competition were allowed to get in the way. Before the succeeding government of General Francisco Morales Bermúdez Cerrutti (1975–80) began to clean up the battery of protective exclusions in 1978, the average tariff rate reached 66 percent, accompanied by quantitative restrictions on 2,890 specific tariff positions.

In addition to the protective measures, the Velasco government promoted industrial investment by granting major tax exemptions, as well as tariff exemptions on imports used by manufacturers in production. The fiscal benefits given industrialists through these measures equaled 92 percent of total internal financing of industrial investment in the years 1971 through 1975.

Investment rose strongly in response to these measures, as well as to the concurrent rise in aggregate demand. But the tax exemptions also contributed to a rising public-sector deficit and thereby to the beginning of serious inflationary pressure. In addition, the exemptions from tariffs given to industrialists on their own imports of equipment and supplies led to a strong rise in the ratio of imports to production for the industrial sector.

Nationalizations and State Firms

The industrialization drive was meant to be primarily a Peruvian process not totally excluding foreign investors but definitely not welcoming them warmly. In that spirit, the Velasco regime immediately nationalized IPC in October 1968 and, not long after that, the largest copper-mining company, while taking over other foreign firms more peacefully through buy-outs. The government put into place new restrictions on foreign investment in Peru and led the way to a regional agreement, the Andean Pact (see Glossary), that featured some of the most extensive controls on foreign investment yet attempted in the developing world.

The decision to nationalize the foreign oil firm was immensely popular in Peru. It was seen as a legitimate response to many years of close collaboration between the company, which performed political favors, and a series of possibly self-interested Peruvian presidents, who, in exchange, preserved the company's exclusive drilling rights. Nationalization was perhaps less a matter of an economic program than a reaction to a public grievance, a reaction bound to increase public support for the new government.

Subsequent nationalizations and purchases of foreign firms were more explicitly manifestations of the goals of building up state ownership and reducing foreign influence in Peru. The leaders of the military government subscribed firmly to the ideas of dependency analysis (see Glossary), placing much of the blame for problems of development on external influences through trade and foreign investment. Foreign ownership of natural resources in particular was seen as a way of taking away the country's basic wealth on terms that allowed most of the gains to go abroad. Ownership of the resources was expected to bring in revenue to the government, and to the country, that would otherwise have been lost.

In contrast to its abrupt nationalization of the IPC and then of the largest copper mining company, the government turned mainly to purchases through negotiation to acquire the property of the International Telephone and Telegraph Company (ITT) and foreign banks. Partly in response to United States reactions to the earlier nationalizations, and perhaps also partly in response to the realization that foreign investment might play a positive role in the industrialization drive, the government began to take a milder position toward foreign firms. But at the same time, it pursued a policy of creating new state-owned firms, in a sense competing for position against domestic private ownership, as well as against foreign ownership.

State ownership of firms was, of course, consistent with the nationalizations but reflected a different kind of policy objective. Whereas the nationalizations were intended to gain greater Peruvian control over the country's resources and to reduce the scope of foreign influence, the proliferation of state-owned firms was meant to increase direct control by the government over the economy. State firms were seen as a means to implement government economic policies more directly than possible when working through private firms, whether domestic or foreign-owned. The goal was not to eliminate the private sector—it was encouraged at the same time by tax favors and protection—but to create a strong public sector to lead the way toward the kind of economy favored by the state.

The new state firms created in this period established a significant share of public ownership in the modern sector of the economy. By 1975 they accounted for over half of mining output and a fifth of industrial output. One set of estimates indicates that enterprises under state ownership came to account for a higher share of value added than domestic private capital: 26 percent of GDP for the state firms, compared with 22 percent for domestic private firms. The share produced by foreign-owned firms dropped to 8 percent from 21 percent prior to the Velasco government's reforms.

Contrary to the expectation that the earnings of the state firms would provide an important source of public financing for development, these companies became almost immediately a collective drain. In some measure, the drain was a result of decisions by the government to hold down their prices in order to lessen inflation or to subsidize consumers. In addition, deficits of the state-owned firms were aggravated by the spending tendencies of the military officers placed in charge of company management and by inadequate attention to costs of production. The collective deficits of the state enterprises plus the subsidies paid directly to them by the government reached 3 percent of GDP by 1975. State enterprises were not able to finance more than about one-fourth of their investment spending. The government attempted to answer the investment requirements of the state firms by allowing them to borrow abroad for imported equipment and supplies. They did so on a large scale. The external debt rose swiftly, for this and for other reasons discussed below.

Nationalizations and the creation of new state firms stopped abruptly after Velasco lost power. In 1980 the Belaúnde government announced a program to privatize most of the state firms, but it proved difficult to find private buyers, and few of the firms were actually sold. In the opposite direction, the subsequent García government, in addition to nationalizing in 1985 the offshore oil production of the Belco Corporation, a United States company, tried in 1987 to extend state ownership over banks remaining in private hands. The attempted banking nationalization created a storm of protest and was eventually ruled to be illegal. The failures under both Belaúnde and García to change the balance left the state-enterprise sector basically intact until Fujimori implemented major changes.

Macroeconomic Imbalance: Domestic and External

Whatever the promises and the costs of the many kinds of reform attempted by the Velasco government, the ship sank because of inadequate attention to balances between spending and productive

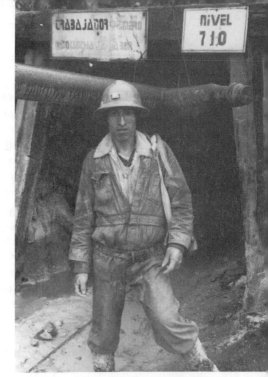

*Miner about to enter
the 4,000-meter-high
Mina Proaño
multimineral mine
Courtesy Inter-American
Development Bank*

*Miners drill dynamite holes
at the Mina Raúl open-pit
copper mine near Arequipa.
Courtesy Inter-American
Development Bank*

189

capacity, and between export incentives and import demand. The Velasco government inherited recessionary conditions in 1968, with a positive external balance and productive capacity readily available for expansion. It maintained effective restraint on spending and deficits for several years but then let things get out of control. The central government's deficit was no more than 1 percent of gross national product (GNP—see Glossary) in 1970, but its own deficit plus that of the greatly expanded group of state firms reached 10 percent of GNP by 1975. Correspondingly, the external current-account balance was positive in the period 1968–70 but showed a deficit equal to 10 percent of GNP by 1975.

The external deficit was driven up primarily by high rates of growth of domestic demand and production through 1974. But in addition, the government's policy of holding to a fixed nominal exchange rate, in an increasingly inflationary context, allowed the real exchange rate to fall steadily from 1969 to 1975. The government refused to consider devaluation for fear it would worsen inflation and managed to avoid it by borrowing abroad to finance the continuing deficit. By 1975 external creditors had lost confidence in Peru's ability to repay its debts and began to put on the brakes. Whether because of such external pressure or because of growing internal opposition to the increasingly arbitrary decisions of the government, the Peruvian military decided to replace Velasco in 1975. The experiment ended on a note of defeat, not so much of its objectives as of its methods.

The Search for New Directions, 1975–90

The head of the second phase of the military government, General Morales Bermúdez, reoriented Peru's economic strategy in much more conservative directions. Many of the specific Velasco reforms were dropped, although land reform and the state enterprise sector remained intact. Because of pressure from the IMF, average tariff rates were cut from 66 percent in 1978 to 34 percent by 1980, and the enormous battery of specific quantitative restrictions on trade was trimmed down greatly: the number of tariff positions under quantitative controls fell from 2,890 in 1978 to 124 by 1980.

On the side of macroeconomic management, the second-phase military government put into effect a desperately needed correction of the exchange rate in order to stimulate exports and greatly reduce public-investment spending. The exchange-rate policy worked well, achieving the country's first significant growth of manufacturing exports. Peru's share of the manufacturing exports of nine leading Latin American countries increased from 2 percent for 1970–74 to 10.9 percent for 1975–79. Accompanied by better prices for traditional exports, manufacturing exports helped create a substantial current-account surplus by the end of the decade. But devaluation fed back into inflation through price increases for imports and exports, and continuing rapid growth of the money supply helped spread the inflationary effects of devaluation through the whole economy.

The Second Belaúnde Government, 1980–85

The return to democracy allowed Peruvians to choose among strongly left, strongly conservative, or middle-of-the-road parties. They chose Belaúnde and his party as the middle road, but it led nowhere. The Belaúnde government tried to return the economy to a more open system by reducing barriers to imports, implementing financial reforms intended to foster private markets, and reversing the statist orientation of the Velasco system. But the new approach never had a chance to get very far because of a series of macroeconomic problems. On one side, the government was rightly concerned about continuing inflation but made the mistake of focusing the explanation on monetary growth arising from the export surplus it inherited at the start. That position made it seem undesirable to continue trying to promote exports and desirable to raise domestic spending and imports. On the other side, President Belaúnde's personal and political objectives included using public investment actively to develop the interior of the country and to answer evident needs for improved infrastructure. Seeing the export surplus as the key macroeconomic source of imbalance, the government decided to eliminate it by removing import restrictions, slowing nominal devaluation to allow the real exchange rate to appreciate, and increasing government investment spending.

The real exchange rate appreciated through 1981 and 1982, public-sector investment rose 54 percent in real terms from 1979 to 1982, and public-sector consumption rose 25 percent during the same three-year period. The combination effectively turned the current-account surplus into a large deficit, as increased spending plus import liberalization practically doubled imports of goods and services between 1979 and 1981. The appreciation also turned manufacturing exports back downward, and a plunge in external prices of primary exports brought them down too. The mistake of focusing on the earlier export surplus as the main cause of inflation became clear: the increases in spending led to a leap of inflation despite the return to an external deficit. The rate of inflation went from 59 percent in 1980 to 111 percent by 1983.

Nothing improved when the government then tried to go into reverse with contractionary macroeconomic policies and renewed depreciation. Output plunged, but inflation once again went up instead of down, to 163 percent by 1985. By this time, pessimism about the government's capacity to solve anything, inflationary expectations turning into understandable convictions, and the price-increasing effect of devaluation all combined to give Peru a seemingly unstoppable inflation despite the elimination of anything that might be considered excess demand. The government apparently lost its sense of direction, retreated from its attempt to reopen the economy by returning to higher tariff levels, and otherwise did little except wait for its own end in 1985.

The García Government, 1985–90

With the market-oriented choice of economic strategy discredited by results under Belaúnde, Peruvians voted for the dynamic populist-reformist promise of García and responded enthusiastically to his sweeping changes. García's program worked wonders for two years, but then everything began to go wrong.

The main elements of the economic strategy proposed by the García government were full of promise. They recognized the prior neglect of the agricultural sector and called for redirecting public programs toward promotion of agricultural growth and reduction of rural poverty. Correspondingly, economic activity was to be decentralized to break down its high concentration in Lima, and within the cities resources were to be redirected away from the capital-intensive and import-intensive modern sector to the labor-intensive informal sector. A strategy of *concertación* (national understanding) with private business leaders on economic issues was to be used systematically to avoid disruptive conflict. Problems of external balance were to be answered both by restructuring production to lessen dependence on imports and by reorienting toward higher exports over the long-term.

These goals for structural change could have improved the efficiency of resource allocation while doing a great deal to lessen poverty. But the goals clearly required both time and the ability to restore expansion without worsening inflation and external deficits. The government initially emphasized such macroeconomic objectives as necessary conditions for the structural changes. The first step was to stop the built-in inflationary process, but to do it without adopting orthodox measures of monetary and fiscal restraint.

To stop inflation, the government opted for heterodox policies of control within an expansionary program. Prices and wages in the modern sector were to be fixed, after an initial one-shot increase in wage rates. The increase in wages was intended to raise living standards of workers and stimulate production by raising sales to consumers. To offset the effects of higher wages on costs of production, financial costs of the business sector were cut by intervention in order to reduce and control interest rates. After making one adjustment of the exchange rate to minimize negative effects on exports, the government stopped the process of continuing devaluation in order to help hold down inflation. Imports were rightly expected to go up as the economy revived; to help finance them, García made his controversial decision to stop paying external debt service beyond 10 percent of the value of exports. Unorthodox as they were, all the pieces seemed to fit. At least, they went together well at the start under conditions of widespread idle capacity, with an initially strong balance-of-payments position.

The macroeconomic measures worked wonders for production. GDP shot up 9.5 percent in 1986 and a further 7.7 percent in 1987. Manufacturing output and construction both increased by more than one-fourth in these two years. An even greater surprise was that agricultural production per capita went up, running counter to its long downward trend. And the rate of inflation came down from 163 percent in 1985 to 78 percent in 1986, although it edged back up to 86 percent in 1987. In response to stronger market conditions and perhaps also to growing confidence that Peru's economic problems were at last being attacked successfully, private fixed investment went up by 24 percent in 1986, and capital flight went down.

The government avoided any spending spree of its own: central government spending was actually reduced in real terms each year. But because the government also reduced indirect taxes in order to encourage higher private consumption and to reduce costs for private business, its originally small deficit grew each year. The economic deficit of the nonfinancial public sector as a whole (excluding interest payments) went up from 2.4 percent of GDP in 1985 to 6.5 percent by 1987.

Although the government reduced its total spending, it managed to support a new public-works program to provide temporary employment and to direct more resources to rural producers as intended in its program for structural change. Three lines of policy helped especially to raise rural incomes. The first was to use generous guaranteed prices for key food products. The second was to provide greatly increased agricultural credit, financed essentially by credit from the Central Bank. The third was to exempt most of the non-guaranteed agricultural prices from controls, allowing their prices to rise sharply relative to those of industrial products from the modern sector. From July 1985 to December 1986, prices of goods and services not under control increased more than three times as much as those under control. Wholesale prices in manufacturing increased 26 percent, but those for agricultural products increased 142 percent.

Besides higher employment and living standards, the first two years of economic revival seemed to offer a break in the cycle of rising rural violence. The flow of displaced peasants from the Sierra eased, and a good many peasants began to return to the countryside. That reverse might be explained by García's initial efforts to reduce reliance on military force to combat the guerrillas and thereby to lessen the degree of two-way violence driving people out of their villages. But the trend may also have been a response to the reality of better economic conditions and earning possibilities in the agricultural sector.

The first two years of the García government gave new hope to the people of Peru, with rising employment, production, and wages suggesting a clear turn for the better after so many years of increasing difficulties. It was hence doubly tragic to see the whole process unravel so quickly, once things started going wrong again. The first sign of trouble came, as it often had, from the balance of payments. The economic boom naturally raised imports swiftly, by 76 percent between 1985 and 1987. But the real exchange rate was allowed to fall by 10 percent in 1986 and by a further 9 percent in 1987. The boom pulled potential export supply into the domestic market, and the fall in the real exchange rate reduced incentives to earn foreign exchange. Exports fell slightly in 1985 and remained below that level through 1987. The external current account went from a surplus of US$127 million in 1985 to deficits of nearly US$1.1 billion in 1986 and nearly US$1.5 billion in 1987.

The García government reacted to the growing external deficit in exactly the same way as had the governments of Velasco and of Belaúnde—by postponing corrective action while the problem continued to worsen. As before, a major fear was that devaluation would worsen inflation. Inflationary pressures were, in fact, beginning to worsen behind the façade of control. To some degree, they were growing in response to the high rate of growth of demand and output, reducing margins of previously underutilized productive capacity. But more explosive pressures were being built up by relying on price controls that required a dramatic expansion of credit to keep the system in place. Prices of public-sector services—gasoline above all, oil products in general, electricity, telephones, and postal services—were frozen at levels that soon became almost ridiculous in real terms. The restrictions on prices charged by state firms drove them ever deeper into deficits that had to be financed by borrowing. The borrowing came from wherever it could, but principally from the Central Bank. At the same time, Central Bank credit rose steadily to keep financing agricultural expansion. Still another direction of Central Bank credit creation was the financing used to handle the government's new structure of multiple exchange rates. Differential rates were used to hold down the cost of foreign exchange for most imports, again with the dominant goal of holding down inflation, while higher prices of foreign exchange were paid to exporters to protect their incentives to export. The Central Bank thus paid more for the foreign exchange it bought than it received for the exchange it sold.

The term used for these leakages—for extensions of Central Bank credit that did not count in the government's budget deficit—is the "quasi-fiscal deficit." Its total increased from about 2 percent of GDP in 1985 to about 4 percent in 1987. Meanwhile, the government's tax revenue fell steadily in real terms, partly because of tax reductions implemented to hold down business costs and partly because of the effect of inflation in cutting down the real value of tax payments. Added together, the fiscal deficit plus the quasi-fiscal deficit increased from 5 percent of GDP in 1985 to 11 percent by 1987.

The two horsemen of this particular apocalypse—the external deficit and the swift rise of Central Bank credit—would have made 1988 a bad year no matter what else happened. But President García guaranteed financial disaster by his totally unexpected decision in July 1987 to nationalize the banks not already under government ownership. No one has yet been able to explain why he decided to do so. It would not seem to have been a move necessary for any component of his program, or needed for government control in a banking sector in which it already had a dominant position. In any case, the action underlined the unilateral character of economic policy action under Peru's presidential system (see The García Government, 1985–90, ch. 4) and wrecked any possibilities of further cooperation with private sector leadership. Private investment began to fall, and the whole economy followed it down shortly thereafter.

The García government tried a series of major and minor new policy packages from early 1988 into 1990 to no avail. The new policies never succeeded in shutting off the rapid infusion of Central Bank credit that was feeding inflation, even when they did succeed in driving production down significantly in 1989. Manufacturing production fell 18 percent in that year, agricultural output 3 percent, and total GDP 11 percent. Simultaneously, inflation increased from a record 666 percent in 1988 to a new record of 3,399 percent for 1989. The one positive change was the external current-account deficit: the fall in domestic production and income was so steep that the current account went from a deep deficit to a substantial surplus. The internal cost was perhaps clearest in terms of real wages: the minimum wage in real terms for urban labor fell 61 percent between 1987 and 1989, and average real wages in manufacturing fell 59 percent.

The Fujimori Government, 1990–91

The Fujimori administration began with yet another reversal of practically all the economic policies of the preceding government, in conditions that clearly required drastic corrective action. Its main immediate target was to stop the runaway course of inflation. Beyond that, the goals included repudiating protection and import substitution, returning to full participation in the world trading and financial systems, eliminating domestic price controls and subsidies, raising public revenue and holding government spending strictly to the levels of current revenue, initiating a social emergency program to reduce the shock of adjustment for the poor, and devoting a higher share of the country's resources to rural investment and correction of the causes of rural poverty. In practice, new measures came out in bits and pieces, dominated by immediate concern to stop inflation; actions taken in the first year did not complete the program.

Preoccupation with inflation was natural enough, after the steep rise of 1989 and the months immediately preceding the change of government. The monthly rate of inflation ranged between 25 percent and 32 percent in the second half of 1989, exceeded 40 percent in June 1990, and amounted to 78 percent by July. The deficit of the central government increased from 4 percent of GDP in January 1990 to 9 percent by May. The money supply of the country increased six times over from January to the end of July. The new government had to act quickly, and did.

The most dramatic immediate action was to eliminate price controls for private-sector products and to raise prices of public-sector products to restore financial balance for public firms. The price of gasoline, previously driven down to about one-eighth its price in the United States, was multiplied by thirty times. For the consumer price index (CPI—see Glossary), the shocks caused an increase of 136 percent in one day.

Eliminating price controls in the private sector and raising prices charged by state firms had three objectives. First, the price increases for the public-sector firms and government services were meant to restore revenue to a level that would allow the government to stop borrowing from the Central Bank. Second, the rise in prices was intended to reduce aggregate demand by cutting the liquidity of business and the purchasing power of the public. Third, with everything priced far higher relative to public purchasing power, it was expected that market forces would begin to operate to drive some prices back down, reversing the long trend of increases in order to help break the grip of inflationary expectations.

To back up the impact of the price shocks, the government declared that it would keep its own expenditure within the limit of current revenue and stop the other two large streams of Central Bank credit creation: Central Bank financing for agricultural credit and for the system of subsidies supporting differential exchange rates. The multiple exchange rates in effect under García were to be unified, and the unified rate was to be determined by market forces. Further, competition from imports to restrain inflation and access to imported supplies for production would both be improved by taking away quantitative restrictions and reducing tariff rates.

The new policies helped greatly to bring down the rate of inflation, although they fell short of accomplishing full stabilization. Against an inflation rate that had reached approximately 2,300 percent for the twelve months to June 1990, the rate of 139 percent for the twelve months to December 1991 can be seen as a dramatic improvement. But the latter was still more than double the government's intended ceiling for 1991 and still extremely high relative to outside world rates of inflation. The last quarter of 1991 looked more promising, with the monthly rate down to 4 percent, but it had risen to 7 percent by March 1992. Inflationary dangers clearly remained troublesome, especially in view of two factors that should have stopped inflation more decisively: a deeply depressed level of domestic demand and an unintended increase in the real exchange rate, making dollars cheaper.

Domestic demand has been held down by the combination of the price shock at the start of the stabilization program, steeply falling real wages, reduced government deficits, and much tighter restraint of credit. All these were deliberate measures to stop inflation, accepting the likely costs of higher unemployment and restraint of production as necessary to that end. In 1990 GNP fell 3.9 percent, aggravating the plunge of 19 percent between 1988 and 1990. In 1991 production turned up slightly, with a gain of 2.9 percent in GNP. That situation left output per capita essentially unchanged from 1990 and at 29 percent below its level a decade earlier.

197

The incomplete success in stopping inflation created an extremely difficult policy conflict. Recovery could in principle be stimulated by more expansionary credit policies and lower interest rates, which would favor increased investment, depreciation of the currency to help producers compete against imports, and improved exports. But continuing inflation and the fear of accelerating its rate of increase argued instead for keeping a very tight rein on credit and thereby blocked the actions needed for recovery. This conflict became particularly acute over the question of what to do about the exchange note: the real exchange rate went in exactly the wrong direction for recovery by appreciating when depreciation was both expected and needed.

The decision to remove controls on the exchange rate had been expected to lead to a much higher foreign-exchange price, to encourage exports, and to permit import liberalization without a surging external deficit. But when the rate was set free, the price of dollars went down instead of going up. That initial effect could be explained by the tight restraints imposed on liquidity, which drove firms and individuals who held dollar balances to convert them to domestic currency in order to keep operating. This movement should presumably have gone into reverse when holdings of dollars ran out, but fully eighteen months later no reversal had occurred. Dollars remained too cheap to make exports profitable and too cheap for many producers to compete against imports for several reasons, including the continuing influx of dollars from the drug trade into street markets and then into the banking system. A second reason has involved the continuing low level of domestic income and production, and corresponding restraint of demand for imports as compared with what they would be in an expanding economy. But perhaps the most fundamental reasons have been the continuing squeeze on liquidity in terms of domestic currency and the resulting high rates of interest for borrowing domestic currency, which strongly favor borrowing dollars instead or repatriating them from abroad. All this means that the economy has had no foreign-exchange problem, but also that incentives to produce for export have been held down severely, when both near-term recovery and longer-term growth badly need the stimulus of rising exports.

The government was more successful in the part of its program aimed at trade liberalization. As has been noted, the average tariff rate was cut greatly in two steps, in September 1990 and March 1991. Quantitative restrictions were eliminated, and the tariff structure was greatly simplified. Effective protection was brought down to a lower level than at any point since the mid-1960s, with a more coherent structure that left much less room for distorted incentives.

Although stabilization and structural reform measures have thus shown some success, the government's program has not taken adequate action to prevent worsening poverty. Its announced programs of short-term aid in providing food and longer-term redirection of resources to get people out of poverty by programs designed to help them raise their productivity have not yet been implemented in any meaningful way. Private charitable agencies, the United Nations (UN), and the United States Agency for International Development (AID) have helped considerably through food grants to stave off starvation. But the government itself has done little, either to alleviate current strains on the poor or to open up new directions that promise gains for them in the future.

Outstanding Issues

For many Peruvians, the frustrations of prolonged economic deterioration in the face of such varied attempts to do something about it mean that something fundamental has gone wrong, perhaps so wrong that mere changes of public policy can do little to help. Such fears are certainly understandable and also costly. They encourage support for violent reaction, and they also foster great pressure on each new government to act quickly, in dramatic new ways, without sufficient attention to the likely costs of their actions. Such pressure may be a key part of the problem. Issues of current policy orientation need to be considered in the perspective of Peru's extremely dislocated society, but that context argues for great caution, as well as for change. The specific issues center on familiar conflicts: between the appeal of trying to return to the open economy and liberal economic system preceding the 1960s, and the contrary appeal of a more directive use of public policy to correct basic structural problems.

Convictions that something fundamental has gone wrong with the country can lead to violence, to emigration as an escape, or possibly instead to new consensus on the need to change particular constraints of public policy. The SL has advocated an extreme answer: traditional society has failed and needs to be swept away. For many others who reject violence, the answer has not seemed to be much more positive: emigration has become an increasingly popular way out for many, including professional people and businesspeople who take their capital with them. Although it is truly difficult to be certain that a reasonably peaceful recovery remains possible, two alternative answers, in different ways, suggest somewhat more hope for the future.

One interpretation of the deterioration since the mid-1960s is that it has been caused by stubbornly misdirected economic policies, specifically excessive protection for import substitution, a proliferation of internal controls adverse to efficiency and free markets, government deficits, and wildly exaggerated monetary expansion. That position gains solid support from the results of the governments of Velasco and García, plus much of the administration under Belaúnde. In that light, the Fujimori government's return of national policy to an open economy with greatly reduced protection and controls and more attention to budget balance is genuinely hopeful. The redirection initially offered the promise of renewed external help from international financial and development agencies, although that possibility was set back at least temporarily in April 1992 when the Fujimori government suspended democracy in Peru.

A second nonviolent alternative goes against attempts to return to the kind of economic system Peru had prior to the 1960s. The old system was neither an equitable system that served to integrate the society nor one that favored learning and technical progress. The depth of Peru's problems in 1991 seemed to call for more directive economic strategies to lessen poverty, pull the industrial sector into export competition, and establish a stronger tax base to provide noninflationary financing for an active government. Such redirection would be fully consistent with reduced protection, although it would gain from adding on strong incentives for industrial exports. It would need much the same kind of effort to maintain fiscal balance as the first alternative, although more through higher public revenue and less through cutback of public-sector functions.

Both of these two alternative orientations raise serious questions about what is possible. Such questions might be considered on three levels: first, can economic growth be revived without making inflation accelerate again; second, can the spread and deepening of poverty be reversed; and third, can the Peruvian people regain enough confidence in their society to induce renewed investment, productive effort, and acceptance of the constraints necessary to rebuild?

To the question on the first level, it is certainly no easy matter to revive economic growth without provoking inflation again, given all the special handicaps of political uncertainty, growing violence, and intense public awareness of past failures to curb inflation. Still, nearly all the purely economic conditions for revival without inflation are present: the industrial sector has a great deal of under-utilized capacity, both skilled and unskilled labor is available in abundance, and the country is in the unusual position of having abundant supplies of foreign exchange to finance increased imports of supplies needed for rising production. If investment and exports can be encouraged, it should be possible to raise production quickly, without running into any near-term limitations on the supply side.

The experience of the first two years of the García government, from 1985 to 1987, suggests both the scope for raising output in such conditions and the danger of doing too much, too rapidly. That experience does not point to any necessary relapse back into inflation: it simply underlines the need for methods that are more consistent and more careful. The García government's revival was crippled quickly because of particular choices that could have been avoided. The exchange-rate policy was wholly and unnecessarily misdirected. More fundamentally, the degree of stimulus lacked any clear relationship to the constraints on how much it was possible to do, how fast, and with what financing. The need for adequate tax revenue and the need for prices of government services adequate to cover costs were never faced. To pay more attention to internal and external macroeconomic balance would have required a slower pace of expansion, but it might then have been possible to keep going without explosion. The experience does not demonstrate that sustained recovery is practically impossible in Peru, only that it has to be done with extreme care because of the damage of past misjudgment.

To the question on the second level—the possibility of seriously reducing poverty—the experience under García again suggests both grounds for hope and reasons for doubt. That government's combination of measures was initially favorable for both the rural poor and those in the informal urban sector. These measures made a notable dent in the degree of extreme poverty in the first two years. If the overall expansion had been more moderate, the gains would have been less but still positive. Redirection of public investment and of credit toward the rural sector must have played a helpful role in that brief experience of reducing poverty and inequality, as they would under any government if placed within a framework of overall balance.

Promotion of a more labor-intensive structure of production, with more rapidly growing employment opportunities for any given level of investment, could do a great deal to lessen poverty and inequality in the longer run. A necessary condition to move in this direction is to avoid overvaluation of the exchange rate, something that the García, Velasco, and Belaúnde governments were unable to do. Overvaluation hurts the poor by making imported capital equipment and supplies artificially inexpensive, thereby encouraging the replacement of workers with machinery. Overvaluation is not beyond correction by a government concerned with the problem, although it may require intervention to offset perverse market forces like those operating in the first year of the Fujimori government. The price of foreign exchange needs to be kept high enough to encourage growth of industrial exports, or else more specific measures have to be taken to keep them growing, even if this means intervening to change the way that market forces are operating.

Beyond such questions of differential incentives and employment opportunities, and of investment and credit for the rural area, serious action to alleviate poverty clearly requires a strong public commitment to provide more nearly equal access to education, to public health programs directed to the poor, and to social action to alleviate conditions of mass hunger. The problem with the alternative of going back to an open economy with much less of a role for government is that it could leave the extent of poverty as great as ever, or even discourage public action to do more about it. Velasco and García went wrong in many ways, but their efforts to change the society were attempts to respond to a real need. To go back to the pre-1960s kind of economic regime might well be less costly than to repeat the nightmares of 1988-90, but it would leave the human problems of Peru unresolved.

To the question on the third level—the possibility of restored confidence in the society—the answer cannot be in terms of economic analysis. It may be that the shocks of the 1980s and those of 1990, combined with the worsening of violence and deterioration of the capability of the government to act, will make it difficult for a long time to generate rising investment, whether by Peruvians or foreign investors. It may be that fear of inflation will paralyze promotional action by the government or, alternatively, that long delay will generate overwhelming pressures for violent change. Such possibilities are all too real. But the surge of hope in 1985-86 (and the surge of investment and of production that immediately came with it) make fatalism about Peru seem misplaced. Even through the confusions of economic policy at that time, including a great many costly kinds of interference adverse to efficiency, and even in the face of destructive violence, Peru was able to respond positively to the temporary turn in a more promising direction. Production went up, poverty went down, and the reign of terror in the Sierra temporarily lessened. Both poverty and violence were worse in 1991, but the background of economic policy distortions had in part been corrected.

It is probably true that Peru has a fundamental problem that underlies the long downward trend of its economic performance.

It is not just the misdirection of excessive protection, government intervention, and excess spending. It is the severity of poverty and inequality. Too many people have serious grounds to reject the society because it has done so little to provide them any hope. The governments since the mid-1960s all tried to find some new way to deal with this basic weakness. Their methods were terribly damaging. It is fairly easy to see what went wrong in each case, if not so easy to see how to work out the interlocking problems at the beginning of the 1990s. Recovery of production is surely possible with better designed economic policies, but to keep society intact requires that the government go beyond reactivation of the economy to include more effective ways to reduce poverty on a sustained basis.

* * *

The Peruvian Experiment, edited by Abraham F. Lowenthal, and *The Peruvian Experiment Reconsidered,* edited by Cynthia McClintock and Lowenthal, cover the Velasco period and its consequences. Rosemary Thorp and Geoffrey Bertram's *Peru 1890–1977* is a comprehensive economic history. Paul E. Gootenberg's *Between Silver and Guano* examines the roles of nationalism and liberalism in shaping the country's development.

On agrarian problems, consult Tom Alberts's *Agrarian Reform and Rural Poverty* and Adolfo Figueroa's *Capitalist Development and the Peasant Economy in Peru.* On the informal sector, the classic book is Hernando de Soto's *The Other Path.*

The García government's economic program from 1985 to 1990 is analyzed in Eva Paus's "Adjustment and Development in Latin America," and in Manuel Pastor, Jr. and Carol Wise's "Peruvian Economic Policy in the 1980s." Thorp's *Economic Management and Economic Development in Peru and Colombia* examines this period through a comparison of the ways the two countries have managed their long-term problems of development. *Peru's Path to Recovery,* edited by Carlos E. Paredes and Jeffrey D. Sachs, is a thorough survey of Peru's problems at the start of the Fujimori government in 1990, with many proposals for corrective action. Particularly useful monthly Peruvian publications include *The Andean Report* and *Perú Económico.* (For further information and complete citations, see Bibliography.)

Chapter 4. Government and Politics

Mochican ear ornament of gold and precious stones representing a warrior with a sling

PERU, IN 1980, was one of the first countries in South America to undergo the transition from long-term institutionalized military rule to democratic government. By 1990, however, Peru was in the midst of a social, economic, and political crisis of unprecedented proportions that threatened not only the viability of the democratic system but also civil society in general.

More than a decade of steep economic decline had resulted in a dramatic deterioration in living standards for all sectors of society and a vast increase in the large proportion of society that was underemployed and below the poverty line. Per capita incomes were below their 1960 levels. Accompanying the economic decline in the 1980s was a rise in insurgent violence and criminal activity. There was also a marked deterioration in the human rights situation—over 20,000 people died in political violence during the decade.

The crisis had partial roots in the failure of successive governments to implement effective economic policy and to fully incorporate the marginalized (informal; see Glossary) sector of the population into the formal economic and political systems. Politics were dominated by personalities rather than programs and by policy swings from populist policies to neoliberal stabilization strategies.

The concentration of decision-making power in the persona of the president and the major swings in policy took an enormous toll on the nation's political system and state institutions. The judicial and legislative branches, already inadequately funded and understaffed, were constantly bypassed by the executive. State institutions, meanwhile, already burdened by excessive bureaucracy, were virtually inoperative because government resources had all but disappeared. Political parties had been increasingly discredited, having failed to provide credible alternatives to the malfunctioning state system with which they were associated. Both extrasystem movements, such as neighborhood organizations and grassroots groups, and antisystem movements, such as guerrilla forces, particularly the Shining Path (Sendero Luminoso—SL), had increased in size and importance. The breach between the Peruvian state and civil society had widened. The political system was fragmented and polarized to an unprecedented degree, and society, which was immersed in a virtual civil war, had become increasingly praetorian (see Glossary) in nature.

Despite the desperate nature of the socioeconomic situation and the extent of political polarization, Peru successfully held its third consecutive elections in April and June 1990. Agronomist Alberto K. Fujimori, a virtual unknown, defeated novelist Mario Vargas Llosa by a wide margin. The victory of Fujimori and his Cambio '90 (Change '90) front was seen as a rejection of traditional politicians and parties, as well as of Vargas Llosa's proposed orthodox economic "shock" program.

Despite his wide popular margin, Fujimori faced substantial constraints early on. One was his lack of an organized party base or a working majority in either of the two houses of Congress. Another was that, as a result of hyperinflation, the lack of government resources, and the clear preferences of international lending agencies, such as the International Monetary Fund (IMF—see Glossary) and World Bank (see Glossary), he had little choice but to implement the orthodox shock program that he had campaigned against.

Although Fujimori made impressive strides during his first year in the implementation of structural economic reforms, there was substantial popular disaffection because of the high social costs of the "Fujishock" program and the government's failure to follow through on promises of a social emergency program to alleviate those shocks. Resource constraints inherited from the previous government severely limited the Fujimori administration's ability to act on the social welfare front. Fujimori lost the support of much of his Cambio '90 front when he turned to orthodox economics. In addition, he was forced to rely on a series of "marriages of convenience" with various political forces in Congress in order to pass legislation. He also had to rely on a sector of the army for institutional support.

On April 5, 1992, Fujimori suspended the constitution, dissolved the Congress and the judiciary, and placed several congressional leaders and members of the opposition under house arrest. The measures, which were fully supported by all three branches of the armed forces, were announced in the name of fighting drug traffic. They amounted to an *autogolpe* (self-coup): a military coup against the government led by the president himself.

Governmental System

During the first ninety-four days of 1992, Peru was a republic with a civilian government, which had a popularly elected president, a bicameral legislature, and an independent judicial branch (see fig. 12). Peru's civilian government ended indefinitely as a result of Fujimori's *autogolpe* of April 5, 1992. The constitution of

1979 remained suspended, and its Congress and judiciary remained dissolved during the rest of 1992. The government held elections for the Democratic Constituent Congress (Congreso Constituyente Democrático) on November 22, 1992, and municipal elections on January 29, 1993. The following sections describe Peru's legitimate civilian government as it existed prior to April 5, 1992.

Constitutional Development

Until April 5, 1992, Peru was governed according to a constitution that became effective with the transition to civilian government in 1980. From the time of the declaration of independence by José de San Martín on July 18, 1821, up until the constitution of 1979, Peru had had ten constitutions. All of them had established a presidential form of government, with varying degrees of power concentrated in the executive. The French- and Spanish-influenced constitution of 1823, which abolished hereditary monarchy, was the first formal organic law of the Peruvian state drawn up by a constituent assembly under a popular mandate.

The departure of Simón Bolívar Palacios (1824–25, 1826) on September 3, 1826, ushered in a long period of revolt and instability with only brief periods of peace. The presidency changed twelve times between 1826 and 1845. During this period, Peru was governed under three constitutions—those of 1828, 1834, and 1839. There was little variation in the basic form of these constitutions. All provided for separate executive, legislative, and judicial branches; for indirect election of the president and Congress; for a centralized regime; and for extensive personal rights and guarantees. The only major variations were in details regarding specific powers of the executive.

The 1828 constitution moved toward decentralization and showed considerable influence by the United States. For example, it provided for presidential election by popular vote. In subsequent constitutions, there was a varying emphasis on executive versus legislative power, and gradual, progressive improvements, such as the subordination of the military to civilian rule, direct popular elections, and the granting of the right to association. The 1839 constitution extended the presidential term from four to six years, with no reelection.

When Marshal Ramón Castilla (1845–51, 1855–62) emerged as dictator in 1845, a period of relative peace and prosperity began. The 1856 constitution, promulgated during Castilla's rule, was more liberal and democratic than any of its predecessors. It provided for the first time for direct popular election of the president and Congress. However, a more conservative constitution was

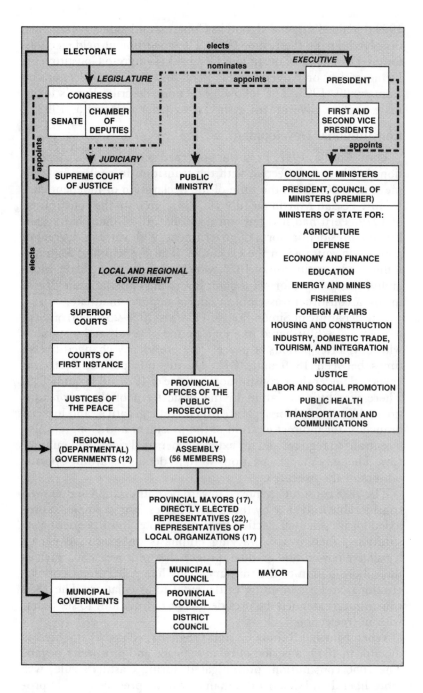

Figure 12. Government Structure, 1991

promulgated in 1860 and remained in force, with two brief interruptions—1862–68 and 1879–81—for sixty years. Although it reduced the presidential term to four years (with reelection after an intervening term), it greatly increased the powers of the president and provided for a much more centralized government. Nevertheless, it laid important bases for the future executive-legislative relationship. In particular, it established a requirement that cabinet ministers, although responsible to the president, report to Congress. Furthermore, it explicitly permitted Congress, at the end of each legislative session, to examine the administrative acts of the president to determine their conformity with the constitution and the laws.

The 1920 constitution was generally more liberal than its predecessor, the 1860 charter, and provided for more civil guarantees. Although it established a strong executive and lengthened the presidential term from four to five years, it placed several new checks on that branch. It deprived the president of his traditional right to suspend constitutional guarantees during periods of national emergency and strengthened the principle of ministerial responsibility to Congress. In particular, it gave Congress the right to force the resignation of ministers by a vote of no confidence. Having promulgated the constitution, however, Augusto B. Leguía y Salcedo (1908–12, 1919–30) ignored it almost completely and established himself as one of Peru's strongest dictators.

The 1933 constitution was, at least in theory, operative until 1980, although civilian government was interrupted from 1933 to 1939, 1948 to 1956, and 1968 to 1980. The 1933 constitution reduced presidential powers and instituted a mixed presidential-parliamentary system. It also instituted compulsory and secret balloting, as well as provisions for religious tolerance and freedom of speech. The president could not remove or nominate cabinet members without parliamentary consent. This situation resulted in a considerable number of executive-legislative stalemates, the most notable of which occurred during the first government of President Fernando Belaúnde Terry (1963–68, 1980–85).

After a prolonged stalemate over issues ranging from tax and agrarian reforms to a contract with the International Petroleum Corporation, Belaúnde was overthrown on October 3, 1968, by the armed forces, led by General Juan Velasco Alvarado (1968–75). The resulting "revolutionary government" was a progressive, left-wing military regime, which attempted to implement a series of structural reforms; it maintained dictatorial powers but was only mildly repressive. After an intraregime coup in 1975 and a turn to orthodox economic management in the face of rising fiscal deficits and inflation, as well as increasing levels of social unrest, the military government called for a civilian-run Constituent Assembly to draft a new constitution and hold elections.

The constitution of 1979, signed by the president of the Constituent Assembly, Víctor Raúl Haya de la Torre, on July 12, 1979, while he was virtually on his death-bed, sought to restore strong presidential power. Largely influenced by the French Fifth Republic, the constitution of 1979 established a presidential system with a bicameral legislature and a Council of Ministers, which was appointed by the president. An excessively broad document, the 1979 charter covered a host of rights and responsibilities of government, private persons, and businesses. It also established the structure of government and mandated measures to effect social changes, including the eradication of illiteracy and extreme poverty. The constitution could be amended by a majority of both houses of Congress.

The constitution guaranteed a series of liberties and rights, including the freedom of expression and association and the right to life, physical integrity, and "the unrestricted development of one's personality." Although the Roman Catholic Church is entitled to the cooperation of the government, Catholicism is not the official religion of the country, and religion is a matter of personal choice. Workers were guaranteed collective bargaining rights and had the right to strike and to participate in workplace management and profits. Public servants, with the exception of those with decision-making power and the armed forces and police, also had the right to strike.

Constitutional guarantees could be suspended during a state of emergency, defined as the disruption of peace or the domestic order, a catastrophe, or grave circumstances affecting the life of the nation. A state of emergency could not last longer than sixty days but could be renewed repeatedly. During such a time, the armed forces retained control of internal order. Guarantees of freedom of movement and of assembly and of freedom from arbitrary or unwarranted arrest and seizure were suspended. Constitutional guarantees could also be suspended during states of siege, defined as an invasion, a civil war, or imminent danger that one of these events may occur. At least half of the nation lived under state-of-emergency conditions beginning in the second half of the 1980s, owing to the increase in insurrectionary activities by the nation's two major guerrilla groups.

The Executive

The president, who had to be Peruvian and at least thirty-five years of age, was elected to a five-year term by direct popular vote, along with the first and second vice presidents. The president could not serve two consecutive terms.

The constitutional president had a wide range of powers and served as chief of state and commander in chief of the armed forces. He had the power to appoint members to the Council of Ministers and the Supreme Court of Justice, submit and review legislation enacted by Congress, rule by decree if so delegated by the Congress, declare states of siege and emergency, and dissolve the Chamber of Deputies, if it voted to censure the Council of Ministers three times in one term of office.

In practice, the constitutional president had even more power, as he had a remarkable amount of freedom to rule by decree. Hernando de Soto, an adviser to the Fujimori government, stated in October 1988 that 95 percent of Peruvian laws were passed by presidential decree. Article 211 of the constitution gave the president the authority "to administer public finances, negotiate loans, and decree extraordinary measures in the economic and financial fields, when the national interest so mandates and with responsibility to give account to Congress." An extraordinary number of measures—134,000 per five-year mandate, or 100 per working day—were passed in this manner in the 1970s and 1980s. In the words of De Soto, "Every five years we elect a dictator."

As no midterm elections for Congress were held, opposition parties had no means of strengthening their position once the president was elected. Moreover, local and regional governments have remained underdeveloped and largely dependent on the central government for resources. Thus, power has remained concentrated in the central government. As the president could bypass Congress with relative ease and rule by decree, power was even more centralized in the persona of the chief executive. Without consecutive reelection or midterm elections, there was no mechanism by which to make the president accountable to the electorate.

Under the Fujimori government, De Soto was instrumental in initiating a reform of this process, the democratization of the system of government, which required laws to be submitted to public referendum before they could be passed. A modified version of this reform was passed in March 1991. Although this version was not expected to have notable effects on the actual process, the debate over reform played an important role in heightening public awareness of the accountability issue.

The Council of Ministers consisted of a prime minister and the specific sectoral ministers, in areas such as economics, education, health, and industry. In 1986, during the government of Alan García Pérez (1985–90), a Ministry of Defense was created, unifying

213

the three armed forces under the auspices of one ministry. Prior to this, the army, navy, and air force each had its own ministry. The ministers could be called to appear in Congress for an interpellation (*interpelación*) at any time, as could the entire cabinet (the latter no more than three times per term). It is traditional for all ministers to resign if the prime minister resigns.

It has also been traditional for the prime minister to serve concurrently as economics minister, although there have been several exceptions. After the resignation of a very popular and powerful prime minister, Juan Carlos Hurtado Miller, in February 1991, President Fujimori separated the posts of prime minister and minister of economy, appointing Carlos Torres y Torres Lara and Carlos Boloña Behr, respectively, to those positions. The president was purportedly uncomfortable with the degree of power that Hurtado Miller had and wanted to retain firmer control of the cabinet in general and economic policy in particular. At the same time, Fujimori combined the positions of prime minister and minister of foreign affairs. In a strong presidential system such as Peru's, the position of prime minister, without control of some other functional ministry, is a relatively impotent one.

The Legislature

The legislature had two houses: a Senate composed of 60 members and a Chamber of Deputies composed of 180 members. Members of Congress were elected to five-year terms of office, which ran concurrently with those of the president and vice presidents. Members of both chambers had to be native Peruvians; senators had to be at least thirty-five years of age; deputies, twenty-five. There was no prohibition on the reelection of congressional representatives.

Congress had the power to initiate and pass legislation; interpret, amend, and repeal existing legislation; draft sanctions for violation of legislation; approve treaties; approve the budget and general accounts; authorize borrowing; exercise the right of amnesty; and delegate the legislative function to the president. A vote of two-thirds of each house was required to pass or amend legislation. The constitution mandated a balanced budget. If Congress did not come up with a balanced budget by December 15 of each year, the president promulgated a budget by executive decree. Congress convened twice annually, from July 27 to December 15 and again from April 1 to May 31.

Members of Congress were elected according to their position on party lists, rather than on the basis of local or regional representation, and thus did not have a strong regional or executive base

of support. This is not to say that they had no regional representation. Whereas members of the Senate were elected by regions, members of the Chamber of Deputies were distributed in accordance with the d'Hondt system of proportional representation, which is based primarily on electoral density, with at least one deputy from each district.

Voters cast votes for a particular party, which presented a list of candidates in numerical order of preference. Voters were allowed to indicate a first-choice candidate, and these votes were tallied as "preferential votes," which might determine a candidate's position on the list in future elections, or which region he or she represents. According to the percentage of votes per region or department, a certain number of seats were allotted in the Congress for that party. A candidate's position on the party list determined whether or not he or she obtained a congressional seat. There was, however, no direct regional representation in the central government, a situation that would not be changed by the introduction of regional governments, as their role was to be strictly limited to the regions.

Congress had the power to censure the Council of Ministers and to demand information through interpellation. Yet, this power was more a reactive power than anything else. If the Chamber of Deputies used its vote of no confidence three times, the president could dissolve the body. Although Congress could make life difficult for the executive branch through censure, interpellation, or the creation of special investigative commissions, these processes occurred largely after the fact.

Particularly with the increase in insurgent violence and the large proportion of the country under emergency rule, the power of the Congress to pass legislation with an impact on significant sectors of the population was increasingly limited. At times, though, after-the-fact processes had resulted in the halting or repeal of damaging legislation. For example, President García's decree nationalizing banks in July 1987 was repealed in late 1990, and President Fujimori's Decree Law 171, which legislated that all crimes committed by the military in the emergency zones be tried in military courts, was repealed in early 1991. In addition, the Congress's special investigative commissions on issues such as human rights and judicial corruption, although perhaps unable to have immediate impact on policy, have been quite successful at bringing such matters to public attention.

The discretionary power accorded the president was designed to avoid the stalemate that occurred prior to 1968, yet it resulted in a system that was highly concentrated in the power of the executive, with little or no public accountability and little significant input on the part of the legislature. Although the Congress could hold ministers accountable for their actions, there was little it could do, short of impeachment, to affect the operations of the president. The president, meanwhile, unconstrained by midterm elections or immediate reelection, had little incentive to build a lasting base of support in the legislature.

The Judiciary

The Supreme Court of Justice was the highest judicial authority in the nation. The twelve Supreme Court justices were nominated by the president and served for life. The nominations had to be approved by the Senate. The Supreme Court of Justice was also responsible for drawing up the budget for the judiciary, which was then submitted to the executive. The budget could be no less than 2 percent of the government's expenditures. Under the Supreme Court of Justice were the Superior Courts, which were seated in the capitals of judicial districts; the Courts of First Instance, which sat in provincial capitals and were divided into civil, criminal, and special branches; and the justices of the peace in all local centers.

Several other judicial functions are worthy of note. The public prosecutor's office was appointed by the president and was responsible for overseeing the independence of judges and the administration of justice, representing the community at trials, and defending people before the public administration. Public attorneys, who were also appointed by the president, defended the interests of the state. The office of the Public Ministry was made up of the attorney general and attorneys before the Supreme Court of Justice, Superior Courts, and the Courts of First Instance. Public attorneys defended the rights of citizens in the public interest against encroachment by public officials.

The National Elections Board established voting laws, registered parties and their candidates, and supervised elections. It also had the power to void elections if the electoral procedures were invalid. The six-member board was composed of one person elected by the Supreme Court of Justice, one by the Bar of Lima, one by the law faculty deans of the national universities, and three by Peru's regional boards.

Although in theory the judicial system was independent and guaranteed at least minimal operating financial support, in practice this was far from the case. The system had been hampered by scarce resources, a tradition of executive manipulation, and inadequate protection of officials in the face of threats from insurgents and drug traffickers. Even without the existence of guerrilla movements, the system was inadequately staffed to deal with the number of cases from criminal violations. It was not uncommon for detainees to spend several years in prison awaiting a hearing. In addition, in the emergency zones, where guerrillas were operating, security forces have had virtual carte blanche in the areas of interrogation and detention, and suspects often have been held incommunicado. Imprisoned suspects awaiting trial have subsisted in medieval conditions. In 1990 the Ministry of Justice recorded 60 deaths from starvation and a backlog over several years of 50,000 unheard cases.

The executive branch traditionally manipulated the judiciary for its own purposes, using its ability to appoint and remove certain judges for its own political ends. For example, when a Superior Court judge ruled that President García's nationalization of Peru's banks was unconstitutional, García merely replaced him with a judge from his party, the American Popular Revolutionary Alliance (Alianza Popular Revolucionaria Americana—APRA). The newly appointed judge then ruled in García's favor.

It also was common for known terrorists or drug traffickers to be released for ''insufficient evidence'' by judges, who had no protection whatsoever but the responsibility for trying those suspected of terrorism. Largely because of corruption or inefficiency in the system, only 5 percent of those detained for terrorism had been sentenced by 1991. Those responsible for administering justice were under threat from all sides of the political spectrum: guerrilla movements, drug traffickers, and military-linked paramilitary squads. Notable cases included the murder of the defense attorney for the SL's number two man, Osmán Morote Barrionuevo, by an APRA-linked death squad, the Rodrigo Franco Command; the self-exile of a public attorney after repeated death threats during his investigation of the military's role in the massacre of at least twenty-nine peasants in Cayara, Ayacucho Department, on May 14, 1988; a bloody letter-bomb explosion at the headquarters of the Lima-based Pro-Human Rights Association (Asociación Pro-Derechos Humanos—Aprodeh); and the March 1991 resignation of an attorney general of the Military Justice Court, after he received death threats for denouncing police aid and abetment of the rescue by the Túpac Amaru Revolutionary Movement (Movimiento Revolucionario Túpac Amaru—MRTA) of one of its leaders, María Lucero Cumpa Miranda. The judicial terrorism was hardly surprising, given the lack of protection for judges dealing with terrorism cases; many of them normally rode the bus daily to work, totally unprotected. Finally, because of neglect of the judicial system by successive governments, the Supreme Court of Justice lacked a significant presence at the national level.

In the context of widespread terrorism, what was legal in theory and what happened in practice had little to do with each other. As the situation increasingly became one of unrestrained violence, the capability of the judicial system to monitor the course of events was reduced markedly. In addition, the judicial system was unable to escape the loss of confidence in state institutions in general that had occurred among the Peruvian public. The discrediting of the judicial system was a significant step toward the total erosion of constitutional order.

Public Administration

Public administration in Peru, already one of the weakest on the continent as of 1968, has experienced a dramatic increase in the size of state enterprises and the number of civil servants. That increase has been accompanied by a gradual decrease in available funds to run the administration, partly because of the inefficiency of several of the state-sector enterprises. The Petroleum Enterprise of Peru (Petroleos del Perú—Petroperú), for example, lost US$700 million in 1987 alone. Tax collection has been virtually nonexistent, with the government having to rely on a tax base of 7 percent of gross national product (GNP—see Glossary), a figure comparable to Bangladesh's 8.6 percent and Uganda's 8.2 percent. Public expenditures per person were US$1,100 in 1975; in 1990 they were only US$180.

These trends were exacerbated markedly during the 1985–90 APRA government of García, as party patronage practices dominated the administration of the state. The number of state employees increased from about 282,400 in 1985 to almost 833,000 in 1990, and government resources all but disappeared because of enormous fiscal deficits and hyperinflation. State-sector workers were not even paid during the last few months of the García government.

The result was a rise in corruption and inefficiency, leaving Peru with one of the most inefficient state sectors in the world. Improvements in the future were likely to be guided by budgetary constraints, as the resources simply did not exist to maintain the existing number of civil servants in the public administration. The short-term costs would be a cutback in already scarce public services and a possible increase in political protest among displaced civil servants. Most Peruvians simply did without the services that even a minimal public administration would normally offer, or else they found some way of attaining them in the informal sector, usually at a much higher price.

Local and Regional Government

Municipal Governments

The process of independent municipal government was initiated with the first nationwide municipal elections in December 1963. This process was halted by twelve years of military rule after 1968, but was reinitiated with the November 1980 municipal elections (see table 19, Appendix). Each municipality has been run autonomously by a municipal council (*consejo municipal*), a provincial council (*consejo provincial*), and a district council (*consejo distrital*), all of whose members were directly elected. Municipalities had jurisdiction over their internal organization and they administered their assets and income, taxes, transportation, local public services, urban development, and education systems.

Yet, the autonomy of municipalities may have been reduced by their financial dependence on the central government. Their funds have come primarily from property taxes, licenses and patents required for professional services, market fees, vehicle taxes, tolls from bridges and roads, fines, and donations from urban migrant clubs. In the majority of municipalities, where the bulk of the inhabitants are poor, those with legal title to a home are in the minority; few people even own their own vehicles; roads are not paved; and there is a dramatic shortage of basic services, such as water and electricity. Most municipalities can hardly generate the revenue to cover operating costs, much less to provide desperately needed services. Thus, a degree of dependence on the central government for resources may limit somewhat the potential for autonomous initiative. Although this situation is hardly unique in Latin America, the shortage of resources in Peru is particularly extreme.

The municipal process has also come under substantial threat from the SL. An important component of its strategy was to sabotage the 1989 municipal and presidential elections. The group launched a ruthless campaign in which elected officials or candidates for electoral offices were targeted. During the 1985–89 period, the SL assassinated forty-five mayors. In a campaign of violence prior to the 1989 elections, it killed over 120 elected officials or municipal candidates, resulting in the resignation or withdrawal of 500 other candidates. In December 1988, dozens of Andean mayors resigned, citing lack of protection from terrorist threats; many rural towns were left with no authorities whatsoever. Voters were also threatened with having their index fingers chopped off by the SL. The threats were most effective in the more remote regions, such as Ayacucho, where null and blank voting in the 1990 elections was the highest in the country.

Regional Governments

The constitution of 1979 mandated the establishment of regional governments in Peru. Regionalization was part of the original APRA program of the 1920s. In 1988 the APRA government finally initiated the process with a law providing for the creation, administration, and modification of regions, which would replace the former departments. Between 1987 and 1990, the APRA government also issued corresponding laws creating eleven of the twelve regions called for under law, with the Lima/Callao region remaining under negotiation (see fig. 13). In 1991 debates in Congress continued on the Lima/Callao and San Martín regions, with the latter voting to separate from La Libertad Department. The highly politicized debates centered on whether senators should be elected by region or by national district, and on the method by which regional assemblies are elected. Five of the regions held their first elections for regional assemblies on November 12, 1989, in conjunction with the municipal elections, and the other six regions held elections in conjunction with the April presidential elections.

By law each regional assembly consisted of provincial mayors (30 percent); directly elected representatives (40 percent); and delegates from institutions representative of the social, economic, and cultural activities of the region (30 percent). In 1990 APRA and the United Left (Izquierda Unida—IU) dominated the regions, with APRA controlling six, IU three, and the Democratic Front (Frente Democrático—Fredemo) only one.

The process of regionalization was more one of administrative shuffling than of substance. However, the regional governments faced the same resource constraints that substantially limited the ability of municipal governments to implement independent activities. The central government is in theory supposed to transfer funds and assets, such as state-sector enterprises, to the regions, but in practice this has only happened piecemeal. This tendency had been exacerbated by the severity of the economic crisis and the poor fiscal situation inherited by the Fujimori government. The dynamic was made more conflictive because the regional governments were controlled by parties in opposition to the central government. The cutting of resources allocated to regional governments in the 1991 budget was a good indication of the constraints that regional governments would face for the foreseeable future. Moreover, the executive had taken back some powers that were originally given to the regions, such as control over the national tourist hotels. The regional governments, meanwhile, had heightened the debate with actions such as the refusal to pay the executive what was owed for electricity tariffs.

The Electoral System

Suffrage was free, equal, secret, and obligatory for all those between the ages of eighteen and seventy. The right to participate in politics could be taken away only when one was sentenced to prison or given a sentence that stripped a person of his or her political rights. No political party was given preference by the government, and free access to the government-owned mass media was given in proportion to the percentage of that party's results in the previous election. The National Elections Board, which was autonomous, was responsible for electoral processes at the national and local levels.

National elections for the presidency and the Congress were held every five years. If no one presidential candidate received an absolute majority, the first- and second-place candidates were in a runoff election. The president could not be reelected for a consecutive term, but deputies and senators could be.

Direct municipal elections were held every three years. Regional governments were elected every five years. Elections of regional governments were held in conjunction with either the December 1989 municipal or April 1990 national elections.

In the late 1980s and early 1990s, the electoral process came under substantial threat from the SL, which made the sabotaging of elections an explicit goal. Despite terrorist threats in the 1990 presidential elections, voter turnout was higher than in 1985, with the exception of some emergency zones in the southern Sierra, where the abstention rate was as high as 40 percent. Null and blank voting was about 14.5 percent of the total in the first round in 1990 and 9.5 percent in the second (see table 20; table 21, Appendix).

The threat from the SL was such that in some remote rural towns there were no local officials at all because potential candidates were not willing to jeopardize their lives in order to run for office. Although there was no doubt that the SL failed to jeopardize the 1990 elections, it managed to pose a significant threat to the process, particularly in remote rural areas. Given the severity and brutality of the SL's threat, it was actually a credit to the Peruvian electoral process that elections were held regularly and with such high voter-turnout ratios, although fines for not voting were also a factor.

Political Dynamics

Political Parties

Until April 5, 1992, Peru had had a multiparty system and numerous political parties, some of which had been in existence for several decades. Yet, in 1990 the Peruvian electorate by and

large rejected established parties and voted for a virtual unknown from outside the traditional party system. Alberto Fujimori's rapid and sudden rise to power and the resulting government that lacked a political party base signified a crisis for Peru's party system, and a crisis of representation more generally. These crises resulted from the severity of the socioeconomic situation and also from the poor performance of several of the traditional parties in government.

American Popular Revolutionary Alliance

APRA, Peru's oldest and only well-institutionalized party, was founded by Víctor Raúl Haya de la Torre in Mexico City in May 1924. The APRA program espoused an anti-imperialist, Marxist-oriented but uniquely Latin American-based solution to Peru's and Latin America's problems. APRA influenced several political movements throughout Latin America, including Bolivia's Nationalist Revolutionary Movement (Movimiento Nacionalista Revolucionario—MNR) and Costa Rica's National Liberation Party (Partido Liberación Nacional—PLN). Years of repression and clandestinity, as well as single-handed dominance of the party by Haya de la Torre, resulted in sectarian and hierarchical traits that were analogous to some communist parties. In addition, opportunistic ideological swings to the right by Haya de la Torre in the 1950s, in exchange for attaining legal status for the party, resulted in an exodus of some of APRA's most talented young leaders to the Marxist left. These shifts created cleavages between APRA and the rest of society and were significant obstacles to democratic consensus-building during APRA's 1985–90 tenure in government.

In any case, the party maintained a devoted core of followers that remained permanent party loyalists. In May 1989, APRA chose as its standard bearer Luis Alva Castro, a long-time rival to President García. APRA was as much a social phenomenon as a political movement, with a significant sector of society among its membership whose loyalty to the party and its legacy was unwavering. Despite APRA's disastrous tenure in power, in the first round of the 1990 elections it obtained 19.6 percent of the vote, more than any other of the traditional parties.

Popular Action

Fernando Belaúnde Terry founded Popular Action (Acción Popular—AP) in 1956 as a reformist alternative to the status quo conservative forces and the controversial APRA party. Although Belaúnde's message was not all that different from APRA's, his tactics were more inclusive and less confrontational. He was able to appeal to some of the same political base as APRA, primarily the middle class, but also to a wider base of professionals and white-collar workers. The AP had significant electoral success, attaining the presidency in 1963 and 1980, but the party was more of an electoral machine for the persona of Belaúnde than an institutionalized organization. In addition, whereas in the 1960s the AP was seen as a reformist party, by the 1980s—as Peru's political spectrum had shifted substantially to the left—the AP was positioned on the center-right. With the debacle of the second Belaúnde government, the AP fared disastrously in 1985, attaining only 6.4 percent of the vote. In 1990 the AP participated in the elections as a part of the conservative coalition behind Mario Vargas Llosa and suffered, as did all political parties, an electoral rejection.

The Christian Democrats

The Christian Democratic Party (Partido Demócrata Cristiano—PDC) was a relatively small, center-right party influenced by Christian Democratic thought. Slightly more conservative than the AP, the PDC, which was founded in 1956, also was perceived to be more to the right as Peru's spectrum shifted left. The PDC on its own was not able to garner an electoral representation of over 10 percent after 1980. A splinter group, the Popular Christian Party (Partido Popular Cristiano—PPC), was founded by Luis Bedoya Reyes (the mayor of Lima from 1963 to 1966) in 1966.

The Democratic Front

The AP and the PPC together provided the organizational basis for Mario Vargas Llosa and his independent Liberty Movement (Movimiento de Libertad). Vargas Llosa, who entered politics to protest García's nationalization of Peru's banks in 1987, started out as an independent, backed by the Liberty Movement. In late 1988, however, Vargas Llosa made a formal alliance, known as Fredemo, with the AP and the PPC because he felt such an alliance would provide him with a necessary party organizational base. By doing so, he alienated several members of his own coalition, including one of his primary backers, Hernando de Soto, who felt that Vargas Llosa was allying with the "traditional" right. Analysis of the electoral results indicated that the majority of voters were also reluctant to support Peru's traditional, conservative politicians. The Fredemo campaign spent inordinate amounts of money on advertising—US$12 million, versus US$2 million spent by the next highest spender, APRA. The free spending, in conjunction with the use in television campaign advertisements featuring white, foreign-born singers, revealed how these parties continued to represent the interests of the nation's elite, who were of European ancestry, and how out of touch they were with the nation's poor, who were of indigenous heritage (see Culture, Class, and Hierarchy in Society, ch. 2).

The Left

The 1990 results also demonstrated that the population was unwilling to vote for the nation's hopelessly divided left. Split into Leninist, Maoist, Marxist, Trotskyite, and Socialist camps, the left in Peru had been severely fragmented since its origins. It had its first experience as a legally recognized electoral force in the 1978–80 Constituent Assembly, in which the left made up approximately one-third of the delegates. Despite its relative strength at the grassroots level, the left was unable to unite behind one political front in the 1980 elections, and it contested the elections as nine separate political factions. Such splintering limited its potential in those elections and played into the hands of Belaúnde. The left together attained a total of 16.7 percent of the vote; APRA, divided and leaderless after the death of Haya de la Torre, garnered 27.4 percent; Belaúnde won 45.4 percent.

Shortly after the 1981 elections, the majority of the factions of the Socialist, Marxist, and Maoist left (with the obvious exception of the SL, which had gone underground in the early 1970s), formed the IU coalition. By 1986, under the leadership of Alfonso Barrantes Lingán, the IU was strong enough to take the municipality of Lima, as well as to become the major opposition force to the APRA government. Barrantes had been the runner-up in the 1985 national elections, winning 22.2 percent of the vote.

Yet, there were irreparable divisions from the outset between the moderate Barrantes faction, which remained committed, first to democracy, and the more militant factions, which were sympathetic to, if not overtly supportive of, "armed struggle" as a potential route. The existence of two active guerrilla movements made this a debate of overriding importance. Although much of the militant left condemned the brutal tactics of the SL, they remained sympathetic with and indeed often had ties to the more "conventional" tactics of the MRTA.

The breach came to a head in 1989, when Barrantes, the most popular politician the left had in its ranks, and the bulk of the moderates split off and formed the Leftist Socialist Accord (Acuerdo Socialista Izquierdista—ASI). The larger and best-organized parties, including the radical Mariateguist Unified Party (Partido Unificado Mariateguista—PUM) and the Peruvian Communist Party (Partido Comunista Peruano—PCP), remained in the IU.

A divided left quarrelling over ideological differences hardly seemed the solution to Peru's quagmire in 1990. In the 1990 elections, the left had its poorest showing since the formation of the IU, with the ASI and IU together garnering less than 12 percent of the vote.

Cambio '90

Cambio '90 only entered the Peruvian political spectrum in early 1990, but by June 1991 it was the most powerful political force in the nation. Cambio's success hinged largely on the success of its candidate for the presidency, Alberto Fujimori, an agricultural engineer and rector of the National Agrarian University (Universidad Nacional Agraria—UNA) in Lima's La Molina District from 1984 to 1989. Fujimori's appeal to a large extent was his standing as a political outsider.

At the same time, Cambio's success was also attributed largely to its eclectic political base and its active grassroots campaign. Cambio's two main bases of support were the Peruvian Association of Small- and Medium-Sized Businesses (Asociación Peruana de Empresas Medias y Pequeñas—Apemipe) and the informal sector workers who associated their cause with Apemipe, and the evangelical movement. Less than 4 percent of the Peruvian population was Protestant. The Evangelicals were extremely active at the grassroots level, particularly in areas where traditional parties were weak, such as the urban shantytowns and rural areas in the Sierra. Although Cambio began activities only in January 1990, by the time of the elections it had 200,000 members in its ranks.

However, Cambio's success at the polls did not translate into a lasting party machinery. Cambio was much more of a front than a political party, and its ability to hold together was called into question within a few weeks after attaining power. Cambio's two bases of support had little in common with each other except opposition to Vargas Llosa. Their links to Fujimori were quite recent and were ruptured to a large extent when Fujimori opted, out of necessity, for an orthodox economic shock program. Less than six months into his government, Fujimori broke with many of his Cambio supporters, including the second vice president and leader of the Evangelical Movement, Carlos García y García, and Apemipe. The latter became disenchanted with Fujimori because small businesses were threatened by the dramatic price rises and opening to foreign competition that the ''Fujishock'' program entailed.

Nonparty Organizations

The rapid rise of Cambio reflected a more far-reaching phenomenon in Peru: the growth of extrasystem democratic political activity.

In conjunction with the rise in economic importance of the informal sector was a rise in activity and importance of a host of "informal" political groups: neighborhood organizations, communal kitchens, popular economic organizations, and nongovernmental organizations. Although originating largely outside the realm of traditional parties and politics, these groups became critical actors in local-level democratic politics. Usually autonomous and democratic in origin and structure, they were often wary of political parties, which attempted to co-opt them, or at least to elicit their support for wider-reaching political goals. These organizations were primarily concerned with daily survival issues, such as obtaining basic services like water and electricity. They tended to support political parties as a convenient way to attain their goals, but just as easily withdrew that support when it did not provide tangible ends. They had a tendency, but by no means a constant one, to vote for parties of the left. This fact could be explained in part by the Peruvian left's approach to grassroots movements, which was usually—but not always—less sectarian and hierarchical than that of traditional parties, such as APRA.

Thus, the relations that informal groups had with political parties were by no means simple or clear-cut. As the varied results from the 1980–90 elections demonstrate, the urban poor had a tendency, which was not without shifts, to vote for the left. They had few binding ties to political parties and were quite willing to vote for nonparty actors, from Manuel A. Odría (president, 1948–50, 1950–56) in the 1950s to Ricardo Belmont Cassinelli (as mayor of Lima in 1989) and Fujimori in 1990. Because the urban poor's need for basic services was so grave, their vote was most often determined by the most credible promise for basic-service delivery. Broader political goals of the parties were only a concern once basic needs had been met. Still, the gap between these groups and parties was significant. Parties play a role in virtually all consolidated democracies, and the difficulties of governing a fragmented society and polity such as Peru's became increasingly evident as the Fujimori government was forced to implement unpopular economic policies in the absence of an organized political base.

Electoral defeats usually trigger internal party changes and democratization. In 1990 all Peruvian parties faced electoral losses. The parties were well aware of the need to reform in order to remain politically viable entities. In early 1991, the Christian Democrats, for example, launched a process of internal party reform and an evaluation of their relations with groups where their support base was weak, such as the shantytowns. The left underwent a process of ideological and strategic reflection at approximately the same time. Most of the other political parties likely would have followed suit. To the extent that parties failed to reform to adapt to new political realities and to the needs and strategies of the plethora of grassroots groups and local organizations in Peru, a crisis of representation in Peruvian democracy, if and when it was restored, appeared more likely for the foreseeable future, threatening its viability.

Interest Groups

The Military

The military in Peru has traditionally played an influential role in the nation's politics, whether directly or indirectly. Prior to the 1968 revolution, the military was seen as caretaker of the interests of conservative elites, and its involvement in politics usually entailed the repression of "radical" alternatives, particularly APRA. An APRA uprising and brutal military retaliation in Trujillo in 1932 initiated a long period of violence and strained relations between the two. As late as 1962, when General Ricardo Pérez Godoy led a military coup to prevent Haya de la Torre from becoming president, the military was willing to resort to extraconstitutional means to prevent APRA from coming to power.

By 1962, however, it was evident that the military was no longer solely the preserver of elite interests, and that it was increasingly influenced by a new military school of thought, the National Security Doctrine, which posited that development and social reform were integral to national security. The Advanced Military Studies Center (Centro de Altos Estudios Militares—CAEM) in Lima was a proponent of this philosophy in the 1950s and 1960s. In addition, the Peruvian military's involvement in fighting guerrilla uprisings in the southern Sierra in the mid-1960s gave many officers a first exposure to the destitute conditions of the rural poor and to the potential unrest that those conditions could breed.

Thus, the military's 1968 intervention was far from a typical military coup. Rather, it was a military-led attempt at implementing far-reaching economic and social reforms, such as the Agrarian Reform Law of 1969 and the Industrial Community Law of 1970. The military's lack of understanding of civil society, demonstrated by its authoritarian attempts to control popular participation through a government-sponsored social mobilization agency, the National System for Supporting Social Mobilization (Sistema Nacional de Apoyo a la Mobilización Social—Sinamos), was largely responsible for the failure of its reforms. When the military left power in 1980, it left a legacy of economic mismanagement, incomplete reforms, and a society more radicalized and politicized than when it had taken over.

Yet, the military's revolutionary experiment changed the image of the institution, as well as its own views about the benefits of direct government control. It was, at least for the foreseeable future, immune from direct intervention in politics. It was no longer seen, however, and no longer perceived itself, as a monolithic conservative institution, but rather as the institution that had attempted to do what no political force had been able to do: radically transform the nation's economy and society. Its failure may have strengthened the voice of conservatives within its ranks, but it retained the awareness that social reform and economic development were critical to Peru's social stability and ultimately its national security. And as keeper of national security, it, more than any other force in the nation, was constantly reminded of this by the presence of the SL and other insurgent groups.

The large proportion of the country under state-of-emergency rule, coupled with the military's desire to fight against the SL unconstrained by civilian control, had understandably created tensions between successive civilian governments and the military. As in the case of several other transitions to democracy in Latin America, the Peruvian military took precautions to protect its institutional viability and to increase its strength vis-à-vis civilian government. From the outset, the Belaúnde government was forced to accept certain conditions set by the military pertaining to budgetary autonomy and states of emergency. Nineteen days before the surrender of power to the Belaúnde administration, the military passed the Mobilization Law, with minimum publicity in order to avoid civilian reaction. The law enabled the military to expropriate or requisition companies, services, labor, and materials from all Peruvians or foreigners in the country at times of national emergency. These times included cases of "internal subversion and internal disasters." In addition, because the Belaúnde government had failed to take the SL seriously until it was too late, the government defaulted to the military in the design and implementation of a counterinsurgency strategy.

The García government began with a different approach. García fired three top generals responsible for civilian massacres in the emergency zones, and in a blow to traditional budgetary autonomy halved an air force order for French Mirage jets. However, García's image suffered a major blow after he personally gave orders for the military to do whatever was necessary to put down a revolt of the SL inmates in Lima's prisons in June 1986, resulting in the massacre of 300 prisoners, most of whom had already surrendered.

As the government lost coherence and as economic crisis and political stalemate set in, pressure on the military subsided, and its de facto control over the counterinsurgency campaign increased.

Because the Fujimori government had no organized institutional base, it was in a difficult position vis-à-vis the military. Although the military had no desire to take direct control of the government, it indicated the one scenario that would force it to intervene—if no one were running the state. Even at the height of the APRA government's crisis, when President García was in virtual hiding in the government palace, the military could rely on APRA to run the state. If a similar loss of control by President Fujimori occurred, there would be no such institution with a stake in running the state, a scenario that might force the military to act. Fujimori had clearly made a point of building strong support in one sector of the army and in return seemed to be backing increased independence for the military in the counterinsurgency war.

A good example of the military's independence was the passage of Decree Law 171, which stipulated that military personnel in emergency zones were on active duty full-time and therefore could be tried only in military courts, which try only for neglect of duty and not for offenses, such as murder or torture. In addition, the government exacerbated tensions with some sectors of the military in September 1990 by refusing to sign a US$93-million aid agreement with the United States that included US$36 million in military aid. The Fujimori government felt the accord's coca eradication policy did not sufficiently take economic development into account. Some within the armed forces, which in general were desperately short of funds, felt that the government should take what it could get. In May 1991, Fujimori conceded to both United States and Peruvian military pressure and signed the accord.

In short, the situation under Fujimori was one of de facto military control, not just of the emergency zones, but of the areas of government that the military perceived to be its domain. Demonstrative of the military's increasing influence over certain areas of government was the fact that the Ministry of Defense and the Ministry of Interior were both headed by generals.

The Church

Although Peru does not have an official religion, the Roman Catholic Church—to which over 90 percent of Peruvians belonged—is recognized in the constitution as deserving of government cooperation. Traditionally, the Roman Catholic Church has monopolized religion in the public domain.

In the Peruvian Catholic Church hierarchy, staunch conservatives, such as Archbishop Juan Landázuri Ricketts, wielded a great deal of influence. Six of the total eighteen bishops, including Landázuri, belonged to the ultraconservative Opus Dei movement. At the same time, the founder of liberation theology (see Glossary), Gustavo Gutiérrez, was a member of the official church in Peru, and liberation theology had a strong presence at the grassroots level. Unlike Brazil, where the official church could be described as liberal and critical of the more conservative Vatican, or Colombia, where the church was a loyal follower of the Vatican's policies, in the Peruvian Church hierarchy both trends coexisted, or at least competed for influence. Conservatives followed the dictates of Pope John Paul II, a strong proponent of theological orthodoxy and vertical control of the church. This view contrasted sharply with the progressives in the Latin American church, who espoused the mandate of Vatican II, which exhorted the clergy to become actively involved in humanity's struggle for peace and justice, and to help the poor to help themselves rather than accept their fate.

At the grassroots level, the church was extremely active at organizing neighborhood organizations and self-help groups, such as communal kitchens and mothers' clubs (see Catholicism and Community, ch. 2). Church activities at this level had little to do with theoretical debates at higher levels, although they tended to emanate from the more progressive sectors within. Church-related organizations, such as Caritas (Catholic Relief Services), were active in providing local efforts with donations of food and funds from abroad. Indeed, Caritas had a nationwide network of coverage superior to or at least rivaling that of any state ministry or institution.

In addition to Caritas, the other major nongovernmental organizer of communal kitchens and mothers' clubs in Lima was the Seventh-Day Adventist Church, which reflected the increasing importance of the Evangelical Movement. Although only about 4.5 percent of Peru's population was Protestant, the Evangelical Movement was extremely active at the grassroots level and, as aforementioned, was critical to the victory of Fujimori and Cambio '90 in poor areas. The Catholic Church hierarchy felt sufficiently threatened by the Evangelicals' support for Fujimori that it unofficially backed Vargas Llosa, an agnostic, against Fujimori, a Catholic.

The church, to the extent that it was an organizer of the poor, had increasingly come into conflict with the SL. Initially, the SL paid little attention to the clergy. In Ayacucho, for example, where the traditionally oriented church hierarchy had little involvement with social issues, the church was of little relevance to the SL. However, in the late 1980s, the SL's strategy shifted, and the group

233

became more concerned with the church's organizational potential. The SL had a more difficult challenge in organizing support, particularly in areas where the church had been active in encouraging close community bonds, such as parts of Cajamarca and Puno. In such areas, as in the shantytowns surrounding Lima, clergy had increasingly become targets of SL assassinations as well.

In the face of the weakening of other state institutions, the church's role, at least at the grassroots level, had increased in importance (see Community Life and Institutions, ch. 2). Caritas was the primary mobilizer of food donations and aid during the most critical stage of the Fujimori government's shock stabilization plan. Although the government promised its own social emergency programs, none materialized, and the church surfaced as the primary vehicle for channeling aid to the poor. This activity increased the visibility of the clergy as a target of SL attacks and posed difficult choices for members of the clergy who continued to operate in the regions where the SL had a strong presence—the majority of the areas where most of the poor of Peru resided.

Economic Associations

The major economic associations in Peru were the National Industries Association (Sociedad Nacional de Industrias—SNI), the National Confederation of Private Business (Confederación Nacional de Instituciones Empresariales Privadas—Confiep), and the Apemipe (Peruvian Association of Small and Medium-Sized Businesses). Traditionally, such organizations had played a minimal role in politics. In the 1980s, however, they became actively involved in the nation's politics.

García's national understanding (*concertación*) strategy called for cooperation between government and business in economic policymaking. Nevertheless, García bypassed organized business sectors, the foremost among them being Confiep, and dealt instead directly with the twelve most powerful businesspeople in the country, the so-called twelve apostles. Thus, when García threatened the entire private sector with his surprise nationalization of the nation's banks, Confiep became one of the most active supporters of the bankers protesting García's move, and subsequently of Vargas Llosa's Liberty Movement. Meanwhile, two former presidents of Confiep—now senators Francisco Pardo Mesones of Somos Libres (We Are Free) and Ricardo Vega Llona of Fredemo—launched independent candidacies in the 1990 elections.

Ironically, Apemipe became politically active in opposition to Vargas Llosa and his proposed policies, which threatened the viability of many small-businesspeople. The former president of

Reed homes erected by squatters in Lima's Pamplona Alta area
Children in the shantytown of Huáscar, Lima
Courtesy Carol Graham

235

Apemipe, Máximo San Román, ran as first vice president for Cambio and became president of the Senate.

Organized business, per se, has never been particularly influential in Peru. Instead, strong influence has been wielded by foreign companies, such as the International Petroleum Corporation (IPC), or by families, such as the Romeros and the Wieses, who had substantial holdings across a variety of industries. Yet with the economic situation in May 1991 and the substantial reduction of foreign investment, the domestic private sector had increased in its relative economic importance. Thus, the sector's tendency to use its organizations to influence political trends was likely to continue for the foreseeable future.

Labor Unions

The labor movement in Peru has traditionally been weak, and its fate, until 1968, was inextricably linked to APRA. Very much affected by the enclave or anti-union enterprises and by the rural or community background of many of its members, labor was unable to articulate a coherent set of class interests. APRA, with its organizational capacity and popular following, was perhaps the only existing mobilization vehicle for organized labor. APRA dominated the Confederation of Peruvian Workers (Confederación de Trabajadores del Perú—CTP), which it founded in 1944 and which was officially recognized in 1964. The major labor dispute was traditionally between the CTP and APRA, and there was a direct correlation between union activity and the legal status of APRA, which was usually banned by military governments. APRA was more concerned with using the labor movement for its own ends than with enhancing the objectives of organized labor. APRA curtailed strike activity, for example, during its years of collaboration with the government of Manuel Prado y Ugarteche (1939–45, 1956–62).

Union activity increased dramatically during the military years with the introduction of a new labor code and the Industrial Reform Law, culminating in the union-led general strikes of 1977 and 1978. Yet, the labor and industries laws, which made it more difficult to dismiss a worker in Peru than in any industrialized nation, acted as a major disincentive to formal-sector employment. These laws, coupled with the dramatic economic decline of the 1980s, led to a substantial decrease in the relative power of labor unions by 1990.

After 1968 the communist labor movement, the General Confederation of Peruvian Workers (Confederación General de Trabajadores del Perú—CGTP) was legalized and began to erode APRA's monopoly on union support, owing in part to the party's relinquishing its radical stance. The Federation of Workers of the Peruvian Revolution (Central de Trabajadores de la Revolución Peruana—CTRP), which was set up by the military as an attempt to control the workers' movement, never really got off the ground, particularly in the face of the powerful CGTP. In 1991 the CGTP remained the most important union confederation in Peru.

The traits that were held typical of APRA union supporters—marginal, socially ambitious, and socially frustrated—began to characterize the Maoist left and its affiliated unions under the CGTP umbrella in the 1970s. These groups, such as the powerful teachers' union, the Trade Union of Education Workers of Peru (Sindicato Único de Trabajadores de la Enseñanza del Perú—SUTEP), and the miners' confederation, the National Federation of Syndicated Mining and Metallurgical Workers of Peru (Federación Nacional de Trabajadores Mineros y Metalúrgicos Sindicalistas del Perú—FNTMMSP), were key actors in the general strikes that virtually brought down the military regime in the late 1970s. In addition, the expansion of state industries, each of which had its own affiliated union, substantially increased the number of organized workers.

By the early 1980s, economic decline began to erode the power of unions, as did the neoliberal strategy adhered to by the Belaúnde government. The APRA government completely bypassed organized labor, as it did organized industry in its *concertación* strategy. García's populist tactics left little room for organized labor. Although there was a high number of strikes by state-sector workers during the García government, particularly during the last two "crisis" years, the strikes were generally more defensive, in the face of economic decline, than political. Most of the general strikes that were called during the García government were largely a failure, attaining only minimal support.

One reason that organized labor was less able to pursue political goals was the SL, which launched several "armed strikes" in various cities throughout the García years. Although these strikes had varying degrees of success, they rarely had union support because supporting the strikes meant supporting the SL. Increasingly, street protest for political purposes signified support for armed insurrection, which the majority of unions rejected. Indeed, there were even violent clashes between the SL and the CGTP during one general strike.

The SL had its own affiliated union, the Class Movement of Workers and Laborers (Movimiento de Obreros y Trabajadores Clasistas—MOTC), which operated primarily in the industries along Lima's Central Highway (Trans-Andean Highway), the industrial belt of the city. Of the four major companies along this highway, the MOTC had made substantial inroads in three. The MOTC did not necessarily control unions, but was tenacious in its support of strikes and was able to establish a strong presence in these industries. Yet, it also created rifts in the labor movement in general because many workers did not necessarily want to be affiliated with the SL. Indicative of the extent of conflict was the SL's killing of fifty-one union leaders, primarily mineworkers, between January and May 1989, and its assassination of a prominent textile leader in October 1989.

The one labor sector that was able to exert substantial pressure during the APRA government was the miners' federation, the FNTMMSP, which in 1989 staged a strike involving 90,000 miners and costing the government hundreds of millions of dollars in lost export earnings. Meanwhile, the federation was also targeted by the SL. Although able to infiltrate the union to some extent, staging armed strikes and attacking mining facilities, the SL was by no means able to gain control of it. Nevertheless, the SL's presence caused violence from both the left (there were clashes between the SL and nonsympathetic miners) and the right (the leader of the miners' federation was assassinated by the APRA-and military-linked paramilitary squad, the Rodrigo Franco Command). Some critics felt that the government and the National Mining and Petroleum Company (Sociedad Nacional de Minería y Petróleo— SNMP) found the SL infiltration of the mines a convenient excuse for declaring a state of emergency in the region.

Only 15 to 20 percent of the labor force was unionized in 1990, making that force a rather privileged sector of the working class. Underemployment was as high as 75 percent; and only 9 percent of Lima's economically active population was fully employed.

The prospects for the union movement in Peru in the early 1990s were dismal at best. On the one hand, the economic crisis made access to a job a luxury. Protest by organized labor was a last attempt at protecting salary levels that had deteriorated by over 50 percent in the 1985–90 period. On the other, the SL's drive to establish influence among organized labor presented a challenge to all the unions that wished to retain their independence.

In the event of an economic recovery and the adoption of a more realistic labor code that did not make access to a job a privilege for a small minority, organized labor might be able to enhance its status as the protector of workers rights rather than the proponent of political radicalism. Still, these developments also hinged on the defeat of the foremost proponent of radicalism, the SL—an unlikely scenario in the short term.

Students

Like the labor unions, the student movement has seen its rise and fall in Peru, and its fate was also inextricably linked to that of the SL. Compared with Peru's other social welfare indicators, Peru had a relatively high rate of literacy (80 percent), owing in large part to the strong emphasis that both Belaúnde regimes placed on education. The numbers of students enrolled in universities increased dramatically in the 1960s, and, consequently, so did their level of organization. Critics had justifiably contended that the emphasis on education was at the expense of other key social welfare expenditures, such as health (see Health and Well-Being, ch. 2).

Students had a strong tradition of political organization in Peru. For example, APRA began as a student and workers union. Student leaders, both of APRA and of the left, also played an important role in the protests against the military regime in the late 1970s. Congruent with the growth in relative strength of the Marxist left in politics was an increase in their presence in student organizations. In early 1991, there was a host of university student organizations, most allied with different factions of the left or with APRA. Some organizations were also allied with the SL or MRTA. Student supporters of the ''new'' right, such as the Liberty Movement, had also emerged, although they were by far in the minority. The increase in student organization had occurred in conjunction with the curbing of financing for universities and the shrinking of economic opportunities for university graduates, which had resulted in a radicalization of the university community in general. Although a few prestigious private universities continued to guarantee their students top degrees and professional opportunities, the quality of the education attained by large numbers of students at state universities varied and was often quite poor. Thus, many universities increasingly had become havens for frustration (see Universities, ch. 2).

The extreme manifestation of this phenomenon was the birth and growth of the SL in the University of Huamanga (Universidad de Huamanga) in Ayacucho in the 1970s. Abimael Guzmán Reynoso, a professor at the university and eventually director of personnel, was the founder and leader of the SL. The SL virtually controlled the university for several years, and students were indoctrinated in the SL philosophy. The university trained students, mainly from the Ayacucho area, primarily in education; but a degree from Huamanga was considered inferior to one from a university in Lima, and students had few opportunities other than returning to their hometowns to teach. As jobs for graduates were few, becoming an active militant in the SL provided an opportunity of sorts (see also Internal Threats, ch. 5).

An analogous phenomenon occurred in most of the universities in Lima in the 1980s. Poorly funded and staffed, universities had far more students than they could adequately train. Employment opportunities had virtually disappeared, and university graduates often ended up driving taxis. The oldest university in the Americas, the state-funded San Marcos University, had become the center of Peru's student radicalism. SL graffiti covered the walls; police raids on the university yielded large caches of weapons and ammunition, as well as arrests. Professors who openly sympathized with the SL were the norm. In 1989 student elections, members of the student organization that supported the SL won in first place and controlled facilities such as the cafeteria.

Like union members, university students often were confronted with a dire predicament. They were the focus of SL organizational efforts, and at the same time their economic opportunities had virtually disappeared. Peaceful organizational efforts to improve their position had little potential in the current context, yet violent efforts were inextricably linked to the SL. Radicalism was in theory an appealing alternative, but in reality the ultraviolent form in which it manifested itself in the SL was hardly an alternative. Unfortunately, finding a job was also less and less a realistic alternative.

News Media

In 1990 Peru had one of the freest and most varied presses in the world, with virtually no curbs on what was published. The best established and largest circulating newspaper was the slightly conservative daily, *El Comercio. Expreso,* owned by former minister of economy and finance Manuel Ulloa, was also slightly to the right of center. A variety of left-leaning dailies included *Cambio, El Diario de Marka,* and *La República. Hoy* was the pro-APRA daily. *El Diario* was a pro-SL newspaper that used to be published daily in Lima and circulated approximately 5,000 copies a day. The government closed it in late 1988, after the editor was accused of being a member of the SL, but it reappeared the next year as a weekly. A state-owned newspaper, *El Peruano,* published a daily listing of decrees and government proceedings. *Oiga* magazine was a right-wing weekly, *Caretas* and *Sí* were centrist weeklies. *Quehacer* was a bimonthly research publication sympathizing with the left.

Peru had a total of 140 state and privately owned television channels. Channel 4, the state-owned channel, provided relatively well-balanced news, as it had fierce competition from its private competitors. The popular weekly news program, "Panorama," which broadcast in-depth interviews with a wide range of intellectuals, politicians, and even guerrillas, was quite influential. The MRTA, for example, made its entrance into national politics when its takeover of Juanjuí in San Martín Department was aired on Panorama.

Peru's media were in general varied, competitive, and highly informative, and options from all sides of the political spectrum were available. Peru's population was a highly informed one, with even the poorest people usually having access to television. In early 1991, when the intelligence police found a video of Abimael Guzmán Reynoso dancing in a drunken stupor, it was aired on national television. When in early 1991 President Fujimori passed Decree Law 171, the media played a major role in raising public awareness as to the impunity that it imparted onto the armed forces and the threat that it posed to investigative journalism in the emergency zones. The publicity was in part responsible for the repeal of the decree in Congress. Indeed, the extent to which freedom of the press continued to exist in Peru, despite the many other obstacles to democratic government, was an important and positive force for Peru's democracy.

Political Trends

Roots of the 1990–91 Crisis

There was no single explanation for the nature and severity of the crisis Peru faced in the early 1990s. The temptation to blame García and APRA was a strong one, given their dismal performance in government, but the crisis had much deeper roots. APRA inherited a nation beset with economic and social problems, but a political climate in which the consensus on the need for reform was unprecedented. The manner in which APRA governed resulted in an exacerbation of an existing breach between state and society. Consensus gave way to polarization and fragmentation of the party system, and economic policy fell prey to internal party politics, with disastrous results.

The Transition to Democracy

Like many other military establishments on the continent, the Peruvian military halted the civilian political process for a prolonged period of time (1968–80), attempted major structural economic change without a great deal of success, accumulated a large debt without public accountability, and then turned the political system back over to the same politicians it had previously ousted. The transition to democratic government, meanwhile, raised popular

241

expectations that a fragile new democracy with severely constrained resources could hardly hope to meet.

The 1980 elections were won, ironically, by Fernando Belaúnde, whom the military had overthrown in 1968. His victory was no surprise, given that the elections were contested by a leaderless and divided APRA, recovering from the recent death of Haya de la Torre, and by a fragmented left that presented what political scientist Sandra Woy Hazelton described as a "cacophony" of candidates and parties. Although Belaúnde was a charismatic personality, he had spent the military years in exile, and was hopelessly out of touch with Peru's political realities in 1980. His government stuck stubbornly to a neoliberal, export-oriented economic model at a time when the world recession caused the prices of Peru's major export products to plummet. At the same time, the government fueled inflation through fiscal expenditures on major infrastructure projects, ignoring the better judgment of the president of the Central Reserve Bank (Banco Central de Reservas—BCR, also known as Central Bank) (see The Search for New Directions, 1980–85, ch.3). Popular expectations raised by the transition to democracy were soon frustrated.

Despite the SL's launching of activities in 1980 and its substantial presence in Ayacucho by 1982, Belaúnde refused to take the group seriously, dismissing them as narcoterrorists. When the government finally realized that the SL was a substantial security threat as a guerrilla and terrorist group, its reaction was too little, too late, and ultimately counterproductive. The government sent special counterinsurgency forces, the Sinchis, to the Ayacucho region, where they were given a free hand. The repressive nature of the military activities and the military's lack of understanding of the SL resulted in unwarranted repression against the local population. The actions of the Sinchis, if anything, played into the SL's hands.

Natural disasters (floods and droughts) and economic decline and triple-digit inflation heightened the negative image of a government that was distant and detached from the population. This image was also exacerbated by Belaúnde's continuous insistence, amid economic crisis and the onset of guerrilla violence, that the solution to Peru's problems was the building of the Jungle Border Highway (*la carretera marginal de la selva* or *la marginal*), linking the Amazon region of the country to the coast. The severity of the economic crisis of the Belaúnde years and his government's poor public relations image opened the door for a major shift of the political spectrum to the left. By late 1983, García, as leader of the opposition in Congress, began to tap the increasing support for a radical solution to Peru's problems.

The García Government, 1985-90

By 1985 García and APRA were well-positioned to win the presidential elections. García was a charismatic orator who was convinced that he needed to "open up" APRA in order to win the nation's vote. He dropped all of APRA's sectarian symbols, such as the Aprista version of the Marseillaise and its six-pointed star, and replaced them with the popular song, "Mi Perú," and with slogans such as "my commitment is with all Peruvians." His attacks on neoliberal economics were directed primarily at foreign capital and the IMF, a convenient beating board because Peru was unlikely to get any capital inflow in the near future; he carefully avoided attacks on domestic capital. Thus, while cultivating the image of a radical among the poor, García also was perceived as the *mal menor*, or lesser evil, by the private sector, as opposed to the Marxist left. Finally, even conservatives recognized the need for reform in Peru by 1985, given the increasing presence of the SL. García defeated Alfonso Barrantes of the IU, taking 47.8 percent of the vote versus 22.2 percent for the IU (see table 19, Appendix). A run-off election (required if an absolute majority is not attained) was not held because Barrantes declined to run.

The first two years of the APRA government were a honeymoon of sorts. García enjoyed unprecedented popularity ratings of over 75 percent, owing in part to his populist personality and oratorical talents, and in part to the *concertación* strategy the government pursued (see The Search for New Directions, ch. 3). It was highly successful as a short-term strategy for a severely depressed economy, but obviously had its limits as a long-term plan. The private sector, meanwhile, gave García and his *concertación* strategy cautious support.

By mid-1987 it was clear that *concertación* had run its course, and a change of emphasis was necessary. At the same time, García was also under pressure from the left and from some sectors within his own party to implement more radical structural change. In June he suffered a defeat within the party when his main rival, former prime minister Luis Alva Castro, was elected president of the Chamber of Deputies. García at this point opted for a radical measure that was intended to retake the political initiative from his rivals. In his annual independence day address on July 28, 1987, García announced the surprise nationalization of the nation's banks. The measure was designed with a small group of advisers in the two weeks prior to its announcement, and few members of the

APRA party or government were consulted. For example, the octogenarian vice president of the republic, Luis Alberto Sánchez, learned of the measure just prior to García's announcement, and he was told by none other than former president Belaúnde. The measure in and of itself may not have been all that significant because only 20 percent of the nation's banks remained in private hands in 1987. However, the manner in which García presented it clearly indicated a change of political course. His rhetoric pitted the rich, lazy bankers against the poor, exploited people, and from that point on he began to speak of the ''bad'' capitalists. He launched a tirade of attacks on the domestic private sector, using precisely the kind of rhetoric he had avoided in the campaign and for the first two years of his presidency.

The private sector's fragile trust in García and the historically confrontational APRA was undermined. The situation was exacerbated by the manner in which APRA silently supported the measure and by the fact that those members of the party who spoke out against the measure were expelled. Foremost among these was the influential senator Jorge Torres Vallejo, who ironically was the person who had launched García's candidacy as secretary general of APRA in 1983.

The nationalization of the banks marked the beginning of the end. Political polarization set in, and the government increasingly lost coherence. The then moribund right found a cause and a candidate for its renovation, and latched onto the protest movement against the measure that was launched by Mario Vargas Llosa and his Liberty Movement. The left had no real cause to support the measure or to ally with the highly sectarian APRA. The poor, who lacked savings accounts, were hardly likely to rally to García's cause. The private sector withdrew its plans for investment as economic policy-making fell prey to political infighting in APRA and to García's own erratic behavior. In September 1988, the time when an austerity package was announced, García went into hiding in the palace and did not appear for a period of over thirty days.

Although reserves had run out, the government continued to maintain unrealistic subsidies, such as the five-tier exchange rate, funded by a growing fiscal deficit, which fueled hyperinflation. The situation was exacerbated by the constant resource drain from inefficient state enterprises, whose bureaucracy increased markedly during the APRA government. The combination of hyperinflation and public-sector debts that could not be paid resulted in a state that had virtually ceased to function. Living standards dropped dramatically as real wages were eroded by inflation, and services for the public, such as public hospital staff, were curbed markedly.

By the end of the APRA government, shortages of the most basic goods, such as water and electricity, were the norm. Economist Jeffrey D. Sachs, on a visit to Lima in June 1990, described the country as "slipping away from the rest of the world."

To make matters worse, a host of corruption scandals involving APRA became publicly evident at this point. The atmosphere of chaos and economic disorder, the virtual nonfunctioning of the state, and the perception of corruption in the highest ranks of government and law enforcement all served to discredit state institutions and political parties, particularly APRA.

Economic decline was accompanied by a dramatic surge in insurgent and criminal violence. In addition to violence from the SL and MRTA, there was a rise in death squads linked to the government and armed forces. These included the Rodrigo Franco Command. Deaths from political violence in the 1980s approached 20,000, and in 1990 alone there were 3,384 such deaths, a figure greater than that from Lebanon's civil war that year. Peru also ranked as the country with the highest number of disappearances in the world (see Changing Threats to National Security, ch. 5). In the context of political violence and economic disorder, criminal violence also surged (see Crime and Punishment, ch. 5).

The 1990 Campaign and Elections

Although Alberto Fujimori was elected by a large popular margin, he had no organized or institutionalized base of support. There have been countless theories as to why Fujimori was able to rise from virtual anonymity to the national presidency in the course of three months. More than anything else, the Fujimori tsunami, as it was called, was a rejection of all established political parties: the right, despite its refurbished image; the squabbling and hopelessly divided far left; and certainly the left-of-center APRA because of its disastrous performance in government. Fujimori was able to capture the traditional support base of APRA: small entrepreneurial groups and those sectors of the middle class for whom APRA was no longer an acceptable alternative, but for whom the conservative Fredemo was also unacceptable. In addition, Fujimori's success was attributed largely to a great deal of support at the grassroots level.

After serving as a UNA rector and host of a popular television program called "Concertando," Fujimori entered politics in 1989, running on a simple, if vague, platform of "Work, Honesty, and Technology." His appeal had several dimensions. First, his experience as an engineer, rather than a politician, and his lack of ties to any of the established parties clearly played into his favor.

APRA's incoherent conduct of government had led to an economic crisis of unprecedented proportions; at the same time, the polarized political debate and the derogatory mudslinging that characterized the electoral campaign did not seem to offer any positive solutions. The right preached free-market ideology with a fervor and made little attempt to appeal to the poor. The left was hopelessly divided and unable to provide a credible alternative to the failure of "heterodox" economic policy. Thus, not only was APRA discredited, but so were all established politicians.

In addition, and key to his popular appeal, were Fujimori's origins as the son of Japanese immigrants. His Japanese ties also aroused some hopes, whether realistic or not, that in the event of his victory the Japanese would extend substantial amounts of aid to Peru. He capitalized on Vargas Llosa's lack of appeal to the poor by promising not to implement a painful "shock" economic adjustment program to end inflation and with slogans like "un presidente como tú" ("a president like you"). The claim of this first-generation Japanese-Peruvian that he was just like the majority in a predominantly mestizo (see Glossary) and native American nation seemed less than credible, and his vague promises of "gradually" ending hyperinflation seemed glibly unrealistic. Nevertheless, his message was much more palatable to an already severely impoverished population than Vargas Llosa's more realistic but bluntly phrased calls for a shock austerity program to end inflation. "El shock" had become a common term in the electoral campaign and among all sectors of society.

Fujimori's success was also enhanced by his rather eclectic political team, Cambio '90, which was extremely active in campaigning at the grassroots level. Cambio had an appeal at this level precisely because it was an unknown entity and was not affiliated with the traditional political system.

In the first round of elections, Vargas Llosa attained 28.2 percent of the vote; Fujimori, 24.3 percent; the APRA, 19.6 percent; IU, 7.1 percent; and ASI, 4.1 percent. Null and blank votes were 14.4 percent of the total (see table 21). It was then clear that the left and APRA would back Fujimori, if for no other reason than to defeat Vargas Llosa in the second round. Vargas Llosa was seen as a representative of the traditional, conservative elite, and thus was unacceptable for ideological reasons. In Luis Alva Castro's words to APRA: "*Compañeros* (partners), our support for Fujimori is a given, but there is no need to make an institutional commitment." A similar stance was taken by the left.

The support of the left and APRA virtually guaranteed Fujimori's victory in the second round, but it by no means signified an organized or institutionalized support base, either inside or outside Congress. The lack of such a base presented a formidable obstacle for a Fujimori government that already had an uncertain future. The electoral campaign, meanwhile, was waged in extremely negative and ad hominem terms and took on both racial and class confrontational overtones. It became a struggle between the "rich whites" and the "poor Indians," exacerbating the existing polarization in the system. The political mudslinging and personal attacks, first by Fredemo against APRA and President García, and then between the Fujimori and Vargas Llosa teams, offended the average voter.

The conduct of the 1990 electoral campaign, in conjunction with the prolonged period of political polarization that preceded it, severely undermined faith in the established system and the political parties and leaders that were a part of it. This loss of faith, more than anything else, played into the hands of Fujimori and was responsible for his victory. In the second round of voting, on June 10, 1993, he attained 56.5 percent of the vote over 33.9 percent for Vargas Llosa.

The Fujimori government came to power without a coherent team of advisers, a program for governing, or any indication of who would hold the key positions in the government. Fujimori's advisers were from diverse sides of the political spectrum, and he made no clear choices among them, as they themselves admitted. At the same time, he made it clear that he would reestablish relations with the international financial community, and that he was not interested in a radical economic program. How he would reconcile those goals in the context of hyperinflation, with his promise not to implement a shock-stabilization plan, was the cause of a great deal of uncertainty.

The 1990 electoral results reflected a total dissatisfaction with and lack of faith in traditional politicians and parties on the part of the populace. Fredemo's dogmatic and heavy-handed campaign was partially to blame for undermining that faith, as were a succession of weak or inept governments for the past several decades. Yet, in the short-term, the disastrous failure of APRA, the country's only well-institutionalized political party, was most directly to blame. The results of the 1990 elections merely demonstrated the exacerbation of a preexisting breach between state and society in Peru that had occurred from 1985 to 1990. The rejection of traditional parties did not necessarily reflect a rejection of the democratic system. Instead, it reflected an ongoing evolution of participation occurring outside the realm of traditional political institutions, as well as the increased importance of autonomous local groups and the informal economy (see table 22; table 23, Appendix).

The 1990 electoral results also indicated a crisis of representation. Political parties play a fundamental, representative role in virtually all consolidated democracies; their utility in formulating and channeling demands in both directions—from society to state and state to society—is an irreplaceable one. In Peru, as in many developing countries, demands on the state for basic services had clearly outpaced its ability to respond. Thus, the role of parties in channeling those demands, and—through the party platform or doctrine—indicating their relative importance, was critical. How Fujimori would govern a fragmented and polarized political system without an institutionalized party base remained unclear at best.

Impact of the "Fujishock" Program

In 1990 Peru's political spectrum and party system were polarized to an unprecedented degree. In addition, the vote for Fujimori was to a large extent a vote against the shock stabilization plan that Vargas Llosa had proposed to implement. After less than a month in government, however, Fujimori was convinced, both by domestic advisers and prominent members in the international financial community, that he had to implement an orthodox shock program to stabilize inflation and generate enough revenue so that the government could operate (see The Search for New Directions, ch. 3). During his visits to the United States and Japan in July 1990, it was made very clear to Fujimori that unless Peru adopted a relatively orthodox economic strategy and stabilized hyperinflation, there would be no possibility of Peru's reentry into the international financial community, and therefore no international aid. At this point, Fujimori opted for an orthodox approach and appointed Juan Carlos Hurtado Miller as minister of economy and prime minister. Later that month, many of Fujimori's original advisers, who were heterodox economists, left the Cambio team. Thus, on August 8, 1990, Fujimori implemented precisely the program that he had campaigned against (see The Search for New Directions, 1990–91, ch. 3).

The shock program was more extreme than even the most orthodox IMF economist was recommending at the time. Plans for liberalization of the trading system and for privatization of several state industries were made for the near future. Overnight, Lima became a city that had, in the words of several observers, ''Bangladesh salaries with Tokyo prices.''

Despite widespread fears that the measures would cause popular unrest, reaction was surprisingly calm for several reasons. First

Alberto K. Fujimori
Courtesy Embassy of Peru,
Washington

of all, the measures were so extreme that they made day-to-day economic survival the primary concern of the majority of the population, including the middle class. Taking time to protest was an unaffordable luxury. Second, street protest and violence were increasingly associated with insurrectionary groups and political violence, with which the average Peruvian had no desire to be associated. Third, the benefits from ending hyperinflation and recovering some sort of economic stability were immediately evident to Peruvians at all levels, even the very poor. Even several months after the shock, the most popular man in Peru was the architect of the program, Hurtado Miller. Although Fujimori's popularity suffered a decline after his first few months in office, it was not necessarily a result of the economic program. Finally, and perhaps most importantly, most people voted for Fujimori not only because of his vague promises, but also because of the perception that, unlike Vargas Llosa, he was much more a man of the people. Thus, his implementing an ''antipopular'' economic program was far more acceptable politically than Vargas Llosa's doing virtually the same thing.

Prospects for the Fujimori Government

In some ways, these trends signified positive prospects for the Fujimori government. The degree of consensus on the economic approach was remarkable for a country as polarized both ideologically

249

and politically as Peru. Fujimori's original cabinet was an eclectic and pragmatic one, including members of virtually all political camps. Despite this diversity, a consensus eventually emerged. Yet, there were some extremely worrisome trends as well. In addition to the economic shock program, the government promised a social emergency program to protect the poorest by providing temporary food aid and employment. However, no such program had materialized over a year into the government. Although the failure to implement such a program was explained in part by resource constraints, it was also explained, in large part, by lack of political will: no one person had any bureaucratic responsibility for the needs of the poor.

In other countries implementing shock economic programs, temporary measures to compensate the poor have played important social welfare and political roles in making economic reform more acceptable and viable. In addition, they have played an important role in providing foreign donors with a single bureaucratic entity through which to channel necessary aid. The lack of such a program on any significant scale in Peru was unfortunate because socioeconomic indicators had already deteriorated markedly prior to the adjustment program and in areas where the threat of increasing insurrectionary violence was a realistic one (see Health and Well-Being, ch. 2).

Despite the new political dynamics, the tradition of centralized and authoritarian presidential leadership remained intact. Fujimori had a strong tendency to attempt to control his ministers and to appoint loyalists. Some of the most talented and independent-minded ministers left the cabinet after a few months because Fujimori had undermined their authority. These included Carlos Amat y León y Chávez, the minister of agriculture; Gloria Helfer Palacios, the minister of education; Carlos Vidal Layseca, the minister of public health; and even Prime Minister Hurtado himself in March 1991. After Hurtado's resignation, Fujimori separated the positions of prime minister and economics minister, presumably so that he could have more relative control than he had with the popular Hurtado. Also telling was Fujimori's insistence on the appointment of Jorge Chávez Alvarez, a young and relatively inexperienced doctoral student, as president of the Central Bank, despite the misgivings of virtually all respected economists. Chávez was seen as a Fujimori loyalist through whom the president could manipulate and control the Central Bank.

In addition, Fujimori's need to make an ''unholy'' alliance with APRA in Congress to get measures passed acted as a barrier to the reform of the state sector. APRA had been the only political force to back the Chávez appointment, and it was widely perceived that Fujimori would have a political price to pay for that backing in the future. Indicative of the price was a debate within the Ministry of Education, in which Fujimori supported APRA against his own minister, Gloria Helfer. She was trying to trim the size of the ministry, which had grown to unrealistic proportions during the APRA government because of its filling of posts for party reasons. The row resulted in the resignation of Helfer and a stalling of the reform of the public education sector.

The age-old tradition of centralism also prevailed. For financial reasons and lack of political will, the regionalization process was stalled. Under existing conditions, regional governments were little more than politicized bureaucracies.

Finally, and most worrisome, was the resurgence of another tradition in Peru—government reliance on the military for power. Fujimori lacked any institutionalized base and had cultivated strong ties with the military by granting it what it wished, as demonstrated by his attempt to legalize its impunity through Decree Law 171.

There are many plausible explanations for the *autogolpe*. The most significant one, which has been noted here, was Fujimori's lack of organized or party-based support, resulting in his increasing reliance on the armed forces and on rule by decree. By early 1992, APRA stopped supporting Fujimori and coalesced the opposition in Congress, somewhat ironically, under the leadership targeted by government repression after the coup, indicative of the extent to which the government felt threatened by APRA opposition. In March there had been a politically damaging scandal among Fujimori's close circle of advisors, in which his wife publicly accused his brother, his closest advisor, of misuse of foreign aid donations. Another of Fujimori's close advisors, Vladimiro Montesinos Torres, the de facto head of the National Intelligence Service (Servicio de Inteligencia Nacional—SIN), had been pressuring the president for some time to free the counterinsurgency struggle from judicial interference. This pressure coincided with a major SL assault on Lima. At the same time, relations with the United States were at an all-time low because of disagreements over counternarcotics strategy; the negative environment possibly led Fujimori to conclude that he had little to lose from jeopardizing relations with the United States.

There was the possibility that Fujimori would abide by the timetable that he set out and reinstate the parliament one year later. Yet, the undermining of the constitutional system had far-reaching costs. First, democratic development is not attained by rescinding the constitution and the institutions of government whenever a crisis

251

is perceived. Second, Fujimori had been able to pass virtually all the laws pertaining to his economic program by the decree powers awarded to him by the Congress; continuing the economic program was not the reason for its closing. If anything, the program was seriously jeopardized by the international isolation that the coup precipitated because of the critical role that international financial support played. Third, the elimination of important constitutional rights, such as habeas corpus, for over a year was likely to result in a worsening of Peru's already poor human rights record. The coup also played into the SL's strategy of provoking a coup in order to polarize society into military and nonmilitary camps. Finally, a yes or no plebiscite is a tool that has been used to establish popular support by a number of dictators, including Benito Mussolini and Ferdinand Marcos. Given short-term popular support for almost any kind of drastic solution to Peru's many problems, there was a very high risk that Fujimori and the military would use the plebiscite as a tool to justify further undermining Peru's constitutional system.

Peru was clearly in a critical situation, where extreme economic deterioration and spiraling political violence had to be reversed as a prerequisite to democratic consolidation. Neither was a simple process, and there was no guarantee that Peru's fragile institutions would survive the challenge; they were jeopardized severely by the measures taken on April 5, 1992. In the short term, in addition to the rapid restoration of constitutional democracy, an important first step would be a more visible and tangible commitment to the poorest sectors, which were suffering the most from the economic program, had the smallest margin for deterioration in their living standards, and were the primary focus of insurgent groups as well. The outbreak of a cholera epidemic in 1991 was a prime example of the extent to which social welfare infrastructure and other needs of the poor had been sorely neglected for several years. Otherwise, despite all good intentions on the economic front, the social peace necessary to reestablish and consolidate democratic government would be unattainable.

Foreign Relations

The emergence of highly nationalistic forces in Peru's political system during the 1960s was accompanied by a marked shift in the nation's approach to foreign relations. A desire to alter Peru's traditionally passive role in foreign affairs, which had led to what was perceived as inordinate influence by foreign countries—and particularly the United States—in the political and economic life of the nation, became a central objective of the Velasco Alvarado regime. During the 1970s, Peru's military government sought an independent, nonaligned course in its foreign relations that paralleled the mixed socioeconomic policies of its domestic reform program. Diplomatic dealings and foreign trade were thus diversified; official contacts with the nations of the communist world, Western Europe, and Asia were significantly expanded during the decade, while the United States' official presence receded from its once predominant position. Multilateral relations, particularly with Latin American neighbors that shared economic and political interests common to many Third World nations, also assumed a new importance.

Peru's foreign policy initiatives were undertaken in part as an effort to gain international support for the military government's experiment in "revolution from above." The initial success of many programs of the military government brought it considerable international prestige and thus, during the early 1970s, Peru became a leading voice for Third World nations. As the fortunes of the Peruvian experiment fell during the late 1970s, however, its international profile receded markedly. The Belaúnde government deemphasized further the nonaligned stance of the military government while working toward closer relationships with the United States and the nations of Latin America.

Foreign Relations under García

Traditionally, Peru was an active and initiating member of regional multilateral organizations, such as the Andean Pact (see Glossary). Yet, the nation's economic crisis and García's loss of prestige, both within and outside Peru, forced the country to turn inward and abandon its high-profile stance. Peru's stance on the international front was influenced to a great extent by the rise and fall of García's anti-imperialist strategy. His anti-imperialist and anti-IMF rhetoric, as well as his unilateral limitation of debt payments, placed a major strain on relations with the international financial community and the United States in particular.

Under Belaúnde, a de facto moratorium on debt service already had existed. By 1985 it was clear that no new capital was headed in Peru's direction and that the country could not afford to pay its debt. García took an openly confrontational approach, with the hope that the rest of Latin America would follow. At the time, there were speculations that the threat posed by García was one reason the Ronald Reagan administration (1981–89) presented the Baker debt-reduction plan (see Glossary) in October 1985.

Although García's debt policy limited payments to 10 percent of export earnings, in reality the government paid approximately

20 percent for the first few years, but then stopped making any payments at all. García's insistence on maintaining a confrontational stance, even after its political utility was exhausted, was counterproductive. On several occasions, accords in principle with the IMF were prepared with representatives of the APRA government and the IMF, and then cancelled at the last minute by García. García's stance initially had some appeal among Third World debtor countries, and a few even followed his example. As the limits to Peru's economic strategy became evident both at home and abroad, however, his stubborn adherence to the policy became the subject of ridicule rather than respect. Peru was declared ineligible for IMF funds in August 1986, and was threatened with expulsion from the organization in October 1989.

García also made heightening Peru's visibility in the Nonaligned Movement and in the Socialist International a priority. Ties were expanded with a number of Third World socialist nations, including Angola, Mozambique, and Zimbabwe; and García took a staunchly pro-Sandinista position in the Central American conflict. Improving Peru's relations with its neighbors, particularly Ecuador and Chile, was also a priority early on. Although some productive discussions were held with Ecuador, including a historic visit by Peru's minister of finance to Quito in October 1985, progress was limited by competition with both the Ecuadorian and Chilean military establishments. García's attempts to curb military expenditures were not reciprocated by Chile, for example.

As the economic crisis in Peru deepened, meanwhile, García took a lower profile stance on the foreign policy front. Relations with the United States remained remarkably good despite García's stances on debt and on Central America. This fact was in part owing to Washington's desire to maintain good bilateral relations because of the threat of instability caused by the SL. Thus, foreign aid flows were maintained despite Peru's violation of the Brooke Alexander Amendment, which makes a country ineligible for United States aid if it is over a year late in repaying military assistance. García's willingness to collaborate, at least rhetorically, on the drug issue, in sharp contrast to his stance on debt, helped ameliorate relations. Finally, relations were maintained because of a good working relationship between United States ambassador Alexander Watson and President García.

Peru's relations with its neighbors were strained also by the extent of the economic crisis and the cholera epidemic. In late 1989, over 6,000 Peruvians crossed the border to Chile in order to buy bread, which was scarce and expensive in Peru. Chile's dictator Augusto Pinochet Ugarte (1973–90), when campaigning prior to the 1988 plebiscite, warned of the dangers of populist democracy by pointing out neighboring Peru. Contraband trade along the Chilean and Ecuadorian borders at times has been a contentious issue. The thousands of Peruvians emigrating to neighboring countries seeking employment were another concern. The fear of the spread of subversion over neighboring borders also worried Peru's neighbors, a concern heightened by events such as the SL's assassination of a Peruvian military attaché in La Paz and by the MRTA's support of the 19th of April Movement (Movimiento 19 de Abril), a Colombian guerrilla group.

Foreign Relations under Fujimori

Fujimori set out to repair Peru's foreign relations, particularly with its creditors. He campaigned on, and was committed to, a strategy of "reinsertion" into the international financial community. This commitment forced him to change his adherence to "gradualist" economics and to open dialogue with the major multilateral institutions.

Peru's foreign relations situation changed dramatically with the April 5 self-coup. The international community's reaction was appropriately negative. Most international financial organizations delayed planned or projected loans, and the United States government suspended all aid other than humanitarian assistance. Germany and Spain also suspended aid to Peru. Venezuela broke off diplomatic relations, and Argentina withdrew its ambassador. The coup threatened the entire economic recovery strategy of reinsertion. In addition, the withdrawal of aid by key members of Peru's support group made the process of clearing arrears with the IMF virtually impossible. Yet, despite international condemnation, Fujimori refused to rescind the suspension of constitutional government, and the armed forces reasserted their support for the measures.

Even before the coup, relations with the United States were strained because they were dominated by the drug issue and Fujimori's reluctance to sign an accord that would increase United States and Peruvian military efforts in eradicating coca fields. Although Fujimori eventually signed the accord in May 1991 in order to get desperately needed aid, the disagreements did little to enhance bilateral relations. The Peruvians saw drugs as primarily a United States problem and the least of their concerns, given the economic crisis, the SL, and the outbreak of cholera.

The cholera outbreak at first resulted in neighboring countries' banning Peruvian food imports, further straining relations. Even after the ban was lifted for certain products, fear of the spread of

255

cholera was confirmed by cases reported in Colombia, Ecuador, Chile, and Brazil.

By the early 1990s, economic trends in Latin America were moving increasingly toward free-trade agreements with the United States and regional market integration, such as the Southern Cone Common Market (Mercado Común del Sur—Mercosur; see Glossary). Although the Andean Pact agreed to form a common market in late 1990, Peru's role, because of the extent and nature of its crisis, remained marginal, at least in the short term. Fujimori was so overwhelmed with domestic problems early into his government, moreover, that he was unable to attend the Group of Eight (see Glossary) meeting in late 1990.

Although Peru could have been eligible for special drug-related assistance and trade arrangements with the United States under the Andean Initiative (see Glossary), Peruvian-United States relations were hardly smooth on the drug front during Fujimori's first year in office. Meanwhile, Peru's eligibility for debt reduction and grants for investment-related reforms under the George H.W. Bush administration's Enterprise for the Americas Initiative (see Glossary) were restricted by its arrears with multilateral credit agencies and private banks.

On the debt front, relations with international institutions were improving, and after six months of negotiations, Peru was able to obtain the US$800-million bridge loan required to re-establish its borrowing eligibility from the IMF. Yet, Peru still had to pay US$600 million to international creditors. It seemed that for the foreseeable future, any credit inflows would merely be recycled to pay existing debts and arrears (see Foreign Trade and the Balance of Payments, ch. 3). Prior to the coup of April 5, 1992, however, almost all of the US$1.3 billion necessary to clear arrears with the IMF had been attained.

Peru had established a strong military relationship with the Soviets and Eastern Europe during the Velasco years and was the Soviets' largest military client on the continent in the 1970s. Because of a reliance on Soviet military equipment, this relationship has continued, although Peru has diversified its source of supply of weapons and now buys from countries ranging from France to North Korea (see Changing Foreign Military Missions and Impacts, ch. 5). In addition, like its relationship with Cuba, Peru's relationship with the Russians is certain to diminish in importance as Russia and Peru turn inward to deal with domestic crises and economic rather than strategic issues dominate the agenda. Reflecting this change is the new importance placed on relations with the United States and also with Japan, the latter largely because of

Fujimori's heritage and the emphasis that he himself placed on the Japanese role during the electoral campaign. More than anything else, Peru's foreign relations were expected to be dominated by the nation's need for foreign aid, capital, and credit, all of which hinged on the republic's solving its internal economic problems, cooperating with the United States on the drug issue, and dealing with the challenge from insurgent groups. Additionally, most of the international community remained unwilling to provide credit or aid until democratic government was restored.

* * *

David Scott Palmer's *Peru: The Authoritarian Tradition* offers a good overview of Peruvian political development through the early 1980s. The most comprehensive treatment of the development of Peru's state sector and public policy framework is Rosemary Thorp and Geoffrey Bertram's *Peru 1890–1977*. Cynthia McClintock and Abraham F. Lowenthal's edited collection of essays, *The Peruvian Experiment Reconsidered*, is a balanced description of the military years and covers a wide range of political and economic issues. Peru's transition to democracy is detailed in Stephen M. Gorman's *Post-Revolutionary Peru*. Carol Graham's *Peru's APRA* is the first single-volume description of the García government and APRA in power. Hernando de Soto's detailed description of the Peruvian informal sector and regulatory framework, *The Other Path*, sparked an extensive debate on the role of the informal sector and its relation to the state in Latin America. A good article on Fujimori's self-coup is Eduardo Ferrero Costa's "Peru's Presidential Coup." On the challenges to the political system posed by the human rights situation, see Angela Cornell and Kenneth Roberts's "Democracy, Counterinsurgency, and Human Rights." (For further information and complete citations, see Bibliography.)

Chapter 5. National Security

Mochican warrior art found on a ceramic vase

THE MILITARY AND THE HISTORY of Peru are inextricably intertwined. From 1821, when José de San Martín declared independence from Spain, through 1991, military officials have served in the top political office more often than civilians, that is, fifty-two out of eighty-one heads of state, for ninety-eight out of 171 years. Furthermore, the military has been instrumental in helping to bring to power by force almost half of the twenty-nine civilian presidents.

The constitution of 1979 was approved by an elected civilian Constituent Assembly during Peru's longest sustained period of institutionalized military rule (1968–80); however, the constitution could not have been promulgated or put into effect on July 28, 1980, when power passed to an elected civilian president, without the acquiescence of the armed forces (Fuerzas Armadas—FF.AA.). The receipt of the presidential sash by Alberto K. Fujimori on July 28, 1990, represented the first time since 1903 that three elected civilians in succession had become head of state without interruption by military action. Put another way, the 1980–91 period represented the longest sustained era of electoral politics in Peru since that of 1895–1914, the country's only other time of continuing civilian rule through regular elections. It was ended by President Fujimori's self-coup (autogolpe) on April 5, 1992, in a manner reminiscent of Augusto B. Leguía y Salcedo (1908–12, 1919–30) when, after being elected president in 1919, he made himself dictator by declaration.

In many ways, nevertheless, this most recent period of elected civilian rule, with the military serving as protectors and defenders of democracy, was even more difficult to sustain. The problems faced by the government of Peru during the 1980–91 period were viewed by some observers to be the most daunting in the Western Hemisphere. These problems included a decline in the gross national product (GNP—see Glossary) of about 40 percent through 1991; an inflation rate of over 100 percent per year in the early 1980s that increased to between 1,600 percent and 7,600 percent per year from 1988 through 1990; a government that increased its employment rolls by over 60 percent from 1985 to 1990, while its taxation capacity declined by over 75 percent and thus sharply reduced its delivery of basic services; narcotics production and trafficking, along with substantial corruption, violence, and addiction; and guerrilla insurgencies by the Shining Path (Sendero

Luminoso—SL) and the Túpac Amaru Revolutionary Movement (Movimiento Revolucionario Túpac Amaru—MRTA) that had resulted in over 25,000 deaths, more than 3,000 disappearances, and some US$22 billion in direct and indirect property damage through 1992.

After great initial reluctance, Peru's elected presidents increasingly used the state of emergency decree to try to cope with the country's difficulties, primarily the insurgency. Under the constitution of 1979, the president could declare states of emergency to deal with threats to public order. These presidential decrees permitted military authorities to temporarily assume political as well as military control of the districts, provinces, departments, or regions specified. Constitutional guarantees of sanctity of domicile, free movement and residence, public meetings, and freedom from arrest without a written court order would be suspended. From five provinces declared to be in a state of emergency in December 1982, the number steadily increased to thirteen in 1984, twenty-three in June 1987, fifty-six in July 1989, sixty-three in July 1990, and eighty-seven by May 1991. As of mid-1991, over 47 percent of Peru's 183 provinces, which included some 56 percent of the country's population of more than 22.3 million, were part of emergency military zones under military control. Although some critics argued that Peru was operating under a de facto military government, the armed forces insisted that they were only fulfilling their constitutional mandate to protect civilian rule and had no interest in carrying out another coup.

Between 1980 and 1990, the size of the FF.AA. increased by some 30 percent, from about 92,000 to about 120,000, with close to two-thirds made up of conscripts. In 1992 the total figure was 112,000. The Peruvian Army (Ejército Peruano—EP) remained by far the largest service, growing from 70,000 in 1980 to around 80,000 in 1990, but declining to 75,000 in 1992. The Peruvian Navy (Marina de Guerra del Perú—MGP) more than doubled in size during the decade, from 12,000 to 25,000, but declined to 22,000 in 1992. The Peruvian Air Force (Fuerza Aérea del Perú—FAP) increased by about 50 percent, from 10,000 to 15,000 (its strength in 1992). Peru's unprecedented economic crisis of the late 1980s and early 1990s substantially reduced military salaries and maintenance capacity and began to threaten the excellent training and strong professionalism at all levels—officer, technician, and noncommissioned officer (NCO)—that had been gradually built up during the post-World War II period.

The FF.AA.'s close relationship with United States counterparts from the 1940s well into the 1960s contributed significantly to this professional and material development. Between 1947 and 1975, the United States military trained 930 Peruvian military personnel in the United States, 2,455 in facilities in the Canal Zone of Panama, and 3,349 in Peru. The United States military mission in Peru peaked at sixty-six members in the mid-1960s, with military sales and assistance from 1955 to 1979 totaling some US$261 million. For a variety of political and military reasons, the Peruvian military regime expelled the United States military mission in July 1969 and began to diversify its training and supply relationships from the late 1960s onward. Beginning in 1973, the EP and FAP, but not the navy, undertook what was to become a substantial relationship with the Soviet Union that included the purchase of equipment totaling between US$1.2 and US$1.5 billion, a sizable training component in the Soviet Union (between 100 and 400 Peruvian officers), and a significant Soviet military mission in Peru (between 25 and 100). Peru's was the only Latin American military besides Cuba's to equip its forces with Soviet matériel. At the same time, the FF.AA. received substantial equipment from other supplying countries to become, by the end of the 1980s, the most diversified in the region in terms of foreign sources of arms and equipment.

Despite the substantial domestic insurgency, the FF.AA. continued to focus on potential external problems with Ecuador and Chile, and based the bulk of their forces (80 percent) in these border areas in 1991. The Peruvian military was concerned about Chile's rapid military expansion beginning in the mid-1970s and its efforts at that time to give Bolivia an outlet to the sea through former Peruvian territory lost in the War of the Pacific (1879–83) with Chile. The FF.AA. were also concerned about Ecuador's unwillingness since the 1960s to accept the Protocol of Rio de Janeiro of 1942 (Rio Protocol; see Glossary), which defined a border between Peru and Ecuador that gave Peru most of the previously disputed Amazon territory. In 1981 Ecuadorian forces, using Paquisha as a base, attempted to secretly regain access to the Amazon through a seventy-eight-kilometer border zone, erroneously demarcated for the Rio Protocol (see fig. 4). Although Peru rebuffed the Ecuadorian forces militarily with loss of life on both sides, border problems with Ecuador have continued to surface from time to time. By mid-1992, however, the proportion of Peruvian forces deployed in the border areas had declined to 66 percent of personnel.

The Peruvian Police Forces (Fuerzas Policiales—FF.PP.) faced new and unexpected challenges in the 1980s, chief among them the insurgencies, the substantial and increasing drug production and trafficking, and the rapid deterioration of public order, with its attendant increase in criminal activity. The political violence claimed 1,464 victims among police and military forces through 1990; most occurred between 1985 and 1990, when there were 794 police deaths and 492 military deaths. The excessive force used to quell coordinated SL prisoner riots in El Frontón, Lurigancho, and Santa Bárbara prisons in the Lima area in June 1986, with close to 300 deaths among the inmates, contributed to a crisis of confidence among the police and military services. That crisis was one of the factors in the decision of President Alan García Pérez (1985–90) to combine the EP, MGP, and FAP into a single Ministry of Defense; to coordinate the intelligence-gathering efforts of hitherto separate agencies; and to join the various police forces into the National Police (Policía Nacional—PN). Because Peru grew between 60 percent and 70 percent of all the coca leaf used worldwide in the manufacture of cocaine, the United States government provided increasing support to the police forces during the 1980s to assist in the effort to reduce drug production and trafficking. Deteriorating economic conditions during most of the 1980s undoubtedly contributed to the escalation of criminal activity (almost 3 percent of Peru's population was arrested for various crimes between 1985 and 1988).

For Peru's military and police forces, the most serious continuing national security challenge was the domestic insurgency, in which the SL accounted for over 80 percent of the 9,184 terrorist incidents from 1985 through 1990 and the MRTA for most of the rest. The political violence between 1980 and the end of 1990 claimed about 18,000 lives by the most conservative calculation and property damage of US$18 billion, almost half of Peru's 1990 GNP in current dollars. Peru's accelerating economic deterioration between 1988 and 1990 exacerbated the national security problem among the increasingly impoverished population and sharply reduced the resources available to the military and police to deal with this mounting challenge. Although Peru entered the 1990s confronted by its worst national security crisis since the War of the Pacific over 100 years ago, by late 1992 it did not appear to be in danger of imminent collapse. The capture of SL founder Abimael Guzmán Reynoso in September 1992 gave the beleaguered government a major victory, but did not presage the end of the political violence.

The Armed Forces in Society and Politics
Changing Role over Time: Preconquest

Military establishments have played a significant role in the different societies and polities that have operated in Peru over the

Workers repairing a military section in Machupicchu
Courtesy Inter-American Development Bank

centuries. Before the Incas gained prominence in the region in the fifteenth century, hundreds of native American groups controlled small areas of the coastal valleys, the small fertile intermontane plains of the highlands, and the banks of the jungle rivers. Armed conflict was an integral part of society to resolve disputes among groups or to deal with issues of territorial expansion. Hundreds of years later, local folk dances and ceremonies continued to portray many of these pre-Incan battles. The Quechua-speaking Incas were, for the thirteenth and fourteenth centuries at least, one more of these many native groups based in the Cusco (Cuzco) Valley of the south-central Andes. During the fifteenth century, however, the Incas embarked on a major campaign of conquest by military force, which resulted by the end of the century in the hemisphere's most extensive empire (see The Incas, ch. 1). Conscription provided the resources for initial conquest and for the *mita* (see Glossary) system to construct public works—roads, granaries, rest stations, and forts. This infrastructure allowed for consolidation of these rapid advances. The latter were aided by several devices: the reeducation in Cusco of conquered nobility and their return to their communities; the stationing of lesser Inca nobility and military detachments in newly acquired territories; forced resettlement of obstreperous groups and communities to areas where they would

265

pose less of a risk; and inculcation of a common language (Quechua), government organization, tribute system, and religious hierarchy (see The Incas, ch. 1).

Colonial Period

Although the Spanish were able to impose effective control over much of the region by 1537, the conquerors soon fell to fighting among themselves over the spoils of their success. Order under the Spanish viceroys was gradually established and extended, but not without regular and persistent challenges at the local or regional level from dissident indigenous groups, often in the name of the Incas. Because of the economic importance of Peru to the crown, second only to Mexico, there was a larger Spanish military presence here than in the rest of Spain's New World empire. Even so, until the colonial reforms of 1764 by the Bourbon dynasty in Spain, the military garrisons were small and stationed in the cities. Many career officers and troops served their tours of duty in these Peruvian cities and then returned to Spain. Landowners were left to their own devices for protecting their local interests, so they raised private militias as necessary. Military forces during the last sixty years of Spanish rule were more regularized and institutionalized into three categories: Spanish regiments on temporary service, others on permanent colonial service, and colonial militias.

The independence movements that began to sweep Latin America in 1810 during Napoleon Bonaparte's occupation of Spain and his brother Joseph's brief reign were slow to reach Peru, but they inevitably arrived. New regiments raised locally to protect the viceroyalty initially defeated independence forces attempting to liberate the area from outside, but eventually played an important role in ousting the Spaniards themselves. However, the main impetus for independence came from Simón Bolívar Palacios and José de San Martín from the viceroyalties of New Granada and Río de la Plata (River Plate), respectively. It was San Martín who brought his army to Peru from Chile and took Lima after refusing to negotiate with the viceroy, declaring independence on July 28, 1821, and making himself military dictator. He used this position to advance the cause of independence and to prepare militarily for the final campaigns against the Spanish. This preparation included establishment of a series of military units, the first of which, called the Peruvian Legion, was formed on August 18, 1821. In addition, he formed Los Montoneros, a mounted guerrilla force, to harass the royalists and shield the operations of the republican regulars.

San Martín resigned and went into exile in France before full independence was secure, when he realized that he and Bolívar would not be able to cooperate. Nevertheless, San Martín's earlier organizational and training efforts earned him the sobriquet of protector of Peruvian independence and founder of the EP. As San Martín had expected, Bolívar went on to win the Battle of Junín in August 1824, with significant help from the forces that San Martín had prepared. These Peruvian units also made important contributions to the final battle for independence at Ayacucho on December 9, 1824, under the command of General Antonio José de Sucre Alcalá (see also Independence Imposed from Without, 1808–24, ch. 1).

Postindependence: Military Defeat and Nation-Building

The military's role in Peruvian affairs during most of the nineteenth century was a large one, owing both to the difficulties of building a domestic political consensus and significant foreign military threats. However, until the establishment of the army's Military Academy (Escuela Militar) in Lima's southern district of Chorrillos in 1896, Peru's armed forces tended to be more the personal, noncareer armies of local and regional caudillos than a true national and professional force. Disputes over boundary and sovereignty issues provoked conflicts between Peru and Colombia (1828), Chile (1836–39), and Bolivia (1841), all with outcomes unfavorable to Peruvian interests and objectives. Domestically, military leaders occupied the presidency almost continuously from 1821 to 1872, when the first elected civilian president, Manuel Pardo (1872–76), took office. The most successful of Peru's early military presidents, General Marshal Ramón Castilla (1845–51, 1854–62), brought some degree of stability and order and a more disciplined military force.

Castilla's force was successful in a brief border conflict with Ecuador and a naval blockade of that country in 1859, as well as in a more serious attempt by Spain to reassert its influence in Peru, Ecuador, and Chile in the mid-1860s. Spain had not yet recognized Peru's independence, and its naval forces blockaded Peruvian ports and occupied the economically vital Chincha Islands off the Peruvian coast in April 1864. These islands held rich deposits of guano, which became a Peruvian government monopoly that was largely responsible for Peru's growing prosperity in the 1850s and 1860s. When the Spanish fleet attacked Callao on May 2, 1866, Peruvian forces repulsed the invaders in a significant military victory and brought about the lifting of the Spanish blockade along with the withdrawal of Spanish ships. This defeat ended Spain's last attempt to regain dominance in its former colonies. Extension of diplomatic recognition was to follow, but not until 1879.

Peru's military preparedness did not keep pace with its increasing economic prosperity in the 1870s. President Pardo reduced military expenditures sharply as part of his Civilista Party's (Partido Civilista—PC) policy of trying to downgrade the historically dominant role of the armed forces. His elected successor, General Mariano Ignacio Prado (1865–67, 1876–79), found his military options limited indeed when he attempted to deal with the growing problem of Chilean investment and ownership of the nitrate workings in Peru's arid, southernmost province of Tarapacá and, at the same time, with Chilean military threats against Bolivia to protect its equally significant nitrate investments in Bolivia's coastal province of Antofagasta.

Despite its discouraging military options, Peru felt obliged to honor its secret treaty obligations with Bolivia when Chile declared war on Bolivia on April 5, 1879. Thus ensued the War of the Pacific, a military, political, and economic disaster unprecedented in Peruvian history. Although Bolivia resigned itself to defeat within months and gave up its coast to Chile, Peru fought on. Peruvian naval forces were soon overwhelmed, even though Admiral Miguel Grau, aboard the iron-clad monitor *Huáscar,* acquitted his outclassed forces brilliantly in defeat and death (to become a Peruvian national hero after whom the cruiser *Almirante Grau* of today's Peruvian Navy is named). Chile's army advanced northward to occupy much of southern Peru, including Iquique in 1879, Arica in 1880, and although slowed and harassed by the courageous actions of General Andrés Avelino Cáceres and his troops, began a more than two-year occupation of Lima in January 1881. By the Treaty of Ancón of October 1883, Peru accepted defeat, giving up all of Tarapacá Province (which included Iquique) and agreeing to Chilean occupation of Tacna and Arica for ten years, until a plebiscite was to be held (see fig. 3). (This provision was not honored and was the source of much bitterness between Chile and Peru before a solution was reached in 1929 with United States arbitration, giving Tacna back to Peru and awarding Arica to Chile.) Chilean forces finally withdrew from Lima in August 1884 (see The War of the Pacific, 1879–83, ch. 1).

Guardian of the New Liberal Elite

Peru was left prostrate as a result of the War of the Pacific. To pay war debts of over US$150 million, it gave up its income from guano to British creditors, along with its railroads (for sixty-six years) and a great tract of Peruvian jungle. Most of the country's economic elite was ruined financially. The government became one of the smallest in Latin America in terms of revenues, and the stage was set for an attempt at nation-building. Military leadership returned to the presidency for a time, vested in General Cáceres (1886–90, 1894–95) and Colonel Remigio Morales Bermúdez (1890–94), and the capability and morale of the armed forces began to be restored. However, much of the credit for the creation of Peru's modern professional military goes to civilian president José Nicolás de Piérola (1895–99). Under his leadership, conscription was initiated, a French military mission was invited to train Peruvian counterparts, and the Military Academy at Chorrillos was established.

Peru's one extended period of civilian rule (1895–1919), with regular national and municipal elections, had begun with elected governments, except for one brief coup period in 1914–15. If the civilian dictatorship of Augusto B. Leguía y Salcedo (1919–30), brought on by his election followed by a self-coup, is included, then the period of civilian rule extended to 1930. Elected or not, these civilian governments represented the newly emerging and consolidating liberal elite. This elite was protected by Peru's armed forces as long as it provided the resources the military believed it needed. This partnership, although sometimes an uneasy one, continued under civilian governments (1939–45, 1956–62) or military rule (1930–39, 1948–56) almost continuously until the 1960s.

For well over half a century, the FF.AA. viewed with suspicion political parties organized from the middle or lower classes. The Democratic Party's 1912 presidential victory by populist Guillermo Billinghurst provoked a coup two years later. A far more serious concern arose in 1930 and after, with the challenge of the avowedly reformist American Popular Revolutionary Alliance (Alianza Popular Revolucionaria Americana—APRA) party. APRA emerged publicly in the aftermath of the 1930 coup overthrowing the Leguía *oncenio,* or eleven-year rule. The coup occurred as the Great Depression was ending the previous foreign investment- and export-led growth years, and was led by Colonel Luis M. Sánchez Cerro, Arequipa garrison commander. Sánchez Cerro then headed the 1930–31 military junta and ran for president in the 1931 elections. APRA mounted a surprisingly strong challenge but lost, claimed fraud, and provoked a strong mass protest.

On July 7, 1932, in an atmosphere of tension, APRA militants confronted an army garrison in Trujillo, the north coastal stronghold of the party, and killed about sixty officers after they had surrendered and had been disarmed. Army reinforcements soon carried out massive reprisals in the city in which at least 1,000 APRA militants and sympathizers were also killed. This event poisoned relations between the army and APRA for over thirty years and was a major factor in postponing the advent of sustained civilian rule in Peru. Sánchez Cerro's assassination in 1933 by a young APRA militant only exacerbated the hostility. APRA was not allowed to run openly for election again until 1962; the military's fear of increased APRA influence in the executive branch through a pact with the conservative National Odriist Union (Unión Nacional Odriísta—UNO) was a major factor in its July 1962 coup, which followed an indecisive election.

Reformer and Agent of Change

If hostility to APRA extended the FF.AA.'s role as guardian of the liberal elite, it also combined with a number of other developments to move the military in the 1960s in the direction of reformer and agent of change. United States military assistance during and after World War II, which contributed to modernization and professionalization and encouraged such new activities as civic action, was one factor. A second factor was the establishment of a specialized advanced military officer training center in 1950 that slowly made officers more aware of Peru's own national reality. The Advanced Military Studies Center (Centro de Altos Estudios Militares—CAEM) in Lima offered an annual concentrated program of study to selected officers and a few civilian government counterparts that was largely devoted to important social, political, and economic issues. A third element was the emergence in the 1956 elections of a non-APRA civilian reformist political alternative, Fernando Belaúnde Terry's Popular Action (Acción Popular—AP) party, as APRA moved right in its attempt to gain political power. A fourth important influence on changing military perspectives was the brief rural insurgency in 1962–63 and again in 1965, which helped the military appreciate the potential future costs of continued government failure to respond to local needs and demands in a timely fashion. The armed forces' awareness of Peru's external dependency was heightened by two decisions by the United States: first, the United States government's unwillingness to sell Northrop F5 jets to Peru in 1967 and, second, its involvement on an ongoing basis in the 1960s with the International Petroleum Company (IPC) negotiations with Peru over nationalization.

When the first elected government of Belaúnde (1963–68), which the military supported and helped make possible during its junta (1962–63), stumbled in its reformist efforts and mismanaged the IPC nationalization, the stage was set for the October 3, 1968, coup by the armed forces that had widespread popular support.

French AMX–13 light tank is paraded on Lima's Avenida Brasil, 1967.
A women's unit of the armed forces parades on Avenida Brasil, 1967.
Courtesy Paul L. Doughty

For most of the military *docenio* (twelve-year rule) that was to follow (1968–80), Peru had a reformist military government. Led by the army, the FF.AA. became agents of change and state expansion based on a concept of security that they had gradually developed, a concept that defined national defense in terms of national development.

Even though the military regime under army General Juan Velasco Alvarado (1968–75) and army General Francisco Morales Bermúdez Cerrutti (1975–80) carried out a number of significant and far-reaching reforms, it ultimately failed. The military rulers tried to do too much too quickly and with insufficient resources. They overextended themselves with foreign loans when domestic capital came up short. They also had more than their share of bad luck, from General Velasco's fatal illness to floods, droughts, and earthquakes, to delays in getting oil exports underway. They preached full participation, but often imposed reforms made in Lima rather than being responsive to local circumstances and implemented them with central-government bureaucrats rather than local leaders. They stretched their military officers too thin over too many responsibilities and ran them to the point of exhaustion.

Protector of Democracy

Peru's military rulers did not try to destroy civilian political organizations and even encouraged the development of the largely Marxist left, as an alternative to APRA. So when circumstances forced civilian political parties in 1977 and 1978 to consider the political future of Peru, they were ready to take responsibility through Constituent Assembly elections and the drafting of a new constitution. The military, exhausted by the most extended period in its history in control of the government, were thus more than willing to assume a new role as protectors and defenders of their country's first mass democracy. Among other results, this period of the military in power had the effect of raising substantially the threshold of any future military intervention in Peru.

The FF.AA., humbled but not humiliated as in some Latin American countries, certainly did not expect Peru's democracy to be challenged by insurgency. Nor did it expect to be forced to protect this democracy by carrying out military operations involving large-scale loss of life among civilians, insurgents, and military/police forces alike, as well as substantial human rights violations. Since 1980 formal or procedural democracy in Peru had been sustained, with the military's assistance, for a longer period than at any time since the first decade of the twentieth century. However, the gradual increase in provinces and departments declared to be under states of emergency and thus subject to military rather than civilian control substantially eroded the formal democratic reality. The 1987–91 economic crisis, in addition to its adverse effects on the population, also substantially reduced government funding of the armed forces, making the FF.AA.'s commitment to protect civilian democratic government increasingly uncertain.

Changing Constitutional Basis

The Peruvian military's relationship to the country's politics over the years was more related to the economic, social, and political issues of the moment and to internal armed forces dynamics than it was to specific legal dispositions. Constitutions themselves changed frequently, in keeping with the divergent and shifting views on the best way to build the Peruvian nation (see Constitutional Development, ch. 4). However, Peru's constitutional history became more regularized in the twentieth century with the constitutions of 1933 and 1979. Each reflected the circumstances prevailing at the time of its drafting, including those provisions related to the military.

The constitution of 1933 was written in the aftermath of the 1930 coup, the 1931 elections in which the upstart reformist APRA party had made such a strong showing, and the violence of the 1932 Trujillo massacres. Members of the Constituent Assembly, now purged of APRA party members, were concerned about law and order and with protecting the political system from such mass-based parties as APRA. Article 213 of the constitution of 1933 clearly defined for the military a major role in national affairs: "The purpose of the armed forces is to secure the rights of the Republic, the fulfillment of the Constitution and the laws, and the preservation of public order." Each of the subsequent military interventions in politics justified the action on the basis of Article 213: in 1934, canceling elections; in 1936, annulling elections; in 1939, restricting eligible parties and candidates; and in 1948, 1962, and 1968, instigating coups. The 1975 coup that gently removed the ailing General Velasco was not justified on the basis of Article 213.

With the constitution of 1979, however, a very different situation prevailed. The military had been in power for a number of years and most of the civilians elected to the Constituent Assembly in 1978 were concerned with how to get the FF.AA. out of government and how to keep them out in the future. The Constituent Assembly did codify the major reforms of the military regime, but members also noted in Article 273 and Article 278 that the role of the armed forces was to "guarantee the independence, sovereignty, and territorial integrity of the Republic." This mandate was much more limited than the mandate in the constitution of 1933. The police forces were given responsibility for internal order. However, under unusual circumstances, as determined by the president, a temporary state of emergency or a state of siege could be declared in which the military would play an internal order role (Article 231). The president was commander in chief of the armed forces, with the authority to declare war or sign peace agreements with the authorization of Congress.

Under the constitution of 1979, promotions to general officer had to be confirmed by the Senate and could fill only existing vacancies. Military personnel could not vote and could not run for public office until six months after resignation or retirement. Military and police were subject to the Code of Military Justice. These dispositions were clearly designed to limit the political role of the military and to place them in a position subordinate to civilian authority.

The principle of the supremacy of civilian authority established in the constitution of 1979 was compromised to a significant degree, however, by several subsequent decrees and laws passed in response to the unexpected development of the domestic insurgency in the 1980s. The Law of Political-Military Commands of June 1985 established and legalized the operation of Political-Military Commands in the areas of the country declared to be in a state of emergency. Another was Decree Law 171, which stipulated that the military in the emergency areas were on active duty full-time and therefore could be tried only in military courts. Furthermore, although a state of emergency or a state of siege could be declared for a ninety-day period, these could be renewed indefinitely by presidential decree. As of late 1991, military personnel had the right to vote.

Each of these dispositions limited in practice the primacy of the role of civilian authority set forth in the constitution 1979 and produced a potential scenario in which civil authority was formal and the real power was that of the military. With the steady expansion in the number of provinces declared by the president to be in a state of emergency between 1982 and 1991, this possible scenario became more and more a reflection of reality. After President Fujimori's *autogolpe* of April 1992 suspended Congress and the judiciary, decree laws defined terrorist acts as treason, provided for trials of alleged terrorists in military courts, and increased maximum sentences on conviction from twenty years to life imprisonment without parole. SL head Guzmán and key lieutenants were tried, convicted, and sentenced to the maximum penalty in October 1992 under these decrees.

Changing Foreign Military Missions and Impacts

Like most other Latin American nations, Peru received substantial assistance from a number of countries over the years to help improve its military capability. Each foreign mission played an important role during its time in Peru. The first missions were those of France, originally invited by President Nicolás de Piérola in 1896 to help rebuild the armed forces, which had suffered a major defeat in the War of the Pacific and which were rent by internal conflict. Except for its withdrawal during World War I, the French army mission operated almost continuously in Peru until 1940, and was supplemented by a French naval mission (1905–12) and an air mission (1919–21) as well.

Perhaps the most significant foreign military presence, the French occupied most of the key command positions, established and then staffed the Military Academy in Chorrillos for over twenty years, and in 1904 set up and then directed the National War College (Escuela Superior de Guerra—ESG), also in Chorrillos. Many of the FF.AA.'s subsequent concerns—expansion of the country's effective national territory, the educational role of conscription, data collection, the institution's civilizing mission, and the connection between national development and internal security—could be traced to the French missions. The origins of the modern professional army of Peru could be found in the work of a succession of French officers and instructors, beginning in 1896 with Colonel Paul Clément, the first head of the French military mission. FF.AA. members trained by the French military mission were on active duty through the 1950s; even CAEM, founded in 1951, had its origins over thirty years earlier in a French mission recommendation. The professional military that the French helped to create in Peru was an activist, interventionist one; it saw no conflict between military responsibilities and involvement in the country's economic, social, and political affairs.

The United States military presence in Peru began with a naval mission in 1920. It operated almost continuously until the difficulties that led to the termination of all United States military missions by the Peruvian military government in 1969. A United States air mission first arrived in 1924, and another began to function in 1941. The United States Army mission worked continuously with its Peruvian counterparts from 1946 to 1969. During the period from the 1940s through the 1960s, when the United States military role was most extensive, and on into the 1970s, almost 7,000 Peruvian officers and personnel were trained by the United States in programs lasting from a few weeks to four years. There were training centers in Peru, in the Canal Zone, and in the United States. United States training objectives included providing specialized technical competence, giving exposure to United States military approaches and relationships with civilian agencies, helping to professionalize in ways that would lead to less military intervention in politics, and assisting in giving the armed forces a development role, as in road-building or civic action.

When increasingly nationalistic Peruvian military leaders felt that the United States role was in growing conflict with their view of Peru's national development goals, they chose in 1969 to expel the United States military missions. However, Peru continued to purchase some equipment from the United States, with attendant instruction, and to send a small number of officers to the United States and its bases in the Canal Zone for training. Peru also accepted small United States military and paramilitary training units in Peru from the mid-1980s onward for short-term specialized instruction related to drug-trafficking interdiction. The February 1990 Cartagena Agreement (or Andean Initiative—see Glossary) signed by the presidents of the United States and the Andean countries, along with the Peru-United States umbrella agreement on drug control and economic assistance of May 1991, envisioned substantially expanded United States economic and military assistance to Peru to help with the drug-trafficking and insurgency problems. Expanded military training assistance was approved by the United States Congress for 1992 as part of a US$30-million military assistance package, but was suspended in April 1992 after President Fujimori's self-coup.

Shorter-term foreign military advisers during the twentieth century included a German general from 1926 to 1930 and an Italian air mission from 1935 to 1940. Beginning in 1973, the EP and FAP developed a close relationship with the Soviet Union that included substantial military missions for both services. From the mid-1970s through the 1980s, some US$1.5 billion in Soviet equipment was purchased by Peru, more than from any other single country. From 100 to 400 Peruvian military personnel from the EP and FAP were trained in the Soviet Union each year at the height of the relationship. In the mid-1980s, the Soviet permanent mission in Peru consisted of 650 personnel. Up to seventy-nine technicians at a time from Cuba's Antiaircraft Defense and Revolutionary Air Force served in Peru in the late 1970s to help with the preparation of Soviet equipment purchased by the FAP. The matériel and support gave Peru significant opportunities to upgrade the EP and FAP at relatively low cost and on extremely favorable credit terms.

A United States Marine captain observes a Peruvian army lieutenant practice
firing a grenade launcher, 1981.
Courtesy United States Department of Defense

Because of economic problems, repayment was largely in goods rather than cash.

Peru was the only Latin American country outside of Cuba in which the Soviet Union had a significant military presence. In fact, in the mid-1980s there were more Soviet military advisers in Peru (150 to 200) than there were United States military advisers in all of Latin America. Although the ongoing Soviet-Peru military relationship had been reduced substantially by early 1991 and Peruvian military authorities were interested in new arrangements with other countries, severe economic problems made these very difficult to work out.

The impact of foreign military training missions on the FF.AA. over the years was significant, even decisive at times. The most important contributions were in the areas of establishing training facilities, providing instruction in an array of military subjects both in Peru and abroad, building the technical capability of the military with training related to equipment purchases, and making each of the institutions of the armed forces more professional. In Peru, however, as in most Latin American countries, military professionalization also better equipped the institution to become involved in politics when its leaders deemed that circumstances required intervention. Neither the French missions of 1896–1940, nor the

277

United States missions of 1946–69 resulted in reduced Peruvian military intervention; the Soviet relationship originally developed while the Peruvian armed forces were in control of the government.

What the Peruvian military tried to do for many years, usually with success, was to maintain diversity in both foreign missions and sources of equipment in order to retain as much independence as possible as an institution. Although this strategy worked in the 1920s and 1930s, it was even more successful in the 1970s and early to mid-1980s. For example, of the more than US$1 billion in military equipment Peru obtained from 1974–78, some 63 percent came from the Soviet Union, 10 percent from the United States, 7 percent from France, 6 percent from the Federal Republic of Germany (West Germany), 4 percent from Italy, 1 percent from Britain, and 9 percent from other countries. This pattern continued in the 1980s, giving Peru the most diversified military in Latin America in terms of equipment, as well as making the country the largest single importer of arms in the region. One of the prices of greater independence with greater diversity, however, was the technical and logistical challenge of trying to mesh widely varied matériel into effective and efficient military operations.

The Armed Forces

Mission and Organization

The constitution of 1979 gave the FF.AA. responsibility for protecting the country and providing for its defense. The president was commander in chief, and the heads of the EP, MGP, and FAP were next in the chain of command. On April 1, 1987, President García signed legislation that streamlined this chain of command by combining the ministries of war (army), navy, and air force into a single Ministry of Defense. Under the ministry's purview were each of the services and the Joint Command of the Armed Forces (Comando Conjunto de la Fuerzas Armadas—CCFA). The CCFA, dating from 1957, brought together the chiefs of staff of each service with a small group of assistants (colonels or navy captains) to advise the president on military matters. It had a planning rather than an operational function, reviewed national intelligence reports, and oversaw the CAEM. The CCFA head rotated each year among senior officers of the three services.

The National Defense System (Sistema de Defensa Nacional—SDN) of 1980 created a National Defense Council (Consejo de Defensa Nacional—CDN) of eight voting members—four civilian, including the president, and four military, including the armed forces commanders. The council responded to specific issues related to national defense (see fig. 14). The CDN was also the body charged with responsibility for reviewing the plans to deal with the insurgency that would be implemented by the Political-Military Commands in provinces or departments declared to be in states of emergency. The National Defense Secretariat (Secretaría de Defensa Nacional) served as the Ministry of Defense's planning, advisory, and doctrinal unit. Headed by a general or admiral in active or retired status, the secretariat relied on the CAEM for training and doctrinal support.

In July 1992, the Fujimori government approved the restructuring of the National Intelligence Service (Servicio de Inteligencia Nacional—SIN) with a view to strengthening national security. Under the decree-law, SIN is tasked with establishing intelligence and counterintelligence objectives, strategies, and plans, as well as managing and monitoring their implementation. The decree-law expanded the scope of intelligence services to encompass politics, the armed forces, the economy, and "psychosociology." It also established the ministerial-level SIN as part of the SDN. Decree 746, issued on November 12, 1991, but repealed by Congress, would have had SIN answerable to the president and given it supremacy over the police and armed forces, as well as overall responsibility for counterinsurgency. Those powers apparently were enacted with the June 1992 restructuring.

Training

The Peruvian military long has had the reputation of being a well-trained force. For example, Peruvian army officers spent about 30 percent of their active careers in school: four or five years in the military academy, one and one-half years in specialization school courses, two years in the ESG, one or two years in intelligence school or study abroad, a year at CAEM, and six months to a year in other special courses. Entrance to each service was based on highly competitive national examinations; advancement was also merit-based, and, in addition, course completion requirements had to be satisfied for promotion and for becoming a general officer. Each service also had technical training centers, such as the Army Advanced Technical School (Escuela Superior Técnica del Ejército—ESTE) for preparing its noncommissioned skilled specialists, preponderantly volunteers rather than conscripts. Draftees received basic training and were encouraged to reenlist after their two-year obligation if their abilities indicated possibilities for advancement through technical training. As of May 1986, women did not serve as officers in any of the services, but there were a few volunteer enlisted servicewomen in the navy and a significant number of

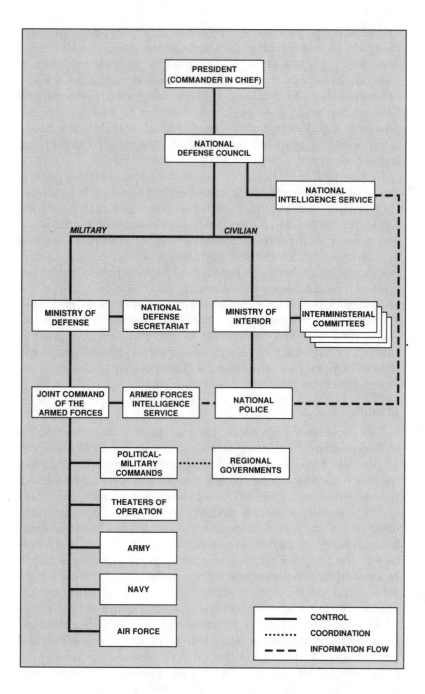

Figure 14. Organization of the National Defense System, 1991

enlisted female personnel in the air force (about 14 percent of total FAP personnel).

Each service had its own training authority to supervise the educational programs. The Peruvian Military Instruction Center (Centro de Instrucción Militar Peruana—CIMP) oversaw the military high schools in Callao, Arequipa, Trujillo, and Chiclayo; the Military Academy; and the specialized branch schools—infantry, artillery, armor, engineer, signal, ordnance, medical, veterinary, and paratroop. The CCFA had purview over the ESG. The Naval Studies Center (Centro de Estudios Navales—CEN) supervised the Naval Academy of Peru (Escuela Naval del Perú), the elite Naval War College (Escuela de Guerra Naval—EGN), and the Naval Technical and Training Center (Centro de Instrucción Técnica y Entrenamiento Naval—CITEN), all located in Callao. The navy and the Ministry of Transit and Communications had joint responsibility for the Merchant Marine Academy. The Aeronautical Instruction Center Command oversaw the Peruvian Air Force Academy (Escuela de Oficiales de la Fuerza Aérea del Perú—EOFAP), Air University, and the Air Technical Training School.

Competitive examinations, strict physical and health requirements, rigorous education and training, as well as promotion and advancement on the basis of proven performance combined to build a strong professional military institution in Peru. Officer recruitment and training were the backbone of the armed forces. In terms of social origins, the officer corps was derived primarily from the middle class, with the army somewhat more from the lower strata and from smaller communities in the provinces; 56 percent of army generals promoted between 1955 and 1965 were born in the highlands or jungle. Both navy and air force personnel came more from the upper strata, even upper class, and from urban areas, particularly Lima; about 90 percent of naval officers and over 65 percent of air force officers fit this description. A large proportion of officers also came from military families; 59 percent of army officers promoted to colonel or general between 1961 and 1971 fit into this category. In addition, a significantly greater percentage of the most prominent military officers were of immigrant origin than was the case in the general population. Among cabinet ministers of the Velasco Alvarado military government, 31 percent from the army, 23 percent from the navy, and 64 from the air force were also of immigrant origin.

Among the entrance requirements of the service academies, only the EP imposed a geographical distribution stipulation; 20 percent of each entering class had to be "from" (defined as where the applicant attended the fifth year of secondary school) the northern departments, 50 percent from the north-central departments, 25 percent from south-central and south departments, and 5 percent from the eastern and northern jungle departments. These social and geographical distinctions tended to be reduced significantly within the military by each service's extensive and rigorous training.

The one significant training opportunity that brought together representatives of each service, the police forces, and civilians was the CAEM. Within two or three years of its founding in 1950, the CAEM became a highly sought-after appointment. Its year-long National Defense Course considered social, economic, and political themes, as well as their strategic and military relevance. There were about forty graduates each year from the National Defense Course, taught by leading military and civilian professors, as well as by distinguished foreign visitors. Of the 1951–71 classes, 46 percent of students were army officers, 9 percent navy, 8 percent air force, 7 percent police, and 30 percent civilian. Many students went on to play significant roles in government and in their respective services. Of officers promoted to general or admiral between 1965 and 1971, 80 percent in the army, 46 percent navy, and 33 percent air force had attended this National Defense Course. Thirteen of the first nineteen cabinet ministers in the 1968–80 military government were CAEM graduates, although there has been some debate over the actual impact of the CAEM on the reformist orientation of this regime and on the military more generally.

Army

The EP was the largest of the military services in 1992, with about 75,000 total personnel—some 8,000 officers and 52,000 conscripts, with the balance technicians and NCOs. However, it grew by less than the other services during the 1980s—only by about 15 percent, after almost doubling in size during the 1970s.

Most of the army's manpower, as well as some of the navy's and air force's, has been provided by two-year conscripts. Although all male citizens between the ages of twenty and twenty-five were liable for military training and compulsory military service, a selective draft system was used in practice. On completion of their two-year service, conscripts remained in the Army Reserve (Reserva), without compensation, for ten years. Then they passed to a second-line reserve, the National Guard (Guardia Nacional). The Army Reserve was formed by men between eighteen and fifty years of age and women between eighteen and forty-five years of age who do not serve in the active forces.

In contrast with the navy and FAP, no women served in army ranks. By law, women were required to register for obligatory military service in one of the three armed forces and could be called up between the ages of eighteen and forty-five for two years. As of 1991, women had never been called up. In the army, women served only in civilian capacities, working as secretaries, clerks, and nurses. The view that it would be very difficult to integrate women into regular military service, including combat roles, continued to prevail in the EP in 1992.

Since the late 1920s, combat units have been organized on the tactical formation of the light division (*división ligera*), made up of four infantry battalions and an artillery group, with the possibility of adding as needed a cavalry regiment or an engineer battalion or both. In 1991 there were a total of twelve light divisions, including one airborne, one jungle operations, two armored, one cavalry, six motorized light infantry, and one special forces division. The divisions are the equivalent in size of a United States brigade.

The infantry, armored, and engineer forces were organized as of 1990 into some thirty-six battalions, including three commando and one paratrooper battalion, plus some nineteen groups. The cavalry was formed into eight regiments, including the horse regiment that made up the presidential escort and two armored regiments in the Tacna Detachment (Third Military Region). The artillery was made up of fourteen groups, including four antiaircraft units, an airborne group, and two jungle units. There were also two tank battalions and seven engineer battalions, including three armored, three combat, and one construction.

The five military regions originally determined by the French military mission at the start of the twentieth century continued to comprise the geographic areas of deployment of the EP. The First Military Region, headquartered in the city of Piura, consisted of the northwestern departments of Tumbes, Piura, Lambayeque, Cajamarca, and Amazonas (see fig. 1). The Lima-based Second Military Region comprised the north-central and coastal departments of La Libertad, Ancash, Lima, Ica, and Huancavelica, as well as the constitutional province of Callao. The Third Military Region, headquartered in Arequipa, included the southwestern coastal-highland departments of Arequipa, Moquegua, and Tacna. The Fourth Military Region, headquartered in Cusco, covered the entire central and southern spine of the Andes and its slopes and foothills toward the jungles of the east and comprised the departments of San Martín, Huánuco, Junín, Pasco, Ayacucho, Puno, Apurímac, and the largely jungle department of Madre de Dios. The Fifth Military Region, headquartered in Peru's largest Amazon city of Iquitos, covered the jungle departments of Loreto and Ucayali. Each region was normally commanded by a major general.

The general staff of the EP had four sections—personnel, intelligence, operations, and logistics—directed by an assistant chief of staff. Additional special staffs, whose directors reported to the chief of staff, included engineering, communications, ordnance, finance, medical, research and development, reserves, premilitary training, and the chaplaincy.

Beginning in 1973, after approaching the United States, France, and Israel without success, the EP negotiated agreements to purchase substantial quantities of arms and equipment from the Soviet Union. Price and credit terms were deemed to be far more favorable than any arrangements that could be made with other potential suppliers. With its Soviet T-54, T-55, and T-62 tanks, as well as its French AMX-13 light tanks, Peru had a significant armored capability, concentrated largely in the two tank battalions in the Third Military Region (see table 24, Appendix).

Peru produced some small arms and ammunition, but most were purchased from several foreign suppliers, including the United States. The diverse sources of Peruvian equipment posed challenging logistical problems, in addition to reported difficulties with maintenance on some Soviet equipment, especially tanks and helicopters.

Navy

As of 1992, the MGP had a total complement of 22,000 personnel, including 2,000 officers, 10,000 conscripts, and 3,000 marines. Volunteers included at least fifty enlisted servicewomen in the navy, some with ranks and regular two-year service duties, others with one-day-a-week and Saturday duties for one year. The former could reenlist for additional two-year periods, the latter for one. They performed mostly administrative tasks.

The number of naval personnel increased by more than 100 percent (and the marines by 150 percent) during the 1980s, more rapidly than did any other service (see table 25, Appendix). In large measure, the increase had resulted from the completion during the decade of a major modernization program begun during the military government of 1968-80. By the end of the 1980s, the MGP had replaced the Chilean navy as the third largest in Latin America, behind only Brazil and Argentina.

Reporting directly to the commander in chief of the navy were the chief of staff and the commanders of the Pacific Naval Force, Amazon River Force, Callao Naval Base, and the Naval Studies Center (Centro de Estudios Navales—CEN). The two key components were the Pacific Naval Force and the Amazon River Force.

A Peruvian special warfare unit marches in downtown Lima during Operation Unitas XXV, 1984.
Courtesy United States Department of Defense

By far the most important was the Pacific fleet, with nine submarines, two cruisers, six destroyers, four missile frigates, and six missile attack craft (see table 26, Appendix). Most were based at the Callao Naval Base, with the submarines at San Lorenzo Island; there was also a small base at Talara in the northwestern department of Piura. The Amazon River Force had four river gunboats and some twenty small craft, most at the main base at Iquitos, with a subsidiary facility at Madre de Dios. Additional components included the Lake Titicaca Patrol Force, with about a dozen small patrol boats, based at Puno; and the Naval Air Service with about sixty aircraft between Jorge Chávez International Airport at Lima (fixed wing) and the Callao Naval Base (a helicopter squadron and a training unit). The greatly expanded Marine Infantry of Peru (Infantería de Marina del Perú—Imap) included an amphibious brigade and local security units with two transports (one used as a school ship), four tank-landing ships, and about forty Brazilian Chaimite armored personnel carriers. Since 1982 Imap detachments have been deployed, under army command, in counterinsurgency capacities in Ayacucho and Huancavelica departments.

Nine submarines gave Peru the largest underwater fleet in Latin America. Six of the submarines that entered into service between

1974 and 1977 were Type 209 (Casma class), built for Peru in West Germany. All were conventionally powered with eight twenty-one-inch torpedo tubes and had a complement of five officers and twenty-six technicians and enlisted personnel. The other three submarines were former United States Navy craft that had been refitted and transferred to the Peruvian Navy. They were newer modified Mackerel class (Dos de Mayo class), launched between 1953 and 1957, with six twenty-one-inch torpedo tubes and a crew of forty.

The two cruisers were the former Netherlands *De Ruyter* and *De Zeven Provincien,* purchased in 1973 and 1976 and renamed the *Almirante Grau* and the *Aguirre,* respectively. The *Almirante Grau* was reconditioned in the late 1980s to include eight surface-to-surface missiles (Otomats), in addition to its eight 152–mm surface guns and 57–mm and 40–mm antiaircraft guns. The *Aguirre* carried the same guns (four 152–mm) but had been modified for a hangar and flight deck for three Sea King helicopters equipped with Exocet missiles. Each cruiser had a crew of 953, including forty-nine officers.

Peru's six destroyers were all older ships from the 1940s and early 1950s. The two former British destroyers, renamed *Ferré* and *Palacios,* had been refitted to accommodate eight Exocet missile launchers and a helicopter deck in addition to their regular armament of six 114–mm guns and two 40–mm antiaircraft guns. The other four destroyers were those remaining in active service of the eight purchased from the Netherlands between 1978 and 1982 (the other four were cannibalized for parts); their armament included four 120–mm guns.

Contrasting with these older, even antiquated former Dutch destroyers were the four modern Lupo-type frigates and six fast missile attack craft. Two of the frigates, *Melitón Carvajal* and *Manuel Villavicencio,* were completed in Italy in 1979; the other two sister ships were constructed at the Callao Naval Base under license to the Maritime Industrial Services (Servicios Industriales de la Marina—Sima), a public company with operational centers located at Callao, Chimbote, and Iquitos, and launched in the early 1980s. Equipment and armament for each included an Agusta Bell 212 helicopter, eight Otomats, two batteries of surface-to-air missiles, and a 127–mm gun. The six missile attack craft, each equipped with four Exocet missiles, were built in France for Peru and completed in 1980 and 1981. These ships were the most important component of Peru's surface navy because of their speed, versatility, and relatively recent construction.

Air Force

The FAP had a total personnel strength of about 15,000 in 1990, including some 7,000 conscripts, with 116 combat aircraft and 24 armed helicopters. These figures compared with some 10,000 air force personnel in 1980 and 138 combat aircraft. Of Peru's three services, only the FAP had made a significant commitment to include women volunteers in regular enlisted service. As of May 1986, there were 2,100 women in the ranks, including 20 senior airwomen, 60 airwomen first class, 300 airwomen, and 1,720 airwomen basic. Basic training courses were the same as those provided to men. Most women served in administrative positions, including secretarial, teletype, nursing, meteorology, and supply assistance.

During the 1968–80 military government, the FAP, like the MGP, underwent a substantial modernization that continued into the elected civilian administrations of the 1980s. Unlike what was true in the navy, however, much of the modernization involved the acquisition of Soviet equipment, the extension of a long-standing air force policy of diversifying material sources rather than relying primarily on a single country.

In addition, the FAP made substantial purchases of planes and helicopters from other countries. Although this remarkable diversity posed major logistical and maintenance challenges, by the late 1980s Peru had the third largest air force in Latin America and the most advanced equipment of them all (see table 27, Appendix).

The FAP entered into an agreement with Italy's Macchi Aviation Company (Aeronautica Macchi—Aermacchi) in 1980 to assemble in Peru sixty-six MB–339 AB trainers and MB–339K light attack planes, with the wings, rear fuselage, and tail unit manufactured in Peru. Construction began in November 1981 of an Aeronautics Industry Public Enterprise (Empresa Pública de la Industria Aeronáutica—Indaer-Perú) factory at Collique with Aermacchi assistance, but financial problems forced its cancellation in late 1984.

The FAP commander, with headquarters in Lima, was responsible to the minister of defense and oversaw a service divided, as of 1990, into some nine groups and twenty-two squadrons across Peru's three air defense zones. The FAP's principal bases were at Iquitos in the north jungle; Talara, Piura, Chiclayo, and Trujillo on the north coast; Huánuco in the central highlands and Lima/Callao, Las Palmas, and Pisco on the central coast; and La Joya and Arequipa in the south. Secondary bases included Cajamarca in the north highlands; Ancón and Limatambo on the central coast; San Ramón, Ayacucho, and Cusco in the central and south-central highlands; and Puerto Maldonado in the south jungle.

The six groups with combat equipment were distributed among the major bases: Attack Group 7 (three squadrons of Cessnas) at Piura and Chiclayo; Bomber Group 9 (two squadrons of Canberras) at Pisco; Fighter Group 11 (including one squadron of Fitter-Js) at La Joya; Fighter Group 12 (two squadrons of Fitter-Fs) at Talara; and Fighter Group 13 (two squadrons of Mirages) at Chiclayo, with deployments to La Joya and elsewhere. The other combat group was Helicopter Group 3, which was based at Callao but deployed at various bases throughout the country, including an attack squadron, which as of 1990 was probably assigned to the army for counterinsurgency duty.

FAP responsibilities during the 1980s also included increasing activities to support the government's effort to reduce drug trafficking, particularly illegal flights to Colombia from clandestine air strips in the north central region of the Upper Huallaga Valley. In addition, the FAP continued to fulfill its long-standing mission of providing air links to remote parts of Peru that lacked roads, particularly the eastern jungle areas. Transportation Group 42, based in Iquitos, operated the National Jungle Air Transport (Transportes Aéreos Nacionales Selváticos—TANS) service with C-47s, DHC-6s, and PC-6s. Transport Group 8 was based at Lima's Jorge Chávez International Airport to perform similar duties, as well as to service some of the military's own air supply and training needs, with L-100-20 Hercules, DHC-5s, AN-26s, AN-32s, Beech 99s, Queen Air 80s, and King Air 90s. The president's fleet, including a Fokker F28 and Falcon 20F, was also a part of Transportation Group 8. Some of the helicopter squadrons were deployed at various bases to assist in such nonmilitary missions as the support of oil exploration activities, medivac, and sea-air rescue; others concentrated on military support activities, particularly against guerrilla operations. Peru's location astride the Andes and its multiple ranges, with a jungle area comprising over half the national territory and a heavily populated coast largely cut off from the rest of the country, required a substantial air force presence. The national airline, Air Transport Company of Peru (Empresa de Transporte Aéreo del Perú—Aeroperú), was considered an auxiliary of FAP.

Uniforms, Ranks, and Insignia

The three services used a variety of uniforms for routine duties as well as for parade, fatigue, field, and shipboard duties. Colors were army khaki and army green, navy blue, and air force blue. Officers had an optional white uniform for summer wear in addition to dress uniforms for ceremonies and formal occasions. Government-issue uniforms worn by enlisted personnel were made of less expensive material and were simpler in design than uniforms worn by officers.

Army officer ranks up to the grade of colonel were the same as in the United States Army, that is, three company grades and three field grades (see fig. 15). The two general officer grades were equivalent to major general and lieutenant general in the United States system. Rank insignia, worn on shoulder boards or shirt collar, consisted of from one to six gold bars for second lieutenant through colonel and two and three miniature gold sunbursts for major general and lieutenant general, respectively. Navy and air force officers had eight comparable ranks; insignia were worn on lower sleeves similar to the practice followed by the United States Navy.

All services utilized several ranks of technicians between the commissioned officer and NCO levels. These were highly trained specialists who in many respects could be compared to warrant officers in the United States services. Technicians—five levels in the army and the air force and four in the navy—were career personnel who had been carefully screened for technical aptitude before being accepted for special training. Selected from among conscripts and volunteers, those accepted usually had attained higher educational levels than the average conscript.

In the navy, there were three petty officer ranks and two seaman ranks, but the other two services had, in effect, two levels of NCOs: subofficers, and sergeants and corporals. Subofficers were generally those who had served an initial tour and decided to follow a military career; in the structure, they were comparable to the supergrades among United States enlisted personnel. The sergeants and corporals were generally conscripts on their initial tour who had been selected for leadership traits (see fig. 16).

The Military in the 1990s

The armed forces entered the 1990s with a strong institutional tradition, excellent training at both the officer and technician levels, and substantially renovated and updated equipment and matériel in each service. However, the services faced major challenges that would have seemed almost inconceivable only a decade earlier when concerns revolved primarily around how to effect an orderly transition back to civilian democratic rule and return to the barracks and bases after twelve years of military government.

The most significant of these challenges from the standpoint of the military as an institution was Peru's severe economic crisis, particularly the 1988–90 hyperinflation. The 1990 estimated defense budget of US$245 million was less than half of 1989 estimated expenditures, which totaled US$544 million. In other words, defense

PERUVIAN RANK	ALFÉREZ (SUBTENIENTE)	TENIENTE	CAPITÁN	MAYOR	TENIENTE CORONEL	CORONEL	GENERAL DE BRIGADA	GENERAL DE DIVISIÓN		GENERAL DEL EJÉRCITO *
ARMY	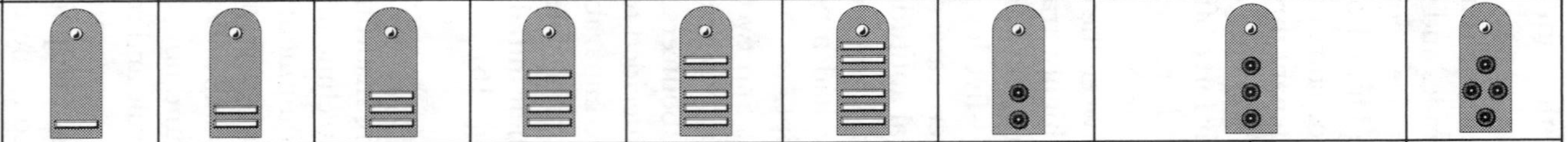									
U.S. RANK TITLE	2D LIEUTENANT	1ST LIEUTENANT	CAPTAIN	MAJOR	LIEUTENANT COLONEL	COLONEL	BRIGADIER GENERAL	MAJOR GENERAL	LIEUTENANT GENERAL	GENERAL
PERUVIAN RANK	ALFÉREZ	TENIENTE	CAPITÁN	MAYOR	COMANDANTE	CORONEL	MAYOR GENERAL	TENIENTE GENERAL		GENERAL DEL AIRE *
AIR FORCE	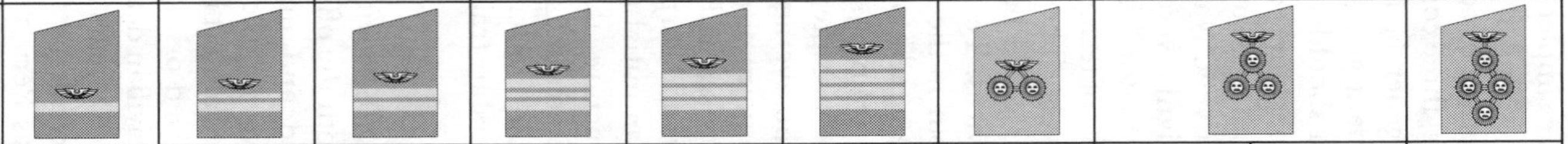									
U.S. RANK TITLE	2D LIEUTENANT	1ST LIEUTENANT	CAPTAIN	MAJOR	LIEUTENANT COLONEL	COLONEL	BRIGADIER GENERAL	MAJOR GENERAL	LIEUTENANT GENERAL	GENERAL
PERUVIAN RANK	ALFÉREZ DE FRAGATA	TENIENTE SEGUNDO	TENIENTE PRIMERO	CAPITÁN DE CORBETA	CAPITÁN DE FRAGATA	CAPITÁN DE NAVÍO	CONTRALMIRANTE	VICEALMIRANTE	NO RANK	ALMIRANTE *
NAVY										
U.S. RANK TITLE	ENSIGN	LIEUTENANT JUNIOR GRADE	LIEUTENANT	LIEUTENANT COMMANDER	COMMANDER	CAPTAIN	REAR ADMIRAL LOWER HALF	REAR ADMIRAL UPPER HALF	VICE ADMIRAL	ADMIRAL

* Rank created by Decree Law No. 20765, published in the official gazette, *El Peruano*, on December 15, 1984, for the purpose of providing representational and institutional recognition for the two top positions of each service.

Figure 15. Officer Ranks and Insignia, 1991

Figure 16. Enlisted Ranks and Insignia, 1991

PERUVIAN RANK	SOLDADO	CABO	SARGENTO SEGUNDO	SARGENTO PRIMERO	SUBOFICIAL TERCERO	SUBOFICIAL SEGUNDO	SUBOFICIAL PRIMERO
ARMY	NO INSIGNIA	NO INSIGNIA	*(insignia)*	*(insignia)*	*(insignia)*	*(insignia)*	*(insignia)*
U.S. RANK TITLE	BASIC PRIVATE / PRIVATE	PRIVATE 1ST CLASS / CORPORAL, SPECIALIST	SERGEANT	STAFF SERGEANT	SERGEANT 1ST CLASS	MASTER SERGEANT / FIRST SERGEANT	SERGEANT MAJOR / COMMAND SERGEANT MAJOR
PERUVIAN RANK	AVIONERO	CABO	SARGENTO SEGUNDO	NO RANK	NO RANK	NO RANK	NO RANK
AIR FORCE (CONSCRIPTS)	*(insignia)*	*(insignia)*	*(insignia)*	*(insignia)*			
U.S. RANK TITLE	AIRMAN BASIC	AIRMAN	AIRMAN 1ST CLASS	SENIOR AIRMAN / SERGEANT			
PERUVIAN RANK	NO RANK	SUBOFICIAL TERCERO	SUBOFICIAL SEGUNDO	SUBOFICIAL PRIMERO			
AIR FORCE (CAREER)	*(insignia)*	*(insignia)*	*(insignia)*	*(insignia)*	*(insignia)*	*(insignia)*	*(insignia)*
U.S. RANK TITLE	AIRMAN BASIC	AIRMAN 1ST CLASS	STAFF SERGEANT	TECHNICAL SERGEANT	MASTER SERGEANT	SENIOR MASTER SERGEANT	CHIEF MASTER SERGEANT
PERUVIAN RANK	APRENDIZ	CABO SEGUNDO	CABO PRIMERO	TÉCNICO TERCERO	TÉCNICO SEGUNDO	TÉCNICO INSPECTOR / TÉCNICO SUPERVISOR	TÉCNICO SUPERVISOR MAYOR
NAVY	NO INSIGNIA		*(insignia)*	*(insignia)*	*(insignia)*	*(insignia)*	*(insignia)*
PERUVIAN RANK	APRENDIZ	CABO SEGUNDO / CABO PRIMERO	OFICIAL DE MAR TERCERO	OFICIAL DE MAR SEGUNDO	OFICIAL DE MAR PRIMERO	MAESTRE SEGUNDO	MAESTRE PRIMERO
U.S. RANK TITLE	SEAMAN RECRUIT / SEAMAN APPRENTICE / SEAMAN	PETTY OFFICER 3D CLASS	PETTY OFFICER 2D CLASS	PETTY OFFICER 1ST CLASS	CHIEF PETTY OFFICER	SENIOR CHIEF PETTY OFFICER	MASTER CHIEF PETTY OFFICER

expenditures in 1990 dropped from 1.6 percent of gross domestic product (GDP—see Glossary), which was US$34.7 billion in 1989 current dollars, to 0.7 percent of 1989 GDP. (This figure compared with 3.3 percent in 1969 and 5.7 percent in 1978.) Such a dramatic drop in available resources meant sharp cutbacks in every area of defense spending, from salaries to maintenance. Officers complained of having only about US$0.20 daily to feed each foot soldier in the field; soldiers were being paid less than US$10 a month in 1991. Some officers and technical personnel resigned because of the financial hardships (180 officers and 370 technicians between January 1 and June 7, 1991, in the army alone and about 400 navy officers, one-fifth of the entire active officer corps, from 1990 to mid-1991). Finally in mid-1991, both the army and navy temporarily halted acceptance of resignations or early retirement. With salaries sharply eroded to a fraction of their former levels as a result of the inflation (US$192 a month for a general before tax and pension deductions in July 1991, compared with US$910 for his Bolivian counterpart) and the inability of the government to keep up with tax collections (less than 4 percent of GNP in 1990) such discouragement was not surprising. One Lima news magazine, *Sí*, noted that the situation had gotten so bad by 1991 that a janitor at Peru's Central Reserve Bank (Banco Central de Reservas—BCR, also known as Central Bank) earned twice the monthly salary of a general. The government turned down the military's 1991 request for US$279 million in an emergency supplemental budget allocation, approving just US$75 million. One disturbing indicator of the potentially dire consequences of this pattern of underfunding was the armed forces' readiness status, which measured the level of preparedness of the military against an ideal level. In 1985 readiness status was determined to be 75 percent; in July 1990, it was only 30 percent.

The other quite unanticipated and unwanted challenge was that posed by the guerrillas. The SL timed the start of its "people's war" to coincide with national elections in May 1980, calculating correctly that neither the outgoing military regime nor the incoming civilian government would be anxious to take it on or even willing to recognize a problem. The circumstances of returning to civilian rule and opening access to both local and national government by multiple parties of the Marxist left did not support the SL's own analysis at the time that worsening conditions were conducive to guerrilla war. Nevertheless, the SL's dogged pursuit of the people's war soon created conditions favorable to its continuance. Sabotage and destruction of infrastructure slowed economic growth and contributed to individual hardship. Selective assassination paralyzed many local governments and led to withdrawal of police, military, and rural development personnel (Peruvian and foreign), particularly in more remote rural areas.

Military responses, beginning late in December 1982 in the region encompassing Ayacucho, Huancavelica, and Andahuaylas, slowed the SL's progress but also displaced the SL to other areas. The armed forces' detachments also intimidated many of the citizens whom they were supposed to protect, with hundreds of human rights violations recorded. Furthermore, over 500 military personnel at all levels and 1,000 police personnel lost their lives between 1982 and 1990. Although the military's response to the insurgent challenge—first against the SL and later against the MRTA as well—often included important successes, the guerrilla problem was much more widespread at the end of the decade than it was at the beginning.

The economic crisis fed the flames of the insurgency in at least four ways: it made daily existence much more precarious for the civilian population and thereby increased its susceptibility to the SL's revolutionary appeal; it reduced sharply the resources available to the armed forces to combat the SL at the very moment they were most needed; it made military personnel more susceptible to corruption by drug traffickers; and it severely limited the state's capacity to provide the economic aid for development programs designed to address popular needs, particularly in the economic, social, and geographical periphery. Given this situation, new economic resources from abroad were viewed as crucial to keep matters from deteriorating further.

Peru successfully reinserted itself into the international financial community with a US$2.1-billion negotiated debt-refinancing package in September–October 1991, along with several hundred million dollars in economic assistance from a support group of developed countries, including the United States. For 1992 the United States Congress approved a US$95-million executive branch request, including US$30 million in counternarcotics assistance. These resources were expected to help Peru achieve net economic growth in 1992 for the first time in five years. However, Fujimori's *autogolpe* of April 5, 1992, resulted in the temporary suspension of most of the funds, including all but humanitarian and counternarcotics aid from the United States. The suspension postponed by at least a year Peru's domestic economic recovery.

The substantial buildup and strengthening of the military's forces in the 1970s and 1980s gave it reserves from which to draw when forced to face both the economic and guerrilla challenges. However, much of the new capability of the FF.AA. was designed for more conventional purposes, such as border and ocean defense, and it was difficult if not impossible to adjust sufficiently to the insurgency problem. In 1991 most of the equipment and over 80 percent of the military personnel remained positioned on the borders or at sea where they could do little to affect the course of the insurgency. Although the military had shifted more personnel into conflicted areas by May 1992, more than two-thirds of military personnel continued to be posted at border bases.

Police Forces

Peru's police forces (FF.PP.) date from the days of Simón Bolívar in 1825 but were formally organized as a responsibility of the central government in 1852, with the establishment of the Gendarmerie. From this force, a Republican Guard (Guardia Republicana—GR) was created in 1919, with specified duties related to border patrol, prison security, and the protection of establishments of national importance. A reorganization was carried out in 1924 under the aegis of a Spanish police mission; the new plan created the Civil Guard (Guardia Civil—GC) as the main national police force (the Republican Guard retained its specialized responsibilities) and a plainclothes investigating and forensic group known as the Investigative Police of Peru (Policía de Investigaciones de Perú—PIP). The constitution of 1979 designated the president of Peru as the head of the police forces and armed forces, but with administrative responsibility for all of the police continuing to be vested in the Ministry of Interior.

After a number of problems in the mid-1980s, which included allegations of corruption, a large spate of human rights violations, and a massacre of inmates (mostly SL members) in Lima prisons in June 1986 after they had surrendered following a riot, President García initiated a reorganization of the police forces that resulted in the creation of the new National Police (Policía Nacional—PN) on December 7, 1988. It encompassed the General Police (Policía General—PG, formerly the GC), the Security Police (Policía de Seguridad—PS, formerly the GR), and the Technical Police (Policía Técnica—PT, formerly the PIP), all of which remained under the authority of the Ministry of Interior (see fig. 17).

The multiple challenges faced by the police forces during the 1980s included rising crime rates, work stoppages, attacks on public buildings and installations, drug trafficking, and a growing guerrilla insurgency. These challenges contributed to a number of crises for the police (detailed later) but also to their expansion in personnel from 46,755 in 1980 to 84,265 in 1986 and about 85,000 in 1991 for the entire PN. By 1992 PN strength was reduced to 84,000.

All personnel were recruited by voluntary enlistment. These figures included a small but indeterminate number of policewomen. Among the special duties policewomen performed were the staffing of a special police center set up in Lima in 1988 to provide assistance to abused spouses and children. In addition to the PN, Peruvian cities employed municipal police for minor duties in the city hall and other city buildings and for overseeing public markets.

General Police

The General Police (PG), formerly the Civil Guard and by far the largest of Peru's police forces (42,537 in 1986), were organized into fifty-nine commands (*comandancias*). The commands were located throughout the country in five police regions whose boundaries and headquarters were the same as the country's five military regions, with overall headquarters in Lima. The general staff was similar to the military's, and included sections for operations, training, administration, personnel, legal affairs, public relations, and intelligence. As of 1989, commands were located in each of Peru's 24 department capitals and in the constitutional province of Callao, as well as in the largest of the 183 provincial capitals. Smaller police stations and posts operated in most of the other provincial capitals and in a significant portion, though by no means all, of the 2,016 district capitals. Detachments varied in size, depending primarily on population density, from a single police officer, to three or four commanded by a sergeant, to thirty or forty commanded by a lieutenant; a department-level command included up to several hundred police and was headed by a colonel or a general. Lima-appointed mayors and deputy mayors had some influence over local posts, but primarily chains of command went through police channels. Some commands had specialized duties, such as riot control, radio patrol, and traffic, and one guarded the presidential palace.

The PG instruction center, located at Chorrillos, included an officers school that provided a four-year curriculum to police cadets comparable to the service academy programs, a school for lieutenants preparing for the required examinations for promotion to captain, and training schools for enlisted officers—recruits, corporals, and sergeants. In the 1960s, the police received training support from the Public Safety Mission of the United States Agency for International Development (AID), and some officers attended the AID's International Police Academy in the United States during its years of operation (1963–74). AID support for the police was renewed in the 1980s in the Upper Huallaga Area Development Project and the Control and Reduction of Coca Cultivation

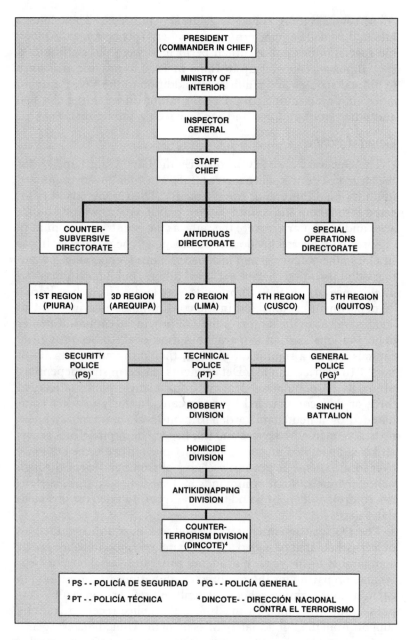

Source: Based on information from "Nuevo Esquema," *Caretas* [Lima], No. 1169, July 22, 1991, 20.

Figure 17. Organization of the National Police, 1991

in the Upper Huallaga Project; the AID assistance was part of the United States government's effort to control coca production and cocaine-paste trafficking. Both projects were created in 1981, but passed from the Ministry of Agriculture to the Ministry of Interior in 1987. The United States Drug Enforcement Administration (DEA) also worked closely with the police to impede drug production and trafficking; a new base, Santa Lucía, completed in the Upper Huallaga Valley in 1989, gave the police and the DEA significantly greater local capability to directly confront the drug problem in the area.

Because the reorganization of the police forces into the PN was not fully implemented by the Congress until 1987, the Ministry of Interior substantially reduced its training programs for new officers and enlisted personnel in the late 1980s by postponing the admission of an entire officer class and two enlisted classes. With normal retirements, losses to the insurgents, and the large number of forced retirements ordered by President García, a decline in police personnel occurred just as insurgency, crime, and drug trafficking were increasing. The first joint police officer class combining the PG, the PT, and the PS did not graduate until 1988. The 1988 class had 682 graduates, some 814 were scheduled to complete their studies in 1989, none in 1990, and about 600 in 1991.

To cover the growing shortage of trained enlisted personnel, the Ministry of Interior established a new National Police School (Escuela de Policía Nacional—EPN), with centers in Lima, Chiclayo, Arequipa, and Cusco and planned to open programs in Chimbote and Pucallpa as well. The eight-month training prepared some 1,288 high school graduates who had already had some secondary school military orientation; there was a somewhat longer program for 1,618 recruits without high school diplomas. With its six locations fully operational, the EPN was capable of providing up to 5,500 graduates a year for the PN enlisted ranks beginning in 1989. As of mid-1991, however, police training remained inadequate, with courses ranging from three to nine months at most.

The insurgency of the 1980s frequently targeted police stations for attack as part of a strategy of acquiring arms and equipment and of forcing the abandonment of smaller and more exposed posts, particularly in rural areas. Individual police were often targeted for the same reasons. From 1981 through 1990, at least 735 police of all ranks were killed at the hands of the insurgents, most by the SL; many analysts believed that seized police arms provided a large share of the guerrillas' weapons stock.

As the incipient insurgency began to grow in Ayacucho, where the SL originated, the new civilian government's initial response in October 1981 was to send the specially trained police counter-terrorist unit to the area to combat it. The Sinchi Battalion, named after pre-Incan warriors by that name, had proven quite effective on previous missions, which had included riot control, squatter eviction, and servings as replacements for the 1980 Cusco police unit work slowdown. However, in Ayacucho the Sinchis appeared to make a difficult situation worse by some acts of indiscriminate violence and abuse, and they were withdrawn before the Belaúnde administration decided to put the area under military control in December 1982. It was believed that the Sinchis underwent a thorough vetting and retraining before being committed to other actions, where their performance was much improved.

Although the police had primary responsibility for dealing with drug-trafficking activities in Peru from the mid-1970s onward, that role expanded markedly during the 1980s. The Peruvian military consistently held that coca eradication and drug interdiction were designated by the constitution of 1979 as responsibilities of the police rather than of the armed forces. However, the army did indicate its willingness to assist with security against the insurgents, so that the police would be better able to carry out antidrug operations. Because Peru was the world's largest producer of coca used to make cocaine, the police concentrated on eradication and interdiction. Because the Upper Huallaga Valley produced most of the cocaine (between 60 and 65 percent of world supply), the police concentrated there. The United States government helped with DEA personnel, an AID assistance program, and, in 1989, resources and assistance for the Santa Lucía base, including a 1,500-meter runway. Three United States mobile training teams of Green Berets helped prepare National Police units in base defense and interdiction techniques, providing short-term training in 1989–91. Contracted United States specialists continued training subsequently.

Although United States financial support for the antidrug production and trafficking program in Peru was modest, it did increase from about US$2.4 million in 1985 to US$10 million in 1990. Even so, both the hectarage under cultivation and the production of coca in the Upper Huallaga Valley increased to 79,000 hectares according to United States government estimates, which were quite conservative compared with those of Peru's Ministry of Agriculture. The latter estimated that 8,400 hectares were cultivated in the Upper Huallaga Valley in 1978 and 150,000 in 1990. Estimates as of early 1992 were 100,000 hectares (United States figures based on aerial surveys) or 315,000 hectares (Peruvian figures based on ground site inspection).

Efforts to reduce drug production and trafficking in the Upper Huallaga Valley were hampered by a number of negative factors. One was the insurgency; both SL and MRTA forces began to operate in the valley in 1985 and 1986. Attacks on police and government employees working on eradication and interdiction forced suspension of most antidrug operations in the Upper Huallaga Valley between February and September 1989. The guerrillas positioned themselves as the protectors of the coca-growing peasants, while collecting ''taxes'' and drug-flight protection payments estimated at between US$10 million and US$30 million per year. Only when the army was able to drive the insurgents out of much of the valley, as occurred for a time in late 1989 and early 1990, could antidrug-trafficking operations resume. When they did, the emphasis shifted to interdiction rather than eradication.

Other problems included the perception among much of the local population that many of the police stationed in the Upper Huallaga Valley were either abusive or corrupt, or both. This perception led to a substantial overhaul of the police forces (and of the army as well) by the García administration during its first year in office, when a reported 2,000 to 3,000 police members were removed, reshuffled, or retired. Shortly after President Fujimori took office on July 28, 1990, another reshuffling took place that forced the retirement of nearly 350 police officers and 51 police generals, some of whom, United States officials believed, were among the drug-trafficking initiative's most able and experienced personnel.

A number of incidents involving the police during the first year of the Fujimori government led Minister of Interior general Víctor Malca Villanueva to disclose that 23 officers and 631 police members had been dismissed and another 291 officers and 600 police members were facing administrative action. Among the events leading to this announcement were the shooting down of a Peruvian commercial plane in the jungle at Bellavista, San Martín Department, with the loss of all seventeen on board; the murder of a medical student and two minors in Callao; the disappearance of fifty-four kilograms of cocaine after a police seizure; the release of a Colombian drug trafficker's plane after large payments to police involved in its capture; and the hold-up of buses on the highways to rob their passengers. General Malca announced on July 12, 1991, that evidence of ''enormous corruption'' and serious excesses committed by some of the PN's members required ''a total restructuring,'' and that the Peruvian government was in contact with the Spanish police to enlist their assistance in the task.

The underlying factors contributing to the problems of the PN included the constant threat and frequent reality of guerrilla attacks;

the low pay (only US$150 per month for top generals and between US$10 and US$15 for new enlisted police) resulting from inflation's impact on the capacity of government to keep up with previous levels; and continuing tensions with armed forces counterparts, particularly the army, over roles, responsibilities, coordination, and support. These difficulties eroded the capability of the police forces, particularly the PG, to operate efficiently and with a high degree of professionalism.

The problems with the armed forces spilled over into a direct confrontation between striking police in Lima and the army in February 1975. The confrontation was settled only after a shoot-out in the police command that resulted in the deaths thirty police members and seventy civilians. Other, less dramatic incidents occurred as well. In March 1989, when the military failed to respond to urgent requests for assistance by a police force besieged by SL guerrillas at Uchiza, in the Upper Huallaga Valley, the police felt that they had been humiliated by another branch of their own government, as well as defeated in that encounter with the guerrillas. General Armando Villanueva Ocampo saw no alternative but to resign as minister of interior. The explanation that no helicopters were available and that no order had been given was unconvincing. Others blamed the failure to respond on interservice rivalries and a perception by some military personnel at the time that the police in the Upper Huallaga Valley were getting more than their share of the technical and material assistance available to fight drug production and trafficking.

Security Police

Although renamed in the police reorganization begun in 1986, the Security Police (PS), formerly the Republican Guard, continued to have responsibility for border control, custody of the prisons, and responsibility for guarding significant government buildings. The PS grew the most rapidly of all the police forces in the 1980s, going from 6,450 members in 1980 to 21,484 in 1986. Some 20 percent of the force was detailed to prison duty, with a large portion of the rest distributed among public buildings and 177 border stations. Another sixty-one border stations were to have been added or reactivated by 1990, thirty-two of them staffed jointly with the army, but budget difficulties may well have delayed these. There was also a small parachute squadron, formed in 1963. Until the early 1970s, this police subgroup recruited its personnel directly from the army and had no training establishment of its own. In 1973 the minister of interior opened an advanced training school for upper-level career officers; a comprehensive training center for all ranks was expected to follow at the end of the decade. In the early 1990s, it was still unclear how the integrated police services officer school, which began operating in the late 1980s, would ultimately affect the PS's own training establishments.

The growing drug-trafficking problem across Peru's borders, particularly with Colombia and Brazil, provided the PS with additional challenges. The additional border posts were envisioned as one way to respond because most were proposed for areas where the drug trafficking was believed to be concentrated. However, the growing prison population during the 1980s posed more difficulties for the PS; many of these difficulties had to do with the prisoners accused and/or convicted of terrorism.

In December 1989, two police officers were found guilty of abuses in the prison massacre by a Military Justice Court and were sentenced to prison terms. The other sixty-nine police members and six army officers accused were acquitted, but in June 1990 the not-guilty verdicts of eight of the police officers were overturned in a Military Appeals Court. One officer was sentenced to one month in jail, the other to seven to six months.

Technical Police

The police reorganization of 1988, which created the Technical Police (PT), gave it the same functions as its predecessor, the Investigative Police of Peru. The PT served as Peru's intelligence service for state security, as well as an investigative unit in criminal and terrorist cases, much like the Federal Bureau of Investigation (FBI) of the United States. A special section, the National Counterterrorism Division (Dirección Nacional Contra el Terrorismo—Dincote, formerly known as Dircote) focused mainly on the SL and MRTA. Headquartered in Lima's Rímac district, the largely plainclothes PT also operated out of the same main regional offices as the military and the PG, or on special assignment from the Lima office. As of 1986, the PT had a total staff of 13,165, including a few women agents, and was fully autonomous from the former Civil Guard (GC).

The effects of the police reorganization on PT training were not clear by 1990, but the PT's distinctive responsibilities probably assured continuity rather than change. Despite suffering from the same restrictions and limitations imposed by the economic crisis and the insurgency, the PT showed fewer signs of trouble than its sister services. The PT's Instruction Center was based in the San Isidro district of Lima and offered both a full four-year course for prospective officers in its Cadet School, as well as specialized training in police technology and criminology in its Detective School.

Successful completion of mid-career courses was a requirement for eligibility for continued advancement in the service.

In September 1992, Dincote succeeded in capturing SL head Guzmán. The capture gave the government and the police forces a badly needed major victory against the Shining Path at a critical juncture and greatly enhanced the standing of the country's beleaguered police forces.

Changing Threats to National Security

External Threats

Historically, the major security challenges to the country and its military were external in nature, usually involving issues of borders and territorial disputes. Peru engaged in more foreign wars after independence than any other Latin American country, although most occurred in the nineteenth century. The conflicts were with Colombia, 1828; Argentina, 1836–37; and Chile, 1836–39; Bolivia, 1827–29, 1835, and 1841; Ecuador, 1858–59; Spain, 1863–66; Chile, 1879–1883. Most of the nineteenth-century conflicts went badly for Peru. The most disastrous was the War of the Pacific against Chile. In many ways, this conflict could be considered more significant than the gaining of independence, given the war's impact on the development of present-day Peru.

In the twentieth century, the Peruvians, as of late 1992, had engaged in two wars and two significant border skirmishes. In the Leticia War of 1932–33, named after the Amazonian city, Peruvian army and naval units were unable to keep Colombia from holding onto territory originally ceded by Peru in 1922 in the Salomón-Lozano Treaty. The 1941 war with Ecuador, however, was a major success for Peruvian forces. Peru had established the first paratroop unit in the region and used it to good effect; the first combat in the hemisphere involving airborne troops resulted in the capture of Ecuador's Puerto Bolívar July 27, 1941. By the end of the month, when military actions had ceased, Peru held Ecuador's southernmost province of El Oro and much of the disputed eastern jungle territory that had been part of Ecuador since the 1830s. The Rio Protocol of February 1942 awarded to Peru some 205,000 square kilometers of previously disputed Amazon territory.

Ecuador repudiated the Rio Protocol in 1960, and border incidents occurred periodically thereafter. None were as serious as the January 1981 incursion by Ecuadorian troops that led to a partial mobilization of forces by both countries. The dispute was resolved, much to Ecuador's displeasure, by the original guarantors of the Rio Protocol—the United States, Argentina, Brazil, and Chile.

Periodic incidents since have indicated that problems remain, particularly along a seventy-eight kilometer stretch of the border known as Cordillera del Cóndor, which was never marked off under the terms of the Rio Protocol. Tensions between Peru and Ecuador increased in 1992 after Ecuadorian troops were alleged to have crossed the border in July in a section that had been marked off; Ecuador denied the charge. However, urgent conversations between the two governments led to an interim agreement in October in hopes of avoiding a new border crisis.

This continuing border disagreement exacerbated the lingering bitterness over the loss of Peruvian territory to Chile in the south and Peruvian alarm over the coup that brought the Chilean military to power in September 1973. The coup was followed by major increases in military spending by Chile and an aborted effort to give Bolivia access to the Pacific through former Peruvian territory. Concern over these two developments contributed to Peru's decision to continue to mass most of its military forces near the northern and southern borders, even as domestic insurgency increased through the 1980s. Peru also mounted a diplomatic initiative with Bolivia in 1991–92 to open up a trade corridor for Bolivia to the Peruvian coast, with special free port access to the coastal city of Ilo. This action was viewed as another effort by Peru to defuse border issues so as to be freer to pursue the internal security threat.

Internal Threats

The Peruvian armed forces have had to face several internal threats to national security since the 1930s. APRA, Peru's first mass-based political party, mounted at least seven attempts to take power by force between 1931 and 1948, after being frustrated in its efforts to gain access through elections. Its reformist agenda was perceived as revolutionary and totally unacceptable to the senior military command, although the party did have some success in gaining support among junior officers, NCOs, and even an occasional senior official. The most serious of the APRA coup attempts were the revolt of February 1939, led by army General Antonio Rodríguez, second vice president and minister of government in the administration of General Oscar Raimundo Benavides (president, 1914–15, 1933–39), and the October 1948 naval revolt in Callao by APRA cells among junior officers. Both were put down violently by loyal army forces, but had the effect of further inflaming military opposition to APRA because of the party's attempts to subvert the integrity of the military institution itself. This military opposition lingered well into the 1960s even though the 1948 revolt was APRA's last attempt to gain power by force.

Guerrillas in the 1960s

The organization of farmers in Cusco's Valle de la Convención, beginning locally in 1951 and with the aid of Trotskyite Hugo Blanco starting in 1960, was the most visible of various efforts in rural Peru in the 1950s and 1960s pushing for land reform. The farmers' movement in La Convención whose principal tactic was to occupy land was successful only after a period of violent confrontation with landowners, police, and the military and the capture of Blanco and most of his partisans in May 1963. It was the first example of substantial, locally organized pressure for agrarian reform. The Government Junta (Junta de Gobierno) (July 1962 to July 1963) officially ratified this de facto local reform as part of its newly progressive approach to dealing with Peru's problems. This initiative gave an early indication of how the armed forces preferred to deal with issues of development that became related to internal security.

The peasants' success in La Convención inspired many others around the Peruvian highlands to carry out their own land occupations, a large number of them coordinated with the return to elected government on July 28, 1963, as President Belaúnde took office. More radical groups, Cuban inspired, also saw the growing rural ferment as an opportunity to begin armed revolution in the countryside. One was the Movement of the Revolutionary Left (Movimiento de la Izquierda Revolucionaria—MIR), created in 1962 and led by Luis de la Puente Uceda with other disaffected former APRA militants. Operating in Cusco, the MIR was tracked down and destroyed by the military in October 1965, and de la Puente was killed in action. Another radical group was Guillermo Lobatón's Túpac Amaru (not to be confused with the MRTA), which suffered the same fate in Junín in January 1966 after six months of skirmishes. A third group, from the National Liberation Army (Ejército de Liberación Nacional—ELN), a Castroite force founded in 1962 and led by Héctor Béjar Rivera, was also defeated in early 1966 in Ayacucho. Béjar was captured and jailed in late 1965. Freed in the military government's Christmas 1970 amnesty, he became an important official in the regime's organization to foster the labor movement. These guerrilla activities and military responses helped convince the armed forces that centralgovernment reforms, rather than continued protection of the status quo, were the preferred route to defend Peru's domestic security needs.

Although the military junta's reforms were ultimately unsuccessful, the regime did attempt to resolve the problems it created by turning the political process back to the civilians. It did not try to overcome its own legitimacy crisis by force. The military regime also opened up the system to the left—political parties and unions especially—for the first time on a sustained basis in Peru's history. Both the constitution of 1979 and the elections of 1980 were to a significant degree the results of the military's decisions. In this context of the restoration of civilian rule and all the enthusiasm that accompanied it, what was totally unexpected was the simultaneous preparation for the inauguration of guerrilla war by an obscure provincial Maoist university group known to outsiders as the SL and to militants as the Peruvian Communist Party (Partido Comunista Peruano—PCP).

Guerrilla Insurgency, 1980–92

The SL launched its people's war with the burning of ballot boxes in the provincial Ayacucho market town of Chuschi on May 17, 1980, the eve of national elections. Unlike the short-lived guerrilla movements of the mid-1960s, the SL extended its range of activities and actions over the course of the 1980s and contributed to the expansion of violence by other guerrilla organizations, as well as by common criminals. By mid-1992 political violence accounted for over 25,000 casualties. The SL insurgency also caused some US$22-billion worth of property damages from direct destruction and indirect loss of production and employment.

The SL's success in comparison with earlier insurgencies' failures had at least six explanations. First, the movement organized and developed over a fifteen- to seventeen-year period before it launched its "armed struggle." Second, the SL began and grew in a provincial university (San Cristóbal de Huamanga) beyond the regular purview of central government authorities and in an isolated highland department (Ayacucho). In 1990 Ayacucho Department was still one of the most sparsely populated and economically deprived departments, one that generated a meager 1 percent of Peru's GNP. Third, the SL was organized from the outset and directed by a single individual, professor Abimael Guzmán Reynoso, who had the capacity to impose an iron discipline, attract many of the university's most able students and faculty, and build a strategy of revolutionary war in Peru drawn from Mao Zedong and other leading Marxist thinkers and practitioners. Fourth, the government response was delayed for years because it refused to take the SL seriously. When the government did act, it was often on the basis of strong and sometimes indiscriminate military action rather than through a combination of military and economic activities that responded to the real problems of the provinces that the SL was trying to exploit. Fifth, continuing and often increasing economic difficulties during the 1980s made it harder for the political center in Lima to respond effectively to the growing needs of the periphery and gave the guerrillas more opportunities. For example, the SL moved into the Upper Huallaga Valley and became involved in the coca production and cocaine-paste trafficking business, which generated resources estimated to be as much as US$30 million per year that were used to pay SL salaries and strengthen the SL's domestic infrastructure. And sixth, the SL's insistence on autarkic autonomy took it out of the mainstream international communist movement, with all of its uncertainties, and gave it a greater sense of its own significance.

As of mid-1992, the SL was believed to have between 3,000 and 4,000 armed cadre and some 50,000 supporters in various civilian support groups. Although the SL began in Ayacucho, the movement consciously expanded to other departments, so that by 1992 most of its actions took place in other areas—particularly Lima, Ancash, Junín, and the Upper Huallaga Valley. The movement was organized into a Central Committee and Politburo and six regional commands, all of which had a certain degree of autonomy that allowed them to adjust to special local circumstances. A strict hierarchy of commitment was maintained: from sympathizers to activists to militants to commanders to the Central Committee and Politburo. The militants formed the armed cadres and the assassination squads; the sympathizers and activists operated in the SL's Popular Aid (Socorro Popular) organization to help the SL prisoners or families of fallen comrades, to assist in legal defense or recruitment, to march in demonstrations, and to undertake other activities. Nineteen Central Committee members and five Politburo leaders were believed to make the decisions for the organization; they were replaced as needed by the most qualified of the militants and so on down. Assassination squads had backups to increase the chances of successful operations.

The SL recruitment took place primarily among the young and the marginalized (see Glossary); the organization included large numbers of women and fourteen- to eighteen-year-old boys. Sympathizers gradually proved themselves by their actions and advanced to the status of militants. Visits by journalists to prisons where captured SL militants were housed suggested that indoctrination was intensive and total, with songs, marches, plays, and skits that suggest a training both ideological and personal. Members appeared to be transformed by their experience, adopting a new, more aesthetic life-style, total subordination to the cause of the revolution, and an apparent utter conviction. These transformations invited

Campesinos from Pomacocha, near Ayacucho, whose mayor was recently assassinated, meet with an agronomist.
Courtesy Inter-American Development Bank

comparisons with religious fundamentalist converts. For the individual, the experience could be uplifting and liberating; at the same time, the person put himself or herself in a situation of complete subservience to the organization and its leadership.

Guzmán and his colleagues were convinced that they had unlocked the secrets of Marxism-Leninism and Maoism and were pursuing the correct revolutionary course even as communist movements and governments collapsed around the world. To Guzmán, or "Presidente Gonzalo," as he was called in the SL, the failure of world communism resulted from its unwillingness to apply the purifying orthodoxy of China's Cultural Revolution that is, to return regularly to the movement's essential proletarian foundations. The PCP was to Guzmán the new beacon of hope for world revolution; the SL's advance worldwide depended first on its slow, methodical, and above all "correct" movement forward in Peru. It was a movement that took the long view, building and progressing slowly on its own terms. Organization and cadre were more important than territory at this point, particularly among the urban proletariat; hence, the greater focus after 1988 on building the movement in the cities, particularly Lima.

Terrorism and intimidation were part of the strategy used to neutralize those key individuals whom the SL could not co-opt, but almost always on a very selective basis, not indiscriminately, and usually for political, not military, reasons. Key targets were local officials, especially candidates and elected officers of communities, towns, organizations, and unions. Targets also included selected government employees and key foreign technicians in rural development projects. Occasionally, a national figure—such as a general, an admiral, or a deputy to Congress—was assassinated to drive the message home that no one was safe, that the central government and the military were unable to protect their own.

The 1989 municipal and 1990 national elections went ahead as scheduled despite SL threats, but over 400 local districts (out of some 2,016) remained bereft of elected officials. Most foreign development projects, including those of France, the Netherlands, and Japan, with between 500 and 1,000 specialists in the field, pulled their people out of rural areas or quietly withdrew from Peru entirely after one to three of each group's members were killed in 1989-91, and the Peruvian government could not guarantee the safety of those remaining.

Attacks on Peru's infrastructure sent a similar message—electrical pylons were toppled, bridges and railroad tracks blown up, roads catered, factories bombed. Through such actions, the SL, although unable to paralyze the country, did impair its function. Living in Lima became more difficult because of electric-power cutoffs and rationing, water-use limits, and spot shortages of key foodstuffs. About 150,000 Peruvians emigrated each year in 1988 and 1989, according to official statistics; in 1990 the figure was 328,000.

The expansion of violence by the SL also took its toll on the armed forces. Thirty-one military and forty-five police members were killed in political violence in 1985; in 1990 there were 135 military fatalities and 163 police deaths. The expansion in the number of provinces under a state of emergency owing to the insurgency forced the deployment of an estimated 15 percent to 20 percent of the armed forces, predominantly the army, to these areas. Because most of the military's equipment was originally purchased for more traditional border defense purposes rather than for combating insurgency, there were continuing shortages of matériel. In addition, the economic crisis of the late 1980s and early 1990s reduced the defense budget substantially, making such fundamental activities as provisioning and maintaining troops in the field quite difficult at times. Helicopter maintenance was a particular problem. Under those conditions, human rights violations by the armed forces and police increased substantially in the late 1980s after marked improvement in 1985 and 1986.

In spite of the multiple challenges posed by the insurgency, the armed forces also experienced a number of important successes. These included the June 1988 capture of several important SL leaders, including Osmán Morote Barrionuevo, believed to have been the organization's number-two figure and chief military strategist. There were also major raids on SL safehouses in Lima in 1990–91 that yielded key documents and computer files of the organization; one raid reportedly came within minutes of capturing Guzmán himself. Significant military operations in the Upper Huallaga Valley in 1989 under the command of General Alberto Arciniega Huby, the political-military chief of the region, restored government control to most of the area, at least temporarily, and resulted in many SL casualties. Guerrilla fatalities nationwide increased markedly, from 630 in 1985 to 1,879 in 1990. These military successes were attributed to a number of factors, including improved intelligence gathering and coordination with the military units in the field, as well as the overextension of the SL organization in some parts of the country and the SL's use of larger military units in the field. In addition, the SL met with greater civilian resistance as peasant communities organized armed peasant patrols (*rondas campesinas*) that served as volunteer defense forces.

The most dramatic government success was the September 1992 capture in Lima of Guzmán himself along with other important SL figures, including at least three members of the Central Committee. This Dincote operation resulted from painstaking police intelligence work. Guzmán's capture helped restore the tattered prestige of Peru's police forces and gave the Fujimori government a significant psychological boost at a critical juncture. Guzmán was tried in a military court that October and sentenced to life imprisonment without parole. He began his imprisonment in solitary confinement in a military prison on San Lorenzo Island. Documents seized in the September safehouse raid led to the subsequent capture of other important SL militants at the regional and local levels. Many, although far from all, analysts believed that this was the beginning of the end for the SL, especially if the government could take advantage of the movement to begin implementing local development projects.

The military and police forces also experienced considerable success against a much smaller and more conventional guerrilla organization, the Túpac Amaru Revolutionary Movement (Movimiento Revolucionario Túpac Amaru—MRTA). Organized in 1985 by disaffected members of the youth wings of several of

Peru's legal Marxist parties, the MRTA began to compete with the SL for support, primarily in Lima, parts of the Upper Huallaga Valley, and the adjacent jungle. Some of its members were killed by SL forces and by the military. A number were captured, including, in 1988, the MRTA's head, Víctor Polay Campos. By early 1990, much of the organization had been disbanded and its jailed leadership was trying to work out a negotiated settlement with the government for the ending of hostilities. But the MRTA got a new lease on life in July 1990 when some forty-seven jailed members, including Polay, tunneled their way to a mass escape from Lima's Canto Grande Prison. The crowning indignity for the outgoing APRA administration was that the escapees videotaped the entire operation.

In the months to follow, the MRTA resumed operations with expanded military activities in the Upper Huallaga Valley and adjacent jungle, and elsewhere. The MRTA appeared to be more willing to consider conversations with government authorities than the SL, which adamantly refused any contact. However, because they were responsible for only between 10 and 20 percent of the incidents of political violence, it was not likely that any settlement that could be reached would significantly diminish Peru's insurgency problem. In any event, with Polay's recapture in 1992, along with a substantial number of his lieutenants, the MRTA appeared to be close to elimination as a significant guerrilla threat. The same careful police intelligence work that brought in Guzmán enabled Peru's government to advance against the MRTA.

Narcotics Trafficking

As the world's largest producer of coca and cocaine paste, Peru had a major drug-trafficking problem during the 1980s, concentrated in and around the Upper Huallaga Valley, where most of the coca used in the manufacture of cocaine for export was grown. Weekly flights from the area's more than 100 clandestine airstrips by small aircraft laden with cocaine paste were believed to have peaked in 1988 and 1989 at about fifty. Concentrated efforts in late 1989 and 1990 to restrict the trafficking in Colombia, the destination of most flights, and in Peru itself were partially successful, as indicated by a sharp overall decline in price for the coca leaf. Counting Peruvian coca growers (estimated to number between 70,000 and 320,000), cocaine-paste processors (estimated at between 23,000 and 107,000), and cocaine-paste transporters (some 2,400 to 11,000), from 95,400 and 438,000 individuals were employed in the illicit production and preliminary refining of the drug in Peru. Considering the average peasant family size of five, between 477,000 and 2.64 million Peruvians, or between about 4 percent and 20 percent of the country's economically active population depended directly on coca and cocaine-paste production for their livelihoods. About 10 percent of Peru's coca production was legal; the indigenous population purchased most of this amount for traditional uses. Joint Peruvian-United States efforts to reduce the supply of cocaine reaching North America initially focused on coca crop eradication but shifted to interdiction and crop substitution in the late 1980s, in part because of tensions with peasant growers.

Cocaine and cocaine base use among Peruvians was also perceived as a problem. A 1990 national epidemiology study of drug use among 12- to 50-year-olds put one-time use of cocaine paste at 4.6 percent and more frequent cocaine use at 1.5 percent, slightly higher than a similar study conducted in 1986. It was believed that drug use in and around centers of drug production was growing much more rapidly. Arrests for drug consumption were about 1,900 in 1985, peaked at 2,200 in 1986, and then declined to about 1,275 in 1989, but rose to 2,055 in 1991 and 3,707 in 1992. Cocaine seized by Peruvian authorities showed a similarly erratic pattern—0.03 tons in 1987, 0.06 in 1988, 0.30 in 1989, 8.50 in 1990, 5.17 in 1991, and 6.93 tons in 1992. Peruvian authorities recognized the seriousness of the drug production and trafficking problem but were more worried about the economic crisis and the insurgency.

Crime and Punishment

Rising Crime Rates

Just as Peru's armed forces and police were buffeted by a number of challenges during the 1980s, so too were the country's judicial and penal systems. Despite the return to civilian government in 1980 under the constitution of 1979 and the widespread expectation at the time that this would also normalize the application and administration of justice, such was not to be the case. The recurring economic crisis of the 1980s and early 1990s prevented the judicial branch from receiving the constitutionally mandated 2 percent of the government budget. In 1989 the sum appropriated was 1.4 percent; in 1990 it was 0.9 percent, or about US$15 million. The economic difficulties also contributed to increases in crime rates as more of the population struggled to cope with rising unemployment and underemployment. Recorded crimes of all types increased from 210,357 in 1980 to 248,670 in 1986, or by 18 percent; these data, compiled by the General Police (PG) and the Technical Police (PT), were believed to underrepresent actual figures.

Incomplete data resulted in part from the growing number of provinces that were under states of emergency during the 1980s because of insurgent activity (almost half of Peru's 183 provinces by mid-1991). The states of emergency suspended constitutional guarantees of due process and freedom of movement and assembly, and placed all executive branch authority in local military commands. Many actions by military and insurgents alike were often not reported as crimes.

The guerrillas also threatened judicial branch officials at all levels and killed some, so that at times large numbers of openings, particularly at the lower levels, were much delayed in being filled. (In 1989, for example, over one-third of Peru's 4,583 justice of the peace positions were vacant.) The combination of vacancies and intimidation then further delayed judicial resolution of pending cases; a mere 3.1 percent of crimes committed in 1980 resulted in sentences, only 2.6 percent in 1986. Of the approximately 40,000 inmates in Peru's prisons in 1990, 80 percent were waiting to be tried and nearly 10 percent had completed their sentences but remained in jail, according to the head of the Minister of Interior's National Institute of Prisons (Instituto Nacional Penitenciario—Inpe). Concern was also expressed that many of the justices and judicial branch employees replaced during the 1985-90 APRA government were selected more by political rather than judicial criteria. In short, a situation that had always been far from satisfactory became even less so by 1990.

One result of President Fujimori's *autogolpe* of April 5, 1992, was the suspension and reorganization of Peru's judiciary. As of October, over half of the twenty-five Supreme Court judges had been replaced, along with scores of judicial officials at other levels. Among other post-April 5 changes were decrees defining terrorism as treason, thereby placing trials for alleged actions in military courts as well as extending sentences from a twenty-year maximum to life imprisonment without parole.

The economic crises, the insurgency, and drug trafficking were major contributors to rising crime rates in the 1980s. Illegal drug-trafficking crimes recorded by the PG between 1980 and 1986 increased by 67 percent, almost four times the rate of growth of crime overall. Drug-trafficking arrests between 1985 and 1988 totaled about 4,500, but were a small fraction of all arrests for alleged crimes for the period (574,393 total arrests, almost 3 percent of Peru's population). Guerrilla attacks during the Belaúnde government (1980–85) totaled 5,880; deaths attributed to the subversion came to 8,103. These levels increased during the García government (1985–90) to 11,937 insurgent actions associated with over 9,660 deaths. Extrajudicial disappearances during the 1980s, most often linked to the army and police in the emergency zones, approached 5,000. From July 28, 1990, to June 30, 1992, the first two years of the Fujimori administration, 2,990 incidents and 6,240 deaths were recorded.

Penal Code

Peru's penal code in force in 1991 was the much amended 1924 code; it addressed itself primarily to common crime as opposed to political violence. The code was expected to be replaced in 1992 by new statutes that were announced in initial form in April 1991. The amended 1924 code's four volumes dealt with general provisions, descriptions of felonies, descriptions of misdemeanors, and application of punishment. Felonies were divided into categories: crimes against the person, the family, or property; crimes against the state, public security, and public order; and crimes of moral turpitude. Punishments included jail, loss of rights, loss or suspension of employment, fines, probation, and warnings.

The proposed new penal code was intended to bring Peruvian law up to date and to make it internally consistent. The legal inconsistencies resulting from the many amendments over the years, under both civilian and military rule, had produced a very unwieldy legal framework. Major changes included specifying white-collar crimes; expanding punishment to include community service; considering society's responsibility in the commission of crimes by less advantaged individuals; emphasizing the possibilities for rehabilitation; specifying economic crimes by monopolies, misuse of public funds, and tax evasion; incorporating much more severe penalties for drug trafficking, terrorism, and human rights violations; and considering as crimes damage to the environment, natural resources, and the ecology. The new code was to be subject to a national debate by interested parties, as well as to a review by Congress before going into effect in 1992. The Fujimori *autogolpe* of April 5, 1992, changed this timetable. In the following month, it produced a plethora of decree-laws, which responded to a number of these issues, particularly those related to criminal activity and terrorism. The Democratic Constituent Congress (Congreso Constituyente Democrático), elected in November, was to incorporate or adjust these decrees. The fate of the proposed code was unclear, but probably was postponed until after the full return to constitutional rule scheduled for July 28, 1993.

The constitution of 1979 abolished the death penalty administered by firing squad, even though it had seldom been invoked (only twelve times between 1871 and 1971). The exception was Article 235, which allowed for the death penalty for the crime of treason during a war with an external enemy. In the 1970s, the military government (1968–80) had gradually expanded the list of crimes subject to the death penalty, including killing a member of the police, killing during a robbery, and mass killing. At least seven individuals were put to death on conviction under these statutes. The issue of the use of military and police rather than civilian courts to try citizens, with no right to appeal to civilian judicial authority, also came up frequently during the military regime. Article 282 of the constitution of 1979 dealt with this difficulty by prohibiting application of the Code of Military Justice to civilians except for treason.

Other provisions of the constitution of 1979 also emphasized civilian institutions and individual rights. Those provisions included the right to habeas corpus; presumption of innocence until proven guilty in judicial proceedings; arrest only by judicial warrant or in the commission of an offense; the right to go before a judge within twenty-four hours of arrest (except for terrorism, treason, and drug trafficking); immediate advice in writing as to reasons for arrest; access to a lawyer from the time of arrest; authorities' obligation to report location of person arrested; the inadmissibility of forced statements; no detention without communication; no transfer to a jurisdiction not provided for by law; trial only under legal procedures; and no torture or inhumane treatment.

However, Article 231 of the constitution of 1979 allowed for the suspension of some civil and political rights under exceptional circumstances by a presidential decree of a state of emergency or a state of siege for all or any portion of the country. It also allowed the president to order the armed forces to assume responsibilities for public order from civilian authorities and could be renewed by the president every ninety days for an indeterminate period. As a result of the insurgency, this article has been invoked repeatedly; the military has been put in charge of every region that has been in a declared state of emergency since December 1982, except Lima. The effect of the president's use of Article 231 was to substantially erode constitutional guarantees in large sections of the country. Civilian courts were denied access to detention areas, making it impossible for them to pursue writs of habeas corpus. Military courts assumed responsibility for dealing with abuses committed by soldiers and were upheld by the Supreme Court. Occasionally, police were tried for their alleged abuses, as in the successful prosecution of twelve members of the Sinchi Battalion for a 1983 massacre in the Ayacucho community of Socos and their sentencing to ten to twenty-five years in prison. But these cases were exceptional, and most reported abuses went unpunished. With the failure of the court system to respond effectively, the Office of the Public Ministry (an autonomous monitoring institution empowered to press charges), a short-lived special prosecutor for the investigation of disappearances, and the Congress through a special commission all tried, with very limited success, to fill the gap.

The civilian court limitations were manifest in the emergency zones, but also were very evident in the rest of the country. Only a small percentage of reported crimes were brought to trial in any given year (1 to 3 percent). Through June 1984, only 15 of 1,080 persons held for terrorist acts had been sentenced. As of 1989, less than 5 percent of those arrested for terrorist acts had been convicted. Of the 643 women inmates of Chorrillos Prison in December 1990, just 117 had received sentences. A smaller number of cases reached the Supreme Court in 1989 and 1990 than in 1985, in part owing to a six-month strike by the judicial branch in 1989. The Ministry of Justice reported in July 1988 that there was a backlog of almost 45,000 criminal cases and that two-thirds of all prison inmates were still awaiting trial. The weaknesses of the judiciary and the strains to which it was subjected by the recurring fiscal crisis of the government, the increase in common crime during the decade, the insurgency, and the government's response to it made the legal principles of the penal code and the constitution of 1979 virtually impossible to apply in practice. Frustration with the judicial system was a major factor in President Fujimori's April 5, 1992, decision to suspend the constitution, including the judiciary. Decree-laws tightened anticriminal and antiterrorist procedures and practices, including internal subversion redefined as treason and hence subject to trial in military courts. After Guzmán's capture in September 1992, his rapid trial, conviction, and life imprisonment along with several fellow SL leaders would have been legally impossible under the pre-April 1992 status of the laws and the judiciary.

Penal System

In the second half of the 1980s, Peru's insurgency exacerbated the country's already intolerable prison conditions. One of the SL's early successes was its March 1982 raid on the Ayacucho Prison; the raid freed most of the prisoners, including several SL militants. Even though intelligence reports had alerted the GR that an attack was planned and Lima had sent reinforcements to Ayacucho, the local commanding officer chose to disregard the warning.

Another problem related to the prison policy of segregating the SL members from the other prisoners. The SL turned this policy to its own advantage by creating model minicamps of collective ideological reinforcement and community building within their separate cell blocks. Visitors reported an organization and an esprit de corps not found in any other part of the prisons. This separation probably facilitated coordinated SL prisoner riots at Lurigancho, El Frontón, and Santa Bárbara prisons in Lima in mid-June 1986, as well as the overreaction by GR jailors and the army reinforcements that were sent in that resulted in the killing of nearly 300 prisoners, many after they had surrendered. One justification offered at the time alluded to the GR's release of pent-up rage after having been continuously subjected to threats from the jailed militants that their comrades outside prison knew where the guards' families lived and would attack them if the inmates were not granted special treatment. Later, Minister of Interior Félix Mantilla accused PS prison officials at Canto Grande of aiding and abetting the July 1990 tunnel escape of forty-seven MRTA prisoners. After the April 1992 *autogolpe,* President Fujimori took steps to break up the blocks of SL militants in prisons, which provoked a riot in Canto Grande in May and resulted in the deaths of about twenty-five SL inmates and two police officials.

Peru's prisons, totaling 114 nationwide in 1990, were administered by 3,075 employees, with a guard staff made up of about 4,000 PS members (formerly Republican Guards). Article 234 of the constitution of 1979 emphasized the reeducation and rehabilitative functions of the penal system rather than simply punishment, with the goal of eventual reintegration of the prisoner back into society. However, that aim remained a distant goal in 1992 rather than a realized program.

Of a 1990 prison population estimated at 40,000, about half were in the twenty-five jails in Lima. Although the military government began an ambitious program of building new prisons and rehabilitating old ones, financial limitations left the project incomplete. In a 1987 survey of prisons to assess their general physical state, only 13 percent (fourteen) were determined to be in good condition, 53 percent (fifty-nine) were average, and 32 percent (thirty-six) were poor; two Lima prisons were not surveyed. Among the larger prisons, all in Lima, were Lurigancho Prison, completed in 1968; Canto Grande Prison, built in the early 1980s; Miguel Castro Prison; and two womens' prisons—Santa Mónica Prison in Chorrillos District, dating from 1951, and Santa Bárbara Prison.

The most dangerous criminals were sent to El Frontón, on a small island near the port of Callao, where the isolated blockhouse, known as La Lobera (Wolf's Lair), was one of the most dreaded in the country. Another principal prison was the agricultural penal colony of El Sepa in the jungle of Loreto.

The twin challenges of a growing prison population and the government's continuing economic difficulties contributed to increasing deterioration of conditions in the prisons, a deterioration that had reached crisis proportions by the end of the 1980s. The total prison population increased from about 15,000 in 1975 to about 40,000 by 1990. Peru's largest prison, Lurigancho, built for a maximum inmate population of 2,000, held nearly 7,000 in August 1990, while Miguel Castro Prison housed over four times its installed capacity of 500. Some 168 children were jailed with their mothers in Chorrillos Prison.

At the time the Fujimori government began its term in July 1990, Inpe was spending less than US$0.10 daily per inmate on food— one meal a day or less. A thirteen-day hunger strike was conducted by some 9,000 prisoners in Lima in August 1990 to protest the situation. In response, the Fujimori government directed food donations to the prisons and increased food expenditures to US$0.55 per inmate in September 1990.

Of the many other problems, one of the most serious was the "custom in the judicial system to delay five years before handing down a verdict," as Inpe director Carlos Caparó said in September 1990. Another problem was the delay in releasing inmates who had completed their sentences, which was an estimated 10 percent of the prison population. In some cases, prisoners were retained because they could not pay the "fees" demanded by authorities for signing the five evaluations (medical, legal, social, educational, and psychological) necessary before an inmate could be released. With the deterioration in conditions, health problems in the prisons increased; forty inmates died of tuberculosis in Lurigancho alone between January and September 1990. President Fujimori stated that about 5,000 of the country's prisoners had life-threatening diseases.

In September 1990, President Fujimori's office promulgated a decree setting up a special advisory group, the Special Technical Qualifying Commission, to review cases of prisoners held but not tried for less serious offenses (drug trafficking, terrorism, and murder were excluded) for possible presidential pardons. The first 97 received President Fujimori's official pardon in December 1990, with up to 2,000 more expected to be pardoned later. The new draft penal code was another major step toward resolving some penal system problems, but alleviation of many other issues would require infusion of new resources that were not yet available in 1992. Fujimori's April 1992 *autogolpe* further postponed any definitive resolution of this problem, other than immediately implementing a reorganization of Inpe.

* * *

The Peruvian military and its relationship to politics and society have been the subject of numerous book-length studies and articles in English, in part because the military takeover in Peru in October 1968 turned out to be the first and the most sustained of several long-term reformist military governments in the region during this period. Some two dozen books appeared in English describing and evaluating the twelve-year regime (1968-80), of which the most comprehensive to date in 1992 was *The Peruvian Experiment Revisited,* edited by Cynthia McClintock and Abraham F. Lowenthal. Daniel M. Masterson's *Militarism and Politics in Latin America* also covers the reform period in depth, as well as providing the most systematic and complete study available in English on the Peruvian military in the twentieth century. Among the many articles that summarize this period, David Scott Palmer's "Changing Political Economy of Peru under Civilian and Military Rule" is quite helpful. Particularly useful studies in English include the annual country reports on human rights practices in Peru submitted to the United States Congress by the Department of State; Philip Mauceri's *The Military, Insurgency, and Democratic Power;* Adrian J. English's "Peru," in Jane's *Armed Forces of Latin America;* Carlos Iván Degregori's *Ayacucho, 1969-1979;* and *The Shining Path of Peru,* edited by Palmer. (For further information and complete citations, see Bibliography.)

Appendix

Table 1. Metric Conversion Coefficients and Factors

When you know	Multiply by	To find
Millimeters	0.04	inches
Centimeters	0.39	inches
Meters	3.3	feet
Kilometers	0.62	miles
Hectares (10,000 m²)	2.47	acres
Square kilometers	0.39	square miles
Cubic meters	35.3	cubic feet
Liters	0.26	gallons
Kilograms	2.2	pounds
Metric tons	0.98	long tons
	1.1	short tons
	2,204	pounds
Degrees Celsius (Centigrade)	1.8 and add 32	degrees Fahrenheit

Table 2. Total Population and Annual Population Change in Peru, 1530–1990

Year	Total Population	Annual Population Change — Number	Annual Population Change — Percentage
1530 [1]	16,000,000	−2,285,714	−7.1
1548	8,285,000	−428,611	−2.6
1570	2,738,500	−252,114	−3.0
1650	3,030,000	3,644	0.1
1796	1,076,122	−13,382	0.5
1825	2,488,000	48,685	4.5
1836	1,373,736	−97,660	−3.9
1850	2,001,203	44,819	3.2
1862	2,487,916	40,559	2.0
1876	2,651,840	11,709	0.5
1940	6,207,967	55,564	2.0
1961	9,906,746	176,132	2.8
1972	13,572,052	333,209	3.3
1981	17,005,210	381,462	2.5
1990 [2]	22,332,100	743,996	3.4

[1] Estimates for the preconquest population of Peru vary widely but in recent years have been greatly increased from the guesses of the 1950s of 3 million to 4 million based on ethnohistorical study on the impact of epidemic diseases sweeping the region beginning in about 1524. Recent estimates for the population in the territory covering present-day Peru range from 12 million to 30 million.
[2] Estimated.

Source: Based on information from Henry F. Dobyns and Paul L. Doughty, *Peru: A Cultural History,* New York, 1976, 298–99; and Peru, Instituto Nacional de Estadística, *Población total proyectada al 30 junio de 1990,* Lima, 1989, 67.

Table 3. Total Population and Annual Population Change in
Lima, 1614–1990

Year	Total Population	Annual Population Change	
		Number	Percentage
1614	24,441	n.a.	n.a.
1700	37,259	126	0.5
1796	52,627	160	0.4
1836	55,627	75	0.1
1857	94,195	1,837	3.3
1862	89,434	-952	-1.0
1876	100,156	766	0.8
1891	103,956	253	0.2
1898	113,409	1,350	1.3
1903	130,089	3,336	2.9
1908	140,884	2,159	1.7
1908 [1]	172,927	n.a.	n.a.
1920	223,807	4,240	2.5
1931	373,875	13,642	6.1
1940	562,885	13,188	9.4
1961	1,632,370	50,928	9.0
1972	3,002,043	124,516	7.6
1981	4,164,597	129,516	4.3
1990 [2]	6,414,500	249,989	6.0

n.a.—not available.
[1] Province of Lima. After 1908 population growth and settlement size made the province the unit for measurement.
[2] Estimated.

Source: Based on information from Henry F. Dobyns and Paul L. Doughty, *Peru: A Cultural History,* New York, 1976, 298–99; and Peru, Instituto Nacional de Estadística, *Población total proyectada al 30 de junio de 1990,* Lima, 1989, 67.

Table 4. *Population and Percentage Growth of Major Cities, Census Years, 1961–90*
(in thousands)

City	1961	1972	1981	1990	Percentage Growth (1961–90)
Lima and Callao ...	1,641	3,394	4,836	6,414	290
Arequipa	158	304	447	634	301
Trujillo	103	241	355	531	415
Chiclayo	95	189	280	426	348
Cusco	79	120	182	275	248
Piura	72	126	186	324	350
Huancayo	64	115	165	207	152
Chimbote	59	159	216	296	401
Iquitos	57	111	185	269	359
Ica	49	73	111	152	210
Sullana	34	60	80	113	229
Tacna	27	55	92	150	473
Talara	27	29	57	89	229
Pucallpa	26	57	92	129	396
Puno	24	41	66	90	275
Huánuco	24	41	53	86	258
Ayacucho	23	34	68	101	339
Cajamarca	22	37	60	92	318
Huacho	22	36	42	87	278
Pisco	22	41	53	77	250
Pasco	21	47	72	76	211
Juliaca	20	38	77	121	505

Table 5. *Total Population and Urban-Rural*
Breakdown by Department, 1990 *
(in thousands)

Department	Urban Number	Urban Percentage	Rural Number	Rural Percentage	Total Population
Amazonas	111.1	33.1	224.2	66.9	335.3
Ancash	586.3	59.6	396.9	40.4	983.2
Apurímac	105.6	28.4	266.1	71.6	371.7
Arequipa	818.4	84.8	146.6	15.2	965.0
Ayacucho	236.8	41.8	329.6	58.2	566.4
Cajamarca	298.1	23.5	972.5	76.5	1,270.6
Callao	582.0	98.9	6.6	1.1	588.6
Cusco	465.4	44.7	576.4	55.3	1,041.8
Huancavelica	107.5	28.6	268.2	71.4	375.7
Huánuco	234.3	38.5	374.9	61.5	609.2
Ica	464.5	85.6	78.4	14.4	542.9
Junín	688.7	61.8	424.9	38.2	1,113.6
La Libertad	878.0	70.6	365.5	29.4	1,243.5
Lambayeque	741.0	79.2	194.3	20.8	935.3
Lima	6,490.2	96.8	217.1	3.2	6,707.3
Loreto	387.6	59.3	266.5	40.7	654.1
Madre de Dios	27.6	56.3	21.4	43.7	49.0
Moquegua	111.7	83.3	22.4	16.7	134.1
Pasco	176.2	62.3	106.7	37.7	282.9
Piura	977.6	65.4	516.7	34.6	1,494.3
Puno	392.0	38.3	631.5	61.7	1,023.5
San Martín	270.4	58.8	189.6	41.2	460.0
Tacna	178.1	84.9	31.7	15.1	209.8
Tumbes	116.8	81.0	27.4	19.0	144.2
Ucayali	153.4	66.7	76.7	33.3	230.1
PERU	15,599.3	69.9	6,732.8	30.1	22,332.1

* Projected figures.

Source: Based on information from Peru, Instituto Nacional de Estadística, *Población total*
proyectada al 30 de junio de 1990, Lima, 1989.

Table 6. *Distribution of Population by Region,*
Census Years 1940–90
(in percentages)

Year	Coast	Highlands	Selva	Total
1940	25	62	13	100
1961	39	52	9	100
1972	45	44	11	100
1981	51	41	8	100
1990 *	53	36	11	100

* Estimated.

Source: Based on information from Peru, Instituto Nacional de Estadística, *Población total*
proyectada al 30 de junio de 1990, Lima, 1989, 54; and Peru, Instituto Nacional de
Estadística, *Censos nacionales de VII de población, 1981,* Lima, 1981, 45.

Table 7. Education Statistics by Level, 1988

Level	Number of Schools	Enrollment	Number of Teachers	Student-Teacher Ratio
Primary	27,626	3,864,900	126,117	30.6
Secondary	5,462	1,801,080	80,273	22.4
Vocational	1,288	216,920	8,707	24.9
University	46	431,040	24,911	17.3
PERU	34,422	6,313,940	240,008	n.a.

n.a.—not available.

Source: Based on information from Peru, Instituto Nacional de Estadística, *Perú: Compendio estadístico,* Lima, 1987; Encyclopaedia Britannica, *1991 Book of the Year,* Chicago, 1991; and United Nations, Economic Commission for Latin America and the Caribbean, *Statistical Yearbook for Latin America and the Caribbean, 1990,* Santiago, Chile, 1991.

Table 8. Literacy by Urban-Rural Breakdown, Region, and Sex, 1989 (in percentages)

	Males	Females	Total
Urban-rural breakdown			
Urban	50	50	100
Rural	62	38	100
Region			
Coast	51	49	100
Highlands	58	42	100
Selva	59	41	100
Metropolitan Lima	50	50	100
PERU *	53	47	100

* Figures differ sharply from reported 1990 estimated literacy rate of 85 percent (male, 92 percent; female, 80 percent).

Source: Based on information from Peru, Instituto Nacional de Estadística, *Perú: Compendio estadístico,* Lima, 1987; Encyclopaedia Britannica, *1991 Book of the Year,* Chicago, 1991; and United Nations, Economic Commission for Latin America and the Caribbean, *Statistical Yearbook for Latin America and the Caribbean, 1990,* Santiago, Chile, 1991.

*Table 9. Medical Personnel, Hospitals, and Hospital
Beds by Department, 1987*
(per 10,000 persons)

Department	Physicians	Nurses	Hospitals *	Hospital Beds
Amazonas	0.4	0.4	93	4.3
Ancash	2.5	1.4	232	11.5
Apurímac	0.4	1.1	83	6.1
Arequipa	12.5	19.3	248	22.8
Ayacucho	0.6	1.8	176	7.2
Cajamarca	0.7	2.0	149	2.9
Callao	n.a.	9.6	55	30.4
Cusco	1.8	5.7	201	10.3
Huancavelica	0.4	1.0	156	6.4
Huánuco	1.8	2.6	113	7.2
Ica	10.5	6.0	98	21.7
Junín	2.6	7.8	253	13.5
La Libertad	10.4	7.4	209	13.1
Lambayeque	5.2	8.2	73	13.7
Lima	23.8	13.1	620	24.9
Loreto	2.6	3.4	195	18.5
Madre de Dios	2.8	2.6	35	19.8
Moquegua	9.6	11.0	52	30.0
Pasco	3.7	3.0	114	21.4
Piura	2.7	2.2	168	9.3
Puno	0.9	2.5	231	7.3
San Martín	1.0	0.6	244	9.4
Tacna	5.6	12.0	49	23.6
Tumbes	1.6	2.1	46	12.3
Ucayali	1.9	0.5	48	10.3
PERU	9.5	7.4	n.a.	16.0
(Total number)	20,198	15,464	3,941	32,326

n.a.—not available.
* General hospitals, infant hospitals, and clinics.

Source: Based on information from Peru, Instituto Nacional de Estadística, *Perú: Compendio estadístico,* Lima, 1987.

Table 10. Health Indicators, 1975–90

Heath Indicator	1975	1980–85	1985–90
Public health expenditure per capita [1]	n.a.	n.a.	17.90
Average calories per capita	2,263	2,144	2,277
Food supply as percentage of FAO recommendation [2]	100	99	93
Access to potable water [3]	47	52	52
Life expectancy at birth	55.5	58.6	62.2
Birth rate [4]	40.5	36.7	34.3
Mortality rate [4]	12.8	10.7	9.2

n.a.—not available.
[1] In United States dollars.
[2] FAO—Food and Agriculture Organization of the United Nations.
[3] In percentages.
[4] Per 1,000 population.

Table 11. Production of Major Agricultural Crops, 1970, 1980, and 1990 (in thousands of tons)

Crop	1970	1980	1990
Bananas	n.a.	684	656
Coffee	65	86	80
Corn	615	493	621
Cotton	248	265	239
Potatoes	1,929	1,380	1,190
Rice	587	411	966
Sugar	7,591	5,598	6,083
Wheat	125	77	95

n.a.—not available.

Source: Based on information from Richard Webb and Graciela Fernández Baca (eds.), *Perú en números, 1990,* Lima, 1990, 438–59.

Table 12. Major Manufacturing Branches: Value Added,
1988, and Percentage Change, 1980–88

Branch	Value Added, 1988 (in percentages)	Percentage Change, 1980–88
Food processing	30.6	22.5
Textiles and leather	14.2	-7.9
Wood and furniture	6.0	37.7
Paper	5.7	0.0
Chemicals	12.5	14.5
Nonmetal finished products	5.9	48.5
Base metals	13.9	-21.7
Metal products	9.5	-7.0
Other	1.7	-11.6
ALL MANUFACTURING	100.0	4.8

Source: Based on information from Peru, Instituto Nacional de Estadística, *Evolución de la economía peruana*, Lima, November 1989, 95.

Table 13. Gross Domestic Product (GDP) by
Sector, 1950–60 and 1990 *
(in percentages)

Sector	1950–60	1990
Agriculture and fishing	22	14
Manufacturing	20	22
Mining	2	11
Construction	9	7
Services	43	37
Government	4	9
TOTAL	100	100

* Output evaluated at current prices in each period.

Source: Averages for 1950–60 based on information from World Bank, *World Tables*, Washington, 1983; data for 1990 from Banco Central de Reserva del Perú, *Memoria 1990*, Lima, 1991.

Table 14. Production of Crude Petroleum, 1980–90
(in thousands of barrels)

Year	Production	Year	Production
1980	71.4	1986	64.8
1981	70.4	1987	59.7
1982	71.2	1988	51.7
1983	62.5	1989	47.6
1984	67.4	1990	47.1
1985	68.8		

Source: Based on information from Richard Webb and Graciela Fernández Baca (eds.), *Perú en números, 1990*, Lima, 1990, 521.

Table 15. Principal Trading Partners, 1980 and 1990
(in millions of United States dollars)

Country	1980 Exports	1980 Imports	1990 Exports	1990 Imports
United States	1,227	1,043	732	792
Japan	336	251	203	63
West Germany	256	192	267	165
Britain	147	95	169	76
Brazil	117	95	129	146
Ecuador	92	15	32	47
Colombia	82	28	95	72
Chile	59	48	51	69
Argentina	51	99	29	204
France	43	45	61	42
Spain	24	45	42	24

Source: Based on information from Richard Webb and Graciela Fernández Baca (eds.), *Perú en números, 1990,* Lima, 1990, 942, 944, 962, and 963.

Table 16. Major Exports, 1970 and 1990

	1970 Value [1]	1970 Percentage	1990 Value [1]	1990 Percentage
Traditional				
Copper	252	24.4	732	22.3
Iron	72	7.0	57	1.7
Silver	29	2.8	79	2.4
Lead	63	6.1	182	5.6
Zinc	49	4.7	412	12.6
Petroleum products	7	0.7	263	8.0
Fish meal	303	29.3	341	10.4
Coffee	44	4.3	97	3.0
Other	181	17.5	139	4.2
Total traditional	1,000	96.8	2,302	70.2
Nontraditional				
Manufactures	19	1.8	628	19.2
Other	15	1.5	346	10.6
Total nontraditional ...	34	3.3	974	29.8
TOTAL [2]	1,034	100.0	3,276	100.0

[1] In millions of United States dollars.
[2] Figures may not add to total because of rounding.

Source: Based on information from Richard Webb and Graciela Fernández Baca (eds.), *Perú en números, 1990,* Lima, 1990, 922–23 and 931.

Table 17. Composition of Labor Force by Sector, 1950,
1980, and 1990
(in percentages)

Sector	1950	1980	1990
Agriculture and fishing	59	40	34
Mining	2	2	2
Manufacturing	13	12	10
Construction	3	4	4
Services	23	42	50
TOTAL	100	100	100

Source: Based on information from Rosemary Thorp and Geoffrey Bertram, *Peru 1890-1977,*
New York, 1978, 259; and Richard Webb and Graciela Fernández Baca (eds.),
Perú en números, 1990, Lima, 1990, 303.

Table 18. Distribution of Income by Quintile,
1972 and 1985
(in percentages)

Quintile	1972	1985
Highest	61.0	51.9
Second	21.0	21.5
Third	11.0	13.7
Fourth	5.1	8.5
Lowest	1.9	4.4
TOTAL	100.0	100.0

Source: Based on information from World Bank, *World Development Report, 1989,* Washington,
1989, 223; and World Bank, *World Development Report, 1990,* Washington, 1990, 236.

Table 19. Results of Municipal Elections, 1980–89
(in percentages)

Party	1980	1983	1986	1989
Lima				
AP [1]	34.8	11.9	n.a.	n.a.
APRA [2]	16.3	27.2	37.6	11.5
ASI [3]	n.a.	n.a.	n.a.	2.2
Fredemo [4]	n.a.	n.a.	n.a.	26.8
IU [5]	28.3	36.5	34.8	11.5
Obras [6]	n.a.	n.a.	n.a.	45.2
PPC [7]	20.6	21.2	26.9	n.a.
Total Lima	100.0	96.8	99.3	97.2
Nationwide [8]				
AP	35.8	15.0	n.a.	n.a.
APRA	22.6	34.0	42.0	17.0
ASI	n.a.	n.a.	n.a.	0.7
Fredemo	n.a.	n.a.	n.a.	30.0
IU	23.9	30.0	32.0	15.0
PPC	10.9	10.0	9.0	n.a.
Other	n.a.	n.a.	n.a.	25.0
Total nationwide	93.2	89.0	83.0	87.7

n.a.—not available.
[1] Acción Popular (Popular Action).
[2] Alianza Popular Revolucionaria Americana (American Popular Revolutionary Alliance).
[3] Acuerdo Socialista Izquierdista (Leftist Socialist Accord).
[4] Frente Democrático (Democratic Front).
[5] Izquierda Unida (United Left).
[6] Movimiento Independiente de Obras (Independent Obras Movement).
[7] Partido Popular Cristiano (Popular Christian Party).
[8] Preliminary results. Release of official figures long delayed.

Table 20. Results of National Elections, 1985

Party	Candidate	Percentage of Votes	Number of Seats Senate	Chamber of Deputies
AP [1]	Luis Alva Castro	6.4	5	10
APRA [2]	Alan García Pérez	47.8	32	107
CODE [3]	Luis Bedoya Reyes	12.2	8	12
IU [4]	Alfonso Barrantes Lingán	22.2	15	48
Others [5]	n.a.	2.6	0	3
Null and blank [6]	n.a.	8.8	0	0
TOTAL		100.0	60	180

n.a.—not available.
[1] Acción Popular (Popular Action).
[2] Alianza Popular Revolucionaria Americana (American Popular Revolutionary Alliance).
[3] Confederación Democrática (Democratic Confederation), consisting of Popular Christian Party (Partido Popular Cristiano—PPC) and Hayaist Movement (Movimiento de Bases Hayaistas—MBH).
[4] Izquierda Unida (United Left).
[5] Includes National Front of Workers and Peasants (Frente Nacional de Trabajadores y Campesinos—Frenatraca), Tacneñist Front (Frente Tacneñista), and Nationalist Left (Izquierda Nacionalista).
[6] Null and blank vote was half the average of the first four elections. Null means ballots were nullified for some reason, e.g., defaced, and blank means ballots were not filled out.

Table 21. Results of National Elections, 1990

Party	Candidate	Percentage of Votes First Round	Second Round	Number of Seats Senate	Chamber of Deputies
APRA	Luis Alva Castro	19.6	2d	14	33
ASI [2]	Alfonso Barrantes Lingán	4.1		3	4
Cambio '90 [3]	Alberto K. Fujimori	24.3	56.5	15	49
Fredemo [4]	Mario Vargas Llosa	28.2	33.9	22	64
IU [5]	Henry Pease García	7.1		5	18
Others [6]	n.a.	1.0		1	12
Null and blank [7]	n.a.	14.5	9.6	0	0
TOTAL		98.7	100.0	60	180

n.a.—not available.
[1] Alianza Popular (Popular).
[2] Acuerdo Socialista Izquierdista (Leftist Socialist Accord).
[3] Change '90.
[4] Frente Democrático (Democratic Front).
[5] Izquierda Unida (United Left).
[6] Includes National Front of Workers and Peasants (Frente Nacional de Trabajadores y Campesinos—Frenatraca), Tacneñist Front (Frente Tacneñista), and Nationalist Left (Izquierda Nacionalista).
[7] Null and blank vote was half the average of the first four elections. Null means ballots were nullified for some reason, e.g., defaced, and blank means ballots were not filled out.

Table 22. Voting Behavior in the Twelve Poorest Lima Districts, National Elections, 1980, 1985, and 1990 (in percentages)

Party	1980	1985	1990
AP [1]	50.2	4.3	n.a.
APRA [2]	16.1	53.6	13.5
ASI [3]	n.a.	n.a.	5.6
Cambio '90 [4]	n.a.	n.a.	39.6
Fredemo [5]	n.a.	n.a.	22.7
IU [6]	38.9	31.3	7.1
PPC [7]	11.6	8.8	n.a.
TOTAL	116.8	98.0	88.5

n.a.—not available.
[1] Acción Popular (Popular Action).
[2] Alianza Popular Revolucionaria Americana (American Popular Revolutionary Alliance).
[3] Acuerdo Socialista Izquierdista (Leftist Socialist Accord).
[4] Change '90.
[5] Frente Democrático (Democratic Front).
[6] Izquierda Unida (United Left).
[7] Partido Popular Cristiano (Popular Christian Party).

Table 23. Voting Behavior in the Twelve Poorest Lima Districts, Municipal Elections, 1980–89 (in percentages)

Party	1980	1983	1986	1989
AP [1]	n.a.	8.7	n.a.	n.a.
APRA [2]	20.9	26.5	41.8	12.4
ASI [3]	n.a.	n.a.	n.a.	3.0
Fredemo [4]	n.a.	n.a.	n.a.	16.4
IU [5]	18.2	49.9	43.9	15.1
Obras [6]	n.a.	n.a.	n.a.	49.2
PPC [7]	8.0	11.5	13.3	n.a.
TOTAL	47.1	96.6	99.0	96.1

n.a.—not available.
[1] Acción Popular (Popular Action).
[2] Alianza Popular Revolucionaria Americana (American Popular Revolutionary Alliance).
[3] Acuerdo Socialista Izquierdista (Leftist Socialist Accord).
[4] Frente Democrático (Democratic Front).
[5] Izquierda Unida (United Left).
[6] Movimiento Independiente de Obras (Independent Works Movement).
[7] Partido Popular Cristiano (Popular Christian Party).

Table 24. Major Army Equipment, 1992

Type and Description	Country of Origin	In Inventory
Main battle tanks		
T-54/T-55/T-62	Soviet Union	300
Light tanks		
AMX-13	France	110
Armored reconnaissance vehicles		
M-8 (M-200 version)	United States	60
Fiat 6616	Italy	20
BRDM-2	Soviet Union	15
Armored personnel carriers		
M-113	United States	300
UR-416	West Germany	225
Artillery		
Model M-116, 75mm	United States	12
Model 56 pack, 105mm	–do–	50
M-101, 105mm	–do–	130
D-30, 122mm	n.a.	30
BM-21, 122mm	n.a.	14
M-46, 130mm	Soviet Union	30
M-54, 130mm Bofors	Sweden	30
M-114, 155mm	United States	36
M-109A2, 155mm	–do–	12
Mk F3, 155mm	France	12
Mortars		
81mm	n.a.	n.a.
107mm	n.a.	n.a.
120mm Brandt	France	300
Recoilless rifles		
M-40A1, 105mm and 106mm	United States	n.a.
Antiaircraft guns		
ZSU-23-4, 23mm	Soviet Union	35
Towed, 40mm Bofors L60/70	Sweden	40
Surface-to-air missiles		
SA-3/SA-7	Soviet Union	12
Aircraft		
Cessna 182	United States	1
Cessna 185	–do–	5
Cessna U206	–do–	2
Cessna 337	–do–	1
Beech Queen Air 65	–do–	1
U-10	–do–	3
U-17	–do–	3

Table 24—Continued

Type and Description	Country of Origin	In Inventory
Helicopters		
Bell 47G	United States	2
Mi-6	Soviet Union	2
Mi-8	–do–	28
Mi-17	–do–	14
Aérospatiale SA-318C	France	3
SA-315	France	6
SA-316	–do–	5
SA-318	–do–	3
Agusta A-109	Italy	2

n.a.—not available.

Source: Based on information from *Tecnología Militar* [Bonn], No. 4, July–August 1990, 52; and *The Military Balance, 1992–1993,* London, 1992, 185.

Table 25. Armed Forces Personnel Strength, Selected Years, 1829–1992

Army		Air Force		Navy	
Year	Personnel	Year	Personnel	Year	Personnel
1829	8,000	1925	301	1934	2,449
1841	5,400	1927	61	1944	3,500
1851	6,000	1929	175	1958	1,000
1872	4,500	1930	600	1970	7,200
1879	5,241	1939	1,600	1977	10,000
1881	33,500	1941	4,639	1984	20,500
1926	7,556	1947	4,000	1990	25,000
1930	9,045	1980	9,500	1992	22,000
1935	15,000	1990	15,000		
1940	15,273	1992	15,000		
1941	31,578				
1951	32,000				
1960	55,000				
1982	75,000				
1990	80,000				
1992	75,000				

Source: Based on information from Adrian J. English, *Armed Forces of Latin America,* London, 1984, 366–408; and *The Military Balance, 1992–1993,* London, 1992, 185–86.

Table 26. Major Naval Equipment, 1992

Type and Description	Country of Origin	In Inventory
Navy		
Patrol and coastal combatants		
Support	n.a.	9
River and lake flotillas	n.a.	10
Missile combatants		
Velarde-class fast patrol craft	France	6
Amphibious craft		
Paita (former U.S.S. Terrebonne Parish		
class)	United States	4
Principal surface combatants		
Cruisers		
Almirante Grau (De Ruyter class) ...	Netherlands	1
Aguirre (De Zeven Provincien class) .	–do–	1
Destroyers		
Palacios (Daring class)	Britain	2
Bolognesi (Friesland class)	Netherlands	4
Frigates		
Melitón Carvajal (Lupo class)	Italy	4
Manuel Villavicencio (Lupo class)	–do–	1
Montonero (Lupo class)	–do–	1
Submarines		
Casma class (Type T-209/1200)	West Germany	6
La Pedrera (Guppy IA class)	United States	1
Abtao (Mackerel class)	–do–	3
Oceanography vessels		
Unanué (former U.S.S. *Sotoyomo*) ...	–do–	1
Carrillo	n.a.	3
Naval Aviation		
Antisubmarine warfare and marine		
reconnaissance aircraft		
S-2E	n.a.	4
SG	n.a.	4
Super King Air B 200T	United States	3
Helicopters		
Bell AB-212 ASW	–do–	6
SH-3D Sea King	–do–	6
UH-1D	–do–	6
SA-319 Alouette III	France	2
Transport		
C-47 Dakota	United States	5
C-47 Hercules	–do–	2
Liaison		
Bell 206B	–do–	4

Table 26—Continued

Type and Description	Country of Origin	In Inventory
Training		
Cessna 150	United States	2
Beech T-34C	–do–	5

n.a.—not available.

Source: Based on information from *The Military Balance, 1992–1993,* London, 1992, 185–86.

Table 27. *Major Air Force Equipment, 1992*

Type and Description	Country of Origin	In Inventory
Bombers		
Canberra B–2	Britain	30
Attack group aircraft		
Sukhoi Su-22 Fitter	Soviet Union	41
Cessna A–37B Dragonfly	United States	25
Fixed-wing fighters		
Mirage 2000P	France	10
Mirage DP	–do–	2
Mirage 5P	–do–	14
Trainers		
Cessna 150	United States	2
Cessna T–37B/C	–do–	25
Cessna T–41A/A/D Mescalero	–do–	35
EMB–312 Tucano	Brazil	29
Aermacchi MB–339A	Italy	13
SU–22 Uti	Soviet Union	4
Tankers		
Boeing KC 707-323C	United States	1
Transports		
An-26	Soviet Union	n.a.
An-32	–do–	14
C–130A	United States	4
C–130D	–do–	6
Lockheed L–100–20	–do–	5
DC–8–62F	–do–	2
DHC–5 Buffalo	–do–	12
DHC–6 Twin Otter	–do–	8
Douglas C–47	–do–	6
FH–227 (F–27)	–do–	1
PC–6 Turbo Porter	Switzerland	9
Harbin Y–12	China	6

Table 27—Continued

Type and Description	Country of Origin	In Inventory
Reconnaissance		
Gates Learjet 25B	United States	2
36A Halcón (C-101)	Argentina	2
Presidential fleet		
Fokker F-28 Mk1000	Sweden	1
Dessault/Breguet Falcon 20F	France	1
Liaison		
Beech 99	United States	2
Cessna 185	–do–	3
Cessna 320	–do–	1
Beech Queen Air 80	–do–	15
King Air 90	–do–	3
PA-31T	n.a.	1
Liaison helicopters		
UH-1D Iroquois	United States	8
Training helicopters		
Bell 47G	–do–	12
Attack helicopters		
Mi-25	Soviet Union	10
Helicopters		
Bell 206	United States	8
Bell 212	–do–	15
Bell 214	–do–	5
Bell 412	–do–	1
MBB Bo-105C	West Germany	10
Mi-6 Hook	Soviet Union	5
Mi-8 Hip	–do–	5
Aérospatiale SA-316B	France	5
Aérospatiale Alouette III	–do–	10
Missiles		
AS-30	n.a.	n.a.
AA-2 Atoll	n.a.	n.a.
R-550 Magic	n.a.	n.a.
SA-2	Soviet Union	3
SA-3	–do–	6
Missile launchers		
SA-2	–do–	18
SA-3	–do–	24

n.a.—not available.

Source: Based on information from *The Military Balance, 1992–1993,* London, 1992, 186;
and *Tecnología Militar* [Bonn], No. 4, 1990, 52.

Bibliography

Chapter 1

Alexander, Robert, ed. *Aprismo: The Ideas and Doctrines of Víctor Raúl Haya de la Torre.* Kent: Kent State University Press, 1973.

Andrien, Kenneth J. *Crisis and Decline: The Viceroyalty of Peru in the Seventeenth Century.* Albuquerque: University of New Mexico Press, 1985.

Anna, Timothy E. *The Fall of the Royal Government in Peru.* Lincoln: University of Nebraska Press, 1979.

Arzáns de Orsúa y Vela, Bartolomé. *Tales of Potosí.* (Ed., R.C. Padden.) Providence: Brown University Press, 1975.

Bakewell, Peter. *Silver and Entrepreneurship in Seventeenth-Century Potosí: The Life and Times of Antonio López de Quiroga.* Albuquerque: University of New Mexico Press, 1988.

Becker, David G. *The New Bourgeoisie and the Limits of Dependency: Mining, Class, and Power in "Revolutionary" Peru.* Princeton: Princeton University Press, 1983.

Bertram, Geoffrey. "Peru 1930-1962." Pages 385-450 in Leslie Bethell (ed.), *The Cambridge History of Latin America,* 8. Cambridge: Cambridge University Press, 1991.

Bethell, Leslie (ed.). *The Cambridge History of Latin America,* 1. Cambridge: Cambridge University Press, 1984.

_____. *The Cambridge History of Latin America,* 5. Cambridge: Cambridge University Press, 1986.

_____. *The Cambridge History of Latin America,* 8. Cambridge: Cambridge University Press, 1992.

Blanchard, Peter. *The Origins of the Peruvian Labor Movement, 1883-1919.* Pittsburgh: University of Pittsburgh Press, 1982.

Blondet M., Cecilia. *Las mujeres y el poder: Una historia de Villa El Salvador.* Lima: Instituto de Estudios Peruanos, 1991.

Bonilla, Heraclio. "Peru and Bolivia." Pages 539-82 in Leslie Bethell (ed.), *The Cambridge History of Latin America,* 1. Cambridge: Cambridge University Press, 1984.

Booth, David, and Bernardo Sorj (eds.). *Military Reformism and Social Classes: The Peruvian Experience, 1968-80.* New York: St. Martin's Press, 1983.

Bourque, Susan C., and Kay B. Warren. *Women of the Andes: Patriarchy and Social Change in Two Peruvian Towns.* Ann Arbor: University of Michigan Press, 1981.

Bowser, Frederick P. *The African Slave in Colonial Peru.* Stanford: Stanford University Press, 1974.

Brown, Kendall W. *Bourbons and Brandy: Imperial Reform in Eighteenth-Century Arequipa.* Albuquerque: University of New Mexico Press, 1986.

Burga, Manuel, and Alberto Flores Galindo. *Apogeo y crísis de la República aristocrática.* (3d ed. rev.) Lima: Ediciones Rikchay Perú, 1984.

Burkholder, Mark A. *Politics of a Colonial Career: José Baquíjano and the Audiencia of Lima.* (2d ed.) Wilmington, Delaware: Scholarly Resources Books, 1990.

Burkholder, Mark A., and Lyman L. Johnson. *Colonial Latin America.* New York: Oxford University Press, 1990.

Cameron, Ian. *The Kingdom of the Sun God: A History of the Andes and Their People.* New York: Facts on File, 1990.

Campbell, Leon G. *The Military and Society in Colonial Peru, 1750-1810.* Philadelphia: American Philosophical Society, 1978.

Chavarría, Jesús. *José Carlos Mariátegui and the Rise of Modern Peru, 1890-1930.* Albuquerque: University of New Mexico Press, 1979.

Clayton, Larry. *Grace: W.R. Grace, the Formative Years, 1850-1930.* Ottawa, Illinois: Jameson Books, 1985.

Cole, Jeffery A. *Potosí Mita, 1573-1700: Compulsory Indian Labor in the Andes.* Stanford: Stanford University Press, 1985.

Collier, David. *Squatters and Oligarchs: Authoritarian Rule and Policy Change in Peru.* Baltimore: Johns Hopkins University Press, 1976.

Contreras, Carlos. *Mineros y campesinos en los Andes: Mercado laboral y economía compesina en la Sierra Central, siglo XIX.* Lima: Instituto de Estudios Peruanos, 1988.

Cook, Noble David. *Demographic Collapse: Indian Peru, 1520-1620.* Cambridge: Cambridge University Press, 1981.

Cotler, Julio. "Peru since 1960." Pages 451-508 in Leslie Bethell (ed.), *The Cambridge History of Latin America, 8.* Cambridge: Cambridge University Press, 1991.

Cueva García, Aníbal (ed.). *Gran atlas geográfico del Perú y el mundo.* Lima: A.F.A. Editores S.A., 1991.

Cushner, Nicholas P. *Lords of the Land: Sugar, Wine, and Jesuit Estates of Coastal Peru, 1600-1767.* Albany: State University of New York Press, 1980.

Davies, Keith A. *Landowners in Colonial Peru.* Austin: University of Texas Press, 1984.

Davies, Thomas M., Jr. *Indian Integration in Peru: A Half Century of Experience, 1900-1948.* Lincoln: University of Nebraska Press, 1974.

Degregori, Carlos Iván. *El nacimiento de Sendero Luminoso.* Lima: Instituto de Estudios Peruanos, 1990.

Derpich, Wilma, José Luis Huiza, and Cecilia Israel. *Lima años 30: Salarios y costo de vida de la clase trabajadora.* Lima: Fundación Friedrich Ebert, 1985.

de Soto, Hernando. *The Other Path: The Invisible Revolution in the Third World.* New York: Harper and Row, 1990.

Deustua, José. *La minería peruana y la iniciación de la República, 1820-1840.* Lima: Instituto de Estudios Peruanos, 1986.

Deustua, José, and José Luis Rénique. *Intelectuales, indigenismo y descentralismo en el Perú.* Cusco: "Bartolomé de las Casas," 1984.

DeWind, Josh. *Peasants Become Miners: The Evolution of Industrial Mining Systems in Peru, 1902-1974.* New York: Garland, 1987.

Dietz, Henry A. *Poverty and Problem-Solving under Military Rule: The Urban Poor in Lima, Peru.* Austin: University of Texas Press, 1980.

Dobyns, Henry F., and Paul L. Doughty. *Peru: A Cultural History.* New York: Oxford University Press, 1976.

Dore, Elizabeth. *The Peruvian Mining Industry: Growth, Stagnation, and Crisis.* Boulder, Colorado: Westview Press, 1988.

Drake, Paul. *The Money Doctor in the Andes: The Kemmerer Missions, 1923-1933.* Durham: Duke University Press, 1989.

Duviols, Pierre. *La lutte contre les religions autochtones dans le Pérou colonial: "L'extirpation de l'idolatrie entre 1532 et 1660."* Lima: Instituto Francés de Estudios Andinos, 1971.

Economist Intelligence Unit. *Country Report: Peru, Bolivia* [London], No. 1, 1992.

_____. *Country Report: Peru, Bolivia,* No. 2, 1992.

Eckstein, Susan. "The Impact of Revolution on Social Welfare in Latin America." Pages 280-306 in Jack Goldstone (ed.), *Revolutions: Theoretical, Comparative, and Historical Studies.* New York: Harcourt Brace Jovanovich, 1986.

Espinoza Soriano, Waldemar. *La destrucción del imperio de los incas: La rivalidad política y señorial de los Curacazgos andinos.* Lima: Retablo de Papel Ediciones, 1977.

_____. *Los incas: Economía, sociedad y estado en la era del Tahuantinsuyo.* La Victoria, Perú: Amaru Editores, 1987.

Figueroa, Adolfo. *Capitalist Development and the Peasant Economy of Peru.* Cambridge: Cambridge University Press, 1984.

Fisher, John R. *Government and Society in Colonial Peru: The Intendant System, 1784-1814.* London: 1970.

_____. *Silver Mines and Silver Miners in Colonial Peru, 1776-1824.* Liverpool: University of Liverpool, 1977.

Fitzgerald, Edmund V.K. *The Political Economy of Peru, 1956-1978: Economic Development and the Restructuring of Capital.* Cambridge: Cambridge University Press, 1979.

Flores Galindo, Alberto. *Buscando un inca: Identidad y utopia en los Andes.* Lima: Instituto de Apoyo Agrario, 1987.

Flores Galindo, Alberto (ed.). *Independencia y revolución, 1780-1840.* (2 vols.) Lima: Instituto Nacional de Cultura, 1987.

————. *Túpac Amaru II-1780: Sociedad colonial y sublevaciones populares.* Lima: Retablo de Papel Ediciones, 1976.

Gardiner, C. Harvey. *The Japanese and Peru, 1873-1973.* Albuquerque: University of New Mexico Press, 1975.

Gilbert, Dennis. *La oligarquía peruana: Historia de tres familias.* Lima: Editorial Horizonte, 1982.

Glave, Testino, and Luis Miguel. *Trajinantes-caminos indígenos en la sociedad colonial siglos XVI-XVII.* Lima: Instituto de Apoyo Agrario, 1989.

Glave, Testino, Luis Miguel, and María Isabel Remy. *Estructura agraria y vida rural en una región andina: Ollantaytambo entre los siglos XVI-XIX.* Cusco: Centro de Estudios Rurales Andinos ''Bartolomé de las Casas,'' 1983.

Goldstone, Jack (ed.). *Revolutions: Theoretical, Comparative, and Historical Studies.* New York: Harcourt Brace Jovanovich, 1986.

Gonzales, Michael J. *Plantation Agriculture and Social Control in Northern Peru, 1875-1933.* Austin: University of Texas Press, 1985.

Gootenberg, Paul E. *Between Silver and Guano: Commercial Policy and the State in Postindependence Peru.* Princeton: Princeton University Press, 1989.

Gorman, Stephen M. (ed.). *Post-Revolutionary Peru: The Politics of Transformation.* (Westview Special Studies on Latin America and the Caribbean.) Boulder, Colorado: Westview Press, 1982.

Gorriti Ellenbogen, Gustavo. *Sendero: Historia de la guerra milenaria en el Perú, 1.* Lima: Editorial Apoyo, 1990.

Guamán Poma de Ayala, Felipe. *Letter to a King: A Peruvian Chief's Account of Life under the Incas and under Spanish Rule.* New York: Dutton, 1978.

Haya de la Torre, Víctor Raúl. *Obras completas.* (7 vols.) Lima: Editorial Mejía, 1976-77.

Hemming, John. *The Conquest of the Incas.* New York: Harcourt Brace Jovanovich, 1970.

Huayhuaca, José Carlos. *Martín Chambi: Fotógrafo, Cusco 1920-1950.* Lima: Banco de Lima, 1989.

Jacobsen, Nils P. *Mirages of Transition: The Peruvian Altiplano, 1780-1930.* Berkeley: University of California Press, 1993.

Jacobsen, Nils P., and Hans-Jürgen Puhle (eds.). *The Economies of Mexico and Peru During the Late Colonial Period, 1760-1810.* Berlin: Colloquium Verlag, 1986.

Juan, Jorge, and Antonio de Ulloa. *Discourse and Political Reflections on the Kingdoms of Peru.* Norman: University of Oklahoma Press, 1978.

Kápsoli Escudero, Wilfredo. *Los movimientos campesinos en el Perú 1879–1965.* Lima: Delva Editores, 1977.

Keith, Robert G. *Conquest and Agrarian Change: The Emergence of the Hacienda System on the Peruvian Coast.* Cambridge: Harvard University Press, 1976.

Kendall, Ann. *Everyday Life of the Incas.* New York: Dorset Press, 1989.

Klaiber, Jeffrey L. *The Catholic Church in Peru, 1821–1985: A Social History.* Washington: Catholic University of America Press, 1992.

———. *Religion and Revolution in Peru, 1824–1976.* Notre Dame: University of Notre Dame Press, 1977.

Klarén, Peter F. "The Indian Question in Latin America: Peru's Great Divide." *The Wilson Quarterly,* 15, No. 3, Summer, 1990, 23–32.

———. *Modernization, Dislocation, and Aprismo: Origins of the Peruvian Aprista Party, 1870–1930.* Austin: University of Texas Press, 1973.

———. "Origins of Modern Peru, 1850–1930." Pages 587–640 in Leslie Bethell (ed.), *Cambridge History of Latin America,* 5. Cambridge: Cambridge University Press, 1986.

Kristal, Efraín. *The Andes Viewed from the City: Literary and Political Discourse on the Indian in Peru, 1848–1930.* New York: Peter Lang, 1987.

Kuczynski, Pedro-Pablo. *Peruvian Democracy under Economic Stress: An Account of the Belaúnde Administration, 1963–1968.* Princeton: Princeton University Press, 1977.

Laite, Julian. *Industrial Development and Migrant Labour in Latin America.* Austin: University of Texas Press, 1981.

Lee, Rensselaer W. *The White Labyrinth: Cocaine and Political Power.* New Brunswick, New Jersey: Transaction Books, 1989.

Lockhart, James. *The Men of Cajamarca: A Social and Biographical Study of the First Conquerors of Peru.* (Latin American Monographs, No. 27.) Austin: University of Texas Press, 1972.

———. *Spanish Peru, 1532–1566: A Colonial Society.* Madison: University of Wisconsin Press, 1968.

Loveman, Brian, and Thomas M. Davies, Jr. (eds.). *The Politics of Antipolitics: The Military in Latin America.* (2d ed.) Lincoln: University of Nebraska Press, 1989.

Lumbreras, Luis Guillermo, and Carlos Araníbar (eds.). *Nueva historia general del Perú: Un compendio.* Lima: Mosca Azul Editores, 1980.

Macera, Pablo. *Trabajos de historia: Economía y sociedad.* Lima: Instituto Nacional de Cultura, 1977.

Mallon, Florencia E. *The Defense of Community in Peru's Central Highlands: Peasant Struggle and Capitalist Transition, 1860–1940.* Princeton: Princeton University Press, 1983.

Manrique, Nelson. *Campesinado y nación: Las guerrillas indígenas en la guerra con Chile.* Lima: Centro de Investigación y Capacitación/Editora Ital Perú, 1981.

————. *Mercado interno y región: La sierra central, 1820–1930.* Lima: Centro de Estudios y Promoción del Desarrollo, 1987.

————. *Yawar Mayu: Sociedades terratenientes serranas, 1879–1910.* Lima: Institut français d'études andines, Centro de Investigación y Capacitación, 1988.

Mariátegui, José Carlos. *Seven Interpretive Essays on Peruvian Reality.* Austin: University of Texas Press, 1971.

Masterson, Daniel M. *Militarism and Politics in Latin America: Peru from Sánchez Cerro to Sendero Luminoso.* New York: Greenwood Press, 1991.

Mathew, W.M. *The House of Gibbs and the Peruvian Guano Monopoly.* London: Royal Historical Society, 1981.

Matos Mar, José. *Un desborde popular: El nuevo rostro del Perú en la década de 1980.* Lima: Instituto de Estudios Peruanos, 1984.

McClintock, Cynthia. *Peasant Cooperatives and Political Change in Peru.* Princeton: Princeton University Press, 1981.

————. "Why Peasants Rebel: The Case of Peru's Sendero Luminoso." *World Politics,* 37, No. 1, October 1984, 48–84.

McClintock, Cynthia, and Abraham Lowenthal (eds.). *The Peruvian Experiment Reconsidered.* (2d ed.) Princeton: Princeton University Press, 1983.

Mejía Baca, Juan (ed.). *Historia del Perú.* (12 vols.) Lima: Editorial Mejía Baca, 1980.

Miller, Roy (ed.). *Region and Class in Modern Peruvian History.* Liverpool: Institute of Latin American Studies, University of Liverpool, 1987.

Mörner, Magnus. *The Andean Past: Land, Societies, Conflicts.* New York: Columbia University Press, 1985.

Murra, John V. "Andean Societies Before 1532." Pages 59–90 in Leslie Bethell (ed.), *The Cambridge History of Latin America, 1.* Cambridge: Cambridge University Press, 1984.

————. *Research in Economic Anthropology: The Economic Organization of the Inka State.* (Supplement No. 1.) Greenwich, Connecticut: JAI Press, 1980.

North, Liisa. *The Peruvian Revolution and the Officers in Power, 1967–1976.* Montreal: Centre for Developing-Area Studies, McGill University, 1981.

O'Donnell, Guillermo. *Modernization and Bureaucratic Authoritarianism: Studies in South American Politics.* Berkeley, California: Institute of International Studies, University of California, 1973.

O'Phelan Godoy, Scarlett. *Rebellions and Revolts in Eighteenth-Century Peru and Upper Peru.* Cologne: Bohlau, 1985.

Palmer, David Scott. "The Origins and Evolution of Sendero Luminoso." *Comparative Politics* 18, No. 2, January 1986, 127–46.

_____. *Peru: The Authoritarian Tradition.* New York: Praeger, 1980.

Pastor, Manuel, Jr., and Carol Wise. "Peruvian Economic Policy in the 1980s: From Orthodoxy to Heterodoxy and Back," *Latin American Research Review,* 27, No. 2, 1992, 83–117.

Pease, Franklin, G.Y. *Del Tawantinsuyu a la historia del Perú.* Lima: Instituto de Estudios Peruanos, 1978.

Peru. Instituto Nacional de Estadística. *Población total proyectada al 30 de junio de 1990.* Lima: 1989.

Pike, Fredrick B. *The Politics of the Miraculous in Peru: Haya de la Torre and the Spiritualist Tradition.* Lincoln: University of Nebraska Press, 1986.

_____. *The United States and the Andean Republics: Peru, Bolivia, and Ecuador.* Cambridge: Harvard University Press, 1977.

Preeg, Ernest H. *The Evolution of a Revolution: Peru and Its Relations with the United States, 1968–1980.* Washington: NPA Committee on Changing International Realities, 1981.

Prescott, William H. *History of the Conquest of Peru.* New York: Modern Library, 1936.

Quiroz, Alfonso W. *Banqueros en conflicto: Estructura financiera y economía peruana, 1884–1930.* Lima: Centro de Investigación/Universidad del Pacífico, 1989.

_____. *La deuda defraudada: Consolidación de 1850 y dominio económico en el Perú.* Lima: Instituto Nacional de Cultura/Editorial y Productora Gráfica "Nuevo Mundo," 1987.

Ramirez-Horton, Susan E. *Land Tenure and the Economics of Power in Colonial Peru.* Madison: University of Wisconsin Press, 1977.

_____. *Provincial Patriarchs: Land Tenure and the Economics of Power in Colonial Peru.* Albuquerque: University of New Mexico Press, 1986.

Reid, Michael. *Peru: Paths to Poverty.* London: Latin America Bureau/Third World Publications, 1985.

Rénique C., José Luis. *Los sueños de la sierra: Cusco en el siglo XX.* Lima: CEPES, 1991.

Rodríguez Pastor, Humberto. *Hijos del celeste imperio en el Perú (1850–1900): Migración, agricultura, mentalidad, y explotación.* Lima: Instituto de Apoyo Agrario, 1989.

Rostworowski de Diez Canseco, María. *Doña Francesca Pizarro: Una ilustre mestiza, 1534–1598*. Lima: Instituto de Estudios Peruanos, 1989.

Sánchez-Albornoz, Nicolás. *Indios y tributos en el Alto Perú*. Lima: Instituto de Estudios Peruanos, 1978.

Scheetz, Thomas. *Peru and the International Monetary Fund*. Pittsburgh: University of Pittsburgh Press, 1986.

Sempat Assadourian, Carlos. *El sistema de la economía colonial: Mercado interno, regiones y espacio económico*. Lima: Instituto de Estudios Peruanos, 1982.

Silverblatt, Irene M. *Moon, Sun, and Witches: Gender Ideologies and Class in Inca and Colonial Peru*. Princeton: Princeton University Press, 1987.

Spalding, Karen. *Huarochirí: An Andean Society under Inca and Spanish Rule*. Stanford: Stanford University Press, 1984.

St. John, Ronald Bruce. *The Foreign Policy of Peru*. Boulder, Colorado: Lynne Rienner, 1992.

Stein, Steve. *Lima obrera, 1900–1930*. (2 vols.) Lima: Ediciones El Virrey, 1986–87.

_____. *Populism in Peru: The Emergence of the Masses and the Politics of Social Control*. Madison: University of Wisconsin Press, 1980.

Stein, Steve, and Carlos Monge. *La crisis del estado patrimonial en el Perú*. Lima: Instituto de Estudios Peruanos, 1988.

Stein, William W. *El levantamiento de Atusparía*. Lima: Mosca Azul, 1988.

Stepan, Alfred. *The State and Society: Peru in Comparative Perspective*. Princeton: Princeton University Press, 1978.

Stern, Steve J. *Peru's Indian Peoples and the Challenge of Spanish Conquest: Huamanga to 1640*. Madison: University of Wisconsin Press, 1982.

Stern, Steve J. (ed.). *Resistance, Rebellion, and Consciousness in the Andean Peasant World, 18th to 20th Centuries*. Madison: University of Wisconsin Press, 1987.

Sulmont, Denis. *El movimiento obrero peruano, 1890–1979*. Lima: Tarea, 1985.

Tamayo Herrera, José. *Historia social del Cuzco republicano*. (2d ed.) Lima: Editorial Universo, 1981.

Tarazona-Sevillano, Gabriela. *Sendero Luminoso and the Threat of Narcoterrorism*. New York: Praeger, 1990.

Taylor, Lewis. *Bandits and Politics in Peru: Landlord and Peasant Violence in Hualgayoc, 1900–30*. Cambridge: Center of Latin American Studies, Cambridge University, 1987.

Thorp, Rosemary, and Geoffrey Bertram. *Peru 1890–1977: Growth and Policy in an Open Economy*. New York: Columbia University Press, 1978.

Uriarte, J. Manuel. *Transnational Banks and the Dynamics of the Peruvian Foreign Debt and Inflation.* New York: Praeger, 1986.

Vega, Garcilaso de la. *Royal Commentaries of the Incas and General History of Peru.* Austin: University of Texas Press, 1987.

Villanueva, Víctor. *Ejército Peruano: Del caudillaje anárquico al militarismo reformista.* Lima: Juan Mejía Baca, 1973.

———. "Military Professionalization in Peru." Pages 79–85 in Brian Loveman and Thomas M. Davies, Jr. (eds.), *The Politics of Antipolitics.* Lincoln: University of Nebraska Press, 1978.

Wachtel, Nathan. *The Vision of the Vanquished: The Spanish Conquest of Peru Through Indian Eyes.* New York: Barnes and Noble, 1977.

———. "The Indian and Spanish Conquest." Pages 207–48 in Leslie Bethell (ed.), *Cambridge History of Latin America,* 1. Cambridge: Cambridge University Press, 1984.

Webb, Richard, and Adolfo Figueroa. *Distribución del ingreso en el Perú.* Lima: Instituto de Estudios Peruanos, 1975.

Webb, Richard C., and Graciela Fernández Baca de Valdez (eds.). *Perú en números, 1990: Almanaque estadístico.* Lima: Cuánto, 1990.

Weeks, John. *Limits to Capitalist Development: The Industrialization of Peru, 1950–1980.* Boulder, Colorado: Westview Press, 1985.

Werlich, David P. *Peru: A Short History.* Carbondale: Southern Illinois University Press, 1978.

Wightman, Ann M. *Indigenous Migration and Social Change: The Forasteros of Cuzco, 1570–1720.* Durham: Duke University Press, 1990.

Wilgus, A. Curtis. *Historical Atlas of Latin America: Political, Geographic, Economic, Cultural.* New York: Cooper Square, 1967.

Yepes del Castillo, Ernesto. *Perú 1820–1920: Un siglo de desarrollo capitalista?* Lima: Ediciones SIGNO Universitario, 1981.

Zook, David H., Jr. *Zarumilla-Marañón: The Ecuador-Peruvian Border Dispute.* New York: Bookman, 1964.

Zuidema, R. Tom. *Inca Civilization in Cuzco.* Austin: University of Texas Press, 1990.

Chapter 2

Alberti, Giorgio, and Enrique Mayer (eds.). *Reciprocidad e intercambio en los Andes peruanos.* (Peru Problema No. 12.) Lima: Instituto de Estudios Peruanos, 1974.

Alberts, Tom. *Agrarian Reform and Rural Poverty: A Case Study of Peru.* Boulder, Colorado: Westview Press, 1983.

Allen, Catherine. *The Hold Life Has: Coca and Cultural Identity in an Andean Community.* Washington: Smithsonian Institution Press, 1988.

————. "To Be Quechua: The Symbolism of Coca Chewing in Highland Peru," *American Ethnologist*, 8, No. 1, February, 1981, 157–68.

Altamirano, Teófilo. *Cultura andina y pobreza urbana: Aymaras en Lima metropolitana.* Lima: Fondo Editorial de la Pontificia Universidad Católica del Perú, 1988.

————. "Estrategias de supervivencia de origen rural en el contexto urbano," *Antropología* [Lima], No. 1, 1984, 127–59.

————. *Migración de retorno en los Andes.* PISPAL, México e Instituto Andino de Estudios en Población y Desarrollo: Programa de Investigación sobre Población en América Latina: Lima, 1985.

————. *Migrantes campesinos en la ciudad: Aproximaciones teóricas para su estudio.* Lima: Publicaciones del Departamento de Ciencias Sociales, Fondo Editorial de la Pontificia Universidad Católica del Perú, 1985.

————. *Presencia andina en Lima metropolitana: Un estudio sobre migrantes y clubes de provincianos.* Lima: Fondo Editorial de la Pontificia Universidad Católica del Perú, 1984.

————. "Regional Commitment Among Central Highland Migrants in Lima." Pages 198–216 in Norman Long and Brian R. Roberts (eds.), *Miners, Peasants, and Entrepreneurs: Regional Development in the Central Highlands of Peru.* Cambridge: Cambridge University Press, 1984.

Amat y León, Carlos. *Los hogares rurales en el Perú: Importancia y articulación con el desarrollo agrario, grupo de análisis de política agraria.* Proyecto PADI, Lima: Ministerio de Agricultura, Fundación Friedrich Ebert, 1987.

Ambos, Kai. *Terrorismo y ley: Análisis comparativo: República Federal Alemana, Gran Bretaña, Perú y Colombia.* Lima: Comisión Andina de Juristas, 1989.

Ames Cobián, Rolando. *Violencia y estado democrático de derecho.* (1st ed.) Jesús María, Peru: CODEPP, 1988.

Asociación Multidisciplinaria de Investigación y Docencia en Población. *Perú: Las provincias en cifras, 1876–1981.* (3 vols.) Lima: 1986.

————. *Problemas poblacionales peruanos.* Lima: 1980.

Andes, N. "Socioeconomic, Medical Care, and Public Health Contexts Affecting Infant Mortality: A Study of Community-Level Differentials in Peru," *Journal of Health and Social Behavior*, 30, No. 4, 1989, 386–97.

Aramburu, Carlos E. "Expansion of the Agrarian and Demographic Frontier in the Peruvian Selva." Pages 153–79 in Marianne Schmink and Charles H. Wood (eds.), *Frontier Expansion in Amazonia.* Gainesville: University of Florida Press, 1985.

_____. *Las migraciones en la sociedad campesina: El caso de Puno.* (Publicaciones CISEPA, No. 21.) Lima: Fondo Editorial de la Pontificia Universidad Católica del Perú, 1982.

Arnold, P. "Pilgrimages and Processions as Forms of Symbolic Power of the Subordinate Classes: 2 Cases from Peru," *Social Compass,* 32, No. 1, 1985, 45–56.

Ash, Robert B. "Sendero Luminoso and the Peruvian Crisis," *Conflict Quarterly,* 5, Summer 1985, 19–31.

Assies, W. "The Agrarian Question in Peru: Some Observations on the Roads of Capital," *Journal of Peasant Studies,* 14, No. 4, 1987, 500–32.

Babb, Florence E. *Between Field and Cooking Pot: The Political Economy of Marketwomen in Peru.* (Texas Press Sourcebooks in Anthropology, No. 15.) Austin: University of Texas Press, 1989.

Ballón, Eduardo (ed.). *Movimientos sociales y crisis: El caso peruano.* Lima: Centro de Estudios y Promoción del Desarrollo, 1986.

_____. *Movimientos sociales y democracia: La fundación de un nuevo orden.* Lima: Centro de Estudios y Promoción del Desarrollo, 1986.

Basadre, Jorge. *Historia de la República del Perú.* (7th ed.) Lima: Ediciones Universitarias, 1983.

Bastien, Joseph W. *Mountain of the Condor.* Prospect Heights, Illinois: Waveland Press, 1978.

Becker, David G. *The New Bourgeoisie and the Limits of Dependency: Mining, Class, and Power in 'Revolutionary' Peru.* Princeton: Princeton University Press, 1983.

_____. "Peru after the Revolution—Class, Power, and Ideology," *Studies in Comparative International Development,* 20, No. 3, 1985, 3–30.

Belaúnde, Víctor Andrés. *Peruanidad.* Lima: Comisión Nacional del Centenario, 1987.

Berberoglu, Berch. "The Class Nature of the State in Peru, 1968–75," *International Review of Modern Sociology,* 16, No. 2, 1986, 407–13.

Bernard, H. Russell, and Pertti J. Pelto (eds.). *Technology and Social Change.* (2d ed.) Prospect Heights, Illinois: Waveland Press, 1987.

Bernales, B. Enrique. *Juventud: Problemas y esperanzas.* Lima: Fundación Friedrich Ebert, 1985.

_____. "Origins and Evolution of the Peruvian University," *Revista Mexicana de Sociología* [Mexico City], 43, No. 1, 1981, 455–506.

Berry, R. Albert. "International Trade, Government, and Income Distribution in Peru since 1870," *Latin American Research Review,* 25, No. 2, 1990, 31–59.

Bode, Barbara. *No Bells to Toll: Destruction and Creation in the Andes.* New York: Scribner, 1989.

Bonilla, Heraclio. *Guano y burguesía en el Perú.* (2d ed.) Lima: Instituto de Estudios Peruanos, 1984.

————. *La independencia en el Perú.* (2d ed.) Lima: Instituto de Estudios Peruanos, 1981.

————. *Un siglo a la deriva: Ensayos sobre el Perú, Bolivia y la guerra.* Lima: Instituto de Estudios Peruanos, 1980.

Booth, David, and Bernardo Sorj (eds.). *Military Reformism and Social Classes: The Peruvian Experience, 1968-80.* New York: St. Martin's Press, 1983.

Bourque, Susan C. "Experiments with Equality: Complexities in Peruvian Public Policy," *Journal of Asian and African Studies,* 20, Nos. 3-4, 1985, 156-68.

————. "Multiple Arenas for State Expansion: Class, Ethnicity and Sex in Rural Peru," *Ethnic and Racial Studies,* 3, No. 3, 1980, 264-80.

Bourque, Susan C., and Kay B. Warren. "Democracy Without Peace: The Cultural Politics of Terror in Peru," *Latin American Research Review,* 24, No. 1, 1989, 7-34.

————. *Women of the Andes: Patriarchy and Social Change in Two Peruvian Towns.* Ann Arbor: University of Michigan Press, 1981.

Branner, F. "Class and Corporate Elements in Habsburg, Lima's Elite Circulation," *Revista Internacional de Sociología,* 39, No. 40, October–December 1981, 507-22.

Brass, Tom. "Cargos and Conflict: The Fiesta System and Capitalist Development in Eastern Peru," *Journal of Peasant Studies,* 13, No. 3, 1986, 45-62.

————. "Trotskyism, Hugo Blanco, and the Ideology of a Peruvian Peasant Movement," *Journal of Peasant Studies,* 16, No. 2, 1989, 173-97.

Bray, Warwick, and Colin Dollery. "Coca Chewing and High-Altitude Stress: A Spurious Correlation," *Current Anthropology,* 24, No. 3, 1983, 269-82.

Brush, Stephan B. *Mountain, Field, and Family: The Economy and Human Ecology of an Andean Valley.* Philadelphia: University of Pennsylvania Press, 1977.

Bunster, B. Ximena, and Elsa Chaney. *Sellers and Servants: Working Women of Lima, Peru.* New York: Special Studies, Praeger, 1985.

Burga, Manuel. *El nacimiento de una utopia.* Lima: Instituto de Apoyo Agrario, 1981.

Burga, Manuel, and Alberto Flores Galindo. *Apogeo y crísis de la República aristocrática.* (3d ed. rev.) Lima: Ediciones Rikchay Perú, 1984.

Burger, Richard L. "An Overview of Peruvian Archaeology, 1976–1986," *Annual Review of Anthropology,* No. 18, 1989, 37–69.

Buvinic, M., and M. Berger. "Sex Differences in Access to a Small Enterprise Development Fund in Peru," *World Development,* 18, No. 5, 1990, 695–705.

Caballero, José María. *Agricultura, reforma agraria y pobreza campesina.* Lima: Instituto de Estudios Peruanos, 1980.

———. "Agriculture and the Peasantry under Industrialization Pressures: Lessons from the Peruvian Experience," *Latin American Research Review,* 19, No. 2, 1982, 3–41.

———. *Economía agraria de la sierra peruana: Antes de la reforma agraria de 1969.* Lima: Instituto de Estudios Peruanos, 1981.

Cadorette, C. "Towards a Contextual Interpretation of Papal Teaching: Reflections from a Peruvian Perspective," *Social Compass,* 36, No. 3, 1989, 285–94.

Califano, M. "Huachpaire and Zapiteri Shamanism (Harakmbet, Southwest Amazonia of Peru)," *Anthropos,* 83, Nos. 1–3, 1988, 229–32.

Campodonico, F.F. (ed.). *El pensamiento indigenista.* Lima: Mosca Azul Editores, 1981.

Castelli, Amalia, Marcia Koth de Paredes, and Mariana Mould de Pease (eds.). *Etnohistoria y antropología andina.* Lima: Museo Nacional de Historia, 1981.

Castro Morales, Jorge. "Farmacodependencia en el Perú," *Psicoactiva* [Lima], 1, No. 1, 1987, 15–53.

Cavero G., Samuel. *Un rincón para los muertos.* Lima: Editores Associados, 1987.

Caviedes, C.N. "Emergency and Institutional Crisis in Peru During El Niño, 1982–1983," *Disasters,* 9, No. 1, 1985, 70–74.

Celestino, O. "Land and People in Peru: The Chancay Valley from the 16th to the 20th Century," *International Social Science Journal,* 39, No. 4, 1987, 505–22.

Centro de Investigación y Promoción Amazónica and Concejo Nacional de Población. *Población y colonización en la Amazonia peruana.* Lima: 1984.

Cerron Palomino, R. "Language Policy in Peru: A Historical Overview," *International Journal of the Sociology of Language,* No. 77, 1989, 11–33.

Chaplin, David (ed.). *Peruvian Nationalism: A Corporatist Revolution.* New Brunswick, New Jersey: Transaction Books, 1976.

Chibnik, M., and W. Dejong. "Agricultural Labor Organization in Ribereño Communities of the Peruvian Amazon," *Ethnology,* 28, No. 1, 1989, 75–95.

Chico Colugna, Franco. *Elecciones: Compendio concordado de legislación, jurisprudencia y doctrina.* Trujillo, Peru: Instituto de Desarrollo de la Información Legal, Linea Editores, SA, 1989.

Collier, David. *Squatters and Oligarchs: Authoritarian Rule and Policy Change in Peru.* Baltimore: Johns Hopkins University Press, 1976.

Collins, J.L. "The Household and Relations of Production in Southern Peru," *Comparative Studies in Society and History,* 28, No. 4, 1986, 651-71.

Cook, Noble David. *The People of the Colca Valley: A Population Study.* (Dellplain Latin American Studies, No. 9.) Boulder, Colorado: Westview Press, 1982.

Cornelius, Wayne A., and Felicity M. Trueblood (eds.). *Latin American Urban Research,* 5. Beverly Hills, California: Sage, 1975.

Cotler, Julio. *Clases, estado y nación en el Perú.* Lima: Instituto de Estudios Peruanos, 1978.

_____. "The Mechanics of Internal Domination and Social Change in Peru." Pages 35-74 in David Chaplin (ed.), *Peruvian Nationalism: A Corporatist Revolution.* New Brunswick, New Jersey: Transaction Books, 1976.

Cottam, M.L. "Cognitive Psychology and Bargaining Behavior: Peru Versus the MNCs," *Political Psychology,* 10, No. 3, 1989, 445-75.

Cueva García, Aníbal (ed.). *Gran atlas geográfico del Perú y el mundo.* Lima: Editores S.A., 1991.

Cussiánovich, Alejandro. *Amazonia, un paraíso imaginario.* Lima: Instituto de Publicaciones, Educación, y Comunicación José Cardijn, 1985.

Davidson, Judith. "The Survival of Traditional Medicine in a Peruvian Barriada," *Social Science and Medicine,* 17, No. 17, 1983, 1271-80.

de Rios, M.D. "A Modern Day Shamanistic Healer in the Peruvian Amazon: Pharmacopoeia and Trance," *Journal of Psychoactive Drugs,* 21, No. 1, 1989, 91-99.

de Soto, Hernando. *El otro sendero.* Lima: Instituto Libertad y Democracia, 1987.

Deere, Carmen Diana. "The Differentiation of the Peasantry and Family Structure: A Peruvian Case Study," *Journal of Family History,* 3, No. 4, 1978, 422-38.

Deere, Carmen Diana, and Alain de Janvry. "Demographic and Social Differentiation among Northern Peruvian Peasants," *Journal of Peasant Studies,* 8, No. 3, 1981, 335-66.

_____. "The Division of Labor by Sex in Agriculture: A Peruvian Case Study," *Economic Development and Cultural Change,* 30, No. 4, 1982, 795-811.

Deere, Carmen Diana, and Magdalena León de Leal. *Women in Andean Agriculture: Peasant Production and Rural Wage Employment in Colombia and Peru.* Geneva, Switzerland: International Labour Office, 1982.

Degregori, Carlos Iván. *Ayacucho, raíces de una crisis.* Lima: Instituto de Estudios Peruanos, 1986.

Deustua, Alejandro. *El narcotráfico y el interés nacional.* Lima: Centro Peruano de Estudios Internacionales, 1987.

Dietz, Henry A. "Political Participation in the Barriadas: An Extension and Reexamination," *Comparative Political Studies,* 18, No. 3, 1985, 323-55.

Dobyns, Henry F., and Paul L. Doughty. *Peru: A Cultural History.* New York: Oxford University Press, 1976.

Dobyns, Henry F., Paul L. Doughty, and Harold D. Lasswell (eds.). *Peasants, Power, and Applied Social Change: Vicos as a Model.* Beverly Hills, California: Sage, 1971.

Doughty, Paul L. "Against the Odds: Collaboration and Development at Vicos." Pages 129-57 in Donald D. Stull and Jean J. Schensul (eds.), *Collaborative Research and Social Change: Applied Anthropology in Action.* (Westview Special Studies in Applied Anthropology.) Boulder, Colorado: Westview Press, 1987.

_____. "Decades of Disaster: Promise and Performance in the Callejón de Huaylas, Peru," *Studies in Third World Societies,* No. 36, June 1986, 35-80.

_____. "Engineers and Energy in the Andes." Pages 11-36 in H. Russell Bernard and Pertti J. Pelto (eds.), *Technology and Social Change.* (2d ed.) Prospect Heights, Illinois: Waveland Press, 1987.

_____. "A Latin American Specialty in World Context: Urban Primacy and Cultural Colonialism in Peru," *Urban Anthropology,* 8, Nos. 3-4, 1979, 383-98.

_____. "Social Policy and Urban Growth." Pages 75-110 in David Chaplin (ed.), *Peruvian Nationalism: A Corporatist Revolution.* New Brunswick, New Jersey: Transaction Books, 1976.

_____. "Update." Pages 369-73 in H. Russell Bernard and Pertti J. Pelto (eds.), *Technology and Social Change.* (2d ed.) Prospect Heights, Illinois: Waveland Press, 1987.

_____. "Vicos: Success, Rejection and Rediscovery of a Classic Program." Pages 433-59 in Elizabeth M. Eddy and William L. Partridge (eds.), *Applied Anthropology in America.* (2d ed.) New York: Columbia University Press, 1987.

Dutt, James S., and Paul T. Baker. *Cultura andina y represión.* Cusco: Centro de Estudios Rurales Andinos "Bartolomé de las Casas," 1986.

Eddy, Elizabeth M., and William L. Partridge (eds.). *Applied Anthropology in America.* (2d ed.) New York: Columbia University Press, 1987.

Epstein, Erwin. "Peasant Consciousness under Peruvian Military Rule," *Harvard Educational Review,* 52, No. 3, 1982, 280–300.

Farnsworth, Elizabeth. "Peru: A Nation in Crisis," *World Policy Journal,* 5, Fall 1988, 725–46.

Ferrando R., Delicia. *Perú: Participación de la mujer en la actividad económica: Análises censal, 1940-1981.* Lima: Instituto Nacional de Estadística, 1984.

Figueroa, Adolfo. *La economía campesina de la sierra del Perú.* (2d ed.) Lima: Fondo Editorial de la Pontificia Universidad Católica del Perú, 1983.

Flaherty, Joseph A., Susan Birz, and Ronald M. Wintrob. "The Process of Acculturation: Theoretical Perspectives and an Empirical Investigation in Peru," *Social Science and Medicine,* 25, No. 7, 1987, 839–47.

Flores Galindo, Alberto. *Buscando un inca: Identidad y utopía en los Andes.* Lima: Instituto de Apoyo Agrario, 1987.

Flores, L.G., and R.F. Catalenello. "Personal Value-Systems and Organizational Roles in Peru," *Journal of Social Psychology,* 127, No. 6, 1987, 629–38.

Fuhr, Harold. "The State Cooperatives and Peasants' Participation: The Case of Peruvian Agrarian Reform," *Land Reform,* Nos. 1-2, 1986, 57–74.

Gall, Norman, and Eleodoro Mayorga Alba. *Brazil and Peru: Social and Economic Effects of Petroleum Development.* Geneva, Switzerland: International Labour Office, 1987.

García Sayan, Diego. *Tomas de tierras en el Perú.* Lima: Centro de Estudios y Promoción del Desarrollo, 1982.

Germana, César. "The Middle Class and Power in Peru," *Revista Mexicana de Sociología,* 43, No. 3, 1981, 1169–86.

Gifford, Douglas, and Pauline Hoggarth. *Carnival and Coca Leaf: Some Traditions of the Peruvian Quechua Ayllu.* New York: St. Martin's Press, 1976.

Giesecke, Alberto, and Enrique Silgado. *Terremotos en el Perú.* Lima: Ediciones Rikchay Peru, 1981.

Glewwe, Paul. *The Distribution of Welfare in Peru in 1985-86.* (Living Standards Measurement Study, Working Paper No. 42.) Washington: World Bank, 1988.

Goldman, N. "Collection of Survey Data on Contraception: An Evaluation of an Experiment in Peru," *Studies in Family Planning,* 20, No. 3, 1989, 147–57.

354

Golte, Jürgen. *Repartos y rebeliones*. Lima: Instituto de Estudios Peruanos, 1980.

Gonzales de Olarte, Efraín. *Economías regionales del Perú*. Lima: Instituto de Estudios Peruanos, 1982.

_____. *Economía de la comunidad campesina*. Lima: Instituto de Estudios Peruanos, 1984.

Gonzales, Michael J. "Chinese Plantation Workers and Social Conflict in Peru in the Late 19th Century," *Journal of Latin American Studies*, 21, October 1989, 385–424.

Gorriti Ellenbogen, Gustavo. "Responso en Uchiza," *Caretas*, No. 716, September 1982, 16–20.

Gow, Peter. *Of Mixed Blood: Kinship and History in Peruvian Amazonia*. Oxford: Clarendon Press, 1991.

Graham, Carol. "The APRA Government and the Urban Poor: The PAIT Programme in Lima's Pueblos Jóvenes," *Journal of Latin American Studies*, 23, pt. 1, February 1991, 91–130.

Greaves, Thomas. "The Woman's Voice in Andean Labor Unions," *Urban Anthropology*, 15, Nos. 3–4, 1987, 355–76.

Greenow, L., and V. Muñiz. "Market Trade in Decentralized Development: The Case of Cajamarca, Peru," *Professional Geographer*, 40, No. 4, 1988, 416–27.

Grompone, Romeo. *Talleristas y ambulantes*. Lima: Centro de Estudios y Promoción del Desarrollo, 1985.

Guerra-García, Roger (ed.). *Problemas Poblacionales Peruanos II*. Lima: Asociación Multidisciplinaria de Investigación y Docencia en Población, 1986.

Guillet, David. *Agrarian Reform and Peasant Economy in Southern Peru*. Columbia: University of Missouri Press, 1979.

_____. "Terracing and Irrigation in the Peruvian Highlands," *Current Anthropology*, 28, No. 4, 1987, 409–30.

Gutiérrez, Blas. *Parentesco ritual y sistema de ayuda mutua en una población periferie de Lima: El caso de Pamplona Alta*. Lima: Fomciencias, 1986.

Gutiérrez, Gustavo. *A Theology of Liberation: History, Politics, and Salvation*. Maryknoll, New York: Orbis Books, 1973.

Harrell, M.W. "Nutritional Classification Study of Peru: Who and Where Are the Poor," *Food Policy*, 14, No. 4, 1989, 313–29.

Hern, Warren M. "Family Planning, Amazon Style," *Natural History*, 101, December 1992, 31–36.

Hiraoka, M. "Zonation of Mestizo Riverine Farming Systems in Northeast Peru," *National Geographic Research*, 2, No. 3, 1986, 354–71.

Holland, Connie J., and Peter W. Van Arsdale. "Responses to Disaster: A Comparative Study of Indigenous Coping Mechanisms in Two Marginal Third World Communities," *International Journal of Mass Emergencies and Disasters,* 4, No. 3, 1986, 51–70.

Hopkins, Diane E. "Juego de enemigos," *Allpanchis* [Cusco], 20, 1982, 167–87.

―――. "The Peruvian Agrarian Reform: Dissent from Below" *Human Organization,* 44, No. 1, 1985, 18–32.

Hopkins, Raúl. *Desarrollo desigual y crisis en la agricultura peruana, 1944–1969.* Lima: Instituto de Estudios Peruanos, 1981.

Hornberger, N.H. "Schooltime, Classtime, and Academic Learning Time in Rural Highland Puno, Peru," *Anthropology and Education Quarterly,* 18, No. 3, 1987, 207–21.

―――. "Can Peru's Rural Schools be Agents for Quechua Language Maintenance?" *Journal of Multilingual and Multicultural Development,* 10, No. 2, 1989, 145–59.

―――. "Reorienting Expert Production to Benefit Rural Producers: Annatto Processing in Peru," *Journal of Rural Studies,* 6, No. 1, 1990, 85–101.

Iguiñez, Javier. *La cuestión rural en el Perú.* Lima: Fondo Editorial de la Pontificia Universidad Católica del Perú, 1986.

Isbell, Billie Jean. *To Defend Ourselves: Ecology and Ritual in an Andean Village.* Austin: Institute for Latin American Studies, University of Texas, 1978.

―――. "The Role of Hallucinogenic Drugs and Sensory Stimuli in Peruvian Ritual Healing," *Culture, Medicine and Psychiatry,* 8, No. 4, 1984, 399–430.

Kápsoli Escudero, Wilfredo. *Rebeliones de esclavos en el Perú.* (2d ed.) Lima: Ediciones Perej, 1990.

Kay, Cristóbal. "Achievements and Contradictions of the Peruvian Agrarian Reform," *Journal of Development Studies,* 18, January 1982, 141–70.

Keith, Robert G. *Conquest and Agrarian Change: The Emergence of the Hacienda System on the Peruvian Coast.* Cambridge: Harvard University Press, 1976.

Klaiber, L. Jeffrey. *La iglesia en el Perú: Su historia social desde la independencia.* (2d ed.) Lima: Fondo Editorial de la Pontificia Universidad Católica del Perú, 1988.

―――. *Religion and Revolution in Peru, 1824–1976.* Notre Dame: University of Notre Dame Press, 1977.

―――. *Violencia y crisis de valores en el Perú.* (2d ed.) Lima: Fondo Editorial de la Pontificia Universidad Católica del Perú, Fundación Tinker, 1988.

Levieil, D.P., and B. Orlove. "Local Control of Aquatic Resources: Community and Ecology in Lake Titicaca, Peru," *American Anthropologist,* 92, No. 2, 1990, 362–82.

Lloyd, Peter. *The "Young Towns" of Lima: Aspects of Urbanization in Peru.* Cambridge: Cambridge University Press,1980.

Lobo, Susan. *A House of My Own.* Tucson: University of Arizona Press, 1982.

Long, Norman, and Bryan R. Roberts. *Miners, Peasants, and Entrepreneurs: Regional Development in the Central Highlands of Peru.* Cambridge: Cambridge University Press, 1984.

Lopez, L.E. "Sociolinguistic and Educational Problems in the Aymara-Speaking Population of Peru," *International Journal of the Sociology of Language,* No. 77, 1989, 5-67.

Lynch, Barbara D. *The Vicos Experiment: A Study of the Impacts of the Cornell-Peru Project in a Highland Community.* Washington: Bureau for Latin America and the Caribbean, United States Agency for International Development, 1982.

MacCormack, S. "Pachacuti-Miracles, Punishments, and Last Judgment: Visionary Past and Prophetic Future in Early Colonial Peru," *American Historical Review,* 93, No. 4. 1988, 960-1006.

MacEwen Scott, Alison. "Women and Industrialisation: Examining the 'Female Marginalisation' Thesis," *Journal of Development Studies,* 22, No. 4, 1986, 649-80.

Mallon, Florencia E. *The Defense of Community in Peru's Central Highlands: Peasant Struggle and Capitalist Transition, 1860-1940.* Princeton: Princeton University Press, 1983.

———. "Gender and Class in the Transition to Capitalism: Household and Mode of Production in Central Peru," *Latin American Perspectives,* 13, No. 1, 1986, 147-74.

———. "Patriarchy in the Transition to Capitalism: Central Peru, 1830-1959," *Feminist Studies,* 13, No. 2, 1987, 379-409.

Malpica Silva Santisteban, Carlos. *Los dueños del Perú.* (11th ed.) Lima: Ediciones PEISA, 1980.

Mannheim, B. "The Language of Reciprocity in Southern Peruvian Quechua," *Anthropological Linguistics,* 28, No. 3, 1986, 267-73.

Mariátegui, José Carlos, 1894-1930. *Peruanicemos al Perú.* Lima: Empresa Editora Amauta, 1975.

Marzal, Manuel. *Los caminos religiosos de los inmigrantes en la gran Lima: El caso de El Agustino.* Lima: Fondo Editorial de la Pontificia Universidad Católica del Perú, 1988.

———. *El sincretismo iberoamericano: Un estudio comparativo sobre los quechuas (Cusco), los mayas (Chiapas), y los africanos (Bahía).* (2d ed.) Lima: Fondo Editorial de la Pontificia Universidad Católica del Perú, 1988.

———. *La transformación religiosa peruana.* (2d ed.) Lima: Fondo Editorial de la Pontificia Universidad Católica del Perú, 1988.

357

Masuda, Shozo. *Contribuciones a los estudios de los Andes centrales.* Tokyo: University of Tokyo Press, 1984.

Masuda, Shozo, Shimada Izumi, and Craig Morris (eds). *Andean Ecology and Civilization: An Interdisciplinary Perspective on Andean Ecological Complementarity.* Tokyo: University of Tokyo Press, 1985.

Matos Mar, José. "Child and Spouse Replacement Mechanisms: A Life Cycle Perspective on Family Composition in Peru," *International Journal of Sociology of the Family,* 10, No. 1, 1982, 67–80.

————. *Un desborde popular: El nuevo rostro del Perú en la década de 1980.* Lima: Instituto de Estudios Peruanos, 1984.

————. *Taquile en Lima: Siete familias cuentan.* Lima: Fondo Internacional para la Promoción de la Cultura, United Nations Economic, Social and Cultural Organization, and Banco Internacional del Perú, 1986.

Matos Mar, José, and José Manuel Mejía. *La reforma agraria en el Perú.* Lima: Instituto de Estudios Peruanos, 1980.

Mayer, Enrique. "On Social Anthropology in Peru," *Current Anthropology,* 24, No. 4, 1983, 526–27.

McClintock, Cynthia. *Peasant Cooperatives and Political Change in Peru.* Princeton: Princeton University Press, 1981.

————. "The Prospects for Democratic Consolidation in a Least Likely Case—Peru," *Comparative Politics,* 21, No. 2, 1989, 127–48.

————. "Sendero Luminoso: Peru's Maoist Guerrillas (Origin of the Movement, Nature of Its Membership and of Its Allies and Popular Support)," *Problems of Communism,* 32, 1983, 19–34.

McClintock, Cynthia, and Abraham F. Lowenthal (eds.). *El gobierno militar: Una experiencia peruana, 1968–1980.* (1st ed.) Lima: Instituto de Estudios Peruanos, 1985.

————. *The Peruvian Experiment Reconsidered.* Princeton: Princeton University Press, 1983.

McGregor, Felipe, and Laura Madalengoitia. *Violencia y paz en el Perú hoy.* Asociación Peruana de Estudios e Investigaciones para la Paz, Lima: Fundación Friedrich Ebert, 1984.

Mercado, Hilda. *La madre trabajadora: El caso de las comerciantes ambulantes.* Lima: Centro de Estudios de Población y Desarrollo, 1978.

Millones Santagadea, Luia. "Tugurio, The Culture of Peruvian Marginal Population: A Study of a Lima Slum." (Ed. and Trans., William W. Stein.) Pages 56–123 in *Peruvian Contexts of Change.* New Brunswick, New Jersey: Transaction Books, 1985.

Montoya, Rodrigo. "Democracy and the Ethnic Problem in Peru," *Revista Mexicana de Sociología,* 48, No. 3, 1986, 45–50.

Moore, Thomas R. "SIL and a New-Found Tribe: The Amara-kaeri Experience," *Dialectical Anthropology*, 4, No. 2, 1979, 113–25.

Morales, Edmundo. "Coca and Cocaine Economy and Social Change in the Andes of Peru," *Economic Development and Cultural Change*, 35, No. 1, 1986, 143–61.

_____. *Cocaine: White Gold Rush in Peru*. Tucson: University of Arizona Press, 1989.

Moseley, Michael Edward. *The Incas and Their Ancestors: The Archaeology of Peru*. New York: Thames and Hudson, 1992.

Mosley, P. "Achievements and Contradictions of the Peruvian Agrarian Reform: A Regional Perspective," *Journal of Development Studies*, 21, No. 3, 1985, 440–48.

Murra, John V. (ed.). "Andean Societies," *Annual Review of Anthropology*, 13, 1984, 119–41.

Myers, William E. "Urban Working Children: A Comparison of Four Surveys from South America (Findings from Cities in Bolivia, Brazil, Paraguay, and Peru)," *International Labour Review*, 12, No. 3, 1989, 321–35.

Encyclopaedia Britannica. *1991 Book of the Year*. Chicago: 1991.

Oliver-Smith, Anthony. *The Martyred City: Death and Rebirth in the Andes*. Albuquerque: University of New Mexico Press, 1986.

_____. "Post Disaster Consensus and Conflict in a Traditional Society: The 1970 Avalanche of Yungay, Peru," *Mass Emergencies*, 4, No. 1, 1979, 39–52.

_____. "The Yungay Avalanche of 1970: Anthropological Perspectives on Disaster and Social Change," *Disasters*, 3, No. 1, 1979, 95–101.

Orlove, Benjamin. *Alpacas, Sheep, and Men: The Wool Export Economy and Regional Society in Southern Peru*. (Studies in Anthropology Series.) New York: Academic Press, 1977.

_____. "Two Rituals and Three Hypotheses: An Examination of Solstice Divination in Southern Highland Peru," *Anthropological Quarterly*, 52, No. 2, 1979, 86–98.

Ortega, Julio. *La cultura peruana*. Mexico City: Fondo de Cultura Económica, 1978.

Osterling, Jorge P. "The 1970 Peruvian Disaster and the Spontaneous Relocation of Some of Its Victims: Ancashino Peasant Migrants in Huayopampa," *Mass Emergencies*, 4, No. 2, 1979, 117–120.

Oviedo, J.M. "Peru: Can This Nation Save Itself?" *Dissent*, 34, No. 2, 1987, 171–78.

Palmer, David Scott. "Changing Political Economy of Peru under Military and Civilian Rule, 1963–83," *Inter-American Economic Affairs*, 37, 1984, 37–62.

_____. "Peru's Persistent Problems," *Current History,* 89, No. 543, January 1990, 5-8, 31-34.

_____. "Rebellion in Rural Peru: The Origins and Evolution of Sendero Luminoso," *Comparative Politics,* 18, No. 2, 1986, 127-46.

Parodi, Felipe Osterling. *Las obligaciones.* (2d ed.) Lima: Fondo Editorial de la Pontificia Universidad Católica del Perú, 1988.

Pásara, Luis. *Radicalización y conflicto en la iglesia peruana.* Lima: Ediciones El Virrey, 1986.

Pásara, Luis, and Jorge Parodi (eds.). *Democracia, sociedad y gobierno en el Perú.* Lima: Centro de Estudios de Democracia y Sociedad, 1988.

Peru. Instituto Nacional de Estadística. *Censos nacionales de VII de población, 1981.* Lima: 1981.

_____. Instituto Nacional de Estadística. *Peru: Compendio estadístico.* Lima: 1987.

_____. Instituto Nacional de Estadística. *Población total proyectada al 30 junio de 1990.* Lima: 1989.

Poole, D.A. "Landscapes of Power in a Cattle-Rustling Culture of Southern Andean Peru," *Dialectical Anthropology,* 12, No. 4, 1987, 367-98.

Post, D. "Political Goals of Peruvian Students: The Foundations of Legitimacy in Education," *Sociology of Education,* 61, No. 3, 1988, 178-190.

_____. "Student Expectations of Educational Returns in Peru," *Comparative Education Review,* 29, No. 2, 1985, 189-203.

Pozziescot, I. "Students' Preferences in Learning English in Lima, Peru," *System,* 15, No. 1, 1987, 77-80.

Quilter, J., and T. Stocker. "Subsistence Economies and the Origins of Andean Complex Societies," *American Anthropologist,* 85, No. 3, 1983, 545-62.

Quiroz, Alfonso W. "Financial Leadership and the Formation of Peruvian Elite Groups, 1884-1930," *Journal of Latin American Studies,* 20, May 1988, 49-81.

Richman, J.A., and M. Gaviria. "The Process of Acculturation: Theoretical Perspectives and an Empirical Investigation in Peru," *Social Science and Medicine,* 25, No. 7, 1987, 839-47.

Rondinelli, D.A., and P.A. Wilson. "Linking Decentralization and Regional Development Planning: The IRD Project in Peru," *Journal of the American Planning Association,* 53, No. 3, 1987, 348-57.

Rossini, Renzo G., and J.J. Thomas. "The Size of the Informal Sector in Peru: A Critical Comment on Hernando de Soto: El otro sendero," *World Development,* 18, No. 1, 1990, 197-98.

Salinas, P.W., and J.M. Garzon. "Prospects for Political Decentralization: Peru in the 1980s," *International Journal of Urban and Regional Research,* 9, No. 3, 1985, 330-40.

Salinas-Ramos, Francisco. "The Religion of the Peruvian Quechuas, Yesterday and Today," *Cuadernos de Realidades Sociales,* Nos. 16-17, 1980, 273-89.

Sallnow, Michael J. *Pilgrims of the Andes: Regional Cults in Cusco.* Washington: Smithsonian Institution Press, 1987.

_____. "A Trinity of Christs: Cultic Processes in Andean Catholicism," *American Ethnologist,* 9, No. 4, 1982, 730-49.

Sánchez, Rodrigo. *Los movimientos campesinos en Andahuaylas.* Lima: Instituto de Estudios Peruanos, 1982.

Sara Lafosse, Violeta. "El status de la mujer y sus implicaciones demográficas." Pages 293-331 in Asociación Multidisciplinaria de Investigación y Docencia en Población, *Problemas poblacionales Peruanas.* Lima: 1980.

Schmink, Marianne, and Charles H. Wood (eds.). *Frontier Expansion in Amazonia.* Gainesville: University of Florida Press, 1985.

Scott, C.D. "Strategies of Technical Choice in the Peruvian Sugar Industry, 1955-74," *Journal of Peasant Studies,* 12, No. 4, 1985, 26-56.

Scurrah, Martin J., and Mario Padron. "Self-Management as a Development Alternative: Reflections on the Peruvian Experience," *Canadian Journal of Development Studies* [Toronto], 2, No. 2, 1981, 427-42.

Silva, G.R. "Crisis, Democracy, and the Left in Peru," *Latin American Perspectives,* 15, No. 3, 1988, 77-96.

Silverblatt, Irene M. *Moon, Sun and Witches: Gender Ideologies and Class in Inca and Colonial Peru.* Princeton: Princeton University Press, 1987.

Skar, Harold. *The Warm Valley People: Duality and Land Reform among the Quechua Indians of Highland Peru.* (2d ed.) Göteborg: Göteborgs Etnografiska Museum, 1988.

Skar, Sarah Lund. "The Use of the Public/Private Framework in the Analysis of Egalitarian Societies: The Case of a Quechua Community in Highland Peru," *Women's Studies International Quarterly,* 2, No. 4, 1979, 449-60.

Smith, Gavin A. "Socio-Economic Differentiation and Relations of Production among Rural-Based Petty Producers in Central Peru, 1880-1970," *Journal of Peasant Studies,* 6, No. 3, 1979, 286-310.

Stein, William W. *Peruvian Contexts of Change.* New Brunswick, New Jersey: Transaction Books, 1985.

Stocks, Anthony. "Indian Policy in Eastern Peru." Pages 33-61 in Marianne Schmink and Charles H. Wood (eds.), *Frontier Expansion in Amazonia.* Gainesville: University of Florida Press, 1984.

Strassman, W.P. "Types of Neighborhood and Home-Based Enterprises: Evidence from Lima, Peru," *Urban Studies,* 23, No. 6, 1986, 485-500.

Stromquist, N.P. "Feminist Reflections on Peruvian University Politics," *Higher Education,* 17, No. 5, 1988, 581-601.

Stull, Donald D., and Jean J. Schensul (eds.). *Collaborative Research and Social Change: Applied Anthropology in Action.* (Westview Special Studies in Applied Anthropology.) Boulder, Colorado: Westview Press, 1987.

Suárez, Flor, Vilma Vargas, and Joel Jurado. *Cambio de la economía peruana y evolución de la situación de empleo de la mujer.* Lima: Ministerio de Trabajo y Promoción Social, United Nations Children's Fund, 1982.

Tienda, Marta. "Community Characteristics, Women's Education, and Fertility in Peru," *Studies in Family Planning,* 15, No. 4, 1984, 162-69.

_____. "Macro and Micro Contexts of Dependency Rates: An Illustration with Peruvian Data," *Population and Environment,* 4, No. 2, 1981, 79-96.

Torres-Adrian, Mario J. "Demographic and Economic Adaptation by Peasants in Peru," *Eastern Anthropologist,* 31, No. 4, October 1978, 481-509.

Tucker, G.M. "Barriers to Modern Contraceptive Use in Rural Peru," *Studies in Family Planning,* 17, No. 6, 1986, 308-16.

United Nations. Economic Commission for Latin America and the Caribbean. *Statistical Yearbook for Latin America and the Caribbean, 1990.* Santiago, Chile: 1991.

Urton, Gary D. *At the Crossroads of the Earth and the Sky: An Andean Cosmology.* Austin: University of Texas Press, 1981.

Valdemoro, Hubert L., and Fernando G. Fernandini. "Peru Climbs on the Chilean Bandwagon," *Benefits and Compensation International,* 21, No. 7, March 1992, 9-15.

Valdivia Ponce, Oscar. *Hampicamayoc: Medicina folklórica y su substrato aborigen en el Perú.* Lima: Universidad Nacional Mayor de San Marcos, 1975.

Van den Berghe, Pierre. "Tourism as Ethnic Relations: A Case Study of Cuzco, Peru," *Ethnic and Racial Studies,* 3, No. 4, 1980, 375-92.

Van den Berghe, Pierre, and George Primor. *Inequality in the Peruvian Andes: Class and Ethnicity in Cuzco.* Columbia: University of Missouri Press, 1977.

Vandergaag, J. "Wage Differentials and Moonlighting by Civil Servants: Evidence from Ivory Coast and Peru," *World Bank Economic Review*, 3, No. 1, 1989, 67-95.

Vargas Ugarte, Rubén. *Historia general del Perú*. (2d ed.) Lima: C. Milla Batres, 1984.

Varillas Montenegro, Alberto, and Patricia Mostajo de Muente. *La situación poblacional peruana: Balance y perspectivas*. Lima: Instituto Andino de Estudios en Población y Desarrollo, 1990.

Velasco, J.A. "The U.N. Decade for Women in Peru," *Women's Studies International Forum*, 8, No. 2, 1985, 107-9.

Vellinga, M., and D. Kruijt. "The State, Regional Development and Regional Bourgeoisie in Latin America: Case Studies of Peru and Colombia," *Inter-American Economic Affairs*, 37, Winter 1983, 3-31.

Villalobos de Urrútia, Gabriela. *Diagnóstico de la situación social y económica de la mujer peruana*. Lima: Centro de Estudios de Población y Desarrollo, 1975.

_____. *La madre trabajadora: El caso de las obreras industriales*. Lima: Centro de Estudios de Población y Desarrollo, 1977.

Wallace, James. "Urban Anthropology in Lima: An Overview," *Latin American Research Review*, 19, No. 3, 1984, 57-86.

Weeks, John. *Limits to Capitalist Development: The Industrialization of Peru, 1950-1980*. Boulder, Colorado: Westview Press, 1985.

Werlich, David P. *Peru: A Short History*. Carbondale: Southern Illinois University Press, 1978.

_____. "Peru: The Shadow of the Shining Path (Impact of the Guerrilla Movement on Peruvian Politics)," *Current History*, 83, February 1984, 42-78.

Whyte, William Foote, and Giorgio Alberti. *Power, Politics, and Progress: Social Change in Rural Peru*. New York: Elsevier-North Holland, 1976.

Wilgus, A. Curtis. *Historical Atlas of Latin America: Political, Geographic, Economic, Cultural*. New York: Cooper Square, 1967.

Wilson, Patricia A., and Carol Wise. "The Regional Implications of Public Investment in Peru, 1968-1983," *Latin American Research Review*, 21, No 2, 1986, 93-116.

World Bank. *World Development Report, 1989*. Washington: 1989.

_____. *World Development Report, 1990*. Washington: 1990.

Zapata, Francisco. *Guamán Poma, indigenismo y estética de la dependencia en la cultura peruana*. Minneapolis, Minnesota: Institute for the Study of Ideologies and Literatures, 1989.

(Various issues of the following publications were also used in the preparation of this chapter: *Comparative Social Research*, 1979,

1981; *Demografía y Economía, Revista del PISPAL* [Mexico City], 1981; *Economist* [London], 1988; *Economy and Society,* 1974; *El Comercio* [Lima], 1985–86; *Estudios Andinos* [Lima], 1976; *Ethnology,* 1979–81; *Journal of Comparative Family Studies,* 1980, 1985; *Journal of Marriage and the Family,* 1980; *Revista Paraguaya de Sociología* [Asunción], 1979; *Revue Canadienne de Sociologie et d'Anthropologie* [Montreal], 1980; *Social Science Quarterly,* 1979; *Terrorism: An International Journal,* 1988; *Third World,* 1987; and *Women and Politics,* 1984.)

Chapter 3

Alarco, Germán. *Economía peruana, 1985–1990: Enseñanzas de la expansión y del colapso.* (1st ed.) Lima: Fundación Friedrich Ebert, 1990.

Alberts, Tom. *Agrarian Reform and Rural Poverty: A Case Study of Peru.* Boulder, Colorado: Westview Press, 1983.

Altimir, Oscar. "The Extent of Poverty in Latin America." (World Bank Study No. 522.) Washington: World Bank, 1982.

Alvarez, Elena H. "The Economics and Political Economy of Coca Production in the Andes: Implications for U.S. Foreign Policy and Rural Development in Bolivia and Peru." (Research proposal.) Albany: The Nelson A. Rockefeller Institute of Government, State University of New York at Albany, January 1989.

_____. *Política económica y agricultura en el Perú, 1969–1979.* Lima: Instituto de Estudios Peruanos, 1983.

Amat y León, Carlos. *La crisis de la economía peruana.* Lima: Fundación Friedrich Ebert, 1977.

Banco Central de Reservas. *Memoria 1985.* Lima: 1985.

_____. *Memoria 1990.* Lima: 1991.

Becker, David G. *The New Bourgeoisie and the Limits of Dependency: Mining, Class, and Power in "Revolutionary" Peru.* Princeton: Princeton University Press, 1983.

Berry, R. Albert. "International Trade, Government, and Income Distribution in Peru since 1870," *Latin American Research Review,* 25, No. 2, 1990, 31–59.

Caballero, José María. *Economía agraria de la sierra peruana: Antes de la reforma agraria de 1969.* Lima: Instituto de Estudios Peruanos, 1981.

Caller, Jaime, and Rosario Chuecas. *Estrategia de desarrollo industrial: Algunas reflexiones.* Lima: Fundación Friedrich Ebert, 1989.

Cardoso, Eliana, and Ann Helwege. "Below the Line: Poverty in Latin America," *World Development,* 20, No. 1, 1992, 19–37.

Carter, Michael C., and Elena Alvarez. "Changing Paths: The Decollectivization of Agrarian Reform Agriculture in Coastal Peru." Pages 156-87 in William C. Thiesenhusen (ed.), *Searching for Agrarian Reform in Latin America.* Boston: Unwin Hyman, 1989.

Condes Conde, Roberto, and Shane Hunt (eds.). *Latin American Economies: Growth and Export Sector, 1880-1930.* New York: Holmes and Meier, 1985.

Cotler, Julio. *Clases, estado, y nación en el Perú.* Lima: Instituto de Estudios Peruanos, 1978.

Cueva García, Aníbal. *Gran atlas geográfico del Perú y el mundo.* Lima: A.F.A. Editores, 1991.

de Soto, Hernando. *The Other Path: The Invisible Revolution in the Third World.* New York: Harper and Row, 1990.

Dore, Elizabeth. *The Peruvian Mining Industry: Growth, Stagnation, and Crisis.* (Political Economy and Economic Development in Latin America Series.) Boulder, Colorado: Westview Press, 1988.

Economic Commission for Latin America and the Caribbean. *Preliminary Overview of the Economy of Latin America and the Caribbean, 1990.* Santiago: December 1990.

El Comercio [Lima], April 12, 1992, F20.

Feres, Juan Carlos, and Arturo León. "Magnitud de la situación de la probreza," *Revista de la CEPAL,* No. 41, August 1990, 133-52.

Figueroa, Adolfo. *Capitalist Development and the Peasant Economy in Peru.* Cambridge: Cambridge University Press, 1984.

————. "Productividad agrícola y crisis económica," *Economía,* 11, No. 22, December 1988, 9-34.

Fitzgerald, Edmund V.K. *The Political Economy of Peru, 1956-78: Economic Development and the Restructuring of Capital.* Cambridge: Cambridge University Press, 1979.

Frank, Charles R., Jr., and Richard Webb (eds.). *Income Distribution and Growth in the Less-Developed Countries.* Washington: Brookings Institution, 1977.

Garland, Gonzalo H. *El sector industrial en el Perú: Una visión de largo plazo.* Lima: Grupo de Análisis para el Desarrollo, 1991.

Glewwe, Paul. *The Distribution of Welfare in Peru in 1985-86.* (Living Standards Measurement Study, Working Paper No. 42.) Washington: World Bank, 1988.

Golte, Jürgen, and Norma Adams. *Los caballos de Troya de los invasores: Estrategias campesinas en la conquista de la gran Lima.* Lima: Instituto de Estudios Peruanos, 1990.

Goodsell, Charles. *American Corporations and Peruvian Politics.* Cambridge: Harvard University Press, 1974.

Gootenberg, Paul E. *Between Silver and Guano: Commercial Policy and the State in Post-Independence Peru.* Princeton: Princeton University Press, 1989.

Grupo de Análisis para el Desarrollo, with the Brookings Institution. *Estabilización y crecimiento en el Perú: Una propuesta independiente.* Lima: May 1990.

Hartlyn, Jonathan, and Samuel Morley (eds.). *Latin American Political Economy: Financial Crisis and Political Change.* Boulder, Colorado: Westview Press, 1986.

Hunt, Shane. "Direct Foreign Investment in Peru: New Rules for an Old Game." Pages 302-49 in Cynthia McClintock and Abraham F. Lowenthal (eds.), *The Peruvian Experiment: Continuity and Change under Military Rule.* Princeton: Princeton University Press, 1975.

_____. "Growth and Guano in Nineteenth Century Peru." Pages 335-60 in Roberto Condes Conde and Shane Hunt (eds.), *Latin American Economies: Growth and Export Sector, 1880-1930.* New York: Holmes and Meier, 1985.

Inter-American Development Bank. *Economic and Social Progress in Latin America: 1989 Report.* Washington: 1989.

_____. *Economic and Social Progress in Latin America: 1990 Report.* Washington: Johns Hopkins University Press, 1990.

International Monetary Fund. *International Financial Statistics: Yearbook, 1990.* Washington: 1991.

Jain, Shail. *Size Distribution of Income: A Compilation of Data.* Washington: World Bank, 1975.

Kay, Cristóbal. "Achievements and Contradictions of the Peruvian Agrarian Reform," *Journal of Development Studies,* 18, January 1982, 141-70.

Kirk, Robin. *The Decade of Chaqwa: Peru's Internal Refugees.* Washington: U.S. Committee for Refugees, May 1991.

Lasarria-Cornhiel, Susana. "Agrarian Reform of the 1960s and 1970s in Peru." Pages 127-55 in William C. Thiesenhusen (ed.), *Searching for Agrarian Reform in Latin America.* Boston: Unwin Hyman, 1989.

McClintock, Cynthia. "After Agrarian Reform and Democratic Government: Has Peruvian Agriculture Developed?" Pages 50-69 in F. LaMond Tullis and W. Ladd Hollist (eds.), *Food, the State, the International Political Economy.* Lincoln: University of Nebraska Press, 1986.

_____. *Peasant Cooperatives and Political Change in Peru.* Princeton: Princeton University Press, 1981.

McClintock, Cynthia, and Abraham F. Lowenthal (eds.). *The Peruvian Experiment: Continuity and Change under Military Rule.* Princeton: Princeton University Press, 1975.

_____. *The Peruvian Experiment Reconsidered.* (2d ed.) Princeton: Princeton University Press, 1983.

Martino, Orlando D. (ed.). *Mineral Industries of America.* Washington: GPO, 1988.

Melmed-Sanjak, Jolyne, and Michael R. Carter. "The Economic Viability of 'Capitalised Family Farming:' An Analysis of Agricultural Decollectivisation in Peru," *Journal of Development Studies,* 27, No. 2, January 1991, 199–210.

Paredes, Carlos E., and Jeffrey D. Sachs (eds.). *Peru's Path to Recovery: A Plan for Economic Stabilization and Growth.* Washington: The Brookings Institution, 1991.

Pásara, Luis. "When the Military Dreams." Pages 309–46 in Cynthia McClintock and Abraham F. Lowenthal (eds.), *The Peruvian Experiment Reconsidered.* Princeton: Princeton University Press, 1983.

Pastor, Manuel, Jr., and Carol Wise. "Peruvian Economic Policy in the 1980s: From Orthodoxy to Heterodoxy and Back," *Latin American Research Review,* 27, No. 2, 1992, 83–118.

Paus, Eva. "Adjustment and Development in Latin America: The Failure of Peruvian Heterodoxy, 1985–90," *World Development,* 19, No. 5, May 1991.

Peru. Instituto Nacional de Estadística. *Evolución de la economía peruana.* Lima: November 1989.

_____. Ministerio de Agricultura, Grupo de Análisis de Política Agraria. *Lineamientos de política agraria, 1990–1995.* Lima: 1990.

PREALC (Economic Recovery Program for Latin America and the Caribbean), Oficina Internaciónal del Trabajo. *Mercado de trabajo en cifras: 1950–1980.* Santiago: 1982.

Revilla, C. Víctor. *El proceso de liberalización comercial 1978–1983: Lecciones de una experiencia frustrada.* Lima: Fundación Friedrich Ebert, 1990.

Riding, Alan. "Peru Fights to Overcome Its Past," *New York Times Magazine,* May 14, 1989, 40ff.

Rossini, Renzo G. "Las medidas recientes de apertura comercial," *Moneda [Lima],* 4, No. 33, March 1991.

Sánchez-Albornoz, Nicolás *The Population of Latin America: A History.* Berkeley: University of California Press, 1974.

Schydlowsky, Daniel M. "The Tragedy of Lost Opportunity in Peru." Pages 115–38 in Jonathan Hartlyn and Samuel Morley (eds.), *Latin American Political Economy: Financial Crisis and Political Change.* Boulder, Colorado: Westview Press, 1986.

Sheahan, John. "The Economics of the Peruvian Experiment in Comparative Perspective." Pages 387–414 in Cynthia McClintock and Abraham F. Lowenthal (eds.), *The Peruvian Experiment Reconsidered.* Princeton: Princeton University Press, 1983.

_____. *Patterns of Development in Latin America: Poverty, Repression, and Economic Strategy.* Princeton: Princeton University Press, 1987.

_____. "Peru: Economic Policies and Structural Change, 1968–1978." *Journal of Development Studies,* 7, No. 1, 1980.

Stein, Steve. *Populism in Peru: The Emergence of the Masses and the Politics of Social Control.* Madison: University of Wisconsin Press, 1980.

Stein, Steve, and Carlos Monge (eds.). *La crisis del estado patrimonial en el Perú.* Lima: Instituto de Estudios Peruanos, 1988.

Stevens, Evelyne Huber. "The Peruvian Military Government, Labor Mobilization, and the Political Strength of the Left," *Latin American Research Review,* 17, No. 2, 1982.

Tarazona-Sevillano, Gabriela. *Sendero Luminoso and the Threat of Narco Terrorism.* New York: Praeger, 1990.

Tello, Mario D. "La crisis del sector externo, 1955–1988," *CISEPA* [Lima], No. 80, July 1989.

Thiesenhuser, William C. (ed.). *Searching for Agrarian Reform in Latin America.* Boston: Unwin Hyman, 1989.

Thorp, Rosemary. *Economic Management and Economic Development in Peru and Colombia.* Pittsburgh: Pittsburgh University Press, 1991.

_____. "The Evolution of Peru's Economy." Pages 39–64 in Cynthia McClintock and Abraham F. Lowenthal (eds.), *The Peruvian Experiment Reconsidered.* Princeton: Princeton University Press, 1983.

_____. "Peruvian Adjustment Policies, 1978–1985: The Effects of Prolonged Crisis." Pages 59–77 in Rosemary Thorp and Laurence Whitehead (eds.), *Latin American Debt and the Adjustment Crisis.* London: Macmillan, 1987.

Thorp, Rosemary, and Geoffrey Bertram. *Peru 1890–1977: Growth and Policy in an Open Economy.* New York: Columbia University Press, 1978.

Thorp, Rosemary, and Laurence Whitehead (eds.). *Latin American Debt and the Adjustment Crisis.* London: Macmillan, 1987.

Tullis, F. LaMond, and W. Ladd Hollist (eds.). *Food, the State, the International Political Economy.* Lincoln: University of Nebraska Press, 1986.

United Nations Development Programme. *Human Development Report, 1990.* New York: Oxford University Press, 1990.

Vega Castro, Jorge. *El sector industrial informal y las políticas deliberalización del comercio exterior en el Perú: El caso de las industrias de confecciones y de calzado.* Lima: Instituto de Investigación y Docencia, 1989.

Webb, Richard, and Graciela Fernández Baca (eds.). *Perú en números 1990: Almanaque estadístico.* Lima: Cuánto, 1990.

World Bank. *Peru: Long-Term Development Issues.* Washington: 1979.

_____. *Peru: Policies to Stop Hyperinflation and Initiate Economic Recovery.* Washington: 1989.

_____. *World Development Report* (annuals 1981–1982 through 1989–1990). Washington: 1981 through 1989.

_____. *World Tables.* (3d ed.) Washington: 1983.

(Various issues of the following publications were also used in the preparation of this chapter: *The Andean Report,* 1989–91; *Journal of Development Economics,* 1987; and *Perú Económico [Lima],* 1989–91)

Chapter 4

Angell, Alan. "Classroom Maoists: The Politics of School-teachers under Military Government," *Bulletin of Latin American Research* [London], 1, No. 2, 1982, 47–66.

_____. "The Difficulties of Policy Implementation in Peru," *Bulletin of Latin American Research,* 3, No. 1, 1984, 25–43.

Ballón, Eduardo (ed.). *Movimientos sociales y democracía: La fundación de un nuevo orden.* Lima: Centro de Estudios y Promoción del Desarrollo, 1986.

Berrios, Rubén, and Cole Blasier. "Peru and the Soviet Union (1969–1989): Distant Partners." *Journal of Latin American Studies,* pt. 2, 23, May 1991, 365–84.

Blaustein, Albert P., and Gisbert H. Flanz (eds.). *Constitutions of the Countries of the World.* Dobbs Ferry, New York: Oceana, 1989.

Cameron, Maxwell A. "Political Parties and the Worker-Employer Cleavage: The Impact of the Informal Sector on Voting in Lima, Peru." *Bulletin of Latin American Research* [London], 10, No. 3, 1991, 293–313.

Caretas [Lima], March 4, 1991, 38–39.

Cornell, Angela, and Kenneth Roberts. "Democracy, Counter-insurgency, and Human Rights: The Case of Peru," *Human Rights Quarterly,* 12, No. 4, November 12, 1990, 529–53.

Crabtree, John. "From Belaúnde to Alan García," *Bulletin of Latin American Research,* 4, No. 2, 1985, 83–109.

_____. *Peru under García: An Opportunity Lost.* Pittsburgh: University of Pittsburgh Press, 1992.

de Soto, Hernando. *The Other Path: The Invisible Revolution in the Third World.* New York: Harper and Row, 1990.

Dornbusch, Rudiger, and Sebastian Edwards (eds.). *The Macroeconomics of Populism in Latin America.* Chicago: University of Chicago Press, 1991.

Ferrero Costa, Eduardo. "Peru's, Presidential Coup," *Journal of Democracy,* 4, No. 1, January 1993, 28-40.

Gorman, Stephen M. (ed.). *Post-Revolutionary Peru: The Politics of Transformation.* (Westview Special Studies on Latin America and the Caribbean.) Boulder, Colorado: Westview Press, 1982.

Graham, Carol. "The APRA Government and the Urban Poor: The PAIT Programme in Lima's Pueblos Jóvenes," *Journal of Latin American Studies,* pt. 1, 23, February 1991, 91-130.

_____. "Parties and Grass Roots Movements in Chile, Bolivia, and Peru: Poverty Alleviation and Democratic Consolidation," (Paper presented at the Latin American Studies Association Annual Meeting, April 1991.) Washington: April 1991.

_____. *Peru's APRA: Parties, Politics, and the Elusive Quest for Democratic Consolidation.* Boulder, Colorado: Lynne Rienner, 1992.

_____. "Peru's APRA Party in Power: Impossible Revolution, Relinquished Reform," *Journal of Interamerican Studies and World Affairs,* 32, No.3, Fall 1990, 75-115.

Haak, Roelfien, and Javier Díaz Albertini (eds.). *Estrategias de vida en el sector urbano popular.* Lima: Centro de Estudios y Promoción del Desarrollo, 1987.

Haggard, Stephan, and Robert Kaufman. *The Political Economy of Stabilization and Inflation in Middle Income Countries.* (World Bank Working Paper No. 444.) Washington: June 1990.

Huntington, Samuel P. *Political Order in Changing Societies.* New Haven: Yale University Press, 1968.

Iguíñiz, Javier. *Política económica, 1985-1986: Deslindes mirando al futuro.* Lima: Centro de Estudios y Promoción del Desarrollo, 1986.

Johnson, Nancy R. *The Political, Economic, and Labor Climate in Peru.* (Latin American Studies, Multinational Industrial Relations Series, No. 4.) Philadelphia: University of Pennsylvania Press, 1979.

Long, Norman, and Bryan R. Roberts. *Miners, Peasants, and Entrepreneurs: Regional Development in the Central Highlands of Peru.* Cambridge: Cambridge University Press, 1984.

McClintock, Cynthia. "Peru's Fujimori: A Caudillo Derails Democracy," *Current History,* 92, No. 572, March 1993, 112-19.

McClintock, Cynthia, and Abraham F. Lowenthal (eds.). *The Peruvian Experiment Reconsidered.* (2d ed.) Princeton: Princeton University Press, 1983.

Palmer, David Scott. *Peru: The Authoritarian Tradition.* New York: Praeger, 1980.

_____. "Peru's Persistent Problems," *Current History,* 89, No. 543, January 1990, 5-8, 31-34.

Pásara, Luis, and Jorge Parodi (eds.). *Democracía, sociedad y gobierno en el Perú.* Lima: Centro de Estudios de Democracia y Sociedad, 1988.

Peredes, Peri, and Griselda Tello. *Pobreza urbana y trabajo femenino.* Lima: Asociación de Defensa y Capacitación Legal, Asociación de Trabajo y Cultura, 1988.

Peru. Instituto Geográfico. Nacional. *Perú: Mapa regional.* Lima: 1989.

Redden, Kenneth Robert (ed.). *Modern Legal Systems Cyclopedia.* Buffalo, New York: William S. Hein, 1987.

Rojas Samañez, Alvaro. *Partidos políticos en el Perú: Manual y registro.* Lima: Centro de Documentación e Información Andina, 1982.

Rudolph, James D. *Peru: The Evolution of a Crisis.* (Politics in Latin America: A Hoover Institution Series.) Westport, Connecticut: Praeger, 1992.

Saba, Raúl P. *Political Development and Democracy in Peru: Continuity in Change and Crisis.* (Westview Special Studies on Latin America and the Caribbean.) Boulder, Colorado: Westview Press, 1987.

St. John, Ronald Bruce. *The Foreign Policy of Peru.* Boulder, Colorado: Lynne Rienner, 1992.

Thorndike, Guillermo. *La revolución imposible.* (1st ed.) Lima: EMI, 1988.

Thorp, Rosemary, and Geoffrey Bertram. *Peru, 1890-1977: Growth and Policy in an Open Economy.* New York: Columbia University Press, 1978.

United States. Department of State. *Country Reports on Human Rights Practices for 1989.* (Report submitted to United States Congress, 101st, 2d Session, Senate, Committee on Foreign Relations, and House of Representatives, Committee on Foreign Affairs.) Washington: GPO, February 1990.

_____. Department of State. *Country Reports on Human Rights Practices for 1990.* (Report submitted to United States Congress, 102d, 1st Session, Senate, Committee on Foreign Relations, and House of Representatives, Committee on Foreign Affairs.) Washington: GPO, February 1990.

Valenzuela, Arturo. *Political Brokers in Chile: Municipal Government in a Centralized Polity.* Durham, North Carolina: Duke University Press, 1978.

Vargas Llosa, Mario. "A Fish Out of Water," *Granta* [London], 36, Summer 1991, 17-85.

Vega Centeno, Imelda. *Ideología y cultura en el aprismo popular.* Lima: Tarea, Fundación Friedrich Ebert, 1986.

Werlich, David P. "Fujimori and the 'Disaster' in Peru," *Current History,* 90, No. 553, February 1991, 61-64, 81-3.

World Bank. *World Development Report, 1990.* Washington: 1990.

(Various issues of the following publications were also used in the preparation of this chapter: *Caretas* [Lima], 1988; *Cuánto* [Lima] 1991; Foreign Broadcast Information Service, *Daily Report: Latin America,* 1990-91; *Lima Times* [Lima], 1991; *Nation,* 1988; *Newsletter* [Lima], 1990; *New York Times,* 1989; *Posible* [Lima] 1986-87; *Quehacer* [Lima], 1987, 1989; and *Wall Street Journal,* 1988-91.)

Chapter 5

Amnesty International. *Peru: Human Rights in a State of Emergency.* New York: 1989.

"Andean Air Power . . . The Peruvian Air Force," *Air International,* 34, No. 5, May 1988, 224-35ff.

Andrade, John. "Peru." Page 157 in *World Police and Paramilitary Forces.* New York: Stockton Press, 1985.

Astiz, Carlos A. "The Peruvian Military." Pages 131-61 in Carlos A. Astiz, (ed.), *Groups and Power Elites in Peruvian Politics.* Ithaca: Cornell University Press, 1969.

Astiz, Carlos A. (ed.). *Groups and Power Elites in Peruvian Politics.* Ithaca: Cornell University Press, 1969.

Astiz, Carlos A., and José García. "The Peruvian Military: Achievement Orientation, Training, and Political Tendencies," *Western Political Quarterly,* 25, No. 4, December 1972, 667-85.

Barsallo Burga, José, and Eduardo Gordillo Tordoya. *Drogas: Responsabilidad compartida.* Lima: J.C. Editores, 1988.

Berg, Ronald H. "Peasant Responses to Shining Path in Andahuaylas." Pages 83-104 in David Scott Palmer (ed.), *The Shining Path of Peru.* New York: St. Martin's Press, 1992.

Booth, David, and Bernardo Sorj (eds.). *Military Reformism and Social Class: The Peruvian Experience, 1968-1980.* New York: St. Martin's Press, 1983.

Burneo, José. "Fuerzas armadas, estado de emergencia, y seguridad nacional." Pages 17-21 in Comisión Episcopal de Acción Social, Servicio de Derechos Humanos. *Defensa de la vida, democracia, y doctrina de seguridad nacional.* Lima: 1987.

Centro de Estudios y Promoción del Desarrollo. *Violencia política en el Perú, 1980-1988,* 2. Lima: 1989.

Comisión Episcopal de Acción Social. Servicio de Derechos Humanos. *Defensa de la vida, democracia, y doctrina de seguridad nacional.* Lima: 1987.

Cornell, Angela, and Kenneth Roberts. "Democracy, Counterinsurgency, and Human Rights: The Case of Peru," *Human Rights Quarterly,* 12, No. 4, November 12, 1990, 529–53.

Craig, Wesley W. "Peru: The Peasant Movement of La Convención." Pages 274–96 in Henry A. Landsberger (ed.), *Latin American Peasant Movements.* Ithaca: Cornell University Press, 1969.

Crosby, Alfred W., Jr. *The Columbian Exchange: Biological and Cultural Consequences of 1492.* Westport, Connecticut: Greenwood, 1972.

De Wit, Ton, and Vera Gianotten. "The Center's Multiple Failures." Pages 45–58 in David Scott Palmer (ed.), *The Shining Path of Peru.* New York: St. Martin's Press, 1992.

Degregori, Carlos Iván. *Ayacucho, 1969–1979.* Chapel Hill: University of North Carolina Press, 1992.

_____. "The Origins and Logic of Shining Path: Return to the Past." Pages 33–44 in David Scott Palmer (ed.), *The Shining Path of Peru.* New York: St. Martin's Press, 1992.

Dietz, Henry A., and David Scott Palmer. "Citizen Participation under Innovative Military Corporatism in Peru." Pages 172–88 in Mitchell A. Seligson and John A. Booth (eds.), *Politics and the Poor.* (Political Participation in Latin America Series, No. 2.) New York: Holmes and Meier, 1978.

Einaudi, Luigi R. *The Peruvian Military: A Summary Political Analysis.* Santa Monica, California: Rand, 1969.

_____. "U.S. Relations with the Peruvian Military." Pages 15–56 in Daniel A. Sharp (ed.), *U.S. Foreign Policy and Peru.* Austin: University of Texas Press, 1972.

Einaudi, Luigi R., and Alfred Stepan. *Latin American Institutional Development: Changing Perspectives in Peru and Bolivia.* Santa Monica, California: Rand, 1971.

English, Adrian J. "Las armadas iberoamericanas, 1990," *Tecnología Militar* [Bonn], 12, No. 1, 1990, 10–18, 21.

_____. *Armed Forces of Latin America: Their Histories, Development, Present Strength, and Military Potential.* London: Jane's, 1984.

Fowler, Luis R. *Monografía histórico-geográfica del departamento de Ayacucho.* Lima: Imprenta Torres Aguirre, 1924.

García Sayán, Diego. *Hábeas corpus y estados de emergencia.* Lima: Comisión Andina de Juristas y Fundación Friedrich Naumann, 1988.

Gamarra, Eduardo (ed.). *Latin American and Caribbean Contemporary Record, 1989–90,* 9. New York: Holmes and Meier, 1992.

Gonzales, José E. "Guerrillas and Coca in the Upper Huallaga Valley." Pages 105–26 in David Scott Palmer (ed.), *The Shining Path of Peru*. New York: St. Martin's Press, 1992.

Gorriti Ellenbogen, Gustavo. *Sendero: Historia de la guerra milenaria en el Perú*, 1. Lima: Editorial Apoyo, 1990.

―――. "Shining Path's Stalin and Trotsky." Pages 149–70 in David Scott Palmer (ed.), *The Shining Path of Peru*. New York: St. Martin's Press, 1992.

Herring, Hubert Clinton, with the assistance of Helen Baldwin Herring. *A History of Latin America*. (3d ed.) New York: Knopf, 1968.

Hopkins, Jack (ed.). *Latin America: Perspectives on a Region*. New York: Holmes and Meier, 1987.

Isbell, Billie Jean. "Shining Path and Peasant Responses in Rural Ayacucho." Pages 59–82 in David Scott Palmer (ed.), *The Shining Path of Peru*. New York: St. Martin's Press, 1992.

Jane's. *Armed Forces of Latin America: Their Histories, Development, Present Strength, and Military Potential*. London: 1984.

Jaquette, Jane S. *The Politics of Development in Peru*. (Dissertation Series No. 33.) Ithaca: Latin American Studies Program, Cornell University, 1971.

Keegan, John. "Peru." Pages 469–74 in John Keegan (ed.), *World Armies*. Detroit: Gale Research, 1983.

Keegan, John (ed.). *World Armies*. Detroit: Gale Research, 1983.

Landsberger, Henry A. (ed.). *Latin American Peasant Movements*. Ithaca: Cornell University Press, 1969.

Lockhart, James. *The Men of Cajamarca: A Social and Biographical Study of the First Conquerors of Peru*. (Latin American Monographs, No. 27.) Austin: University of Texas Press, 1972.

Loveman, Brian, and Thomas M. Davies, Jr. (eds.). *The Politics of Antipolitics: The Military in Latin America*. (2d ed.) Lincoln: University of Nebraska Press, 1989.

Lowenthal, Abraham F. "Peru's Ambiguous Revolution." Pages 3–43 in Abraham F. Lowenthal (ed.), *The Peruvian Experiment: Continuity and Change under Military Rule*. Princeton: Princeton University Press, 1975.

Marks, Tom. "Making Revolution with Shining Path." Pages 191–206 in David Scott Palmer (ed.), *The Shining Path of Peru*. New York: St. Martin's Press, 1992.

―――. "Making Revolution: Sendero Luminoso in Peru," *Small Wars and Insurgencies*, 3, No. 1, Spring 1992, 22–46.

Masterson, Daniel M. *Militarism and Politics in Latin America: Peru from Sánchez Cerro to Sendero Luminoso*. New York: Greenwood Press, 1991.

Mauceri, Philip. *The Military, Insurgency, and Democratic Power: Peru, 1980-1988.* (Papers on Latin America, No. 11.) New York: The Institute of Latin American and Iberian Studies, Columbia University, 1989.

McClintock, Cynthia. "Theories of Revolution and the Case of Peru." Pages 225-40 in David Scott Palmer (ed.), *The Shining Path of Peru.* New York: St. Martin's Press, 1992.

McClintock, Cynthia, and Abraham F. Lowenthal (eds.), *The Peruvian Experiment Reconsidered.* (2d ed.) Princeton: Princeton University Press, 1983.

McCormick, Gordon A. *The Shining Path and the Future of Peru.* Santa Monica, California: Rand, 1990.

The Military Balance, 1990-1991. London: International Institute for Strategic Studies, 1990.

The Military Balance, 1992-1993. London: International Institute for Strategic Studies, 1992.

North American Congress on Latin America. "U.S. Training Programs for Foreign Military Personnel: The Pentagon's Protégé," *Latin American and Empire Report,* 10, January 1976, 15-28.

North, Liisa, and Tanya Korovkin. *The Peruvian Revolution and the Officers in Power, 1967-1976.* Montreal: Center for Developing Area Studies, McGill University, 1981.

"Nuevo Esquema," *Caretas* [Lima], No. 1169, July 22, 1991, 20.

Nunn, Frederick M. "Professional Militarism in Twentieth-Century Peru: Historical and Theoretical Background to the *Golpe de Estado* of 1968," *Hispanic American Historical Review,* 59, No. 3, August 1979, 391-418.

_____. *Yesterday's Soldiers: European Military Professionalism in South America, 1890-1940.* Lincoln: University of Nebraska Press, 1983.

Ocaña Ferrera, Víctor. "Fuerzas aéreas de América del Sur," *Tecnología Militar* [Bonn], 12, No. 2, 1990, 10-29ff.

Palmer, David Scott. "Changing Political Economy of Peru under Military and Civilian Rule, 1963-83," *Inter-American Economic Affairs,* 37, 1984, 37-62.

_____. "Drug Trafficking, Political Violence, and Domestic Stability in Peru and Colombia." (Paper prepared for the Colombian Studies Project, University of Miami, May 1989.) Miami: University of Miami, May 1989.

_____. "Military in Latin America." Pages 257-72 in Jack Hopkins (ed.), *Latin America: Perspectives on a Region.* New York: Holmes and Meier, 1987.

_____. *Peru: The Authoritarian Tradition.* New York: Praeger, 1980.

_____. "Peru's Persistent Problems," *Current History,* 89, No. 543, January 1990, 5-8, 31-34.

————. "Peru, the Drug Business and Shining Path: Between Scylla and Charybdis?" *Journal of Interamerican Studies and World Affairs*, 34, No. 3, Fall 1992, 65–88.

————. "United States-Peru Relations in the 1990s: Asymmetry and Its Consequences." Section B in Eduardo Gamarra (ed.), *Latin America and Caribbean Contemporary Record, 1989–90*, 9, New York: Holmes and Meier, 1993.

Palmer, David Scott (ed.). *The Shining Path of Peru*. New York: St. Martin's Press, 1992.

Peru. President of the Republic. "Leyes orgánicas de las FF.AA., Ministerio de Defensa y defensa nacional," *El Peruano: Diario Oficial* [Lima], September 27, 1987.

"Peru." *Tecnología Militar* [Bonn], No. 4, July–August 1990, 51–52.

Pettavino, Paula J. "Peru's Military Buildup," *Journal of Defense and Diplomacy*, 7, March 1986, 23–27, 63.

Philip, George. *The Rise and Fall of the Peruvian Military Radicals, 1968–1976*. London: Athlone Press, 1978.

Prado Saldarriaga, Víctor R. *Derecho penal y política: Política penal de la dictadura y la democracia en el Perú*. Lima: Editorial y Distribuidora de Libros, 1990.

Rudolph, James D. *Peru: The Evolution of a Crisis*. (Politics in Latin America: A Hoover Institution Series.) Westport, Connecticut: Praeger, 1992.

Seligson, Mitchell A., and John A. Booth (eds.). *Politics and the Poor*. (Political Participation in Latin America Series, No. 2.) New York: Holmes and Meier, 1978.

Sharp, Daniel A. (ed.). *U.S. Foreign Policy and Peru*. Austin: University of Texas Press, 1972.

Smith, Michael L. "Taking the High Ground: Shining Path and the Andes." Pages 15–32 in David Scott Palmer (ed.), *The Shining Path of Peru*. New York: St. Martin's Press, 1992.

————. "Shining Path's Urban Strategy: Ate Vitarte." Pages 127–48 in David Scott Palmer (ed.), *The Shining Path of Peru*. New York: St. Martin's Press, 1992.

Tarazona-Sevillano, Gabriela. "The Organization of Shining Path." Pages 171–90 in David Scott Palmer (ed.), *The Shining Path of Peru*. New York: St. Martin's Press, 1992.

United States. Congress. 102d, 2d Session. House of Representatives. Committee on Foreign Affairs. Subcommittee on Western Hemisphere Affairs. *The Threat of the Shining Path to Democracy in Peru*. (Hearings March 11–12, 1992.) Washington: GPO, 1992.

————. Congress. 102d, 2d Session. House of Representatives. Committee on Foreign Affairs. Subcommittee on Western Hemisphere Affairs. *The Shining Path after Guzmán: The Threat and the International Response.* (Hearings September 23, 1992.) Washington: GPO, 1992.

_____. Department of State. "Peru." Pages 7808–23 in *Country Reports on Human Rights Practices for 1989.* (Report submitted to United States Congress, 101st, 1st Session, Senate, Committee on Foreign Relations, and House of Representatives, Committee on Foreign Affairs.) Washington: GPO, February, 1990.

_____. "Peru." Pages 736–54 in *Country Reports on Human Rights Practices for 1990.* (Report submitted to United States Congress, 102d, 1st Session, Senate, Committee on Foreign Relations, and House of Representatives, Committee on Foreign Affairs.) Washington: GPO, February, 1991.

_____. Department of State. Bureau of International Narcotics Matters. *International Narcotics Control Strategy Report.* Washington: GPO, March 1990.

_____. Bureau of International Narcotics Matters. *International Narcotics Control Strategy Report.* Washington: GPO, March 1991.

Villanueva, Víctor. "The Military in Peruvian Politics, 1919–45." Pages 126–35 in Brian Loveman and Thomas M. Davies, Jr. (eds.), *The Politics of Antipolitics: The Military in Latin America.* (2d ed.) Lincoln: University of Nebraska Press, 1989.

Werlich, David P. "Fujimori and the 'Disaster' in Peru," *Current History,* 90, No. 553, February 1991, 61–64ff.

Wesson, Robert (ed.). *The Latin American Military Institution.* New York: Praeger, 1986.

Woy-Hazelton, Sandra, and William A. Hazelton. "Shining Path and the Marxist Left." Pages 207–24 in David Scott Palmer (ed.), *The Shining Path of Peru.* New York: St. Martin's Press, 1992.

(Various issues of the following publications during the 1989–92 period were also used in the preparation of this chapter: *Boston Globe; Caretas* [Lima]; *Christian Science Monitor;* Foreign Broadcast Information Service, *Daily Report: Latin America; Informativo Desco* [Lima]; *Latin American Weekly Review* [London]; *Latinamerica Press; New York Times; Oiga* [Lima]; *Perú Económico* [Lima]; *Quehacer* [Lima]; *Resumen Semanal* [Lima]; *Sí* [Lima]; and *Washington Post.*)

Glossary

Alliance for Progress—Established in 1961 at a hemispheric meeting in Punta del Este, Uruguay, under the leadership of President John F. Kennedy as a long-range program to help develop and modernize Latin American states. Program involved various forms of foreign aid from the United States to all states of Latin America and the Caribbean, except Cuba. Its main instruments for fostering modernization were development loans offered at very low or zero interest rates. Program called for multisectoral reforms, particularly in health and education.

Andean Initiative (or Andean Strategy)—At the February 1990 Cartagena (Colombia) Drug Summit, the presidents of Bolivia, Colombia, Peru, and the United States agreed to mount a regional attack on the drug trade. Their governments thereby qualified for United States counternarcotics assistance. After taking office in July 1990, President Alberto K. Fujimori proposed a comprehensive counternarcotics effort, to include narcotics law enforcement, demand reduction, public diplomacy, and economic development. However, progress in organizing this strategy was hindered by police/military rivalries and corruption. Furthermore, in late September 1990 Fujimori turned down US$35.9 million in authorized United States military/antidrug assistance after the United States failed to meet his concerns about the military focus of its antidrug strategy in Peru. After extensive talks, Fujimori signed the Peru-United States umbrella agreement on drug control and economic assistance on May 14, 1991, establishing a political understanding at the highest level and serving as a framework for a coordinated, comprehensive program to dismantle the drug trade in Peru with assistance of the United States, other developed countries, and international organizations. It addresses the role of the police and military in counternarcotics activities, alternative economic assistance, crop substitution, and access to establishing legitimate economies versus the cultivation and illicit processing of coca leaf into cocaine products.

Andean Pact—An economic group, the Andean Common Market, created in 1969 by Bolivia, Colombia, Chile, Ecuador, and Peru as a subregional market to improve its members' bargaining power within the Latin American Free Trade Association (LAFTA) and to encourage increased trade and more rapid development. LAFTA, which dated from 1960, was

379

replaced in 1980 by the Latin American Integration Association (Asociación Latinoamericana de Integración—ALADI), which advocated a regional tariff preference for goods originating in member states. Chile left the Pact in 1976. The threat that Peru might withdraw from the Pact had receded by August 1992.

audiencia—A high court of justice, exercising some administrative and executive functions in the colonial period.

ayllu—A self-governing and land-owning peasant community in the Andean highlands. May refer to either a village, a kinship group, or a class-like organization, usually based on collective agriculture. Although a pre-Columbian term, *ayllu* has been used as a synonym for contemporary highland Peasant Communities.

Baker debt-reduction plan—As part of the Enterprise for the Americas Initiative (*q.v.*), Nicholas F. Brady, the United States secretary of the treasury in the administration of President George H.W. Bush (1989–93), led a United States Government interagency process that determined country eligibility for debt reduction. The Brady Plan has been used to forge agreements between banks and the governments of several Latin American nations.

barriadas—Squatter settlements or shantytowns that surround Lima and other urban centers. Since the late 1960s, these settlements have been also known as *pueblos jóvenes* (young towns).

cabildo—A town council in the colonial period, usually composed of the most prominent citizens.

cholo—A term that has a variety of definitions and social implications. During colonial times, it was equivalent to mestizo but has evolved to include persons of mixed or pure native American ancestry who are trying to move up the social and economic ladder by observing various Hispanic cultural norms. *Cholos* speak Spanish in addition to an indigenous language. *Choloficación* (Cholofication) refers to the transition process from native American to mestizo status.

compadrazgo—Literally, copaternity. A system of ritual coparenthood that links parents, children, and godparents in a close social or economic relationship.

consumer price index (CPI)—A statistical measure of sustained change in the price level weighted according to spending patterns.

Contadora Support Group—A diplomatic initiative launched by a January 1983 meeting on Contadora Island off the Pacific coast of Panama, by which the "Core Four" mediator countries of

Mexico, Venezuela, Colombia, and Panama sought to prevent through negotiations a regional conflagration among the Central American states of Guatemala, El Salvador, Honduras, Nicaragua, and Costa Rica. In September 1984, the negotiating process produced a draft treaty, the Contadora Act, which was judged acceptable by the government of Nicaragua but rejected by the other four Central American states concerned. The governments of Peru, Uruguay, Argentina, and Brazil formed the Contadora Support Group in 1985 in an effort to revitalize the faltering talks. The process was suspended unofficially in June 1986 when the Central American governments refused to sign a revised treaty. The Contadora process was effectively superseded by direct negotiations among the Central American states.

corporatist—An adherent to corporatism, a sociopolitical philosophy that found its most developed expression in Italy under Benito Mussolini. Corporatism is antithetical to both Marxist and liberal democratic political ideals. A corporatist would organize society into industrial and professional corporations that serve as organs of political representation within a hierarchical, centralized polity.

corregidores de indios—Magistrates or chief officers, usually a white or *cholo* (*q.v.*), in preindependence Peru charged with administering local native American affairs in *corregimientos* (*q.v.*).

corregimientos—Colonial administrative districts that later became *intendencias* (intendancies or provinces) and Catholic dioceses or parishes.

dependency analysis—A theory that seeks to explain the continuing problems of Latin American underdevelopment and political conflict by positing the existence of an imperialistic, exploitative relationship between the industrialized countries and the developing nations of Latin America and other developing regions.

Economic Commission for Latin America and the Caribbean (ECLAC)—A United Nations regional economic commission established in 1948 as the Economic Commission for Latin America (ECLA). In 1984 expanded its operations and title to include the Caribbean. Main functions are to initiate and coordinate policies aimed at promoting economic development. In addition to the countries of Latin America and the Caribbean, ECLAC's forty-one members in 1992 included Britain, Canada, France, the Netherlands, Portugal, Spain, and the United States. There were an additional five Caribbean associate members.

economies of scale—Decreases in the unit cost of production associated with increasing output.

effective protection—The percentage increase in value added, compared with what it could have been at international prices, as a result of the higher domestic prices permitted by protection.

encomenderos—Colonial grantees, usually large landowners, to rights over native American labor and tribute in exchange for assuming responsibility to protect and Christianize these native subjects.

encomienda(s)—A system adopted in 1503 whereby the Spanish Crown assigned rights over native American labor and tribute in the Spanish American colonies to individual colonists (*encomenderos*) in return for protecting and Christianizing their subjects. However, most ended up as virtual slaves with no recognized rights. The system was not ended until late in the eighteenth century.

Enterprise for the Americas Initiative—A plan announced by President George H.W. Bush on June 27, 1990, calling for the United States to negotiate agreements with selected Latin American countries to reduce their official debt to the United States and make funds available through the restructuring for environmental programs, to stimulate private investment, and to take steps to promote extensive trade liberalization with the goal of establishing free trade throughout the Western Hemisphere.

export-led growth—An economic development strategy that emphasizes export promotion as the engine of economic growth. Proponents of this strategy emphasize the correlation between growth in exports and growth in the aggregate economy.

fiscal year (FY)—Calendar year.

gamonales (sing. *gamonal*)—Ruthless rural bosses who used armed force as well as the law to obtain land, displacing many native Americans in the process.

gross domestic product (GDP)—A measure of the total value of goods and services produced by the domestic economy during a given period, usually one year. Obtained by adding the value contributed by each sector of the economy in the form of profits, compensation to employees, and depreciation (consumption of capital). The income arising from investments and possessions owned abroad is not included, hence the use of the word *domestic* to distinguish GDP from gross national product (*q.v.*).

gross national product (GNP)—Total market value of all final goods and services produced by an economy during a year. Obtained by adding the gross domestic product (*q.v.*) and the income received from abroad by residents less payments remitted abroad to nonresidents.

Group of Eight—A permanent mechanism for consultation and political coordination that succeeded the Contadora Support Group (*q.v.*) in December 1986. It consisted of Argentina, Brazil, Colombia, Mexico, Panama, Peru, Uruguay, and Venezuela. Its second meeting, attended by the presidents of seven member-countries (Panama's membership was temporarily suspended in February 1988), was held in Punta del Este, Uruguay, in October 1988. Like the Contadora Support Group, the Group of Eight advocated democracy and a negotiated solution to the Central American insurgencies. Its name was changed in 1990 to the Group of Rio, which had eleven members in 1992. Peru was suspended from the Rio Group following President Alberto K. Fujimori's self-coup on April 6, 1992, but was formally reinstated in April 1993.

hacendado—Hacendados (owners of haciendas) often acted as intermediaries for *gamonales* (*q.v.*) in taking over native American lands and extorting wool merchants.

import-substitution industrialization—An economic development strategy that emphasizes the growth of domestic industries, often by import protection using tariff and nontariff measures. Proponents favor the export of industrial goods over primary products.

informal sector—Unofficial sector of underground economic activity beyond government regulation and taxation, to include street vendors in urban areas as well as coca-growers in rural areas.

International Monetary Fund (IMF)—Established on July 22, 1944, the IMF began operating along with the World Bank (q.v.) on December 27, 1945. The IMF is a specialized agency affiliated with the United Nations that takes responsibility for stabilizing international exchange rates and payments. The IMF's main business is the provision of loans to its members when they experience balance-of-payments difficulties. These loans often carry conditions that require substantial internal economic adjustments by the recipients. In 1992 the IMF had 156 members.

latifundios—Large estates held as private property, which may be farmed as plantations, by tenant sharecroppers, or as traditional haciendas. The latifundio system (*latifundismo*) is a pattern of land ownership based on latifundios owned by local gentry, absentee landlords, and domestic or foreign corporations.

liberation theology—An activist movement led by Roman Catholic clergy who traced their inspiration to Vatican Council II (1965), where some church procedures were liberalized, and the Second Latin American Bishops' Conference in Medellín (1966), which endorsed greater direct efforts to improve the lot of the poor. Advocates of liberation theology, sometimes referred to as "liberationists," have worked mainly through Christian Base Communities (Comunidades Eclesiásticas de Base—CEBs).

licenciado—A person granted a higher degree in a university; also a title bestowed on lawyers.

machismo—Cult of male dominance, derived from the word *macho,* meaning male.

marginality—A concept used to explain the poor political, economic, and social conditions of individuals within a society, social classes within a nation, or nations within the larger world community. It refers often to poverty-stricken groups left behind in the modernization process. They are not integrated into the socioeconomic system, and their relative poverty increases. Marginality is sometimes referred to as dualism or the dual-society thesis.

mayorazgo—Colonial system whereby the elder son inherited the titles and properties of the family.

mayordomos—Special officials in colonial Peru appointed, sometimes under threat of physical punishment for refusal, for important celebrations. Their duties included making sure the priest's pay was available and making up shortages out of their personal patrimony.

Mercosur—(Mercado Común del Cono Sur—Southern Cone Common Market)—An organization established on March 26, 1991, by Argentina, Brazil, Paraguay, and Uruguay for the purpose of promoting regional economic cooperation. Chile was conspicuously absent because of its insistence that the other four countries first had to lower their tariffs to the Chilean level before Chile could join. Mercosur aimed to form a common market by December 31, 1994. Bolivia hoped to eventually become a fifth member.

mestizo—Originally, term designated the offspring of a Spaniard and a native American. It now means any obviously nonwhite individual who is fluent in Spanish and observes Hispanic cultural norms.

minifundios—Very small landholdings, legally held, allowing only a bare existence.

mita system—A colonial system whereby all taxpayers had to work a prescribed number of days annually in the *mita,* or labor pool, to run the households of local leaders. Each taxpayer could be called up by his or her *curaca* (chief) to work on imperial or local projects at any convenient time.

mita de minas—A compulsory labor system implemented by the Spaniards to work the mines. Required that all able-bodied native American men present themselves periodically for short periods of paid work in the mines. System led to abuses: inhumane treatment of the conscripts, arbitrary extensions of the service period, and depletion of adult males from individual communities.

obrajes—Rudimentary textile factories set up throughout the highlands in the colonial period to pay the tribute owed to *encomiendas* (*q.v.*).

Organization of American States (OAS)—Established by the Ninth International Conference of American States held in Bogotá on April 30, 1948, and effective since December 13, 1951, the OAS has served as a major regional organization composed of thirty-five members, including most Latin American states and the United States and Canada. Determines common political, defense, economic, and social policies and provides for coordination of various inter-American agencies. Responsible for implementing the Inter-American Treaty of Reciprocal Assistance (Rio Treaty) (*q.v.*) when any threat to the security of the region arises.

patrón—Usually a large landowner who is called on to provide his workers land, water, and sometimes materials and/or equipment and salary payments, as well as protection from outsiders, including local officials, and even from fellow workers.

praetorian—Praetorianism is a form of militarism in which the armed forces act as a corporate body to maintain control over government, actively intervening in politics to select or change the government. The "ruler-type" praetorian army rejects the existing social order for one based on modernization, industrialization, and rapid economic growth, as the Peruvian Army (Ejército Peruano—EP) did following its assumption of power in 1968. Political scientist Samuel Huntington describes a praetorian society as one in which social forces confront each other directly, with no institutions accepted as legitimate mediaries and, more importantly, no agreement existing among the groups as to an authoritative means for conflict resolution.

primary exports—Peru's traditional primary goods exports, as opposed to manufactured exports, included cotton, sugar, copper, silver, lead, zinc, and oil.

Protocol of Rio de Janeiro (Rio Protocol)—An agreement concluded in Rio de Janeiro on January 29, 1942, between Peru and Ecuador with the participation of the mediatory nations of Argentina, Brazil, and the United States. It was ratified by the congresses of both Peru and Ecuador on February 26, 1942, and it established the border between the two countries as internationally recognized today. Following the discovery of the Río Cenepa between the Zamora and Santiago rivers in the Cordillera del Cóndor in 1951, Ecuador disputed the treaty demarcation, which then stopped, leaving a stretch of the border uncharted. Ecuador repudiated the treaty in 1960, but the guarantor powers ruled this repudiation invalid.

pueblos jóvenes—See *barriadas*.

real exchange rate—The value of foreign exchange corrected for differences between external and domestic inflation.

reducciones—Viceroy Francisco de Toledo's orders created hundreds of these colonial settlements for only native Americans. Although conveniently located in the flat valley bottoms, these settlements were established in areas subject to floods and avalanches. Their governing personnel consisted only of native Americans.

repartimiento—State monopoly of selling inferior goods at inflated prices to conquered native Americans. Set off a wave of violent protests in 1776.

residencia—A formal inquiry conducted at the end of a colonial official's term of office.

Rio Group—See Group of Eight.

Rio Protocol—See Protocol of Rio de Janeiro.

Rio Treaty (Inter-American Treaty of Reciprocal Assistance)—A regional alliance, signed in Rio de Janeiro on September 2, 1947, that established a mutual security system to safeguard the Western Hemisphere from aggression from within or outside the zone. Signatories include the United States and twenty Latin American republics. In 1975 a special conference approved, over United States objections, a Protocol of Amendment to the Rio Treaty that, once ratified, would establish the principle of "ideological pluralism" and would simplify the rescinding of sanctions imposed on an aggressor party.

slash-and-burn agriculture—Method of cultivation whereby areas of the forest are burned and cleared for planting, the ash providing some fertilization. Area is cultivated for several years and then left fallow for a decade or longer.

sol (S/)—Peru's unit of currency, technically the nuevo sol (new sol), consisting of 100 céntimos, established officially as Peru's monetary unit on January 4, 1991. In late 1992, the exchange rate for the new sol was S/1.63 = US$1. In the late 1800s, a silver sol was the country's currency until its metallic content exceeded its monetary value and it was exported instead of circulating. Before the 1860s, Bolivian coins circulated in Peru. The sol was established by law in 1931 as an unminted gold coin; bank notes were issued in terms of gold soles. It replaced the Peruvian gold pound created in 1900. The Peruvian pound was equivalent in value to the British pound, and both circulated as legal tender. Beginning in 1975, the value of the sol declined continuously as officials attempted to adjust the exchange rate to the rate of inflation. By mid-1985 the sol had deteriorated to more than S/11,900 per US$1, when a new unit of currency, the inti (equivalent to S/1,000), was introduced. By 1990 US$1 equaled about 188,000 intis. Consequently, President Fujimori adopted the new sol, equivalent to 1 million inti, in July 1991. The free exchange rate in Peruvian currency in February 1993 was 2,100 new soles to the dollar.

terms of trade—The relationship between the price of primary exports and the price of manufactured goods. May be defined as the ratio of the average price of a country's exports to the average price of its imports. In international economics, the concept of "terms of trade" plays an important role in evaluating exchange relationships between developed and developing nations.

value-added tax (VAT)—An incremental tax applied to the value added at each stage of the processing of a raw material or the production and distribution of a commodity. It is calculated as the difference between the product value at a given state and the cost of all materials and services purchased as inputs. The value-added tax is a form of indirect taxation, and its impact on the ultimate consumer is the same as that of a sales tax.

World Bank—Informal name used to designate a group of four affiliated international institutions: International Bank for Reconstruction and Development (IBRD), International Development Association (IDA), International Finance Corporation (IFC), and Multilateral Investment Guarantee Agency (MIGA). IBRD, established in 1945, has the primary purpose of providing loans at market-related rates of interest to developing countries at more advanced stages of development. IDA, a legally separate loan fund administered by the staff of IBRD, was set up in 1960 to furnish credits to the poorest developing countries on much easier terms than those of conventional IBRD loans. IFC, founded in 1956, supplements the activities of IBRD through loans and assistance designed specifically to encourage the growth of productive private enterprises in less developed countries. MIGA, founded in 1988, insures private foreign investment in developing countries against various non-commercial risks. The president and certain senior officers of IBRD hold the same positions in the IFC. The four institutions are owned by the governments of the countries that subscribe their capital. To participate in the World Bank group, member states must first belong to IMF (*q.v.*).

Contributors

Paul L. Doughty is Professor of Anthropology and Latin American Studies, Department of Anthropology, University of Florida, Gainesville.

Carol Graham is Guest Scholar in the Foreign Policy Studies Program, Brookings Institution, and Adjunct Professor of Government, Georgetown University, Washington, D.C.

Rex A. Hudson is Senior Research Specialist in Latin American Affairs, Federal Research Division, Library of Congress, Washington, D.C.

Peter F. Klarén is Professor of History and International Affairs and Director of the Latin American Studies Program, George Washington University, Washington, D.C.

David Scott Palmer is Professor of International Relations and Political Science, Center for International Relations, Boston University, and Director of its Latin American Studies Program.

John Sheahan is William Brough Professor of Economics, Department of Economics, Williams College, Williamstown, Massachusetts.

Index

393

Published Country Studies

(Area Handbook Series)

550-65	Afghanistan	550-87	Greece
550-98	Albania	550-78	Guatemala
550-44	Algeria	550-174	Guinea
550-59	Angola	550-82	Guyana and Belize
550-73	Argentina	550-151	Honduras
550-169	Australia	550-165	Hungary
550-176	Austria	550-21	India
550-175	Bangladesh	550-154	Indian Ocean
550-170	Belgium	550-39	Indonesia
550-66	Bolivia	550-68	Iran
550-20	Brazil	550-31	Iraq
550-168	Bulgaria	550-25	Israel
550-61	Burma	550-182	Italy
550-50	Cambodia	550-30	Japan
550-166	Cameroon	550-34	Jordan
550-159	Chad	550-56	Kenya
550-77	Chile	550-81	Korea, North
550-60	China	550-41	Korea, South
550-26	Colombia	550-58	Laos
550-33	Commonwealth Caribbean, Islands of the	550-24	Lebanon
550-91	Congo	550-38	Liberia
550-90	Costa Rica	550-85	Libya
550-69	Côte d'Ivoire (Ivory Coast)	550-172	Malawi
550-152	Cuba	550-45	Malaysia
550-22	Cyprus	550-161	Mauritania
550-158	Czechoslovakia	550-79	Mexico
550-36	Dominican Republic and Haiti	550-76	Mongolia
550-52	Ecuador	550-49	Morocco
550-43	Egypt	550-64	Mozambique
550-150	El Salvador	550-35	Nepal and Bhutan
550-28	Ethiopia	550-88	Nicaragua
550-167	Finland	550-157	Nigeria
550-155	Germany, East	550-94	Oceania
550-173	Germany, Fed. Rep. of	550-48	Pakistan
550-153	Ghana	550-46	Panama